I0061624

International development cooperation today:
a radical shift towards a global paradigm

International Development Cooperation Today

A Radical Shift Towards a Global Paradigm

Patrick Develtere
Huib Huyse
Jan Van Ongevalle

LEUVEN UNIVERSITY PRESS

© 2021 by Leuven University Press / Presses Universitaires de Louvain / Universitaire Pers Leuven. Minderbroedersstraat 4, B-3000 Leuven (Belgium).

All rights reserved. Except in those cases expressly determined by law, no part of this publication may be multiplied, saved in an automated datafile or made public in any way whatsoever without the express prior written consent of the publishers.

ISBN 978 94 6270 261 5
eISBN 978 94 6166 398 6
https://doi.org/1.11116/9789461663986
D / 2021 / 1869 / 21
NUR: 740

Typesetting: Crius Group
Cover design: Frederik Danko
Cover illustration: Pogonici/Shutterstock.com (1584299791)

Whatever you do for me but without me, you do against me.
—Mahatma Gandhi, 1869–1948

*Many small things done in many small places by many
small people can change the face of the world.*
—Chinese saying

*Somewhere I was sure that if people were willing (…) to see the
light of other cultures, there would be no war on earth.*
—Nguyen Phan Que Mai, *The Mountains Sing*

*For it is often the way we look at other people that
imprisons them within their own allegiances. And it is also
the way we look at them that may set them free.*
—Amin Maalouf, *In the Name of Identity*

Perhaps, indeed, in curiosity lies the prospect of openness and tolerance.
—Amos Oz, *Dear Zealots*

*The men of your kin say that if a person desires to scratch his hands
or an itch on most other parts of his body, he does not need help.
But if he must scratch his back, he must ask others to help him.*
—Chigozie Obioma, *An Orchestra of Minorities*

*Action without vision is only passing time, vision without action is
merely daydreaming, but vision with action can change the world.*
—Nelson Mandela, 1918–2013

One does not develop a people; a people develops itself.
—Sylvain Shomba Kinyamba

*We are caught in an inescapable network of mutuality, tied in a single
garment of destiny. Whatever affects one directly, affects all indirectly.*
—Rev. Martin Luther King Jr., 1929–1968

*Nature has given a right to all men to leave the country
in which chance, not choice, has placed them.*
—Thomas Jefferson, 1720 – 1776

*There is no creation without tradition; the 'new' is an inflection on
a preceding form; novelty is always a variation on the past.*
—Carlos Fuentes, *Myself with Others: Selected Essays*

*Do not scoff at anyone's disaster. Fortune's vicissitudes
happen to all and the future is unknown.*
—Isocrates, 436–338 BC

What is the essence of life? To serve others and to do good.
—Aristotle, 384–322 BC

If I hadn't seen such riches, I could live with being poor.
—James, *Sit Down*

*We do not deal with COVID-19 anywhere if
we do not deal with it everywhere.*
—Justin Welby, Archbishop of Canterbury, CNN, November 2020

Contents

The unbearable lightness of the support for development cooperation

List of figures

List of tables

List of boxes

Abbreviations

ACP	African, Caribbean and Pacific Countries
AKDN	Aga Khan Development Network
ARC	Alliance for Religion and Conservation
AU	African Union
AusAID	Australian Agency for International Development
BINGO	Big International Non-Governmental Organisation
BNB	Banco Nacional de Bolivia
BONGO	Business-Organised Non-Governmental Organisation
BRAC	Bangladesh Rural Advancement Committee
BRICS	Brazil, Russia, India, China and South Africa
CBO	Community-Based Organisation
CDF	Comprehensive Development Framework
CIDA	Canadian International Development Agency
CNDD–FDD	Conseil National pour la Défense de la Démocratie – Forces pour la Défense de la Démocratie
COOPAfrica	Cooperative Facility for Africa
CSO	Civil Society Organisation
CSR	Corporate Social Responsibility
DAC	Development Assistance Committee (OECD)
DCD	Development Cooperation Division (Ireland)
DFID	Department for International Development (UK)
DGD	Direction Général Coopération au Développement (Belgium)
DIE	Deutches Institut für Entwicklungspolitik (Germany)
DONGO	Donor-Oriented/Organised Non-Governmental Organisation
DSSI	Debt Service Suspension Initiative
ECDPM	European Centre for Development Policy Management
EFA	Education for All
EM-DAT	Emergency Events Database
EPA	Economic Partnership Agreement
EU	European Union

FAO	Food and Agricultural Organisation
FBO	Faith-Based Organisation
FDI	Foreign Direct Investment
FID	Finance for International Development
FTF	Fair Trade Federation
GAVI	Global Alliance for Vaccines and Immunization
GDP	Gross Domestic Product
GEF	Global Environment Facility
GIZ	German Organisation for Technical Cooperation
GNI	Gross National Income
GNP	Gross National Product
GINGO	Grassroots International Non-Governmental Organisation
GONGO	Government-Oriented/Organised Non-Governmental Organisation
GRINGO	Government-Run/Inspired Non-Governmental Organisation
HGIS	Homogeneous Budget for International Cooperation (Netherlands)
HIPC	Heavily Indebted Poor Countries
HMO	Health Maintenance Organisation
IBRD	International Bank for Reconstruction and Development
ICA	International Cooperative Alliance
IDA	International Development Association
IFAD	International Fund for Agricultural Development
IFC	International Finance Corporation
IFRC	International Federation of Red Cross and Red Crescent Societies
IGO	International Governmental Organisation
ILO	International Labour Organisation
IMF	International Monetary Fund
IOM	International Organization for Migration
ITUC	International Trade Union Confederation
JICA	Japan International Cooperation Agency
KNOMAD	Global Knowledge Partnership on Migration and Development
LDC	Least Developed Countries
LMIC	Lower-Middle-Income Countries

MDG	Millennium Development Goals
MDRI	Multilateral Debt Relief Initiative
MFA	Ministry of Foreign Affairs
MIGA	Multilateral Insurance Guarantee Agency
MINBUZA	Ministerie van Buitenlandse Zaken (the Netherlands)
NCD	Non-Communicable Disease
NGDO	Non-Governmental Development Organisation
NGO	Non-Governmental Organisation
OACPS	Organisation of African, Caribbean and Pacific States
OCHA	United Nations Office for the Coordination of Humanitarian Affairs
ODA	Official Development Assistance
ODF	Official Development Finance
OECD	Organisation for Economic Co-operation and Development
OEEC	Organisation for European Economic Co-operation
OVOP	One Project One Village
PDI	Private Development Initiative
PFM	Public Financial Management
PMI	Philip Morris International
PRSP	Poverty Reduction Strategy Paper
QUANGO	Quasi Non-Governmental Organisation
SAP	Structural Adjustment Programme
SDC	Swiss Agency for Development and Cooperation
SDG	Sustainable Development Goal
SECO	Sécretariat d'Etat Suisse à l'Economie (Switzerland)
SIDA	Swedish International Development Cooperation Agency
SMO	Social Movement Organisation
SNV	Stichting Nederlandse Vrijwilligers
TB	Tuberculosis
TGI	Transnational Governance Initiative
TOSSD	Total Official Support for Sustainable Development
TUDCN	Trade Union Development Cooperation Network

UAE	United Arab Emirates
UK	United Kingdom
UMIC	Upper-Middle-Income Country
UN	United Nations
UNAIDS	Joint United Nations Programme on HIV and AIDS
UNCTAD	United Nations Conference on Trade and Development
UNDP	United Nations Development Programme
UNEP	United Nations Environment Programme
UNESCO	United Nations Educational, Scientific and Cultural Organisation
UNFPA	United Nations Population Fund
UNHCR	United Nations High Commissioner for Refugees
UNICEF	United Nations Children's Fund
UNIDO	United Nations Industrial Development Organisation
UNIFEM	United Nations Development Fund for Women
UNIMED	Confederaçao Nacional das Cooperativas Médicas
UNRWA	United Nations Relief and Works Agency
US(A)	United States (of America)
USAID	United States Agency for International Development
WFP	World Food Programme
WHO	World Health Organization
WTO	World Trade Organization

Preface

The quiet and secluded village of Toubacouta, with its five to 6,000 inhabitants, four hours' drive from Senegal's capital Dakar, is the gateway to the Sine-Saloum delta with its mangroves, mounts, baobabs and astonishing fauna and flora, as well as numerous petite fishing hamlets. The economy of Toubacouta and the surrounding areas is primarily based on field crop production, dry-season gardening, fishing, charcoal production and fruit trees. Most inhabitants have to survive on a meagre and uncertain income; they have to grab the devil by the tail, as the West-African saying goes. In the winter months, tourism provides a major economic boost and remittances from the Toubacouta diaspora add to the otherwise limited purchasing power of the villagers.

Toubacouta echoes the whole-of-society approach: the phenomenon that more and more conventional and non-conventional actors are entering an already crowded field of development cooperation, and that we are to encounter in this book. In 2013, the Toubacouta Culture Centre was inaugurated in the presence of local dignitaries, several Senegalese ministers and representatives of the United Nations (UN). The UN Educational, Scientific and Cultural Organisation (UNESCO) had coordinated this Millennium Development Goals-Fund project in close cooperation with the UN Development Programme, UN Industrial Development Organisation (UNIDO), World Tourism Organization and UN Population Fund in an effort to 'deliver as one UN family'. The Centre has a big space for events, performances and training, as well as an exhibition hall and a tourism office.

"We have decided to give the name 'l'Esplanade des Asturies' to the area in front of the artisan market to pay tribute to the generosity of the Spanish people", the Minister of Culture said during the event. Asturias is indeed a Spanish province and the Government of Spain provided the necessary funds for this cultural and tourist venture.

International cooperation in this small, resource-poor village predates this project realised by several UN agencies in conjunction with a bilateral donor. In the 1960s, the first US Peace Corps volunteers arrived in Senegal and the Toubacouta region. The Peace Corps volunteers live with local host families and engage in a wide variety of sectors ranging from agriculture to agroforestry, community economic development, mangrove restoration and healthcare. With the African associational revolution in the 1980s, which was also a shock wave to Senegal's social and political fabric, novel local NGOs in Toubacouta, such as the Action Group for Community Development, called for moral, technical and financial support from the NGDO community in Europe. Several European NGDOs commenced cooperation with local grassroots groups, digging wells, restoring feeder roads and organising short training workshops.

In the 1990s, some Europeans who regularly came to Toubacouta for hunting and exploration settled and opened small hotels, attracting a growing group of tourists, mainly from Europe. One of these expat-owned hotels now prides itself on being a social entrepreneur and helps the local authorities with support for its garbage collection service. Hotel guests also have the opportunity to get a three-hour guided tour of the village. Stops are made at the local clinic: a gift of Belgian celebrities who were once hotel guests and whose names are presented on a copper plate at the entrance. They can visit the maternity clinic, named after the foreign benefactor who paid for its construction, and the two primary schools that are run with the support of what we, in this book, will call European fourth pillar organisations or private development initiatives. Visitors to the schools are kindly requested to put their names in a ledger and indicate how much money and which objects for the children, the school or the community they gave to the schoolmaster. Toubacouta is also involved in a twinning arrangement with several European villages and cities. The international youth movement 'Toubacouta network' (or 'Réseau Toubacouta') found roots in this small and remote village some years ago. Liaising with militant local youth-for-the-environment organisations in Egypt, Senegal, Morocco, Togo and Belgium, exchanges are being organised and local awareness campaigns are being set up in order to engage the local communities in environmental protection and rehabilitation.

The history of Toubacouta's experience with development aid and development cooperation is idiosyncratic in its genesis and expansion, as well as exceptional in its density and intensity, but effectively illustrates how development cooperation patterns are the result of ever-increasing interactions between a growing community of international and local actors. Gradually, Toubacouta has become a regional hub for development initiatives of all kinds with the tourists and development workers who first discovered and often contributed to the hustling development scene of this little town and regional centre, and who extend their operations to even smaller and poorer settlements in the surrounding delta which they detect on their adventurous trips in the interior.

The thesis of this book is that Toubacouta symbolises what is happening in the wider sector of development cooperation. An increasing number of actors are involved in a complex web of interactions. These do not go exclusively from North to South anymore; they are more and more South-to-South driven and express the desire of actors from all over the globe to act 'without borders'. Development cooperation is no longer the reserve of development aid specialists. Globalisation has replaced the North-South divide as the dominant pattern that drives and structures relations worldwide. We thus see a whole-of-society engagement in global relations with a growing number, even sprawl, of actors who consider themselves to be 'development workers'.

This is what this book is all about. We try to see where we come from as a sector and where we are heading. We have done this in dialogue with the existing academic literature and research findings but as much as possible in interchange with the many actors, small and big, that are involved. We are conscious, but not at all sorry, that this brings along a researcher bias. It is clear that in all research, and especially in this kind of venture, personal values and norms, even emotions, play a significant role. Our own ethos and pathos, indeed, have certainly affected what we have observed, how we have looked at it, and also the conclusions we draw. This is all the more the case because the three of us have been actively involved in the sector of development cooperation for over two decades. We did research *about* but also *for* the sector, and above all, we have worked as professionals in the sector and been engaged as volunteers in many instances. This is also why we want to thank the hundreds of colleagues in the sector whom we have been working with and who have inspired us. Our gratitude similarly goes to the many people from all over the globe whom we could interview, talk to and consult. This book is about them and for them.

Patrick Develtere
Huib Huyse
Jan Van Ongevalle

Introduction

When talking to people and doing interviews in many developing countries, we have rarely heard critical views about development cooperation: not in the villages like Toubacouta we presented in the Preface, and seldom in the local mass media. To a limited degree, local politicians air negative views about the development aid their constituency receives; most often because they want the local population to believe that they deserve more foreign aid and that, as the people's representatives, they are their best advocates for that. Only occasionally, with slightly more objections and demur, negative comments are expressed by academic circles.

Likewise, in most Western countries, development cooperation is only rarely the subject of heated debate in living rooms, in the pub, in the media or in parliament. Oddly, the one time when we do have debate is when development cooperation becomes negatively linked to diplomatic relations with an important country. We had good examples of this in the 1980s, when Belgium, France and the USA continued to give significant support to the rotten Mobutu regime in Zaire, now the Democratic Republic of Congo: *le pays des mystères, minières et misères*. There was also a considerable outcry in the Netherlands during the same period because of the messy relationship with the Suharto regime in the former Dutch colony of Indonesia. In both cases, it was the dictator who put a stop to the flow of aid, in 1991 and 1992, respectively. In the USA, critical voices were heard in the media when the American development agency USAID had to be brought in to clear away rubble after the fall of the Iraqi dictator Saddam Hussein in April 2003, and it became apparent that plans had already been made for this before war had even been declared. The sector also sometimes becomes the subject of public reflection for a while when development cooperation ends up being negatively linked with commercial interests. Thus, in the mid-1990s, official aid became a topic of debate in various donor countries due to the 'white elephants' or megalomaniac projects that were being funded in Africa, Latin America and Asia. More recent examples include the poorly coordinated humanitarian aid after the Haiti earthquake in 2009, the food aid that came too little and too late to rescue the starving people in East Africa in 2011, the late response to the locust swarms in East Africa in 2019 and the Western donors' greedy monopolisation of personal protection equipment at the beginning of the COVID-19 pandemic in early 2020. Suddenly, everyone had an opinion about whether this kind of aid was right, whether other priorities needed to be set or whether development aid was to blame for the disasters.

The lack of public discussion may have more to do with the fact that development cooperation is not among the domestic themes of contention that have the capacity to really stir up public opinion, the press and politicians in a country, rather than reflecting a general lack of interest in the topic. In fact, there are reasons to believe that there is growing support for development aid. Neither are we solely referring here to the wave of solidarity in late 2004 and early 2005 that followed the tsunami which ravaged Thailand, Myanmar, Sri Lanka, the Maldives and the eastern coast of India, or the uncountable expressions of generosity, private and public, from China and Russia to Europe, from Europe to Africa, or from capitals to rural areas everywhere in the wake of the outbreak of the COVID-19 pandemic. Rich countries also have a high density of organisations (non-governmental development organisations [NGDOs] and others) that have specialised in development cooperation. And is the proliferation of new actors, some of which we have already met in Toubacouta, another indicator that support for development aid is on the rise? There is ample research that shows that interest in development aid is increasing everywhere. But those same studies also hasten to add that people are particularly ignorant about the aid sector and that support is not very deep rooted.

We want to use this book to do something about that lack of knowledge and debate. Development cooperation is a maze. It is a very unusual community of many thousands of institutions and organisations that specialise in it and are engaged in it on a daily basis. Some of these are government institutions; they are to be found, above all, in the 30 members of the Development Assistance Committee (DAC) of the Organisation for Economic Co-operation and Development (OECD), the club of the rich countries, but more and more new 'emerging' official donors, most notably China, Turkey and the UAE, colour the scene. Other institutions belong to the UN and specialise in various forms of development aid. There are also international organisations outside the UN that play an important role in the development community. The International Organization for Migration is one example. Yet other organisations are 'non-governmental' in nature. These NGDOs are private initiatives by people looking for solutions to the North-South divide or to poverty, destitution and human rights violations in the so-called Global South. There are more than 10,000 NGDOs recognised by their respective governments for their expertise in the field of development work.

These official international and non-governmental aid organisations all make their own choices. Some specialise in emergency aid operations, while others work more in the long term. There are institutions and organisations that provide technical aid, and others that just give money. Few provide loans; most only make donations. Over a hundred institutions and organisations are mentioned in this book.

Do not be deterred. These institutions and organisations are discussed according to the category to which they belong. Thus, we examine official 'bilateral' development cooperation (the 'first pillar' of development cooperation) separately from international institutions (the 'second pillar') and NGDOs (the 'third pillar'). Text boxes provide information about specific projects, initiatives and points of interest.

We will describe the development sector not just as a community but also as an arena: a place where quite a number of opposing interests meet. It is the scene for sometimes fierce discussions and even conflicts. And it is also a market. Goods, services and a great deal of money circulate in the sector, and ever greater quantities of these are sought and promised. Thus, this sector, just like any other, is full of opportunists, marketers, dealers and canny accountants.

The field of development cooperation is now also populated by nations such as China, India, Turkey, Thailand and Brazil, as well as by local and regional authorities. What is less widely known is that in most donor countries, other ministries are now also becoming involved in development cooperation. Thus, we are seeing a kind of mainstreaming of development cooperation. Non-specialists are starting to offer aid in all kinds of forms.

The field of international players is also expanding. Both the UN and Europe are themselves giving a boost to new forms of development work and are eagerly creating additional development institutions. There are already over 300 intergovernmental organisations positioned in different ways in the development cooperation market.

By now, we all know that Bill and Melinda Gates have set aside a huge amount of money for Africa and healthcare globally. And each of us knows a local business leader, trade unionist, schoolteacher or hospital director who has set up an initiative from within their company, union, school or hospital to provide aid to acquaintances in the Global South.

In this book, we have suggested using the term 'fourth pillar' for all these newcomers. The vast majority of them were not established within the context of post-war 'North-South relations' but in response to the more recent trend of globalisation. Together with globalisation, concerns other than the persistent global inequalities separating North and South are coming to the fore and imposing themselves on the agenda of the development community: think of sustainable development, climate change, the danger of the worldwide spread of epidemics, the call for decolonisation, and, of course, migration and new waves of internally and internationally displaced people.

The traditional development cooperation community has never defined what constitutes good or bad aid. Hitherto, it has seemed obvious that trying to do good *is* good, or is better than nothing. After all, 'every little helps', as the often-used expression has it. In recent years, though, doubts have been growing. We know that not all help is (equally) helpful. We know that there is an art to giving. We also know that there are certain shortcomings in the aid apparatus. Work is, therefore, being done in some quarters on a 'new aid architecture'. But there is not yet any sign of a collective set of standards that clearly define what constitutes good aid, let alone an arbitration system that defines who is *allowed* to engage in development cooperation or that includes correction or sanction mechanisms to filter out faulty or counterproductive work. In other words, anyone can carry out development work, or claim to do so, in their own way. Anyone can offer any kind of supply. The market is free and highly competitive. But the whole-of-society approach that we are to meet with in this book proposes a positive message. It posits that there is a paradigm shift in the making. The present phase of globalisation no longer allows us to think in terms of North and South, nor in terms of givers and recipients. By hook or by crook, everybody, every single individual, institution, organisation and enterprise, has to take responsibility and co-create a sustainable future for mankind. This is the thesis of this book. Today, international development cooperation is making a radical shift towards a new paradigm.

There are, therefore, so many developments in the world that we have to take into account when drawing a picture of the changes the world of development cooperation is going through. How will we connect all those dots? It takes us ten chapters. In the first chapter, we will give a general overview of the sector by looking at it as a community, an arena and a market. Then we will take a step back and try to trace the more important historical building blocks that have resulted in the current state of affairs of the development cooperation sector. Throughout the book, we want to avoid talking about the sector as if there were only donors; it takes two to tango. Therefore, in the third chapter, we zoom in on the role of the recipients. They are not passive or subdued, as we will see. We think that it is not possible to understand the dynamics of the sector of development cooperation if it is reduced to a single conglomerate, so in the following four chapters, we describe the singularities of each of the four pillars that we have already presented: the bilateral and governmental first pillar, the international second pillar, the non-governmental third pillar of specialised NGDOs and, finally, the emerging and heterogeneous fourth pillar of a new generation of development workers. But this does, in our opinion, not yet give a full picture of the sector. We chose, therefore, to look at humanitarian or emergency aid in a separate eighth chapter because all the pillars are increasingly involved in this aspect and some consider it an aid sector in its own right. In the ninth chapter, we will try to understand how deep and broad public support is for development cooperation, and what the result is of the transformation of national citizens into world citizens in times of globalisation. Then it is time to draw up the balance sheet, which is what we will do in the tenth and final chapter.

Development cooperation in an era of globalisation

Most Western countries have been formally involved in development cooperation for over 60 years now. During this period, specialist organisations and institutions have been created, projects and programmes have been launched, ideas and strategies – the good and the not so good – for achieving efficient development cooperation have been debated, regulatory frameworks have been devised, and further new specialist organisations and institutions were then created, further new projects and programmes were launched, and so on. In other words, a typical cycle has occurred through which a social sector has taken shape: a process in which institutional innovations, a permanent war of ideas, new action models and policies have influenced one another, giving rise to a particular 'system'. Such a system ends up with an established pattern that is rather stubborn and hard to move away from. In the case of development cooperation, for instance, you can count on one hand the number of specialist organisations that have emerged since the early 1960s and subsequently been shut down. Organisations remain and adapt their goals; they rarely admit that their task has been accomplished or (even worse) that they have failed and should, therefore, simply shut up shop.

Even new regulations and agreements hardly ever lead to the dismantling of deficient parts of the system. Regulations usually define new institutions and methods, which are grafted onto the previous ones. Thus, the reforms of the development apparatuses of different European countries in the 1990s led to the creation of a number of new institutions, such as technical and executing agencies. Since then, the sector has also had to acknowledge that it could not handle the immense development problem alone and new actors have gained some recognition in this field, including through governmental support and subsidies. However, 'the sector' was only prepared to accept those new fellow development workers, such as foundations, if this went hand in hand with a win-win situation for the existing players (Ministries, NGDOs etc.). The UN is another example: whenever new agreements are made for combating poverty, the approach to certain diseases or the linking of environmental and development issues, everyone invariably wants to jump onto the bandwagon and a series of new specialist institutions are created as leading agencies.

Nor is it just certain distinctive patterns – ingrained and complex – that are acquired over time; a particular subculture also emerges. The sector gains typical characteristics: its own 'house style' and 'house culture'. Exactly what that style or culture is, is particularly hard to grasp. Throughout this book, we shall repeatedly come upon this cultural component, without really being able to explain it scientifically (i.e., after examining it in a methodologically correct fashion). Foreign colleagues and development workers now and then venture an informal character sketch of one another's style. American development cooperation is seen as messianic and patronising and bears imperialistic traits. The French and British approach is said to be characterised by a constant struggle for leadership, the conviction of the universality of their socioeconomic and political model and the dominance of their language. In the case of Belgium, reference is usually made, we are afraid to say, to the country's colonial past to justify labelling Belgian development cooperation as paternalistic and idiosyncratic. Dutch development cooperation is renowned for its generosity and pedantic character, the Scandinavian version for its progressive approach and high level of trust in local partners, and so on. We have found no confirmation of these caricatures in the available academic literature.

Box 1. No definition of development cooperation?

Readers will notice that we provide no definition of development cooperation. There are good reasons for this. There is no scientific definition of the concept, nor is there any definition that is accepted by all the key players, such as the international institutions and NGDOs. It is thus a wide-ranging term. Anybody can claim – on their own behalf – to be engaging in development cooperation.

Not everything, however, is 'official development assistance': the Development Assistance Committee (DAC) of the OECD has devised a number of criteria for this. 'Official development assistance' (ODA) consists, according to the DAC, of grants and loans to developing countries. These countries appear on the DAC List of Aid Recipients (developing countries).[1]

The DAC has some 30 member states but is increasingly working with international organisations and so-called 'new donors', which are non-member states. These grants and (low interest) loans must also originate from the government sector and primarily be intended to promote economic development and welfare. In financial terms, the aid must be concessional, meaning that it has a grant element of at least 45% for loans to least developed countries (LDCs) (15% for lower-middle-income countries [LMICs] and 10% for upper-middle-income countries [UMICs] and multilateral institutions). Technical cooperation – sending specialist personnel and training managers in developing countries – can also be regarded as aid. Grants, loans and credits for military purposes are excluded. Payments to individuals, for example for pensions, repatriation or insurance payouts to donor country personnel, are likewise excluded from the definition.

Reference is usually made to 'net ODA' because the repayment of the capital element of concessional loans is deducted from the aid total.

At present, more than 150 countries and territories are receiving ODA. The income level of the recipient countries has nothing to do with this. When a Western country makes a grant to relatively prosperous Argentina, this is regarded as development aid just as when it makes a donation to poverty-stricken Malawi. By the way, the majority of the countries on the DAC list are lower- and upper-middle-income countries. The country's growth rate is also irrelevant. Aid to China or India is counted without taking into consideration the impressive dynamics of their economies.

It is significant that the definition of development aid is based on the actions of the givers, not the value of the 'aid' to the recipient. The official aid figures that are presented in this manner give no indication whatsoever of what the developing countries receive but only of what is declared as given. It is estimated that the governments of developing countries receive less than half of what the rich countries report as aid. This is because these figures include both liquid funds and goods and services. A proportion of these amounts never even leaves the donor country (including development workers' pay, resources for the reception of refugees, operational funds for the ministry of development cooperation, and government money used by NGDOs for development education or for training Africans at Western universities, for example). And who determines the value of the goods and services that are purchased in the donor country? Could they not have been purchased more cheaply elsewhere? It is also clear that debt cancellation is inflating the aid figures. In reality, debt cancellation is a transfer from one government department (the ministry of development cooperation) to another (the official 'export credit agency'). Many of these debts are no longer expected to be repaid. Some people ask whether emergency aid can be counted as development aid. It usually consists of Western goods that are intended to solve short-term problems and do not bring about structural changes. Since 2014, there has been an interesting discussion about modernising and broadening the definition of ODA. It tries to capture multiple questions: why not focus on support for sustainable development in developing countries and more precisely the sustainable development goals (SDGs)? Why not include all flows, including those from the private sector that are stimulated by, for example, guarantees by state agencies? And those of Multilateral Development Banks? What about South-South cooperation and Islamic finance? And how should expenditures for global public goods and challenges be dealt with? This new international statistical measure has been named 'total official support for sustainable development' or TOSSD.

The OECD remains firm in its determination not to spoil the ODA principles. It decided in May 2020 that research for a vaccine for COVID-19 would not count as ODA, as such a vaccine would benefit developed countries as much as developing countries and should, therefore, be considered as contributing to addressing a global challenge.

> The lack of any definition of development cooperation and sustainable develop-
> ment is harmful to the sector, while the lack of any definition of what constitutes
> 'good' development cooperation is even more problematic, as it means that any-
> one can label their own initiatives as development aid and even as 'good', 'better' or
> 'the best' development aid.

In what follows, we will find out more about 'the development cooperation system', by characterising it in three different ways. By viewing the system at times as a community, at times as an arena and at times as a market, we can detect different dimensions and frames of reference. In sociological terms, these characterisations are, therefore, 'ideal types', which do not directly represent the reality but do make it easier to understand.

Our position is that development cooperation is never exclusively and fully a community, arena or market. Which characteristic is dominant depends on the moment of observation. Thus, we seek to demonstrate that, at present, the market dimension has gained the upper hand at the expense of the arena, and especially at the expense of the community.

More and more new actors on the scene: is the sector still a community?

A survey commissioned in 2019 by the World Economic Forum showed that more than 25% of adults globally had no awareness of the UN SDGs. In Great Britain, Japan and the United States, barely 50% had heard of them.[2] Moreover, people generally do not know who the minister for development cooperation is in their country. They greatly overestimate the extent of offi-cial aid, can name only a few NGDOs and have little or no knowledge of recent trends in the development world.

The 'popularity' of development cooperation, on the other hand, was evi-denced by a special Eurobarometer study, which revealed that – despite the economic turmoil – 86% of Europeans consider development aid to be fairly to very important (European Commission, 2019a).

The development cooperation community can be seen as a rather closed community, even as it is now challenged by new actors entering the sector: by an incipient whole-of-society approach, as we call it. This does not in itself mean that the sector lacks transparency or does not communicate sufficiently. Many people will even agree that development organisations bombard them with leaflets, begging letters, emails and TV, radio and social media ads. What our findings do indicate, though, is that a development cooperation

Table 1: Overview of an expanding community of development actors (examples)

	Not-for-profit Public				Fourth pillar	For-profit Private
Bilateral donors	**Multilateral donors**	**Global programmes**	**NGDOs**	**Fourth pillar**	**Private sector**
Ministry for development cooperation (USAID in the USA, DFID in the UK, JICA in Japan, Sida in Sweden and CIDA in Canada)	UN	Specialist agencies of the UN (ILO, FAO, UNESCO, WHO, UNIDO)	International NGDOs from traditional donor countries (e.g., Oxfam International, Plan International)	Social movements (trade unions, farmers' organisations)	Companies
Bilateral development banks and agencies (GTZ in Germany, BIO and Enabel in Belgium)	Bretton Woods Institutions (World Bank, IMF)	Global Fund to Fight Aids, TB and Malaria, Global Alliance for Vaccines and Immunisation, etc.	International NGDOs from non-traditional donor countries	Associations (migrants' associations, sports clubs, musical groups, etc.)	Commercial banks, Southern banks working with international NGDOs (Banco Nacional de Bolivia and World Vision)
New donors (China, India, Brazil, Thailand, Dubai, etc.)	Regional development banks and agencies	Global Environmental Facility	National NGDOs in traditional donor countries: World Vision, Save the Children, Care (USA)	Social institutions (schools, hospitals, etc.)	Private investors
Other ministries (agriculture, health, labour, etc.) and government institutions (national banks, etc.)	European Commission	Fast Track Initiative/Education for All, Forest Carbon Partnership Facility, Emerging Africa Infrastructure Fund	National NGDOs from non-traditional donor countries: BRAC and Grameen from Bangladesh	Foundations	
Other governmental levels (Länder in Germany, regions in France, communities and regions in Belgium, provinces in Canada, cities and municipalities)	Other international institutions (IOM, International IDEA, etc.)			Company funds	
				Individuals and groups of friends	

system has evolved that comes across as a specialised and separate entity. It has become a fairly closed world, with its own organisations, elite, personnel, procedures, jargon, symbols, public events and subculture. As a community, the sector also likes to present itself as a set of organisations and people who are driven by a values-based frame of reference, as promoters of standards such as solidarity, humanitarianism, equality and justice. A confirmation bias is at play here. The participants in the development cooperation community selectively look for data and other evidence that support their beliefs and mission. For this, alliances are sought with sympathetic think tanks, academic research units, specialised professional journals and international organisations with undisputable reputations. We will come back to this.

A community of this kind gains cohesion through four unifying processes: by developing a collective consciousness, by insisting on the coherent character and consistent behaviour of those participating in it, by the establishment of a collective agenda, and, finally, by coordinated lobbying. Firstly, a *collective consciousness* arises within the community. In the case of development cooperation, there is a very strong collective awareness that without this community, the rich, mainly Western world, would decline into an introverted condition, driven by national egoism and materialism. The development cooperation community is needed to watch over it and ensure that rich countries and their citizens, and in fact the rich everywhere, behave properly towards people in developing countries. If contact with developing countries was left exclusively to those outside the community (such as greedy companies, rich self-righteous individuals and price-conscious consumer masses), there would be a negative impact on developing countries.

A second means by which the community is bound together is *coherence* and *consistency*. The community issues its own marching orders and social control. Thus, tabs are kept on the non-profit-making character of development actors' initiatives. Whether on the part of government institutions or private actors, the community does not allow the principal or subsidiary purpose of development cooperation to be commercial or self-interested. However, there is no set of standards or recipe book defining what the ideal form of development cooperation would be like. For over 10 years there has been talk of 'a new aid architecture'. Reference is made to a number of generally accepted principles in the sector, such as the right of the initiative of governments in developing countries ('ownership', in the jargon of the sector), an equal partnership between donor and recipient, and joint efforts to reduce poverty. At the same time, according to this 'aid architecture', the donors need to adapt to national administrative and procedural systems, and coordinate their input more effectively. However, as we will see, a paradigm shift might be in the making. There is increasing mention of mutual interest, risk-taking, the involvement of private profit-seeking actors, geopolitics and geo-economics. Moreover, with the notions of whole-of-government and whole-of-society approaches being echoed more and more, the traditional development cooperation community is being challenged by other interested parties.

The next unifying factor is the *collective agenda*. The community – and more specifically its elite – does all it can to defend its collective interests and extend its influence. For obvious reasons, it suffers from a structural handicap in this respect. Development cooperation is not one of the traditional political and social issues that stir up commotion in public opinion. In a society that tends to pay greatest attention to the most contentious issues, this represents a serious obstacle. In addition, the community is not directly driven by a conventional social movement or special interest group that represents private interests and is capable of mobilising its supporters. We will also see how the NGDO movement is more of a network movement than a social one. This enables it to form numerous connections and take countless initiatives but also prevents it from acting as a visible actor on behalf of the sector's interests. The most contentious issues within the community of development actors include increasing the development cooperation budget, scrapping tied and, thus, self-interested aid, and making the foreign policy (indeed, all policy) of rich countries friendly and beneficial for resource-poor countries. With the COVID-19 pandemic, we see a new theme on the agenda: the role of development cooperation in preventing global waves of disruption and health problems. To what extent the development community has succeeded in securing increased funding for development aid can be seen in Figure 1.

Figure 1: Trend in official development cooperation of all rich countries combined

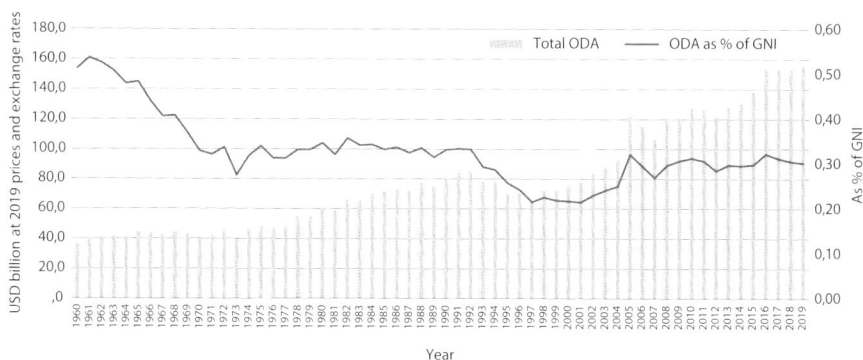

Source: OECD-DAC, Creditor Reporting System Database, 2020

Figure 1 clearly shows that we are supplying a larger combined volume of aid nowadays, but that when we look at our wealth (gross national income [GNI]), we have become far stingier. All the rich countries combined invested around USD 156 billion in official development cooperation in 2019 but that has to be compared against the USD 50,000 billion or so of wealth that these countries created in the same year.

Box 2. ODA is the most stable external resource for developing countries

In the sector of international cooperation, there is much talk nowadays about the importance of other financial flows that are injected into the economies of the countries of the Global South. This creates the impression that ODA is being surpassed by private flows at market prices, private grants and even other official flows (public sector transactions provided at close-to-market terms and/or with a commercial motive). Figure 2 teaches us at least that ODA is not only significant compared to the other flows but also more crisis resistant. Political and solidarity motives thus play a stabilising role in the financial transfers made through concessional aid.

Figure 2: Historically, ODA is the most stable external resource for developing countries

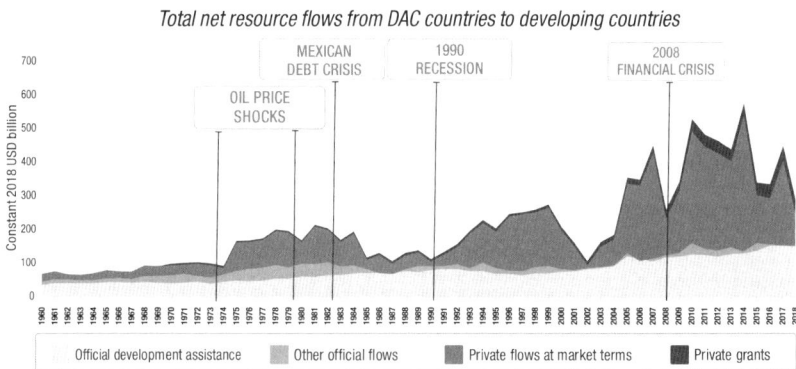

Total net resource flows from DAC countries to developing countries

Source: OECD, 2020c

Big donors, generous donors

Some countries budget larger sums of money for development work than others. As Figures 3 and 4 make clear, countries such as the USA and Japan are significant players in the development sector because they have large budgets (Figure 3), but they dig less deeply into their pockets than some smaller countries such as Luxembourg, Norway or Sweden (Figure 4).

It is around these issues that the elite of the community also coordinate most of their lobbying. For years, indeed, most of their lobbying efforts have been expended on getting the rich countries to commit to spending 0.7% of their wealth on ODA. As Figure 4 shows, only a handful of countries have reached that target: the United Kingdom, Denmark, Norway and Luxembourg. Luxembourg joined this club in 2000, proving that promises are kept at least sometimes. After several rounds of ODA cuts, the Netherlands left the 'G 0.7' club, as described by a former Dutch Minister of Development Cooperation, in the period 2016–2017.

As we mentioned earlier, the question arises of whether in times of globalisation, pandemics, SDGs, climate change, mass migration and the diversification of actors and instruments, we are measuring the right things. In a recent paper, Mitchell, Ritchie and Rogerson (2020), researchers at the Washington-based Centre for Global Development, proposed an alternative measure they called 'finance for international development' (FID). They rightly argue that terms such as 'aid', 'donor' and 'recipient' are anachronisms, but that alternatives such as the aforementioned TOSSD lack precision. The suggested FID encapsulates, on a grant-equivalent basis, the core package of financial assistance that nations – DAC members or not – provide officially and with generous concessions or grant elements across borders to support development. Their FID definition is deliberately narrower than ODA since it excludes all domestic spending in the provider country, such as in-country refugee spending, scholarships, aid administration, development-related research and development, and the promotion of development awareness. They conducted an experimental exercise for the year 2017 and found a total FID for DAC and non-DAC countries of just less than USD 150 billion, about 25 billion of which came from so-called emerging donors. Turkey and the UAE came out as the most generous of all, conventional donors and newcomers alike, investing 1.02% and 0.87%, respectively, of their GNI in international development.

Figure 3: ODA grant equivalent for 2019 (30 countries)

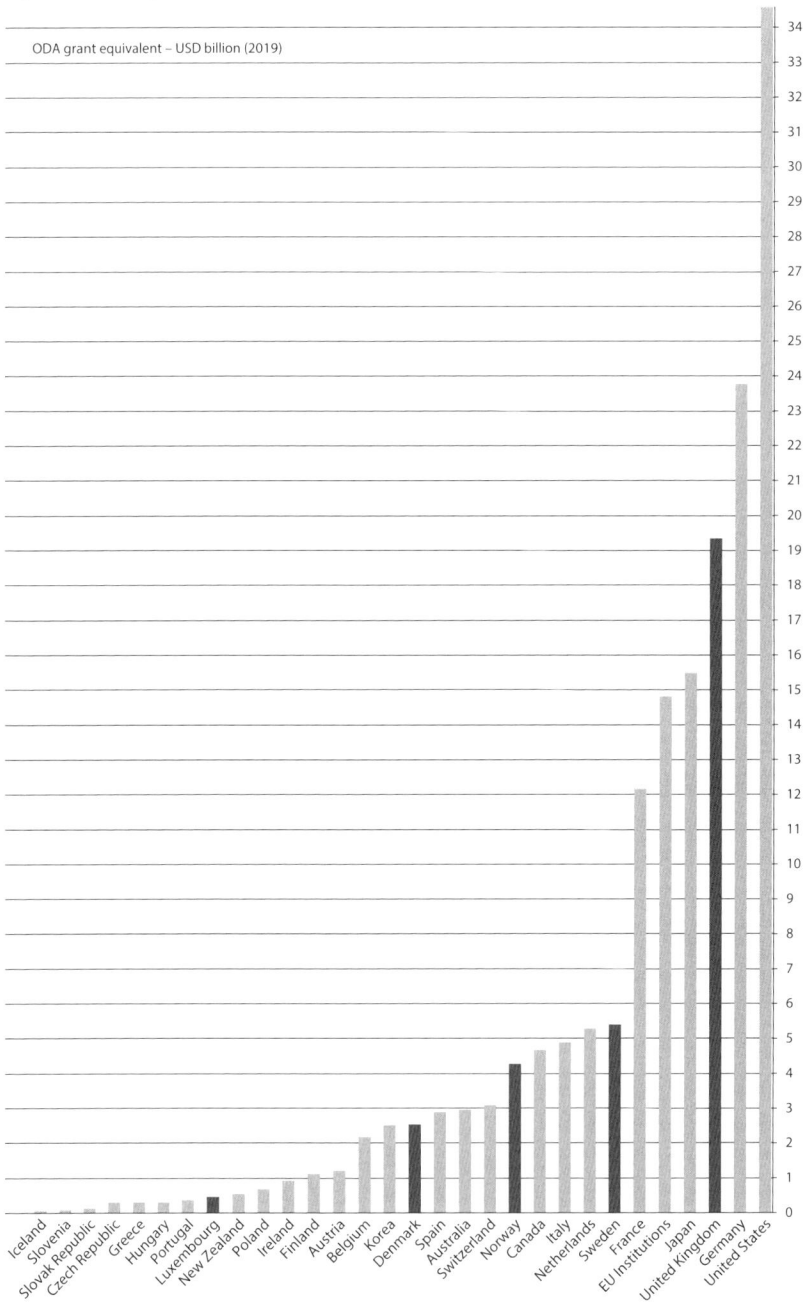

ODA grant equivalent – USD billion (2019)

Source: OECD-DAC, 2020

Figure 4: ODA grant equivalent as a percentage of GNI for 2019 (30 countries)

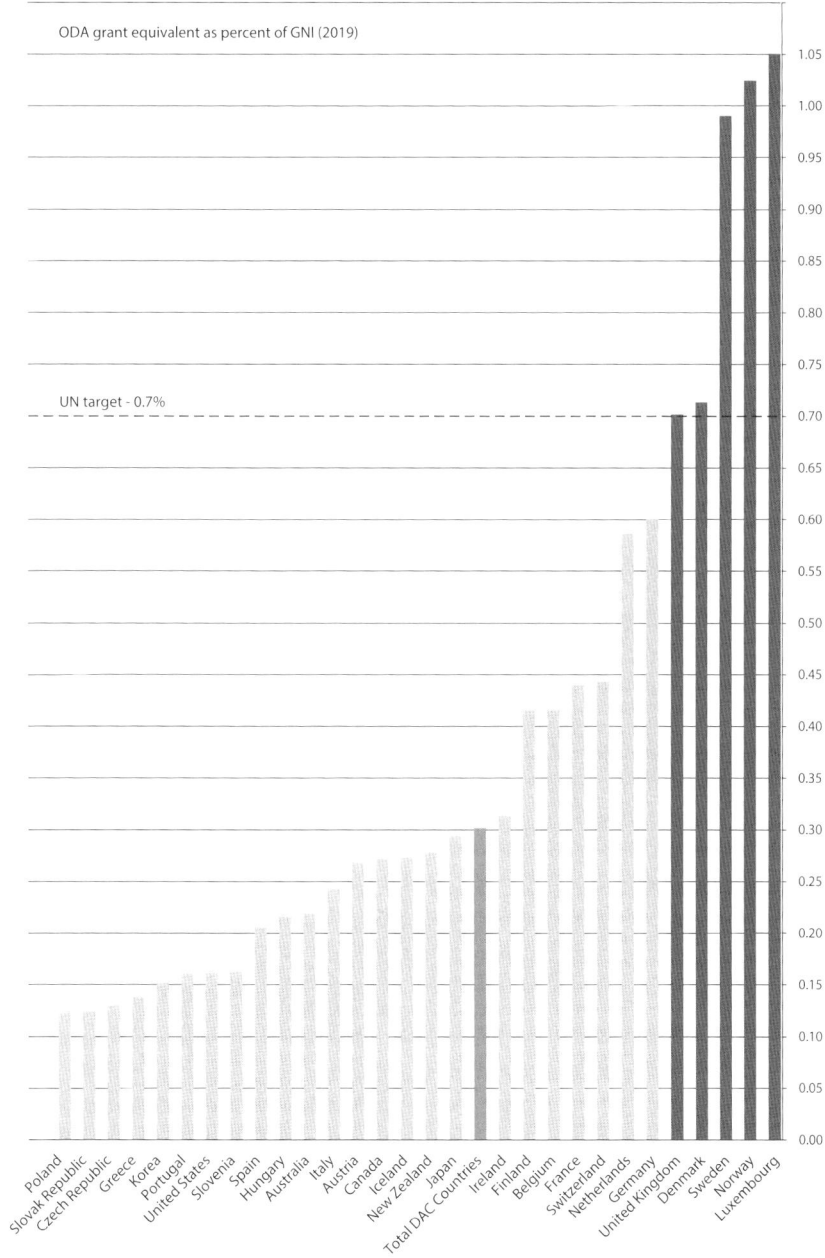

Source: OECD-DAC, 2020

41

Box 3. How relevant is the 0.7% target?

The 0.7% target has become a political mantra, if not a fetish, within the development cooperation community. The idea arose within the World Council of Churches. In 1955, this Protestant institution asked the Dutch agronomist Egbert de Vries, who worked at the World Bank and was a devout Christian, for advice on its own aid initiatives. De Vries stated that donations from the churches would never be enough to raise the standard of living in the poor countries. So the World Council resolved to ask the rich countries to invest 1% of their national income in grants and soft loans. This was exactly twice the amount of all public and private flows of capital into the poor countries at that time. The request from the World Council of Churches soon reached the UN.

In 1960, the UN General Assembly passed a resolution, with the agreement of the rich countries, calling for 1% of their national wealth to be spent on international aid and capital for the poor countries.[3] Academics backed the idea. Econometric studies showed that the developing countries at that time and in the years ahead needed around USD 10 billion to compensate for their savings and investment handicaps, and to get out of the starting blocks. As it happened, at the start of the 1960s this turned out to be precisely 1% of the rich countries' income.

The first session of the UN Conference on Trade and Development (UNCTAD) urged the economically developed countries to make an effort to make funds available of "a minimum net amount approaching as nearly as possible to 1 per cent of [their] national income". It was assumed that around three-quarters of this would be official bilateral aid. There was no mention as yet of an aid target – not until the Commission on International Development. This influential commission, chaired by the former Canadian Prime Minister Pearson, chose 0.7% as a target because it seemed simple, attainable and sufficient. The UN adopted the idea.

At the launch of the Second Development Decade in 1970, it was declared that "each economically advanced country will progressively increase its ODA to the developing countries and will exert its best efforts to reach a minimum net amount of 0.7 per cent of its gross national product... by the middle of the Decade". The undertaking was thus confined to a 'best effort commitment', with no engagement regarding outcomes, either then or later. At the launch of the Third Development Decade (1980–1989) and the Fourth Development Decade (1990–1999), and more recently the UN Addis Ababa Financing for Development Conference and the UN General Assembly of 2015, launching the SDG agenda, the stress was invariably on effort, and none of these international declarations contains a promise to reach 0.7%. The 0.7% goal thus sounds like what the political philosopher Thomas Hobbes once called "senseless speech": abusive or nonsensical language. In May 2015, the European Council, for example, reaffirmed its commitment to increase collective ODA to 0.7% of EU gross national income before 2030. But five years down the road, only four member states have abided to their pledge: Denmark, Luxembourg,

Sweden and the UK (then still a member state). Norway is the only other traditional donor that goes beyond the 0.7% target.

In the meantime, scientists have called the idea of 0.7% into question. The model that was used in the 1960s assumed a mechanistic relationship between capital and growth. By now, we know that development is about more than growth: it is also about resilience and sustainability. This is reflected in the SDGs. In order to meet them, more, adequate and targeted funding will be needed in the short term. In 2019, the International Monetary Fund (IMF) estimated that in order to meet the SDGs, the low-income countries would need to spend an additional half a trillion dollars annually by 2030 (Gaspar, 2019).

The development community is also diligently searching for innovative mechanisms to generate more funds for international cooperation. A recent example is the World Health Organization's WHO Foundation which was launched in early 2020, in the middle of the COVID-19 crisis, to address the most pressing global health challenges. The Foundation, which is legally separate from the WHO, aims to help the organisation broaden its donor base. It is set up to streamline philanthropic contributions from the general public, individual donors and corporate partners.

It is specifically, and not surprisingly, in the health sector that we have seen a lot of innovative work. UNITAID, for example, is another hosted partnership of the WHO. It started in 2006 for purchasing drugs for developing countries. It branched out to invest in innovations to prevent, diagnose and treat HIV/AIDS, tuberculosis (TB) and malaria more quickly, affordably and effectively. A key source of income for UNITAID is innovative financing, specifically the solidarity levy on airline tickets implemented by France, which was later adopted by a number of other countries (including Cameroon, Chile, Congo, Guinea, Madagascar, Mali, Mauritius, Niger and the Republic of Korea).

Gavi, the Global Alliance for Vaccines and Immunization, is yet another public-private health network with a wide variety of partners such as the WHO, UNICEF, the World Bank and the Bill and Melinda Gates Foundation. Together, they support primary healthcare facilities as well as vaccination and immunisation programmes in poor countries. Gavi also works with donors, including governments, foundations and corporate partners; NGOs, advocacy groups, professional and community associations, faith-based organisations and academia; vaccine manufacturers, research and technical health institutes; and developing country governments (Figure 5). One of the central components of Gavi's capital structure is the International Finance Facility for Immunisation. For more than 15 years now, this

Figure 5: The Gavi Alliance

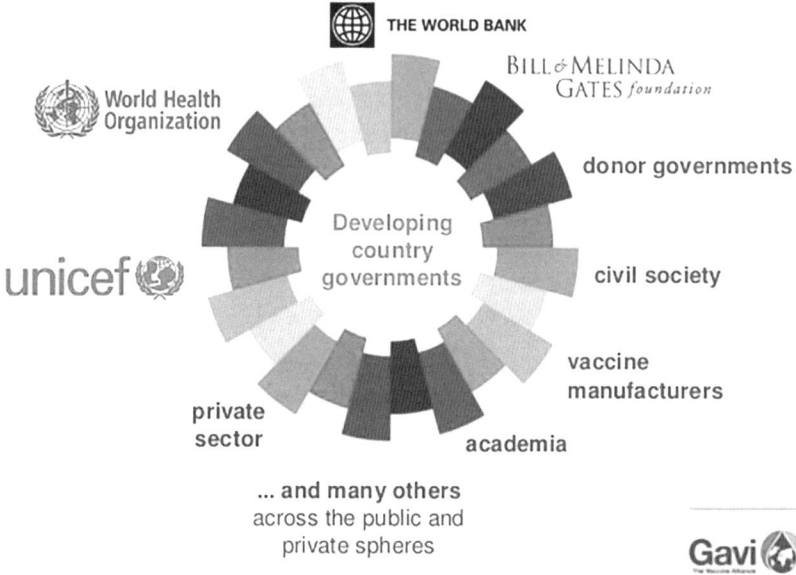

A broadening partnership...

THE WORLD BANK

BILL & MELINDA GATES *foundation*

World Health Organization

donor governments

Developing country governments

civil society

unicef

vaccine manufacturers

private sector

academia

... and many others
across the public and
private spheres

Gavi

Facility, which was created on the initiative of the UK, issues Vaccine Bonds on the capital markets against long-term donor pledges. In this way, Gavi has become the fifth-biggest multilateral financier. Gavi replenishment in the midst of the COVID-19 crisis in June 2020 surpassed the vaccine alliance's target of USD 7.4 billion, securing USD 8.8 billion for 2021 to 2025. The virtual event, hosted by the UK, saw donations from more than 50 countries and organisations.

The development cooperation community is also trying out many other possibilities for raising additional funds. Consideration is being given to a tax on air flights, arms and financial speculation.

It is a sociological fact that a community such as the development cooperation community is driven by the urge for self-determination. Outside interference is not welcomed: the community responds by closing ranks and becoming more or less impenetrable. New would-be participants are regarded with suspicion. However, the community of development actors has come under pressure in recent years.

Firstly, a process of mainstreaming development cooperation has been taking place. Numerous new players and development worker hopefuls are coming forward. We advance the idea that a 'whole-of-society approach' is gaining ground. The novel and unconventional players are rarely organisations, institutions, companies, funds or individuals claiming to specialise in development work (we will take a closer look at the most important newcomers later). Each of them is contesting the existing community's monopoly. However, they do not want to be at odds with the development cooperation specialists; on the contrary, they are introducing new ideas, values, norms, standards and working methods. So far, the reaction of the existing community to their request to join the club has been lukewarm.

Nevertheless, we can already talk in terms of a pluralistic aid community with four main pillars. We first did so in our previous book, where we suggested the advent of a free market in development aid (Develtere, Huyse & Van Ongevalle, 2012). The first pillar is formed from official bilateral development cooperation, in other words, the development cooperation organised by specialist government departments. The second pillar comprises multilateral development cooperation: projects and programmes that are financed by bilateral donors but executed by international institutions. The third pillar consists of the private and specialised development cooperation actors who obtain funds from their government and the general public to carry out specific projects and programmes; the most important of these are the NGDOs. The fourth and most recent pillar is formed of a motley collection of organisations, institutions and companies that have begun to take an interest in development cooperation in recent years. We will devote a separate chapter to these. Importantly and central to the thesis of this book is that these new actors, mainly the new bilateral, multilateral and fourth pillar organisations, are the vanguards of a new vision of development cooperation that is less North-South centred but is looking for mutual interests and development cooperation to benefit from future-oriented opportunities.

As Table 1 also suggests, the pluralisation and fragmentation of the development community are also continuing because the traditional actors are themselves channelling aid from an increasing array of sources. In every country, the specialist ministry of development cooperation has been joined by numerous other government departments, which – untrammelled by the rules applied in the sector – are taking steps of their own in the development world. But perhaps even more challenging is the arrival of new donor countries: Turkey, the UAE, Brazil, Venezuela, Thailand, South Africa, India and many more. Today, they account for about just over USD 20 to 25 billion of aid per year.

The international institutions also form a fragmented community. There are currently estimated to be more than 300 intergovernmental organisations. Previously, the UN Development Programme (UNDP), UNICEF and the World Bank Group were regarded as the main development specialists. On the UN chart (Figure 18), you can count more than 100 agencies, funds, programmes and bodies. Add to that the increasing number of specialised vertical programmes and funds through which UN institutions partner with member states, the business community and civil society to tackle particular environmental, social, economic or health problems. There are over 600 such public-private partnerships, also called transnational public-private governance initiatives (TGI) in the world, most of which are of recent vintage. They deal with issues as disperse as gender, climate change, water, timber and vaccinations, and in the vast majority of cases, UN agencies are involved. They can be very big, like the UN Global Compact which has more than 13,000 participants, mainly states and companies, who aim to adhere to principles of corporate social and sustainable responsibility (Westerwinter, 2019). The Islamic Development Bank Group is another example of an international member-state-based institution that is branching out with ever more new subsidiaries. Finally, the New Development Bank, also called the BRICS (Brazil, Russia, India, China and South Africa) Bank or the bank of the emerging economies, clearly shows that the arrival of new aspiring donors leads to a further expansion and the further pluralisation and fragmentation of the international development community.

More conflicting views and approaches: the arena is getting tough

So far, we have sketched out a picture of a development sector driven by a values-based rationale. This also happens to be the most familiar image of the sector: development cooperation is widely seen as the ultimate 'good cause'. Nonetheless, the sector cannot be exclusively regarded as a collective movement that puts its professed principles into practice. Development cooperation is also subject to a power-based rationale.

Both directly and indirectly, the sector brings together actors belonging to a huge variety of different categories: civil servants, ministerial staff, NGDO employees and volunteers, field workers, consultants, researchers, local employees, target groups, recipient governments and all kinds of local institutions. Each of these actors has a battery of action strategies that they use to obtain or gain control of the largest possible share of the resources and opportunities provided by the sector.

Following the French social anthropologist Olivier de Sardan (1997), we can see development cooperation as a plurality of arenas. These are located in the donor country, in the recipient country, in its capital city and even in the villages where the projects and programmes are run. Interwoven arenas are formed in all places and at all levels, and involve donors, recipients and other parties that have some interests at play. In an arena, we see heterogeneous strategic groups encountering one another. These groups of actors are driven by material and symbolic interests that are not always made explicit. Relational power is unevenly distributed among the different groups because the system assigns more power to one than to another, and because some actors and groups are able to accumulate more economic and social capital than others.

Although there are sometimes storms over the development cooperation arena, the climate is usually tempered because of an unwritten agreement that the community must be able to continue to exist as a single community and move forward collectively. People are, therefore, prepared to negotiate, forgive mistakes and cut one another some slack.

The objects of conflict in the arena are a useful guide to identifying power relations within the sector. They also help us to discern contradictions and inconsistencies. As it is not possible to deal with every object of conflict here, we have selected what we believe to be the most characteristic and perhaps the most relevant themes that give rise to clashes between strategic groups.

Firstly, there is the question of why there should be something like development aid or development cooperation in the first place. The existential question is, thus, is it a moral duty of the resource-rich towards the resource-poor? Or does the West indeed know best because it has proven how not only development and growth but also innovation, social protection and redistribution can take place? But does this not depart from a pathological white saviour syndrome? Does this not lead to pathetic ideas like 'volun-tourism', whereby Western youngsters, who do not yet have any professional track-record, by the mere asset of being Western-born and Western-educated, believe they have to combine their tourist trip to the Taj Mahal in Agra, Uttar Pradesh, with a week or two of unpaid teaching in a primary school, so as to impart some Western know-how to the local kids? In the footsteps of the sociologist and anthropologist Marcel Mauss,[4] some also argue that it is all about reciprocity. Gifts must be returned in some way or another. That is the enigma of the gift. Thus, development aid or cooperation creates ties that can be multiple, even when they are not intentional: geopolitical, commercial, cultural and even military. Or do we seek mutual interests with development aid or cooperation, an argument that frequently surfaces when we discuss the emerging new paradigm? The new narrative is about a win-win or even triple-win situation because not only do the exchanging parties gain from their cooperation but also society at large. But that is again debatable because it is not always clear who benefits most, in the short term and in the long term. As we have seen before, most protagonists of the development cooperation community reject any kind of self-interest and do not want to hear of win-win or mutual interest objectives. For them, development cooperation is all about solidarity and investments *à fonds perdu*: a non-repayable contribution to a better and more equitable world.

Secondly, ever since the beginnings of development cooperation, there has been an ideological rift which partly informs all other debate. The central question that the sector grapples with is whether the best way to resolve the acute but also structural problems of developing countries is through the redistribution of the global wealth pie or through its growth and development. The sustainable development concept – widely used in the sector for over two decades now – is also interpreted differently by groups opting for redistribution from those advocating a growth model. Those in favour of redistribution point out that sustainable development can come about only through greater international solidarity and a radical rearrangement of the available wealth. The defenders of the growth model emphasise that only the joint growth of the economies of the Global North and the Global South can help. The latter position is constantly criticised but has had the upper hand in the development world for years now. Even in the poverty alleviation programmes which are now so popular, considerable emphasis is placed on economic growth, which is supposed to provide fertile soil for social development.

A classic debate then relates to the type of intervention that donors should undertake. Should long-term strategies and more structural measures take precedence over short-term and emergency aid operations? The emergency aid agenda has had the wind in its sails for the last two or three decades. This has further been reinforced by the Ebola virus and COVID-19 crises. The advocates of structural strategies point out that emergency aid can actually reinforce poverty by making people dependent and can lead to wrong policies such as vertical healthcare approaches that focus on a single disease and hinder much-needed horizontal and all-encompassing healthcare policies.

Nevertheless, more structural strategies abound and all have their advocates and their opponents. Is sending technical experts to other countries a good thing or does it force local people out of the employment market? Are short-term projects better than long-term programmes or not? Does debt cancellation reward and encourage bad policy, or is it necessary for a new start?

Another arena is formed by the opposition between public and private actors. The terms 'governmental' and 'non-governmental' actors are used in the sector when referring to donors, and the notions of 'public' and 'civil society/private sector' when referring to recipients. Questions of which type of actor has the best credentials in terms of its contribution to development and how the roles should be divided between public and private are ever-present. Over the last decades, NGDOs have been particularly successful in consolidating their position and turning it to good account financially. However, as will be evident throughout this book, they are now increasingly challenged by the massive emergence of new actors, who are, indeed, not specialists in development cooperation but see an interest in being active with their counterparts in the developing world. We call them the fourth pillar.

The relations between 'donors' and 'recipients' are constantly tense too, with clashes taking place over concepts and principles such as sovereignty, ownership, alignment, accountability, the untying of aid and predictability. As we will see, much of this is being debated in the UN and the OECD-DAC. Although a great deal of lip service is paid to the idea of a more back-seat role for donors, the balance of power is still tipped in favour of the donors: *la main qui reçoit se trouve en bas*, as the French saying goes: 'the receiver's hand is lower than the giver's'. In any case, many donors are not convinced that all governments in the developing world can be trusted with a free hand in the administration of development budgets.

Those involved in development cooperation also disagree on the right local levers for development. On the one hand, there are those who firmly believe in local strengths; in their view, development cooperation is merely a window of opportunity or catalyst, the purpose of which is to help local dynamism unfold (for example by giving local institutions financial means). On the other hand, a gloomier position stresses the weaknesses of local actors and institutions. From this perspective, the purpose of development cooperation is to address local shortcomings and deficiencies (for example by sending in experts).

Different strategic groups can also disagree on the question of whether development work should be 'generalised' or 'concentrated'. Some argue in favour of broad measures that have a general effect on North-South relations. Examples include improving access to Western markets for products from developing countries and the general cancellation of debts. Others believe that concentrated, focused work in specific countries and areas with a high development potential does more good. In this respect, they refer to the LDCs (which accumulate multiple problems) or Small Island Developing States (which are vulnerable because of climate change) and particularly those that show signs of good governance. Protagonists of this more selective work believe that affirmative action is needed for those people and countries that are the 'wrecked of the world'. For them, only stepped-up attention will lift them out of the structural situation they are trapped in.

One theme of contention, which has become very prominent again in recent years, relates to the purity of both the motives for and approach to aid provision. Many hardliners from the idealist school in the sector are unwilling to compromise on this point. Developed donor countries must not seek any advantage for themselves (of any kind at all). Financial gain and profit-based approaches are anathema. So they plead for no tied aid and no commercial strings to be attached to development aid. Others argue that it makes no difference why and how cooperation takes place, provided it delivers the right results. Remarkably, a realist school of thinking has also been prominent in the South for some time already. The advent of new donors such as Turkey and China, who explicitly seek advantages (e.g., market access and proximity to much-needed raw materials) when giving aid to African countries, continues to puzzle traditional donors. Should they condemn the emerging donors or rather accept this approach as the only realistic one? We will come back to this several times because the new emerging paradigm tries to reconcile all of this.

It is clear that strategic groups formed around each of these contentious issues develop a more or less coherent set of arguments to defend their case. Winning such a debate has important symbolic value, but there are also other interests at stake in each case – including financial ones. This brings us to the third rationale that strongly influences development cooperation: the market dimension.

More transactional interests: market appeal

We have by now abandoned the illusion that development cooperation is a system or sector that is exclusively driven by idealists and a values-based rationale. Power relations also play an important role. Furthermore, the field of development cooperation can also be regarded as a market. Thus, a more calculative rationale, that of the market, is also present. Just as they do in a marketplace, the various players treat one another as vendors and customers, as competitors that seek to win profitable transactions, as hard-headed opportunists who are out to increase their turnover, as marketers who are angling for a good position on the market, as investors seeking the maximum return on investment and as business managers who want to win out and make a profit. At first sight, this seems strange, as most of the actors claim to be working towards a public goal (improving the lot of others and general global welfare) rather than a private one.

Whether the actors are government departments that are involved in development work or NGDOs, they do not strive for financial gain. Profit is defined, in line with practice in the public and non-profit sectors, as a 'non-distributable social gain' (number of people employed, social reserves accumulated, etc.). In addition, the means of production that are available in or deployed by the sector are not privately owned but jointly owned by various stakeholders. For that matter, it is hard to say who has legal owner-ship of the output. Is it the local state because it has sovereignty over its ter-ritory and it is on its land that the donor was there to only assist in building a bridge, developing a schooling programme with much-needed infrastruc-ture or setting up a central buying and distribution centre for generic medi-cines? Or is it the donor who can claim ownership since, very often, they are called upon to pay the bill if, after the completion of the project, some work still has to be done for it to become sustainable and self-supporting? In any case, this topic is seldom discussed in development cooperation circles and rarely clearly established in the memoranda of understanding or coopera-tion agreement engaging the parties involved.

Box 4. Who owns this well? Partners in problems!

Things can get pretty complicated in development business. Take an example of the kind of co-ownership or shared ownership that often unwillingly brings part-ners in problems. Who owns the well that was purchased with support from a West-ern NGDO and with additional funding from a Western government but which was built through the combined efforts of the population of the Burkinabe village of Mané? The Western NGDO will assure its supporters that 'its' well has raised the quality of life of the poor rural Burkinabe. The Western government (which prob-ably paid 85% of the bill) claims co-ownership of the well in several ways. It asks for the original purchase receipts, reports and impact evaluations. The Burkinabe government also feels itself to be the owner of the pump, which lies in its territory and must meet the standards that the government has set for water pumps. The water source is counted as part of the national effort to combat poverty and fea-tures handsomely in the many reports submitted by the Ministry of Planning to the World Bank and the UN. The provincial authorities and politicians also boast about this achievement. Their department for water supply had performed the soil surveys and correctly indicated where a large aquifer was present at a depth of 170 metres. Besides, was it not they who were asked to cut the ribbon at the inaugura-tion of this local project? Finally, they were the ones who succeeded in bringing the Western NGDO to the area. The local king reasons along similar lines. The drought has never been so bad as during his reign, but he has managed to attract many *toubabs* (whites) to his area. The local non-governmental organisation is equally proud of 'its' pump. A yellowing map hangs in its local headquarters with 120 drawing pins in it, and the pump at Mané is neatly marked as one of the achievements of its project. And the local people? The members of the well committee who are responsible for hygiene and maintenance regard themselves as co-owners of the pump. They are scarcely able to cope with the limited financial contributions from local users. The rest of the population sees the pump as a gift of the *prozè* (project): a gift from the white man who came past a few harvests ago.

Without this being explicitly intended by the development actors, the risks (failure, theft, loss, natural disaster, etc.) that are necessarily associated with any form of financial interaction are depersonalised in the development sector. Rarely or ever does a development agreement specify who should bear such risks. The water pump in Mané comes from Europe. Replacement parts are hard to obtain in Burkina Faso and expensive. While the project is running, the partnership between the local and European NGDO ensures that the necessary transactions take place if the pump plays up. But both the Western co-financing government and the NGDO's supporters quietly believe that a ten-year investment in the area has been enough. Was it not promised that the project would make the local population more self-reliant?

More often than not development work is practised as a risk-free venture. None of those involved takes full responsibility and engages to pay the bill when things go wrong. But it is also rarely if ever made clear who can lay claim to any gains or benefits resulting from the investments.

Projects and programmes are also often managed via an interactive process in which several parties are associated. For about two decades, as we will see, the development community has placed enormous stress on ownership, meaning that the recipient government or population group is supposed to be 'in the driver's seat', determining which goals should be worked towards, how this should be done and how the results should be evaluated. The donors must 'bring down their flag', take a more behind-the-scenes role and act as a partner. In other words, the idea is to replace 'donorship' with 'ownership'. But, remarkably, we will also see that in recent years, donors are seeking to square the circle by insisting that they want to be not only payers but also players (Develtere, 2020).

These examples hopefully make it clear that the development cooperation market – like any market – is a social construct. The players in the market behave to a significant degree according to the social, cultural, symbolic and power patterns characterising the domain. Yet the market rationality sometimes has a considerable influence on relationships between the play-

Figure 6: Inflows of external finance to ODA-eligible countries

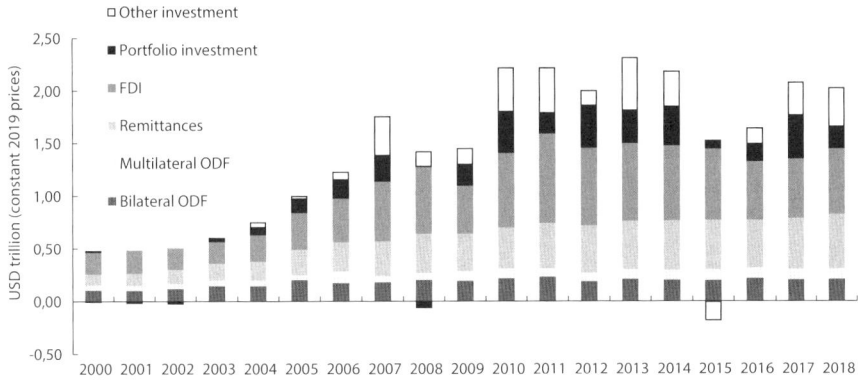

Note: The largest sample possible for ODA-eligible countries was used for each year shown in this figure. ODF: Official Development Finance (ODA – Official Development Assistance – plus OOF – Other Official Flows); FDI (Foreign Direct Investment)

Source: OECD-DAC, Global Outlook on Financing for Sustainable Development 2021[5]

ers. Even the most fervent advocates of the non-profit-making character of development cooperation cannot escape this fact.

Firstly, there is competition between the players (and groups of players) on the market. The public funds available in the donor countries for development cooperation have, in many cases, decreased or only marginally increased during the last decade (Figure 6), but the number of programmes and the number of actors have significantly increased. In all donor countries, ministries for development cooperation, other ministries, public institutions, multilateral 'partners' and NGDOs are embroiled in a permanent struggle over the distribution of these scarce resources.

Furthermore, the so-called charity market lacks elasticity. The amounts donated by private individuals and businesses towards development cooperation are not significantly increasing. Moreover, there has been a proliferation of fundraisers. Competition between organisations is particularly fierce, and they are increasingly resorting to modern marketing techniques in order to increase and activate the generosity of the general public, and channel it (towards themselves).

Annually, between USD 150 and 200 billion has to be converted into goods and services on the international development cooperation market (debt cancellation is obviously excluded from this calculation.) This market can be seen as a segmented one (Taupiac, 2001). Firstly, there are emergency aid operations; where purchasing is concerned, speed and accessibility are paramount for such operations. To save lives, the goods (food, medicines, tents, logistical equipment) need to reach their destination as quickly as possible. They are often simple in design. Although they are increasingly subject to competitive bidding, they are usually also more expensive because of the short delivery period. The other segment – that of the so-called structural and support programmes – works on a somewhat different basis. Goods and services that need to be supplied must above all be suitable for the long-term objectives of the project or programme in question. The range of goods and services is far wider than on the emergency aid market. A significant proportion of the budget is spent on pharmaceuticals, contraceptives, vaccines, medical equipment, management and administrative services, building and maintenance, industrial machinery, vehicles, engineering services, basic chemicals, fertilisers, seeds, IT equipment and school equipment. In recent years, there has been a growing awareness that more local input can and should be provided; in other words, goods and services should be purchased locally if possible.

The UN itself is talking about a UN market and even has a special agency and website for suppliers and demanders: the UN Global Marketplace. The UN represents an annual global market of over USD 17 billion. The biggest suppliers are still Western economies, led by the USA and followed by Belgium, Switzerland, France, Denmark and the UK. Important players in the Global South are India and the UAE. Because of increased local procurement, we see that also countries such as Afghanistan, Kenya and the Democratic Republic of Congo are gaining ground.

Again, the larger trends that we identified earlier in the case of community and arena aspects of development cooperation also apply to the development cooperation marketplace. To start with, it is subject to mainstreaming and localisation. There has been a proliferation of new international, national and sub-national governmental actors. Kharas (2007a) estimated the contribution made by 29 so-called new or emerging bilateral donors, such as China and Turkey, for 2005 at more than USD 8 billion. We found that this increased to an estimated USD 10 billion by 2007 and 15 billion by 2009 (Develtere, Huyse & Van Ongevalle, 2012). Some of these new donors became DAC members. For the remaining 22 new donors, the OECD estimates that they collectively invest just over USD 25 billion in aid (OECD, 2019a). By 2020 this is probably about 30 billion. However, we agree with Kharas (2009) who argues that an exact calculation of the amount of official development aid provided by new bilateral donors is highly problematic because the hybrid nature of some of their transactions disguises whether the purpose is developmental or commercial.

Box 5. Development impact bonds: private investors and conventional donors join forces

The international development cooperation sector increasingly adopts strategies that are deployed in other fields. Development impact bonds are a good example. Inspired by the increasingly popular impact of investing and some of its mechanisms such as social impact bonds in Western countries, development impact bonds are based on a contract between a private investor and conventional donors who jointly want to reach specific development goals, such as giving access to tap water in slum areas in a big city somewhere in a developing country. The investor takes the initial risks of paying for the interventions, such as infrastructural investments, equipment or activities, to hit the goals. To compensate the risk-taking, the investor will be remunerated if and to the extent that the intervention succeeds. Returns on the investment depend on progress and achievement using criteria agreed upon with the donor. The growing impact bond community believes that this more market-driven approach is an original way to attract new sources of funding for development programmes, offers a new business model that encourages innovation, flexibility, efficiency, effectiveness and impact, and proposes a more agile way to be responsive to the fast-changing needs of target groups.

Impact investors are not just reactive actors slavishly following the whimsical preferences and prescriptions of the donors they depend upon to be rewarded for their work; they also shape the investment environment and can influence and orient policies. Henriette Fore, executive director of UNICEF, and Suzanne Biegel, co-founder of the GenderSmart Investment Summit, for example, have made a plea for impact investors and governments alike to help girls shatter the glass ceiling (Fore & Biegel, 2020). They argue that adolescent girls and young women are our next generation of leaders, innovators, and entrepreneurs. Investing in their success makes economic sense and is also a smart way of maximising social impact. Even prior to COVID-19, nearly one in four girls aged 15 to 19 globally were not in education, employment or training, compared with one in 10 boys. The longer the pandemic goes on, the more likely we are to see this gender gap widen even further, as we have seen in previous public health emergencies such as Ebola.

Investors, they write, can choose to build a focused investment strategy in one or several of the key areas that boost the position of girls in the modern global labour market: skills, jobs, education, safety, health and inclusion. Looking across impact investment flows in different sectors, there is currently more than USD 21 billion in existing impact investments relevant to the school-to-work transitions in emerging markets – from education technology to infrastructure. Yet, "only a very small proportion has intentionally and explicitly addressed the opportunities for girls and young women in their due diligence reviews or impact measurements".

As the example of China shows, the new donors are not so new at all. However, they have a different conceptualisation of development aid and are introducing new intervention methods. Not only are the combined donation and exchange operations of the Chinese based on looking for an explicit win-win situation but China also takes pride in the fact that it arranges turnkey projects. Chinese projects are delivered in comprehensive packages including the planning, financing, manpower and training that are necessary to carry out the project (including Chinese language lessons to facilitate contacts). China draws on its strong tradition of implementing and managing large-scale infrastructure projects to greatly shorten the project cycle (from planning to execution). By doing so, it has become a formidable competitor for traditional donors.

Do new donors have other interests?

There is increasingly talk about 'new' or 'emerging' donors, also often referred to as non-DAC-members. Let us be clear right from the beginning: the terms 'new' or 'emerging' are not appropriate. China, for example, was already aiding Vietnam and Korea in the 1950s. Communist Cuba has sent medical teams and other humanitarian aid workers to South American and African nations since the early 1960s. Israel helped many countries to organise their agricultural sector in the 1970s and 1980s, inspiring them with their experiences in their famous Kibbutzim collectives. During the Cold War period, the USSR and its satellites hosted many students from the then-Third World and gave substantial support to developing countries and their regimes choosing alternative paths to development. Nevertheless, the 'new' donors have now become more prominent, more vocal, more influential. When talking about new donors, reference is first made to the BRICS countries: Brazil, Russia, India, China and South Africa. Their global ambitions are partly realised through the multiplication of interactions with other Southern nations, and aid is part of their strategy to forge intimate ties with like-minded regimes. Similar drives can be attributed to other new donors such as the UAE, Qatar, Kuwait, Indonesia, Thailand, Chile, Colombia, Costa Rica and Mexico. As we will see, as a group, these new donors have significantly influenced the move from a North-South paradigm of development cooperation to a global paradigm. Although they are much talked about and have become very visible on the local development scene in Africa and many places in Asia and Latin America, they do not invest significant funds in terms of DAC-defined ODA. China's aid, in DAC terms, is equivalent to the ODA provided by the Netherlands. India's is only one-third of that of the Netherlands. Russia's ODA is one-fifth, while Brazil's is equivalent to that of Luxembourg's foreign aid. Collectively, the new donors spent an estimated USD 25 to 30 billion in concessional aid in 2016, versus the USD 74 billion spent by the EU and its member states.

To better understand the effect of this new wave of donors who tackle development aid and cooperation in a different way than the traditional donors, let us have a look at China. As early as the Mao era, many African leaders were attracted by the Chinese alternative. In exchange for their sympathy, China constructed their national parliaments, gave them a national football stadium to be proud of or installed a railway.[6] Chinese experts, such as doctors and engineers, were sent out. In 1964, Prime Minister Zhou Enlai set out the principles of Chinese aid: Chinese aid must benefit both donor and recipient, China respects the sovereignty of the recipient country and does not impose any conditions,[7] little if any interest is charged, the goal is self-reliance, priority is given to projects that require little investment but yield rapid results, China supplies its own equipment at competitive prices, local technical personnel are trained to manage suitable technology and Chinese experts live like their colleagues in the host country.

Strikingly, all these principles apart from the first and the last could have come straight out of a DAC manual, and Chinese aid today still seems to be inspired by the same principles. So why the current controversy about Chinese aid in Africa?

In the last decades, Chinese-African cooperation has progressed in leaps and bounds in terms of both quality and quantity but the relationship acquired a more functional economic basis when the Chinese economy started to boom in the 1990s. African leaders were in no doubt as to why they were keen to receive Chinese officials or drink tea with them during the summit meetings at the Forum on China-Africa Cooperation (also known as the Beijing Forum). Chinese cooperation is consistently based on the principle of non-interference in domestic affairs. Exports from China to Africa are growing faster than those in the other direction, but China has given the purchase of African goods an enormous boost by exempting some from import duty thanks to its massive appetite for African oil, metal and timber.

Chinese aid has received fierce criticism in traditional Western development cooperation circles. Traditional donors pretend to work towards good governance, while the Chinese do not meddle with local politics, do business with crooks as well as with democrats and reinforce the status of those in power. However, Chinese aid is predictable, more so than Western aid. Because most of its loans are not concessional, China pushes recipient countries into new debt traps. In addition, it not only ties these countries commercially but also uses its 'donation diplomacy' to rally support for its interests in multilateral forums. Looking critically at past and present practices of Western development aid, it sometimes seems that the pot is calling the kettle black. In any case, traditional economic and aid actors are conscious of the Chinese presence. Chinese companies outbid other foreign firms by promising substantial aid in the form of new dams, deep-sea ports or social infrastructure. Traditional donors' aid projects are dwarfed by the big, fast and highly visible Chinese projects. Everybody is increasingly impressed by Chinese assertiveness in the development sector. China's financial resources for concessional foreign aid have increased rapidly since the beginning of this century, reaching more than USD 3 billion from 2014 onwards. However, as we have indicated before, this is just equivalent to the Dutch spending on ODA. As we will see, Chinese ODA-like concessional grants and aid are mixed with 'other official financial' support, which is not concessional; for example, in the framework of the Belt and Road Initiative that is connecting China with the rest of the world. Recently, some journalists and Western scholars report that China – because of growing and worldwide criticism about lack of transparency and sustainability – has drastically curtailed the overseas lending programmes managed by the China Development Bank and the Export-Import Bank of China, after nearly a decade of ambitious growth which at its peak rivalled that of the World Bank (Wheatly & Kynge, 2020).

China gives grants to build hospitals, schools and other medium-sized and small projects for social welfare, interest-free loans for public facilities and concessional loans for productive projects. 'Complete' projects account for a major part of China's foreign aid expenditure. In those projects, the Chinese side is responsible for the whole or part of the process, from study and survey to design and construction; provides all or part of the equipment and building materials; and sends engineers and technical personnel to organise and guide the construction, installation and trial production of these projects. After a project is completed, China hands it over to the recipient country. The Chinese are focused on the inputs and immediate outputs of the projects, while the long-term effects and impact are the responsibility of the receiving partner.

Tellingly, the Ministry of Commerce of China is at the centre of the Chinese system of foreign aid and manages 90% of its bilateral funding. In order to strengthen the coordination of all departments concerned, the Ministry of Commerce, Foreign Affairs and Finance officially established the country's foreign aid inter-agency liaison mechanism. In February 2011, this liaison mechanism was upgraded to an inter-agency coordination mechanism.

In any case, the increase in trade, investment and aid initiatives on the part of China on the African continent is ensuring less dependence on the West and, consequently, more dependence on China. For example, 70% of Africa's IT backbone has been installed by Huawei, financed through a combination of gifts and loans.

The number of Chinese working in Africa is estimated to be in the hundreds of thousands. Contact with China and the Chinese is opening African eyes to an alternative model. The Beijing Consensus is at odds with the so-called Western liberal Washington Consensus but results in high growth figures and a considerable reduction of levels of poverty.

So what do the Africans think about this? 'The West has had 50 years or even far longer to bring us development. It's time to let the Chinese show what they can do'. 'The Chinese seek their own interests, you say? But don't the Westerners do that too?' 'What is the USA doing in Angola, Chad and Equatorial Guinea?' 'Chinese products are of poor quality, you say? I can finally afford a mobile phone'. 'They brought a container of nail clippers with them. Everyone in the village got one!' Opposing voices, such as that of the African trade unionist who complains about working conditions in Chinese businesses and projects, or of the intellectual who says that the 'colonisability' of Africa is not a Chinese but an African problem (Mana, 2008), seem quiet by contrast.

It would be erroneous to look at all these new donors through the prism of the Chinese approach to development aid. They all have their singularities, own approaches and interests.

Turkey, the UAE, Kuwait and Qatar seem to prioritise their Muslim neighbours and have been quick to significantly increase their foreign aid to Egypt following the Arab Spring in 2011. It would appear as though these countries use aid as a tool to achieve stability, security and economic gain. Such a hypothesis is supported by the fact that Turkish aid has largely taken the form of loans and is aimed at the long-term opening-up of African markets for Turkish companies. A case in point is Turkish Airlines, which expanded from 14 African destinations in 2011 to 55 destinations in 2018. This pragmatic, interest-based approach seems to align better with that of China.

Countries such as South Africa, India, Thailand and Brazil are more in accordance with the international agenda as expressed in the UN SDGs. Thus, South Africa focuses on peace, security, reconstruction, regional integration, governance and humanitarian assistance, and does so in triangular partnerships with several DAC members including Germany, Spain, Norway and Sweden. Similarly, Indian cooperation with Africa focuses on capacity-building and infrastructure, in sectors such as health, education,

IT and energy. Africa's largest-ever ICT project, intended to facilitate links between Indian and African institutions in these sectors, is being conducted with India. The project links seven Indian and five African universities, 12 Indian and five African super-speciality hospitals, and 53 telemedicine and tele-education centres in Africa. Thailand aims to export a balanced and stable model of development, focusing on training, scholarships, fellowships and capacity development. Brazil's South-South aid is focused – at least officially – on peacekeeping, cross-border integration, science and technology, and culture and education.

Public and soft diplomacy play an important role in some of the new donors' strategies. Mirroring French and British efforts to promote their respective cultures and languages, China already boasts 54 Confucius Institutes in 38 African countries. By comparison, *l'Alliance française* is present in 37 African countries, although more intensively (with 126 institutes). In 2018, *Rossotrudnichestvo* announced it would open new Russian cultural centres in Africa, Asia and Latin America. In almost every single African country, one finds China Study Centres in one or more universities, while there are European Study Centres in only four African countries.

Foreign aid is becoming increasingly institutionalised and strategic for these new donors. For instance, South Africa's foreign aid is taking place in the context of its Development Agency's 2015–2020 Strategic Plan, which notably emphasises cooperation with the African continent and South-South relations. Similarly, Brazil's 2010 report on international development cooperation sought to comprehensively assess and offer a narrative on the country's efforts. In 2011, Turkey reorganised its foreign aid agency, while India created its own development unit the following year to accompany the increase in its foreign aid. Russia adopted a new concept on development cooperation in 2014, and Thailand's aid is organised via a special entity within the Ministry of Finance. In 2016, the UAE also reorganised its aid efforts, merging its Ministry for International Cooperation with the Ministry of Foreign Affairs.

These emerging affinities between new donors and recipients can be illustrated by the proliferation of summits: for instance, a tri-annual Forum on China-Africa Cooperation was established in 2000 and many other ones followed suit. The India-Africa Forum Summit convenes annually since 2008, the Africa-Turkey Forum was held in 2008 and again in 2014, and a Russia-Africa Summit took place for the first time at the end of 2019.

Importantly, the new donors do not only compete with the traditional ones but also with each other. In response to the Chinese One Road One Belt initiative, in May 2017, India and Japan announced their ambition to create an Asia-Africa Growth Corridor. This is also manifest in the proliferation of diplomatic missions in Africa; illustrative is that China has embassies in all but a few African Union (AU) member states (50), while Turkey already has 41 and India is planning to open 18 new ones and to have 47 in a couple of years.

Finally, some of the new donors substantially channel their aid budgets through multilateral agencies. For the UAE, Kuwait, Turkey and India, this is over 80% of their aid portfolio. On the other hand, South Africa, Brazil, Indonesia and Thailand prefer to go bilateral and only share less than a third of their aid funds with multilateral institutions.

Everybody from payers to players: the emergence of a new paradigm

As globalisation continues to rapidly shrink our world, and pandemics, as well as climate change, show interdependence and collective vulnerabilities, the international donor community shifts its principles, orientations and working methods. Under President Juncker, in 2018, a new Africa-EU Alliance for Sustainable Investments and Jobs was launched. The first out-of-continent mission of his successor, Ursula von der Leyen, was to Addis Ababa to talk to her colleague in the AU. It was more than a symbolic gesture; President Trump brought together 16 government agencies for his new Prosper Africa initiative intended to unlock opportunities for Americans to do business in Africa. The American development agency USAID is just one of them. In the UK, the new narrative of the Johnson government is about a 'mutual prosperity policy' and its development agency DFID, internationally known as one of the most competent development bulwarks, is being merged with the Foreign, Commonwealth and Development Office.

As we have seen, the new donors do not give the recipient countries a free ride with the money they give. Already in 2014, China engaged with the African Development Bank in a fund that was tellingly baptised the 'Africa Growing Together Fund'. Today, China has less foreign direct investment (FDI) stock in Africa than Europe but has surpassed Europe in terms of FDI flows. Its explicit combination of concessional aid and non-concessional, tied investments seem not to irritate African and other developing countries' political elites. More African heads of state participate in the Forums on China-Africa Cooperation than in the meetings of the AU.

And there are more signs that the development cooperation paradigm is changing. We will meet many of them in this book. Take the proliferation of the fourth pillar organisations or web-based interactions between individuals, organisations and companies from around the globe, or the advent of very influential international development agencies originating in the Global South, such as the Bangladesh Rural Advancement Committee (BRAC) or the Nigerian Tony Elumelu Foundation. What should we think about the national bank of Bolivia giving funding to one of the largest American NGDOs, World Vision? The annual letters of Bill and Melinda Gates are as good a barometer of the temperature and the wind direction in the sector of development cooperation as the reports of the World Bank, the UN Development Programme or the OECD-DAC.

Sixty years ago, when development aid became a sector and system, as we have seen, with three explicit dimensions (community, arena and market), we looked at the world as being divided between North and South. This gap model was infused with the idea that the North had and the South lacked. The North thus had to be generous and not self-interested, the discourse went. It had to give and provide its experience, funding and technology. The donor countries had to step in where developing countries were in need or when they failed. Around the turn of the century, this gradually was transformed into a model in which ownership by the recipient partners would become the alpha and omega of any development cooperation relation. The plans and policies of the recipients would be the starting point for every partnership. They would also remain in charge during the execution of the projects and programmes and their criteria would be used to evaluate them. The donors would limit their own role to just paying the bill. In this book, we argue that we are currently witnessing a new paradigm shift. The relationship between donors and recipients is changing again. Globalisation makes state and non-state actors all over the world aware that the ballgame is shifting. Everybody sees their stake in playing a role in the new global configuration, in defending their interests, in benefiting from the opportunities out there and in forging strategic alliances with partners across borders. This whole-of-society paradigm that is in the making transforms all parties involved into players (Develtere, 2019; 2020).

In this incipient whole-of-society approach, an ever-growing range of state and non-state actors from across the world are collaborating and co-creating development. Accordingly, the traditional vertical and unidirectional North-South approach is giving way to a horizontal, networked model in which various stakeholders share common challenges and goals.

Consequently, the donor-recipient approach is in the process of being revised. Mutual interests and win-win operations are becoming more central. In this model, the focus is not on the weaknesses and deficits encountered in Africa or elsewhere in the developing world but increasingly on the strengths and opportunities of all partners – allowing for the bidirectional, multidirectional and reciprocal partnership of equals.

Thus, as we have seen with the new donors and also with the new options that are on the drawing board in Europe, the USA and the UK, aid is no longer a standalone mechanism to help recipient countries: it is explicitly part of a wider framework of geopolitics and geo-economics that has to be aligned with the donors' perceived interests and realised in conjunction with other instruments such as investments, exchanges, training, trade and digital interconnectedness. The traditional development cooperation community thus becomes an enabler, a facilitator and a vector that stimulates others to grasp the opportunities that international cooperation and co-development provide.

This implies, of course, that donors and recipients are supposed to drop the risk-averse attitude that has characterised development cooperation for so long. Processes are more open-ended than ever and in the upcoming new paradigm, they become increasingly interactive and iterative. Agility, flexibility and adaptability are the new prescriptions imposed upon development workers and their programmes. Because of the rules laid down by the development cooperation market, their interactions have to be opportunity- and human-centred rather than need- and plan-centred, as their credo used to be. The donor-recipient relationship has to make room for a mutually beneficial relationship not only between governments but indeed between societies and economies more broadly.

The new model implies that a diversity of players beyond official development agencies and NGDOs have to fight for their bit of control over the dynamics of the global network society. This includes the private profit-seeking sector, of course, but also social partners, academia, think tanks, the diaspora, farmers' organisations, cultural organisations, civil society at large, museums, foundations, social and cooperative enterprises, start-ups, media, local authorities, etc. When we deal with the fourth pillar of development cooperation, we will come across many of these actors and try to learn how each of them is struggling to be a significant player in this world game.

While already gradually becoming a reality on the ground, the whole-of-society approach is still in its infancy (Figure 7). It will take time for it to establish and impose itself as a new paradigm. The mainstreaming of the whole-of-society approach faces several obstacles. On the side of the Global North, the difficulty lies in the persistence of the perception of their actors as 'donors' rather than 'partners', which creates an asymmetric relationship largely defined by wealth and interest. The question will always be who wins most. On the side of the developing countries, the difficulty resides in the

Figure 7: Towards a new development cooperation model

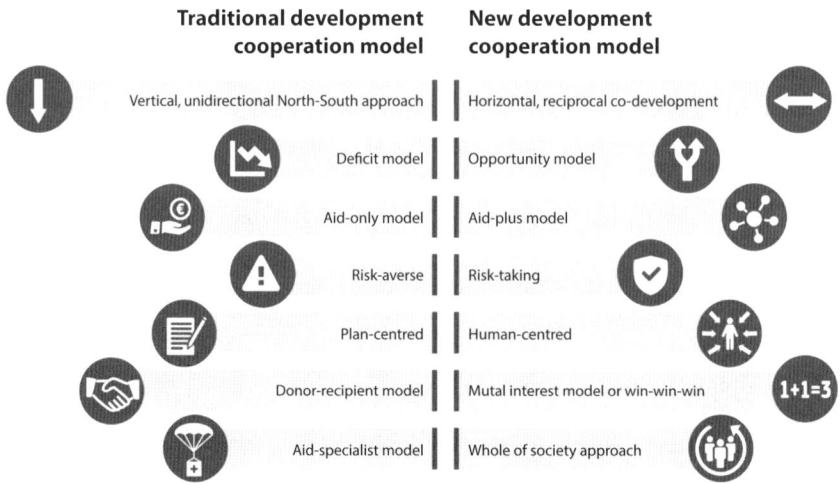

Traditional development cooperation model	New development cooperation model
Vertical, unidirectional North-South approach	Horizontal, reciprocal co-development
Deficit model	Opportunity model
Aid-only model	Aid-plus model
Risk-averse	Risk-taking
Plan-centred	Human-centred
Donor-recipient model	Mutal interest model or win-win-win
Aid-specialist model	Whole of society approach

Source: Develtere, 2019

continuation of a top-down mentality among many governments, which often overpowers the capacity of non-state actors to take leading roles and can result in inefficiency in pursuing dialogue and objectives with their international counterparts.

From colonialism to the Sustainable Development Goals

The complex history of cooperation with developing countries has been and continues to be determined by numerous factors. These can broadly be divided into three categories. Firstly, the international political and economic climate as well as the dominant ideological frameworks are always influential. National development actors (policymakers, NGDOs, consultants and so on) are heavily influenced by what is said about North-South issues, globalisation or international cooperation in other countries and international forums. Secondly, power relations in the home country play a decisive role. To a very significant extent, they determine how cooperation is put into concrete practice in policy frameworks, laws, structures, control mechanisms and so on. Finally, and probably only in third place, the 'recipient' region or institution is also instrumental. Local structures and actors filter the cooperation and determine what effect it can have on local social, economic, political and cultural conditions, but, as we will see, their influence on the donor countries' development policies, cooperation instruments and development practice is only very limited, although not non-existent.

Thus, in order to gain an understanding of the complex fabric of international cooperation, we will undertake a chronological analysis that takes all these factors into account. In this way, we will see how large guiding concepts, such as trusteeship, technical cooperation, development aid, development cooperation and international cooperation, have successively arisen.

Colonial warm-up exercises

Some commentators reach all the way back to the Enlightenment to explain current ideas and practices relating to international cooperation. The Enlightenment is thought to have provided the ideological superstructure or legitimisation for the large-scale colonial project of the European powers. Although colonialism was initially a mercantile venture in which the colonisers' own political and economic interests were paramount, it was justified on the basis of a certain 'duty to civilise'. The English called the colonial mission 'the White Man's burden'[8]: the accursed duty of the white man to spread his civilisation. This was coupled with claims that the peoples concerned lacked the capacity to determine their own course of development. In this way, 'the incapable other' was created.

But colonialism was not the same at all times and in all places. Belgium, Italy and Germany, for example, were latecomers to the colonisers' club. They joined Spain, Portugal, the Netherlands, France and Great Britain only during the second half of the 19th century. Until then, the focus had been on the colonisation of Latin America and Asia; the 'scramble for Africa' began when Britain attempted to gain control of the Cairo (Egypt)-Cape Town (South Africa) axis and France took territory from the East (Djibouti) to the West (Senegal). Germany squeezed in between them in present-day Togo, Cameroon, Namibia, Ruanda, Burundi and Tanzania. Belgium established a position in the centre in Congo, and Italy sought to gain a foothold in Libya and Eritrea.

A good illustration of the narrative and thinking of the time comes from Albert Thys in 1905. Thys was a Belgian businessperson who was actively involved in the first expeditions that would build the constitution of the Congo Free State of King Leopold II. "It is a civilised state (*'Etat civilisé'*) that, without reservation, takes responsibility for all tasks of a civilised state. It also takes care of the order and justice in its territories. But there is more. It is also a civilising state (*'Etat civilisateur'*) (…) It has to take care of the protection of the natives and the improvement of their race" (Thys, 1905).

Until then, imperialistic and colonial circles had been convinced that an overseas colony could be justified on the basis of a 'doctrine of complementarity'. It was taken for granted that the exploitation of the available natural, material and human resources in the colony was beneficial to both the mother country and the colony. The economies of the home country and the colony would gradually become more interdependent, and each would specialise in areas in which it had a comparative advantage. France, Spain and Portugal operated in this way in a closed, protectionist framework. They allowed their own goods into their colonies freely but imposed high import duties on goods from other states. For quite some time, Great Britain, the Netherlands and Belgium observed the principles of free trade.

In the face of some of the worst excesses of colonial exploitation, the idea arose at the start of the 20th century that the motherland must also make additional efforts for 'colonial development', or, as Lord Lugard, the ideologue of the trusteeship doctrine, put it in his famous pronouncement of 1922, "our present task is clear. It is to promote the commercial and industrial progress of Africa, without too careful a scrutiny of the material gains to ourselves" (quoted by Fieldhouse, 1999). However, due to the international recession, nothing came of a dynamic policy of public investment in the case of any of the colonial powers before World War II. Instead, efforts were confined to reformist social programmes, in which somewhat greater investments were put into healthcare, education and basic infrastructure, and in which trade unions and cooperatives were permitted, albeit under the strict control and supervision of colonial officials.[9]

Such a palliative could not solve the social and development problems in the colonies, however. Riots and uprisings, a burgeoning racial, political and social emancipation movement in the colonies and an anti-colonial intellectual climate in the USA ensured that 'the colonial question' could no longer be ignored. The consequence was a kind of 'welfare doctrine'; the British set up their Colonial Welfare and Development Scheme in 1940, and the French their Investment Fund for the Economic and Social Development of the Overseas Territories. Faced with pressure from the community of black *évolués,* Belgium only established its Native Welfare Fund in July 1947.[10] The core idea in each case was twofold. The colonial government had the task of promoting development in overseas territories on behalf of the 'natives', and the local population needed to be more involved in the modernisation process. From this point onwards, substantial investments were made in social development programmes, healthcare, education and so on.

The colonial governments remained faithful to their general principles of colonial administration in all of this. The British were outspoken advocates of 'indirect rule' for maintaining law and order in their colonies. This meant that the colonies were administered via existing local power structures such as kings, maharajas or tribal chiefs. The government and administration systems of the British colonial authorities were also fairly decentralised and allowed plenty of room for local, voluntary participation. The French, true to the Jacobin tradition, opted for a more centralised system and introduced 'modern' government and administration systems. In the name of the great republican principles, they wanted to assimilate the *indigènes* in order to become citizens of a single French empire. The distinction between indirect and direct rule was not always clear. Often, the English intervened heavily, while the French gave local power-holders a free rein. The Dutch inclined more towards indirect rule in Indonesia but towards direct rule in Suriname and the Antilles. Belgium gave the existing power structures a place in its colonial strategy.

The division of roles between the protagonists (state, army, private sector, missionaries etc.) was different in each colonising country. For example, the Belgian colonial process was driven by the so-called trinity; on the basis of a kind of colonial corporatism, the state, large companies and missionaries worked on the same project. Everyone knew their specific role. The large companies, the majority of which were controlled by the Société Générale,[11] controlled the production of cotton, rubber, palm oil, coffee and cocoa, and the exploitation of the mines (zinc, copper, tin, gold, diamond and uranium). Social development was the joint responsibility of the government and the private sector, and large companies established their own schools and health services. From 1906, healthcare was coordinated by the Prince Leopold Institute for Tropical Medicine, while education was largely run by the missions. By contrast, the British Empire did not give any role to missionaries. In its most important overseas territory, India, the activities of the churches were deliberately and actively discouraged.

Box 6. Colonialists, colonisers, colonists, colonials and the colonised

Of course, the way in which a country practises development cooperation today cannot be derived directly from the way in which it was involved in a colonial venture, but there are still interesting links. One only has to look at the countries that receive most support from a donor to find that former colonies still have a prominent albeit receding place in the list of those most favoured.

But perhaps the nature of the colonial presence also plays an important role. *Colonialists* – in other words, people who were sent out by the *coloniser* (usually their home country) in order to defend its commercial and geopolitical interests there and put ideas into practice – always remained just that; they believed in their mission. In his short story in 1897, Joseph Conrad (2019) was already calling them "outposts of progress", ironically describing his two key characters as isolated, demoralised, lazy and incompetent. The nature of the concept of superiority varied: the British were convinced of their racial superiority, the French felt their culture to be of greater value, the Belgians acted as strict tutors and the Americans were always there 'to clear up the mess', for instance in the Philippines between 1899 and 1946.

Colonists were to settle permanently in the colony, for example, the numerous Portuguese who settled in Latin America, Angola, Mozambique and Cape Verde, the Spanish in Latin America and the French in Algeria and West Africa. Other countries, such as the UK, the Netherlands and Belgium, did not have such a tradition. They confined themselves to *colonials* who assumed temporary (and usually official) functions in order to rule the colony. They were fewer than many think. In the late 1930s, French West Africa had a population of 15 million and was run by less than 400 colonial administrators. The whole of British tropical Africa, where more than 40 million people lived, was governed by 1200 administrators. Belgium ran the Congo with just over 700 administrators (Meredith, 2014). For most of the colonised peoples, the relationship with 'the white man' was thus a fairly remote and paternalistic one, which had to be conducted in the cultural and linguistic language of the coloniser. The patterns forged in this way have persisted, as is shown by the fact that many Congolese still address and regard the Belgians as their '*noko*', or uncles.

Most academic research on the colonial systems is looking primarily at the way they functioned and were underscored by a certain ideology. Jan Vansina (2010) attempted to do it differently and focused on the side of the *colonised*, underlining the active agency of the Bakuba in rural Congo. He sheds light on the implication of the indirect rule system and the co-optation of the Kuba Kings, atrocities, the tax system, forced labour, food shortages, lack of adequate shelter in the forest where rubber had to be tapped and the spread of diseases such as smallpox and amoebic dysentery. But he also emphasises the role played by the matrilineal and democratic Kuba society, the influx of other ethnic groups, education creating a new class and missionary preaching by Catholics and Protestants as an apostolate of modernity.

Echoing the *dependentistas* theory, Vansina concluded the following: "The colonial government called the results of all the economic pressure it piled on the villages *development* rather than *exploitation*. However, *development* still meant very little even in terms of rising standards of living. By the end of colonial rule practically no Kuba village was better off than when that era began. Quite the contrary! (…) They had lost most of their freedom, as they were always at the beck and call of government agents, as well as that of the king. Surely, had they known the word, the villagers would not have called this *development* but rather the contrary: *underdevelopment*" (Vansina, 2010, pp.242–243).

The colonial approach towards the local population was usually highly paternalistic. Everyone concerned – colonial officials, entrepreneurs and missionaries – was supposed to help the native population take the difficult step from tradition to modernity. That population had the potential, but as yet lacked the capacity, to act autonomously. A phase of acculturation still needed to be passed through. Modernity needed to be spoon-fed to them so that modern Western values, norms and practices could be adopted.

Box 7. Are colonial attitudes back or are they being magnified by COVID-19?

The COVID-19 pandemic is stirring up discriminatory, racist and even neo-colonial sentiments in many places and instances. During the early months of the pandemic, Chinese citizens living in Africa were accused of bringing ill-health and death to the continent, while American president Donald Trump called COVID-19 the 'Chinese virus'. African residents in Guangzhou and other regions in China told international media that they were subjected to more days of isolation and that their medical clearances were withheld for longer periods of time than non-Africans.

In April 2020, two French scientists suggested that trials would be conducted in Africa to test the effectiveness of a TB vaccine against the coronavirus. There was uproar in Africa and beyond. WHO Director-General, Dr Tedros Ghebreyesus, was particularly outspoken, calling the proposal appalling and a disgrace. In a press conference, he said, "Africa cannot and will not be a testing ground for any vaccine. The hangover from colonial mentality has to stop. WHO will not allow this to happen."

The experience of racism and discrimination is not new in development, especially in global health, and the pace of the COVID-19 crisis is only exacerbating the situation, writes Devex Associate Editor Amruta Byatnal (2020). She refers to a paper, 'The Impact of COVID-19 and Strategies for Mitigation and Suppression in Low- and Middle-Income Countries', that was released in the journal *Science* (Walker, et al., 2020). It lists 49 authors from five prestigious universities in the UK and USA. Missing conspicuously was local representation from the countries that the paper talked about.

For Byatnal, COVID-19 is a mirror and a magnifying glass laying bare persistent colonial attitudes in global health. "Colonizing in this sense refers to the idea that Western researchers and practitioners impose solutions and decisions on countries that are under-resourced without involving people from those places. As countries around the world struggle to contain the coronavirus, inequalities brought about by existing imbalanced power structures are resurfacing, resulting in growing calls to decolonize global health". These calls are echoed and belt out by social media movements such as *#DecolonizeGlobalHealth*.

Colonial thinking was not static, however. As we have seen, it evolved from a rather *laissez-faire* approach into a more interventionist one. There was constant debate about objectives and means. Still, the moral concept of superiority was a firm and important basis for thinking about the colonial mission and duties. Attention was increasingly focused on the interests of the colonised in terms of welfare and well-being, but the asymmetrical, hierarchical, unequal relationship between those concerned was not discussed – even in the 'development projects' of the time.

Technical cooperation and knowledge transfer

After the First World War, the League of Nations was created as part of the Treaty of Versailles in 1919 "to promote international co-operation and to achieve international peace and security". The International Labour Organization (ILO) was established at the same time as an affiliated body.

Although the League of Nations was primarily intended as a means of preventing disputes between 'developed' countries, or keeping them to a minimum, it established a number of important tenets. Thus, the Versailles Treaty stated that the best way to guarantee the well-being and development of peoples who were not yet able to stand by themselves was that "the tutelage of such peoples should be entrusted to advanced nations who by reason of their resources, their experience or their geographical position can best undertake this responsibility…"[12] (Article 22).

Inspired by a multilateral vision of international development and interdependence, the League and its specialised agencies, such as the ILO, began to offer technical assistance to governments responsible for colonies or mandated territories. The method of technical assistance was (as it still is) based on the idea of common progress and the underlying principles of linearity, convergence, predictability and manageability. Technical assistance could be used literally to bring about development 'in the image and likeness of the developed West'. More specifically, technical assistance was provided in the field of social policy, which in accordance with the 'welfare doctrine', was to be pursued in every field. The ILO gave technical advice on the introduction of trade unions, social dialogue and labour legislation and inspection. The Health Organisation of the League of Nations arranged contacts between epidemiologists from different countries and exchanges of health personnel, and encouraged public health as a separate discipline and distinct policy field.

Many African, Asian and Latin American countries, colonies and regions were involved. China's approach was exceptional and promising. As a member of the League, China wanted technical cooperation to contribute to its own modernisation through the transfer of know-how and capital. In 1933, a technical expert visited China at the request of its government to act as a liaison figure between the National Economic Council of China and the technical organisations of the League. His task was to inform the Chinese about the functioning of the League's organisations, convey cooperation requests from China to the League and coordinate League experts' activities locally. Significantly, the Chinese themselves stated that "the duration of his mandate shall be one year and his travel and accommodation costs shall be defrayed by the Chinese government" (letter from W. Koo to the General Secretary, 14 July 1933, quoted in Rist, 1996).

When the League of Nations proved unable to prevent the Second World War, its activities were discontinued. But the League's successor, the UN, pursued the path of technical assistance further in order to address the knowledge and skills deficits of developing countries. In 1949, the UN established the Expanded Programme of Technical Assistance. The following year, it organised the very first aid-pledging conference, at which it was able to raise USD 20 million (approximately USD 175 million at today's rates), mainly in order to finance technical assistance.

Box 8. The role of Chinese training and scholarship programmes in Tanzania

Over 10,000 mid- to high-ranking African officials are invited to China annually to attend short seminars and academic training programmes. But what do trainees think about this way of acquiring knowledge and technological capacity? The Tanzanian scholar H. Makundi and his colleagues (2017) asked a sample of beneficiaries. While critical comments were raised, the trainees were largely positive about the Chinese training experiences. Besides the direct transfer of skills and exposure to China's modernity, the indirect outcome of technology transfer came about through the importation of equipment and technical literature. However, efforts to transfer and apply acquired knowledge have been regularly impeded by structural barriers including cross-cultural and linguistic communication problems, differences in attitude and the fact that in several cases, Tanzania did not have the capacity to absorb some of the advanced Chinese technologies taught in the courses. Two-way communication is needed in order to inform and adapt the Chinese government training programmes to the specific needs of the recipient African economies, they conclude.

Faith in development aid

It was only at the end of the Second World War that the idea finally took shape that all countries would benefit from the participation of all nations in a worldwide development project. As the UN Charter of 1945 puts it, "We the peoples of the United Nations determined to save succeeding generations from the scourge of war (…) agree to employ international machinery for the promotion of the economic and social advancement of all people". The idea of development was invented.

But right after the War, attention was not focused on the problems of the southern hemisphere.[13] Just before the creation of the UN, in the summer of 1944, international monetary and financial agreements were made in Bretton Woods (New Hampshire, USA) which were intended to prevent economic nationalism and waywardness from again leading to political nationalism and major wars. The International Bank for Reconstruction and Development (IBRD, better known as the World Bank) and the IMF were established[14] in an attempt to define a new international order.

Furthermore, Europe, which had been thrown into turmoil by the war, needed to be reconstructed. The USA and the Soviet Union manoeuvred to establish their positions. The Marshall Plan,[15] also known as the European Recovery Plan, was launched in 1948 in order to give the USA's European allies financial breathing space; USD 17 billion was earmarked for this purpose.[16] The funds were not made available unconditionally. The participating countries had to make arrangements together to coordinate the use of the aid, and the money had to be repaid.[17] To this end, the Organisation for European Economic Co-operation (OEEC) was set up. The OEEC assumed a transatlantic dimension when it was transformed into the Organisation for Economic Cooperation and Development (OECD) in the early 1960s. This also represented the first move to institutionalise development aid. Even today, the OECD's Development Assistance Committee remains one of the most important coordinating bodies for the Western donor community.

Box 9. Yet another Marshall Plan

Time and again there are calls for a Marshall Plan for Africa or for a country or region in trouble anywhere in the world. Often these plans are also set up and keep carrying the Marshall Plan stamp but only rarely do they contain the same ingredients of the original Marshall plan.

When COVID-19 wreaked havoc in early 2020, the European Commission set up a new, self-funded Marshall Plan to address the consequences of the pandemic. This was to be more than just a large injection of capital into the economy: it made explicit reference to the post-war Marshall Plan. Just as the original Marshall Plan accelerated European integration, invested in industrialisation and led to a strategic alliance against Soviet aggression, a Marshall Plan for today's economy was to invest in technology, promote digital free trade and align its industrial strategy with allies such as the USA and Japan to resist the growing economic and security threats posed by China.

Two years previously, Germany had launched a plan to support companies that invest in Africa. It got the title 'Marshall Plan for Africa'. The purpose was to tackle the root causes of the refugee crisis that had been convulsing European politics since 2015. The scheme made it easier for companies to write off losses on investments in Africa in order to moderate initial investment risks. Geo-economics also played a role since only an estimated 1000 German companies do business in Africa. When presenting the new plan, the German Development Minister lamented, "we cannot leave Africa to the Chinese, Russians and the Turks".

However, the USA was not just concerned about better economic and financial links between its own economy and those of its European allies; it also had outspoken anti-colonial views and regarded development aid as having a role to play in a new relationship between developed and less developed nations. In his State of the Union address of 20 January 1949, President Harry Truman declared that "we must embark on a bold new program for making the benefits of our scientific advances and industrial progress available for the improvement and growth of underdeveloped areas". The other rich countries were called upon to carry out this grandiose plan together with the USA within the framework of the UN. The old imperialism, said Truman, was based on exploitation and profiteering, and must be replaced by a development programme based on a democratic concept and fair relations between peoples. Sure enough, the USA took the lead in development aid. In June 1950, the US Congress approved a law making it possible for the administration to conclude bilateral development agreements.

Interest in development aid also began to be shown in academic circles. Aid was scientifically legitimated in two ways in the 1960s. Firstly, there was the sociological and functionalist argument that the modernisation of young nations or the transition from traditional to modern societies could be facilitated or accelerated through the transfer of cultural and institutional elements that were necessary in any modern society. The Western, industrialised, modern societies could thus offer their tried and tested patterns to countries in the South, which in this way could artificially speed up their modernisation. Secondly, there was economic rationalisation, which mainly revolved around the so-called two-gap model. This assumed that development in many developing countries was being held back by a lack of local savings and hard currency. Because of this, these countries were unable to set up investments and attract foreign capital. Aid could and should address these two gaps. Both the sociological and economic arguments regarded aid as a win-win situation for developed and developing countries.

Faith in the benefits and effectiveness of aid and the altruism of donor countries was particularly strong among both donor and recipient countries. Resolution 1522 of the UN General Assembly named the 1960s the 'Development Decade' and stated that the developed countries must endeavour to devote 1% of their wealth to aid and investments in developing countries.

Despite the fine-sounding declarations and theoretical support, it quickly became clear that development aid was to a great extent focused on the international and national interests of those providing it. In 1954, the USA was already spending around USD 6 billion on 'development aid'; 86% consisted of military aid.

Local interests also managed to obtain their place in aid provision. In 1954, the US Congress approved Public Law 480 on the Food for Peace Program, in which allies in the southern hemisphere were offered free or cheap American crops. At the same time, however, the American farming lobby acquired a new destination for its food surpluses which had arisen as a result of the recovery of European food production.

In this way, development aid in practice became a unilateral initiative on the part of a donor country by which it sought to contribute to the recipient country's development but also wished to safeguard its own interests. The self-interest and opportunism of 'aid' were never more clearly formulated than by US President Richard Nixon, when he stated in 1968 that "the main purpose of American aid is not to help the other nations but to help ourselves".

During this period, development aid, therefore, could not be credibly associated with altruism. Aid served to give support to allies and friends or to check the progress of other countries' allies and friends. Most British aid went to the Commonwealth countries, most French aid to French-speaking countries, and most Portuguese, Spanish, Dutch and Belgian aid to their former colonies. The majority of US aid was intended for states and regimes on the front line in the struggle against communism. The bulk of the Soviet Union's aid went to its allies and socialist regimes. In fact, development aid thus became an instrument in the bitter struggle of the Cold War.

The official line was that development aid was the duty of rich countries, which had to transfer the necessary technical and financial resources to underdeveloped countries without damaging their own interests. To put it another way, it was assumed that protecting and promoting one's own geopolitical and economic interests was compatible with the development objective of the aid system. It was with this aim in mind that virtually all Western countries set up their own aid bodies and ministries from the 1960s onwards. Canada was the first country with such an institution: the Office for Foreign Aid, established in 1960. In 1961 the US set up the United States Agency for International Development (USAID). Belgium initially had a Ministry for African Affairs (1960–1961) and then a Ministry of Foreign Trade and Technical Assistance. In the Netherlands, the cabinet had a Secretary of State for Development Cooperation by 1963, while in 1964, the Directorate-General for International Cooperation was set up within the Ministry for Foreign Affairs.

What effect development aid had was not yet clear to anyone. The OECD was still taking a downbeat line in 1969: "We have only a vague idea of what we are doing".

Development cooperation: aid in a global setting

In the 1960s, the economy of the developing countries as a whole grew at a rate of 5% per year – faster than ever before. Yet there was no immediate sign of any euphoria. The report by the Pearson Commission (*Partners in Development*, 1969) stated that the gap between developed and developing countries was growing ever wider. The UN introduced the Second Development Decade, with a call to devote more resources to development and make every effort to ensure that the developing countries' economies grew by 6% per year. The decade thus started with a good resolution. At the UN General Assembly, it was declared that the industrialised countries should work to give away 0.7% of their GNI per year to Third World countries.

The 1970s were to be characterised by four significant developments. The first oil crisis pushed oil prices up by 350% in 1973–1974. Suddenly, there was a strong sense of global interdependence, in both the northern and southern hemispheres. The crisis also lent force to calls for a New International Economic Order to sort out the structural inequalities between developed and underdeveloped economies. The developing countries, which had been cooperating ever more closely within the Group of 77 non-aligned countries since the early 1960s and were gradually gaining more of a voice in the UN, stated that they – despite all the development aid – were not receiving any development opportunities. Their call was for "Trade – Not Aid". There was growing political support for international agreements to bring stability to the prices of primary goods sold by developing countries on the international markets. The World Bank spoke of the need for "redistribution with growth" (Chenery, 1974). The ILO presented its basic needs approach and launched the World Employment Programme, with which it sought to encourage developing countries to focus their national development policies on employment, income distribution and basic needs. Finally, a pro-Third-World movement emerged – in both NGDO circles and certain Third World regimes – which argued in favour of self-reliance and popular participation as a double springboard towards national development.

Each of these four developments represented a challenge for development aid.

For the first time, the flow of aid from North to South was considered in a global context. Donor countries realised that the problems went deeper than just a lack of resources for developing countries. International trading relations also needed to be adapted in their favour. The donors proved willing to discuss these matters with the developing countries within the framework of UNCTAD, but the discussions and impressive declarations about a New

International Economic Order did not usher in any noteworthy structural measures. However, development aid did grow. Many donors substantially increased their budgets and gradually changed their discourse. 'Development aid' became 'development cooperation'. The terminological change was supposed to reflect the fact that a more horizontal relationship had arisen between the donors and the more self-confident recipient countries. People argued in favour of 'partnership' and 'cooperation on an equal footing'. The Lomé Convention, which the nine member states of the European Community in 1975 concluded with former colonies in Africa, the Caribbean and the Pacific region, made provision for favourable commercial measures for these so-called ACP countries, as well as for additional aid. The donors' preference, but also that of many developing countries, remained for large-scale, capital-intensive projects with a high degree of technical assistance.

Box 10. Education aid or how development cooperation is fashion sensitive

As we have seen, prior to World War II there was already support for the education sector in the colonies. The emphasis then was on primary education, but missionaries and colonial administrators also pleaded for secondary education. The British and French colonial approach was to gradually build a tertiary education system in their overseas territories and invite a limited number of students from their colonies to study in London or in Paris.

As early as the 1950s, European and North American universities set up twinning arrangements with sister universities in Africa, Asia and Latin America. A wide variety of modes of intervention and aid to the education sector in the young nations were implemented. Classrooms and dormitories were constructed; temporary teaching staff was seconded to schools, colleges and universities; textbooks and educational equipment were provided; educational institutions embarked on curricular and institutional development; scholarships were awarded and joint research projects were initiated. University staff in donor countries also engaged in partnerships with non-university actors in developing countries, sat on the boards of directors of NGDOs and became consultants for multilateral programmes.

After independence, aid to education was heavily concentrated in secondary and higher education. Consequently, the allocation of aid per individual higher education student was many times greater than the aid given per primary school pupil. A growing number of donor countries set up specialised bodies to promote and facilitate links between academia in their own country and developing countries. In close collaboration with academic staff from their own country, they invested in the research, teaching and management capacities of universities in developing countries.

In the late 1980s and early 1990s, studies by the World Bank concluded that the benefits of a young person continuing education after secondary school were significantly higher for the person concerned than for their country. This evidence confirmed the prevailing view that studying at university only helps the local elite. At the same time, these studies suggested that investment in primary education yields a much higher return for the individuals concerned and the economy at large. Globally, this justified a shift in favour of primary education, as was later also reflected in the decision to put universal primary education high on the agenda of the MDGs. This preference for aid and investment in primary education produced the desired effects; the net primary school enrolment rate in sub-Saharan Africa grew from 52% in 1990, to 60% in 2000 and 80% in 2015.

In the meantime, however, the global mindset regarding education and the policy choices to be made evolved again. Several studies and organisations, such as the OECD, advanced arguments that once more defended greater investment in tertiary education. Tertiary education is said to create human capital and foster the dissemination and application of knowledge. Researchers argued that higher education programmes were essential for training much-needed officials such as teachers, economists, medics, engineers and political leaders. In addition, a sound and high-profile academic climate was needed in the Global South to avoid the massive emigration of highly qualified academics to higher education institutions in the West.

Over the last 10–15 years, we have seen a number of evolutions that show that the new paradigm we sketch in this book is also taking shape in the field of university development cooperation. Higher education institutions from donor countries are establishing independent 'satellites' in host countries in the South. Double, dual and joint degrees are made possible. Universities from both donor and recipient countries are developing spin-offs to commercialise research findings or make them available to societal stakeholders. This is also done with the view of realising win-win situations; for example, by having greater success in research grant applications or getting publications in high-impact academic journals.

Many donors also promised to invest more funds in basic facilities. In reality, little came of this. The share of ODA that was spent on basic needs fell from 38% in 1971 to 22% ten years later. The official development bodies were not great advocates of the nationalist-populist path that many countries – led by Tanzania and Chile – sought to take. Support for it came instead from the NGDOs which were emerging in all donor countries and rapidly increasing in scope.

The Washington Consensus and structural adjustments

The years between 1980 and 1990 are described in the development sector as 'the lost decade'. Everything seemed to go wrong. The developing countries' debt burden became intolerable. Those debts were pushed up by the higher costs associated with importing oil and by generous economic policies that were made possible only by a surfeit of petrodollars combined with low interest rates. The loans in question were not granted because of any expected favourable return on the investment but because of a need in the recipient country and the pressure to promote exports from the donor countries (Dijkstra, 2008). Debt repayment, falling prices on the goods markets and the recession in the industrialised countries brought the Third World regimes to their knees.

The Bretton Woods institutions – the IMF and the World Bank – set strict conditions for the issue of additional international loans. Developing countries received concessional loans only if they devised and followed a policy of 'structural adjustment'. Most bilateral and multilateral donors derived their own aid policies from that of the World Bank and the IMF.

As a result, the international aid community collectively aligned itself with the neoliberal economic orthodoxy generally known as the Washington Consensus. Among many politicians in developing countries too, the conviction was growing that their wayward, virtually self-sufficient economic and social model had no future. The idea gained ground that developing countries needed to tune in – otherwise they would be left out.

John Williamson, the intellectual father of the term 'Washington Consensus', himself describes the term as a by-product of that change. In order to convince a sceptical Bush Senior administration in Washington that changes really could be seen in the economic policy of Latin American countries in particular, his Institute for International Economics organised a conference on the subject in 1989. During the conference, Williamson emphasised 10 points that he thought could meet with a general consensus among the Bush administration (Williamson, 2003). He mentioned fiscal discipline, selectivity in government spending (for example, no more general subsidisation of healthcare and education), tax reforms, liberalisation of interest rates, competitive exchange rates, liberalisation of trade, liberalisation of foreign direct investments, privatisation, deregulation and property rights. Points that he himself regarded as important but which he did not believe could count on general support were disregarded. The most striking of these was a focus on income redistribution and rapid growth. The unintended side-effect of this academic and intellectual exercise was far reaching. The Washington

Consensus became a trademark. It was not a consensus, but it became a political manifesto – according to Williamson, a "myth driven by a powerful elite"[18] – which put forward a kind of universal one-size-fits-all solution for developing countries.

Donor institutions increasingly focused their attention on growth rather than on redistribution. So-called 'safety nets' were the solution for those who failed to find their place in 'the market'. Foreign aid was used to push through the 'right' macro-economic measures. The project aid that had previously financed large-scale initiatives such as infrastructure works, power stations or ports was replaced by programme aid. The structural adjustment programmes (SAPs) and adjustment loans were intended to finance the deficits in the balance of payments, while the recipient countries made structural alterations to their policies so that they could export more. In the 1980s, the first generation of reforms was pushed through in this way. The World Bank and the IMF closely followed the progress of the SAPs. Devaluation and trade liberalisation were standard ingredients and conditions, but far more conditions were usually imposed on the recipient countries. The average SAP contained between 10 and 20 conditions, and in some cases as many as a hundred (Boas & McNeill, 2003).

The total volume of 'aid' stagnated in the 1980s. The proportion of aid given to the LDCs fell. Because the developing countries had to repay ever-increasing debts, net financial transfers fell to a historic low. In 1985, the poor countries transferred approximately USD 15 billion more to the rich donor countries, their banks and businesses than they themselves received in the form of aid, loans or investments.

By the start of the 1990s, 100 developing and transitional countries – together representing one-third of the world's population – were poorer in terms of per capita income than they had been 10, 20 or sometimes even 30 years earlier (Jolly, 2002).

International cooperation, the Millennium Development Goals and the Sustainable Development Goals

The SAPs came in for fierce criticism from all sides: NGDOs, social movements, international coalitions,[19] academics and even insiders in the Bretton Woods institutions frankly stated that the SAPs were being imposed to an excessive degree as ready-made, one-size-fits-all solutions on all developing countries, with little or no regard for the differing starting conditions in those countries. There was also criticism of the sometimes disastrous social consequences that they had. Social services such as healthcare and education – which many Third World states had previously provided for free – were made subject to market mechanisms by the SAPs ('customers' should pay). This resulted, in many cases, in serious negative consequences for the social sector in terms of both quantity and quality. The economic results of the SAPs were also a matter of fierce controversy.

The World Bank responded to the criticism by introducing the notion of 'the social dimensions of adjustment'. Special programmes were financed to compensate for the negative social consequences of the SAPs. In the meantime, however, the Bretton Woods institutions pressed ahead with the 'second-generation reforms'; countries could obtain concessional loans if they privatised state corporations and carried out financial reforms (including liberalising financial controls). New 'output conditions' continued to be imposed. The implementation of the second-generation reforms proved highly problematic, especially because such changes required even more institutional capacity than the first-generation adjustments (Addison, 2002).

The governments in developing countries implemented the imposed measures with great reluctance and often resisted them. The application of the conditions was particularly difficult and led to violent popular protests on more than one occasion. The Bretton Woods institutions and the bilateral donors did not succeed in pushing all the measures through in every country, even when they temporarily halted the flow of aid, as they did in Mozambique, Nicaragua, Tanzania, Vietnam, Zambia and Zimbabwe (Riddell, 2008).

Criticism of the SAPs and a sense of aid fatigue laid the basis for a tough debate on the role of development cooperation and the effectiveness of the conditions associated with it (Thorbecke, 2000). Towards the end of the decade, in 1989, the World Bank started to refer to a governance crisis in Africa. It was concluded that the African crisis and the scant effectiveness of the aid were due to an imperfect commitment to the reforms on the part of the local governments and endemic corruption in developing countries.

With the end of the Cold War, the bureaucratic and authoritarian states in the Third World also lost much of their external legitimacy. The fall of the Berlin Wall (in 1989) marked the symbolic end of the bipolar power relations that had been integral to the aid system. The speech given by the French President François Mitterrand (during the Summit of the Francophone Countries at the fashionable Breton resort of La Baule in 1990) made it clear that the donor community was looking for new validation and a new goal for its development cooperation. Mitterrand bluntly said that although France wished to remain loyal to its French-speaking allies in the South, it wanted to do so only if those countries made swift and definite progress towards more democracy and freedom.

In the 1990s, the UN and its specialised institutions organised large-scale summit meetings in the search for these new legitimations and goals for development cooperation. The conferences made it clear that a joint effort – and one on an enormous scale – was needed to tackle the many problems in the world: the degradation of the natural environment, the demographic developments that provoked Malthusian fears, unsustainable and explosive social conditions in many countries, the exponential growth in the number of city-dwellers living in poverty, systematic and structural underdevelopment in the LDCs and the lack of sufficient financial levers to fund development efforts. These problems provided the new legitimisation for future collective efforts and international cooperation among the donor countries and between donors and recipient countries.

The Post-Washington Consensus which arose in this way, like the Washington Consensus itself, is not a coherent political manifesto but rather a form of convergence of ideas, insights and paradigms. Firstly, the consensus is founded to a great extent on new insights regarding human development (also known as the New York Consensus). The *Human Development Reports*, which have been published by the UN Development Programme (UNDP, based in New York) since 1990, define development as a process that increases people's choices and reinforces human capabilities. The reports have been heavily influenced by the work of Nobel Prize winner Amartya Sen and UNDP leading light Mahbub ul Haq. Human development is both an analytical framework and a strategy. The human development strategy is also called a 'rights-based approach' because it assumes that people who are given no development opportunities are treated unfairly in political, civil and socioeconomic terms.

This did not mean that everyone radically moved away from the adjustment policies of the 1980s and 1990. In World Bank and IMF circles, some argued in favour of pursuing the second-generation reforms but paying far more attention to the institutional aspects of development (Williamson, 2003; Easterly, 2002). In their opinion the state must safeguard the institutional infrastructure of the market economy by providing public goods and even by correcting the distribution of income. The World Bank report of 2004, *Making Services Work for Poor People*, for example, was an explicit plea for a holistic approach to 'pro-poor growth'.

The Post-Washington Consensus was also founded on a renewed faith in development aid, this time in the form of international cooperation. The many studies that were conducted in the 1990s into the efficiency, effectiveness and impact of international aid all came to the same conclusions. Firstly, it was found that aid had not contributed to the speeding up of growth in developing countries – contrary to the original expectations. Secondly, aid could also have undesirable negative effects, for example by interfering with local prices and interest rates. Thirdly, aid turned out to be highly 'fungible' or 'mutually interchangeable'. Governments that receive aid do not always use it for the agreed purposes but to finance initiatives that are not immediately relevant to development (senior officials' salaries, the apparatus of repression etc.). Finally, apart from a few anecdotes, no evidence was found that aid programmes had succeeded in reaching the poor population.

The World Bank concluded that financial aid only works if there is a good policy environment. That means sound macro-economic policies (low inflation, budget surpluses and an open trading regime) and sound institutions (legal security, good government services and the absence of corruption). But aid can also serve as the midwife for good policy (Dollar & Pritchett, 1998).

At the end of the last century, the World Bank put forward the Comprehensive Development Framework (CDF) as an institutional vehicle or cooperation platform for all donors and recipient countries. With the CDF, the World Bank explicitly came out in favour of poverty reduction, reducing inequalities and improving opportunities for the poor. For the Bank, poverty reduction had to occupy a central position in a policy that was overseen by the recipient country itself. To this end, the national government had to enter into dialogue with other actors in society, such as the private sector and civil society. This would lead to greater 'national ownership' of the decisions taken. The poorest countries had to forward this national strategy for poverty reduction in a 'poverty reduction strategy paper' (PRSP). In the philosophy of the CDF, international support had to be based on partnership, and all sources of aid had to be deployed in a coordinated fashion, under the leadership of the recipient government (Booth, 2003).

The Millennium Development Goals (MDGs) were adopted by the 189 member states of the UN in New York in September 2000, during the so-called Millennium Summit. The MDGs, as a global deal between richer and poorer countries, were a compilation of the various goals and commitments formulated and adopted during the numerous international conferences in the course of the 1990s. As such, they became an international reference and road map for international cooperation. The strength of this blueprint lay in the fairly concrete, verifiable and controllable indicators that were defined. For each goal, it was clearly stipulated when it had to be attained by and how progress would be checked. Many in the development cooperation community believe and claim that thanks to the MDGs, substantial progress was realised in many fields of human development such as poverty reduction, education and health. However, as Vandemoortele (2018) writes, the claim that the change in pace was caused by the MDGs cannot be upheld scientifically, for lack of clear attribution. There is also disillusionment regarding the dire state of the unbalanced trade system, the lack of progress in development cooperation and the dismal global environmental situation. Thus, Vandemoortele concludes: "progress for people, regress for the planet" after 15 years of MDGs.

Addressing poverty in exchange for debt relief

The development paradigm that has been emerging as of the late 1990s and the early days of the new century has a number of cornerstones. First of all, far more extensive and better-organised dialogue and cooperation are sought between the stakeholders. 'Multistakeholdership' and 'multilevel governance' were the terms widely used for this.

'Multistakeholdership' referred to the need to achieve the broad participation of all kinds of actors. Governments had to listen to the private sector and civil society, for example, chambers of commerce, employers' and workers' organisations, non-governmental organisations, academia, think tanks, associations of farmers, fishermen, women or slum dwellers, and local authorities. Ideally, they had to involve them in policymaking and even its implementation.

'Multilevel governance' meant that such interactions between all kinds of state and non-state actors had to take place at numerous different levels: firstly, at the national level, of course, but also in sub-states, provinces and at the local level. The private sector and civil society organisations (CSOs) also needed a say in regional interstate organisations, such as the AU, or at international conferences. For the donor community, these were not just fine-sounding new words; they became new 'process conditionalities'. Where specific policy outcomes used to be imposed (such as fewer rules for investors), an open relationship of cooperation between government and private actors became a condition for (continuing) support.

A second cornerstone consisted of the ideas of country ownership, accountability and partnership. These expressed the wish – it was generally acknowledged that it was more a wish than a reality! – that the recipient countries define their own policies and are accountable for them to their own populations. Donors became 'partners' who help make that policy possible. But there was also a desire for the policies of national governments receiving support to be consistent with the internationally agreed development goals and, more specifically, with the agenda for poverty reduction and sustainable development. Techniques such as 'rolling programming' and 'performance-based aid allocation' ensured that donors could increase their volume of aid to a specific country at any time (if 'good' work was being done there) or reduce it (if 'good' performances were not recorded).

A third cornerstone was related to the working methods of the donors themselves. More than before – and above all under pressure from the international NGDO community – attention was being paid to the coherence of donors' foreign policies. It was expected of donors that not only their development cooperation but also their policies on trade, migration, the environment or agriculture would be 'Third World-friendly'. Moreover, there was also a desire to use the new agenda to achieve more coordination and streamlining of donors' efforts.

Two development instruments are fine examples or embodiments of the new vision of development cooperation that saw the light some 20 years ago: the PRSPs and budget support. Both show that the innovations of the new paradigm are more than trivial or rhetorical.

The PRSPs were introduced in 1999. Their initial goal was to ensure that the debt cancellation that countries could obtain via the World Bank and the IMF, and especially the Heavily Indebted Poor Countries (HIPC) Initiative was used properly. The idea behind the PRSPs was to diminish the massive extreme poverty in developing countries by sound policies nationally and internationally. Therefore, a large number of low-income countries had to be relieved of their intolerable burden of debt to donors.[20] Secondly, the aim was to support reforms and sound macro-economic and social policy. Social policy? Yes indeed. Debtor countries could get debt relief and extra support when they developed a plan, together with multiple national stakeholders, to combat poverty and invest in social policies that would be instrumental to that aim. Before the HIPC Initiative, heavily indebted poor countries were, on average, spending more on debt repayments than on education and health combined. The debt reduction efforts had some effects. For the 36 countries that received debt relief, debt service paid declined by about 1.5 percentage points of GDP between 2001 and 2015. More recently, with the increase in public debt in low-income countries, debt service burdens have started to rise again, although in 2017 they still remained one percentage point below the pre-HIPC levels.

Nonetheless, the HIPC Initiative has been under constant critique from NGDOs and debt cancellation campaigners. The initiative came too late and was too slow, they assert. Debt cancellation, especially for 'dictator debts', was needed rather than debt relief. Poverty reduction strategy papers were one-size-fits-all because World Bank and IMF staff imposed similar measures all over the place. Some renamed the PRSP the *property* reduction strategy papers. Poor people who participated in the numerous workshops to inspire the national PRSP felt betrayed because the process was manipulated by politicians and international agencies alike.

Criticism has also come from academic circles. Some argue that these measures merely freed up money to pay off debts to other creditors and did not provide the economy with enough oxygen to grow or reduce poverty. Others pointed out that the HIPC countries were usually those with inadequate policies and were being rewarded twice over: with debt reduction and with extra grants. Researcher Geske Dijkstra (2008) found it reprehensible that the bilateral donors were footing the bill. First, they gave money to the World Bank and others so that they could issue loans, then they had to come to the institutions' rescue again in order to finance the cancellation or repayment of the same loans. Thus, the international institutions themselves were not bearing the consequences of their own incorrect choices: a clear problem of 'moral hazard'.

Then comes, of course, the question of the sustainability of the effect of debt relief. Fernandez Lopes Oggier, for example, found that in Tanzania, one of the first beneficiaries of debt relief, health outcomes improved throughout 1995–2015, particularly after the HIPC Initiative. Nonetheless, the effects of debt relief seem to diminish in the long term due to fluctuations in external donors' efforts and preferences (Oggier, 2019).

Box 11. Debt under COVID-19

The COVID-19 pandemic had, of course, a toxic effect, not only on the health situation in most countries worldwide but also on international trade relations, global inequalities and poverty, and the international *rapport de force* in general. It triggered the biggest and deepest global recession since World War II and also hit individual societies and the stability of their polities and economies. In its slipstream, it also affected the debt burden of many developing countries. The international civil society-based Jubilee Debt Campaign had already seen a sharp jump in the number of poor countries in debt distress in 2018, prior to the pandemic. The knock-on effect of the pandemic justified the rapid reaction of the donor and creditor community. The biggest effort to mitigate the effects of the crisis on the debt situation of vulnerable countries is the G-20–sponsored Debt Service Suspension Initiative (DSSI). The Initiative provides for a moratorium or suspension of interest to be paid on outstanding government-to-government debts. This is not without risks, however; some, like the credit rating agency Moody's, announced that they might degrade the credit rating of certain, mainly African, countries if they adhered to the moratorium. Moreover, we have to note that the highest debt burden is related to private sourced credit. The positive note is that China endorsed the DSSI. It is the largest bilateral creditor, often exceeding the combined weight of all other bilaterals, in terms of both debt stock and debt service.

At the turn of the century, another innovation in development cooperation related to the way in which aid was given. Development projects and programmes were, at that time, and are still criticised for their rigidity. They establish goals, working methods and budgets for several years and lack flexibility. Moreover, they tend to disregard national strategies and processes. The high proportion of technical assistance in projects and programmes is typical: they are largely 'donor-driven'. The same goes for programmes, although these are often more flexible and leave room for adjustments *en cours de route*. Inherent weaknesses in programmes relate to the fact that they are often inconsistent with local policies, donors rarely or never harmonise or coordinate their programmes with one another, they are 'fungible' and fail to give national governments the right stimuli for good governance and, finally, they are hard to manage.

Because of this, donors in some countries have switched to 'budget support', in which development money is put directly into the government budget of the country in question. The World Bank assumes that budget support can make aid flows even more predictable. Some donors have been unwilling to go that far because the recipient governments were and are unable to offer sufficient guarantees that the budget will be managed properly. They, therefore, prefer to provide budget support on a sectoral basis. Funds are given to a government for a specific sector, such as healthcare or education. The decision is often made to link this with the functioning of a sector-wide approach. This is a kind of collective working programme – for the relevant local ministry, donors, local civil society and private sector – that is supported by a pre-agreed management and financing system.

Many international institutions still adhere to the ideas behind budget support. The EU budget support, for example, accounts for about 40% of its national cooperation programmes with partner countries. It is, in this way, one of the largest providers of budget support. As the European Commission wrote in an overview of its budget support strategy, the "EU budget support helps the building of more transparent and accountable public administrations, able to deliver services to their citizens more effectively and efficiently. In situations of fragility, it strengthens states' capacity to provide services to the population and fosters countries' resilience. Budget support is a vehicle for dialogue between the EU and its partner countries, involving discussions at technical, policy and political levels, making it pivotal to EU external action and the EU global strategy for foreign and security policy" (European Commission, 2019b).

The budget support aid modality has been critically scrutinised by academics, think tanks and NGDOs. Allegedly, budget support mechanisms are being used to sanction democratic slippage and impose the donors' spending preferences. In addition, budget support is supposed to make for more intense harmonisation and alignment of donors' spending, but these goals are often not or only slowly met since donors are looking for visibility and the realisation of their own development agendas.

International development cooperation and Paris: introducing order to the community and the market

With the turn of the century, it was clear that the parties to be reckoned with, both from the traditional North and the traditional South, from the public and private sector, and from the conventional and new donor groups, as well as from dependent but vocal recipient countries, wanted to shift gears. The belief that we are all part of one single international community was gaining ground. This meant a dramatic revision of the joint agenda and a shift in the collective international modus operandi. A new aid architecture was needed, again.

Many in the aid community began to fear, very soon after they had been announced in 2000, that the MDGs would not be achieved. The UN's annual reports showed that many countries – particularly African ones – were behind schedule and were very likely not to achieve most of the goals by 2015.

Donors seemed to move up a gear during the first few years of the new millennium. Many promised additional funds, and several did actually increase their development budgets. But there was also a desire to do things better. The Paris Declaration on the effectiveness of development aid was signed in 2005 by over 100 countries and multilateral institutions. It was further fine-tuned at several High Level Forums on Aid Effectiveness. The donors regarded the Declaration as an unprecedented consensus on a global scale on increasing the effectiveness of development cooperation via reforms to the delivery and management of aid (CCIC, 2006). Essentially, the Declaration was about replacing the traditional donor-recipient relationship with a partnership. It promotes five principles: ownership, alignment, harmonisation, managing for results and mutual accountability. Visually, this structure is presented as follows.

Figure 8: Visual representation of the Paris Declaration

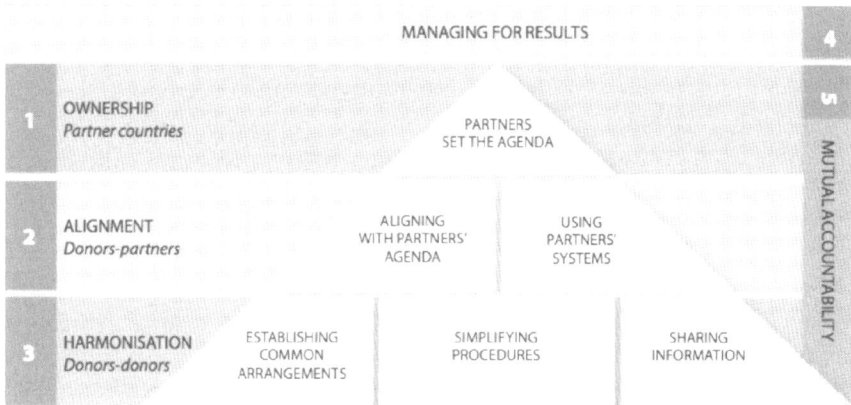

Source: OECD

First of all, developing countries have the right, but also the responsibility, to exercise leadership: they are the owners of the development process. It is often also said that governments in developing countries need to be behind the steering wheel; they need to take the lead in the development and implementation of their development strategies and coordinate the different donors.

Box 12. In the driver's seat?

The development cooperation community is particularly fond of using metaphors. This has unexpected advantages: it brings intercultural differences to the surface. The expression 'the local government needs to sit in the driver's seat' elicited the observation from many Africans that a leader or important person never sits behind the wheel himself. That lowly task is reserved for uneducated but discreet drivers. Americans tend to respond that they do not want to be in a car that is driven by an incompetent driver. Others say that it is not sitting in the driver's seat that is the most important thing but obtaining (getting or buying) a good car and constructing decent roads.

With the second principle, 'alignment', attention is turned to the donors. They must respect ownership and use the partner country's institutions and systems. Why come along with their own procurement procedures and accounting systems if others already exist in the country? Why create parallel institutions to carry out projects when there are governments, businesses and CSOs in the country that can do it themselves? Moreover, the donors need to make their aid more predictable. They need to inform the partner countries accurately and in time about future aid, and also deliver it on time ('in-year predictability'). Less emphasis is placed on the need for long-term predictability, although developing countries find it hard to plan if they do not know what resources they can count on in subsequent years. Alignment also means that the aid must be largely untied. Partner countries can use the funds they have acquired to purchase goods and services from whomever they want.

According to the OECD-DAC, harmonisation would not be an important point in the Paris Declaration if the principles of ownership and alignment were applied properly. But as donors do place such an administrative burden on the recipient countries, they are asked to devise joint sets of rules, send joint missions and conduct evaluations together.

The importance of the first three principles – ownership, alignment and harmonisation – has been acknowledged for quite a long time. Managing for results and mutual accountability are relatively new options. The idea is that everyone (recipient government and donors) should continue to focus on poverty reduction, ensure that it is not surreptitiously deviated from, actually evaluate it quantitatively and report on it transparently. Finally, it is no longer just the recipient countries that should account for their actions: donors must justify their decisions too. Donors have, for years, sought to penalise poor project and programme implementation by recipient countries, but there has been little mention of penalising broken promises or malpractice by the donors themselves.

During the successive High Level Forums on Aid Effectiveness, stock is being taken of the realisation of these principles and a dialogue is taking place between what are now called development partners and partner countries. The fast-changing scene of development cooperation, with new needs and challenges, new commitments such as the SDGs as well as the proliferation of donors and instruments, creates new expectations on all sides. In this sense, the agenda is loaded with new agreements on predictability, the involvement of the private sector, CSOs etc.

Does this amount to anything more than fine intentions and declarations? In any case, the OECD-DAC has developed a monitoring tool that enables the dialogue between the governments of developing countries and the relevant donors on the basis of concrete data on progress or obstacles in the realisation of the Paris agenda.

Box 13. Findings of the 2018 Monitoring Round of the Global Partnership

"Partner country governments have made significant progress in strengthening national development planning. Since 2011, the proportion of partner countries with a high-quality national development strategy has almost doubled (from 36% to 64%). (…)

"Development partners' alignment to partner country priorities and country-owned results frameworks is declining. Alignment of project objectives to partner country priorities, as well as reliance on country-defined results, statistics and monitoring systems, has decreased for most development partners since 2016. While multilateral development banks have increased their reliance of country-owned results frameworks, the decline is most pronounced for bilateral development partners. Availability of government data is a shared bottleneck and signals the need for concerted efforts from both partner countries and development partners to use and strengthen national statistics and monitoring systems. Forward visibility of development co-operation at country level is weakening. Partner countries report a decrease in the availability of forward expenditure and implementation plans from their development partners. This decline is mirrored in the fall of the share of development co-operation finance recorded on partner countries' budgets subject to parliamentary scrutiny. (…)

"Strengthened public financial management (PFM) systems have not been matched with significantly increased use by development partners. (…)

"More systematic and meaningful consultations with development actors are needed both by partner country governments and development partners. Partner country governments and, to a lesser extent, development partners consult a broad range of national stakeholders, such as civil society, the private sector, parliamentarians and subnational governments in the preparation of their country strategies and programmes, respectively. Results indicate that these engagement opportunities could be more regular, predictable and involve a more diverse set of actors. (…)

"The enabling environment for civil society organisations is deteriorating. Civil society organisations (CSOs) report a decline in the legal and regulatory frameworks that provide protection for CSOs as well as limited freedom of expression and inadequate protection from harassment when working with at-risk populations. (…)

"There is mixed progress in making development co-operation more transparent. More development partners report to global information systems and standards

to make information on development co-operation publicly available. Information provided by development partners is also more comprehensive; however, progress on timely and forward-looking information on development co-operation is uneven. (…) However, there is room for improvement regarding consistency and quality of reporting at country level."
OECD and UNDP (2019)

The SDGs and the need for a whole-of-government and whole-of-society approach

The successor to the Millennium Development Goals (MDGs) is the Sustainable Development Goals (SDGs) (Figure 9). These are clearly again an international compromise between different stakeholders. But while in the case of the MDGs, an agreement had to be reached between the governments of the North and the South, the SDGs resulted from a more inclusive and participatory process. Besides a weakened camp of developed countries and a more self-conscious grouping of developing countries, a wide variety of non-state actors were consulted, including NGDOs, CSOs, think tanks, academics, social partners and foundations. For some critics, this explains the fuzziness and lack of clarity of the SDGs (Vandemoortele, 2018). The SDGs are now embraced by all UN agencies, bilateral donors, NGDOs, social and ecological movements, de-growth advocates, philanthropists, think tanks and academics, but even by multinational companies. This might be both the strength and the weakness of this new effort to follow a collective, universal agenda of change.

The agenda of the SDGs is extremely ambitious and has to be realised in the course of only 15 years. The drafters of the 17 goals, 269 targets and 247 indicators did not produce a shock-free programme and did not bear in mind the eventuality of pandemics such as COVID-19, ravages like the locust plague in East Africa and India nor radical changes in international power relations, as we see with the growing isolationism of the USA under the Trump administration, the complexification of the imbroglio in Syria, Iraq and Libya, and the increased assertiveness on the part of China.

The SDGs are an international platform with an unprecedented broad and extensive support base. Criticising the SDGs sounds like criticising Jesus' Sermon on the Mount. Still, a number of remarks are often made. First of all, the goals are non-binding as every country is expected to develop its own national plan. Like the MDGs, the SDGs read primarily as an agenda for the developing countries. Hence the lack of references to challenges such as obe-

Figure 9: Sustainable Development Goals (doughnut visualisation)

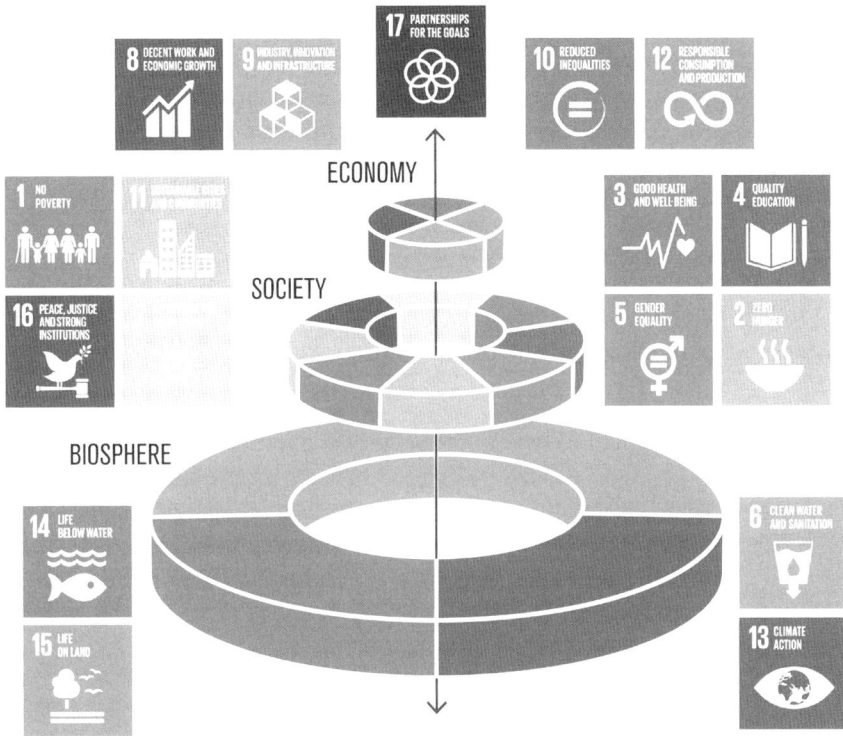

1. No poverty; 2. Zero hunger; 3. Good health and well-being; 4. Quality education; 5. Gender equality; 6. Clean water and sanitation; 7. Affordable and clean energy; 8. Decent work and economic growth; 9. Industry, innovation and infrastructure; 10. Reduced inequalities; 11. Sustainable cities and communities; 12. Respansable consumption and production; 13. Climate action; 14. Life below water; 15. Life on land; 16. Peace, justice and strong institutions; 17. Partnerships for the goals.

Source: Azote for Stockholm Resilience Centre, Stockholm University

sity, overweight and non-communicable diseases. There are also worries that not enough attention is going to negative transboundary spillover effects of trade and consumption patterns. These can also arise when countries pursue new sustainability options. An increasing number of Western European cities and regions, for example, have introduced measures to forbid old polluting cars from circulating in their territory. Hundreds of thousands of these cars end up in Eastern Europe and Africa, creating negative path dependency on diesel in these regions. Some critics also see a tension between the socioeconomic and environmental agendas, and point to the risk that the first will prove to be dominant. Furthermore, focusing on poverty reduction and not insisting on tackling high inequality and taxing the superrich hides a firm belief in the trickle-down effects of the neoliberal economic model. In addition, the SDGs do not really present an alternative to the current status quo. As Block (2018) writes, the SDGs can serve as a lock-in because the goals are developed within UN processes, which are usually unable to challenge prevailing structures of political and economic power. As such, they express a techno-optimistic view of tackling sustainability problems. This is aggravated by the fact that financial resources and the necessary investments that are needed to reach the goals are ambiguous. Finally, many make critical reflections on the measurability and monitoring of the broadly defined goals, as well on the inaptness of many of the indicators used so far.

Box 14. Making university development cooperation SDG-proof

The launch of the SDGs in 2015 was a milestone in establishing a common international framework for action in response to urgent global problems with regard to sustainability, equality, justice and human dignity. Implementing the SDGs will, however, be a daunting challenge, not only for the governments of UN member states but also for local authorities, private businesses, civil society and universities. As knowledge institutions, universities play a leading role in at least four areas: the provision of technical expertise, backed-up by cutting-edge research insights; support for the strengthening of academic capacity in the Global South; the sensitisation of the broader public and the training of the SDG experts of the future; and support for monitoring efforts to follow up on the progress made.

Quite some reflection has already taken place on what SDG-aware development cooperation should look like. The SDGs affect development cooperation both through the way they influence international agenda-setting by spelling out specific goals and targets, as well as through a number of underlying principles. The integrated nature of the SDGs issues a strong call for interdisciplinary and transdisciplinary research and education. The SDG principles of universality and leaving no one behind imply greater attention to research agendas that cover the challenge of lifting vulnerable groups out of poverty, as well as insights in the provision of universal access to public services and global goods. Many of the principles above require strong universities, well embedded in an ecosystem of effective governmental institutions, innovative businesses and a flourishing web of CSOs (SDG 16). All of these are drivers towards university development cooperation-efforts with more attention to integrated approaches; multistakeholdership; local ownership; institutional strengthening at the university level and beyond; mobilising additional funding; and creating an enabling environment.

Jeffrey Sachs, director of the Sustainable Development Solutions Network, and his colleagues are continuously fine-tuning the SDG monitoring and evaluation systems (Sachs et al., 2020). Their 2020 SDG Index and Dashboards include 85 global indicators plus an additional 30 indicators for the OECD countries.

As in previous years, three Nordic countries top the 2020 SDG Index: Sweden, Denmark and Finland. Most countries in the top 20 are OECD countries. Yet even these countries face significant challenges in achieving several SDGs. Every country has a 'red' score on at least one SDG in the dashboards. As we mentioned, high-income countries perform poorly on spill-over indicators. Looking at trends, many high-income countries are not making significant progress on sustainable consumption and production or the protection of biodiversity. Sachs and his colleagues warn that COVID-19 will likely negatively impact progress towards most SDGs in the short and medium term, including in high-income countries.

Low-income countries tend to have lower SDG Index scores. This is partly due to the agenda of the SDGs, which focuses to a large extent on ending extreme poverty and on access to basic services and infrastructure. Moreover, resource-poor countries tend to lack adequate infrastructure and mechanisms to manage key environmental challenges exposed in the SDGs. Except for countries that face armed conflicts and civil wars, the index and dashboards demonstrate that most low-income countries are making progress in ending extreme poverty and providing access to basic services and infrastructure, particularly in relation to good health, well-being, decent work and economic growth. The SDG Index score over time shows that overall, the world has been making progress towards the SDGs. It is, of course, no surprise that some countries perform better and some countries are backsliding. This is shown in Figure 10.

As we already suggested, the SDGs come at a time when the development cooperation paradigm is shifting in new directions. The SDGs have even been a catalyst in this transformation. They are the clearest indicator that the North-South vision and corresponding approaches are behind us and represent a decisive attempt to develop a universal, global agenda to tackle collective problems and challenges. This implies a multi-actor inclusive vision and approaches.

This will, in the first place, have to be realised at the level of the public authorities. Realising the SDGs is not the sole remit of one single Ministry or state agency. Ministries of development cooperation can be instrumental in supporting partner countries' efforts to achieve more sustainability in all areas covered by the SDGs. But, as we will argue many times in this book,

Figure 10: Countries whose SDG Index score has improved or decreased the most since 2015

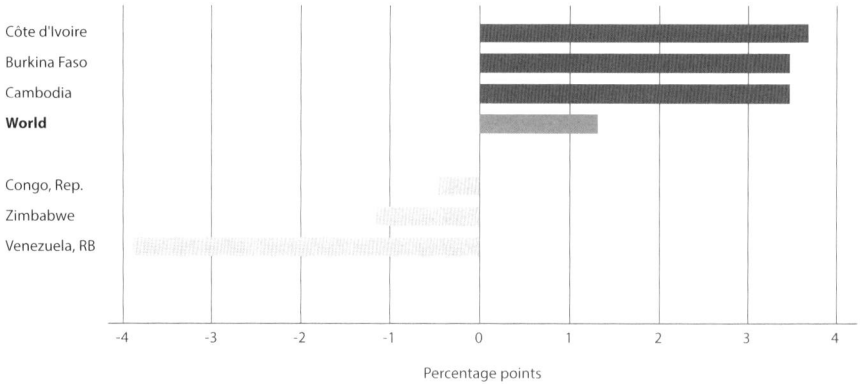

Note: Population-weighted averages
Source: Sachs et al. (2020)

other ministries and state agencies can also step in to implement the national and international SDG agenda. This necessitates a whole-of-government approach and, inevitably, leads to the proliferation of international development cooperation actors, innovations and new expertise. The flipsides of this are multiple. Partner countries have to deal with an ever-expanding set of foreign institutions, amateurism takes time to mature to professionalism and coordination becomes increasingly complicated.

And still, this is what many development cooperation ministry and intergovernmental organisation are trying to do: coordinate and push for a linear top-down management model. As Block (2018) writes, this is a strange approach in view of the extreme complexity of sustainability issues. Already in 2015, Hajer et al. (2015) warned about "cockpit-ism"; the illusion that top-down steering by governments and international organisations alone can address global problems. They wrote that in view of the limited effectiveness of intergovernmental efforts and questions about the capacity of national governments to affect change, the SDGs additionally need to mobilise new agents of change such as businesses, cities and civil society. They call for an "energetic society" perspective that "highlights the transformative potential of the multiple initiatives for sustainable development taken by various agents of change within societies around the world. Such actors are articulate, autonomous citizens, civil society initiatives, self-organized farmers, cities and innovative companies that take action in highly diverse development contexts. Different logics of change are at play: actors may be motivated by a genuine concern for sustainability, or by new opportunities

Figure 11: Whole-of-Society approach

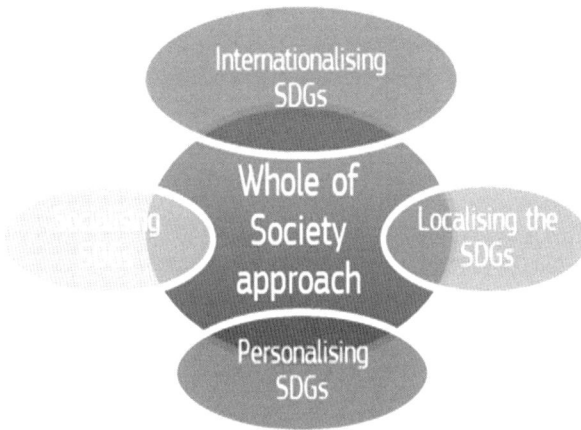

arising from sustainability challenges" (Hajer et al., 2015). This is what we have called a whole-of-society approach (Develtere, 2019; 2020). Figure 11 shows the different links of the whole-of-society approach with the SDGs.

Box 15. The next Einstein will be African

Launched in 2013, the Next Einstein Forum – shaped by its belief that the next Einstein will be African – is an initiative of the African Institute for Mathematical Sciences and the Robert Bosch Stiftung, a European foundation. It aims to connect science, society and policy in Africa and the rest of the world, bringing together key stakeholders from academia, innovation, investment, journalism, industry and government to study critical areas such as energy, health, fintech, climate and smart agriculture. The Forum also has a fellows programme for Africa's most brilliant young scientists and offers a dynamic platform for the African community of scientists.

It takes two to tango

It is clear that national donors have been greatly influenced by the international trends in development thinking and practice outlined above. Starting out as a neo-colonial project, development cooperation has gradually evolved into a tool that is used to a significant degree for combating poverty and making local and global development processes more sustainable. We would even support the contention that the international framework is increasingly determining the standards of national development policy. At any rate, this is certainly true for those, such as the ministries of development cooperation, who started development cooperation as specialists. National development agencies now have to take account of standards, benchmarks and agreements which have been established at the international level. They are increasingly in contact with their counterparts in other countries and with international institutions.

However, to reduce national donors to a national version or a branch of an international cooperative league of donors for development would be to distort the picture. Earlier, we pointed out that each national system has its own way of working. It has its own subculture, its own controversial issues and its own distinctive national power relations. In addition, we observed that it can be regarded as a national marketplace.

Internationally: among specialists

Studies of development aid constantly revive the polemic between the so-called idealists and realists.[21] The former group sees bilateral aid as a form of solidarity by resource-rich countries and people towards resource-poor countries and people. The latter group stresses that bilateral aid is primarily used to support the donor's own foreign-policy interests. Gulrajani and Calleja (2019a) content that pure altruism and total self-interest represent two extreme ends of a spectrum of motivation. They consider them to be more ideal-types than true depictions of any real case. Interestingly they call these motivations the inseparable "yin and yang" of development cooperation; whether yin or yang prevails also depends on the international power relations over a certain time frame.

Schraeder, Hook and Taylor (1998) investigated the aid policy of the USA, Japan, Sweden and France in Africa in the 1980–1989 late Cold War period. Altruism, it was found, was not a decisive element in aid policy, despite the donor countries' humanitarian rhetoric. What they did find was a clear link between the African states' ideological position and the volume of aid they received. Trade relations were very closely correlated with aid flows. This was a remarkable observation, particularly for a country such as Sweden which has always prided itself on its untied generosity.

Omoruyi (2001), a few years later, adapted the study to consider the motivations behind the aid given by the USA, Japan, Norway and France. He also included the post-Cold War period in his study, finding that poorer African countries had more chance of getting a slice of the aid pie from the USA, Japan and Norway. This was not the case for France.[22] He concluded that a kind of international aid regime had arisen which determined the principles and standards by which donors must abide. Even an idiosyncratic donor such as the USA, he argued, had internalised these principles and standards. However, he added that it was not just France that took its own interests into account. Although in the case of Norway, poorer countries were treated preferentially, there was still a positive correlation between the volume of aid that they received and their place on the index of strategic minerals and the value of their imports from Norway. Yin and yang, indeed.

As we have seen, the new paradigm, whose components and contours we are trying to identify, puts win-wins and even win-win-wins at the centre of international development cooperation. Pursuing domestic and global interests simultaneously is the new agenda. Moreover, the parties involved in international cooperation have to look for and concretely experience mutual benefits. Gulrajani and Calleja (2019b) wrote in a policy briefing that these trends represent a marked change from the post-Cold-War period when a strong international consensus existed on the singular importance of poverty alleviation and global solidarity. This is also the central thesis of this book.

So what makes up the current aid regime or paradigm? And is it true that the donor countries are increasingly falling into line with this aid regime? Earlier, we discussed the Paris Declaration, which was signed in 2005. This refers to the need for ownership, alignment, harmonisation, a focus on results and mutual accountability. The donor community has also been singing from the same hymn-sheet for years regarding the preferred destinations for aid; these should be the LDCs, it is argued. To this can be added the point that virtually everyone in the traditional development community is convinced that it is preferable to opt for projects in countries that are institutionally weak and for programmes in stronger countries. Larger projects and programmes are preferred because large numbers of small projects overwhelm the recipients and saddle them with countless administrative and other burdens. The recipients, it is also said, need to know where they stand. That means that aid must be predictable and not constantly fluctuating. Untied aid is not just more productive, it is also better than tied aid, which obliges recipient countries to use the aid (often a loan that has to be repaid) for purchases in the donor country, which may be too expensive and not always the most sensible choice. Tied aid is also at play, but objectionable, when recipient countries receive aid but in return are compelled to buy, for example, weapons from the donor country. On the contrary, many plead for localising aid with the procurement of services and goods on the domestic market of the recipient partner. In the same vein, attention is increasingly put on country programmable aid, so that the recipient country gets more control and ownership of the decision-making and implementation process. In recent years, there has been a conviction that giving budget support is a better form of aid than project or programme support. As we have seen, with budget support, a direct financial injection is provided into the budget of the government or the local NGO with which the donor wishes to work. This is a sign of trust but also compels the partner to take responsibility. Because it is not always easy to trust relatively weak governments or institutions, which lack or flout proper rules, have few if any mechanisms for preventing corruption and few if any competent personnel, budget support is reserved for the better pupils in the class. But whether donors give budget support or project or programme support, it must be coupled with efforts to reinforce the partner's governance and management capacity. Aid for trade and other measures to enhance access to the global trade system are yet another popular mechanism to bring donors and recipient in an aid-plus arrangement. In this way, the international system also comes into the picture. Not only should there be attention on global public goods, such as clean air and the mitigation of climate change, but the international institutions also have to be strengthened and given room to play their legitimate role. There is a growing consensus that this should be done with more core funding of international institutions and less earmarked funding for specific projects or programmes. Consideration should also be given to reducing the alignment of aid with voting patterns in the UN agencies. In addition, as we said, going for mutual interests or win-wins, if well balanced, can motivate the domestic support base in the donor country and make for a more mature and long-lasting relationship of equals between donor and recipient. This is called principled aid.

The proof of the pudding is in the eating, as the saying goes. In other words, to what extent are we seeing a form of development cooperation that complies with the norms and standards that are being defined internationally? We already know that – apart from a few countries – international donors have not kept their word regarding the quantitative norm of 0.7% of their GNI. What about the other norms? Can we be optimistic and get comfortable with the idea that a new paradigm, call it a narrative, will also have effects in terms of policies and practices? This is what Omoruyi (2001) hinted at some 20 years ago. This is also what we could conclude from the 'quality-adjusted aid' index that Roodman (2010) developed a couple of years later. He cleaned up the ODA statistics so that they would better respond to the commitments and the narrative of the donor community and found that not even half of the ODA could be tagged as qualitative. But he saw progress and more and more donor countries adjusting their aid patterns to the international consensus on good aid.

Where do we stand now? When Roodman did his work 10 years ago there was no talk about mutual interests or win-win-win ambitions as yet. Now the donors' interests are back, be it not in terms of tied aid but because donors do not want to just be payers but also players who also aim for some international standards of good development cooperation (Develtere, 2020). Gulrajani and Callega (2019a; 2019b) have already been mentioned; they call this principled aid (PA). They recently developed a composite PA index and looked to DAC donors to discover to what extent donors put their money where their mouth is. Their index comprises three equally weighted dimensions or 'principles'. In summary, they look first at donor countries through the lens of their orientation towards the needs and vulnerabilities of the recipient countries because that generates more trade and investment opportunities. Secondly, they investigate how PA providers allocate their resources in problems that can only be solved by investing in greater global cooperation. Finally, they are interested in the public-spiritedness of donors and the way in which they avoid instrumentalising ODA to their own benefit and the detriment of the recipients.

Studying recent trends and trajectories in aid allocation and donor motivation over the 2013–2017 period, they concluded the following. Luxembourg tops the PA Index, while the UK and Sweden also have a high score. At the bottom of the PA Index is the Slovak Republic, followed by Greece and Austria. Donors, they find, have become more principled on average, largely because of improved scores on the two dimensions of needs and global cooperation; however, donors display a worrying deterioration in their commitment to public-spiritedness.

Box 16. The Trump card

The arrival of the Trump administration in January 2017 sent shock waves through the foreign policy community in the USA and around the world. Powerful, long-suppressed isolationist pressure groups in the USA were coming to the fore, while President Trump himself took the doctrine of 'America First' to an entirely new level. Observers foresaw a seismic paradigm shift (Crane & Maguire, 2017). The Trump administration's call to slash development assistance was by no means a reflection of supposedly generalised isolationist sentiments with the broader American public. Polling data of the Chicago Council of Global Affairs showed that two-thirds of the interviewees favoured "aid that helps needy countries develop their economies" (Kull, 2017).

Because of the president's lack of interest, under Trump, there was no overarching strategic framework for development cooperation emanating from the White House (Igoe, 2020). As a consequence, powerful individuals were able to push through some of their radical views and pet projects. Vice-President Pence pleased his constituency by deploying foreign aid to help religious minorities. Ivanka Trump launched the Women's Global Development and Prosperity Initiative. But in general, existing aid programmes were often subject to the transactional view of international politics the president adhered to. Foreign aid was reformed into a tool of punitive diplomacy. Aid to Central America was cut because the region's governments were too slow in stopping migration. USAID also blocked hundreds of millions of dollars of aid to the Palestinians as a means to pressuring the Palestinian authorities to resume peace talks with Israel and engage with Trump's Middle East peace plan.

Trump's predilection for disruption was also evidenced in his rapport with the UN. Soon after the outbreak of the coronavirus pandemic, President Trump announced that the US had officially terminated its funding to the WHO and would undertake an investigation into whether the health agency mismanaged or covered up the spread of COVID-19. For the Trump administration, the WHO was too 'China-lenient' and mismanaged or covered up the spread of the virus. Cutting around 15% of the WHO's budget and positioning the Bill and Melinda Gates Foundation as the biggest funder of the world's most important health agency was not an act of uncontrollable petulance but one expressing a systematic preference for disruption.

Similarly, hardly a month before the US presidential elections of November 2020, the US imposed an American citizen as the new president of the Inter-American Development Bank. This was in contradiction with customary law that prescribes that a Latin American citizen should head this Washington-based institution. For the White House, Claver-Caroneto, the new head of the Inter-American Development Bank, has to be a counterweight to the significant inflow of loans from Beijing into the region and prove that the 19th century Monroe doctrine claiming America for the Americans is back in town.

Contrary to what many expected, consecutive plans to cut the foreign aid budgets of the State Department and USAID have been boycotted by both Republican and

Democrat lawmakers. This is an indication that the president's view that "in some cases, these are countries that we should not be giving to" is not widely shared, especially not in Congress, neither was his conviction that foreign aid cuts can lead to talks that improve relationships.

Quid Africa? Since President Reagan, each president has had a signature policy initiative or focus for Africa, and with Prosper Africa, a US Government initiative to unlock opportunities to do business in Africa, Trump is no exception. But unlike his predecessors, he did not appear to be personally involved in this policy instrument nor other aspects of US-Africa policy (Campbell, 2020). He did not visit any African country during his term of office. These might also be expressions of the presidents' preference for breaking with the past.

Immediately after taking office, two of Joe Biden's first moves were to initiate a 30-day process to rejoin the Paris climate agreement and cancel the previous administration's plan to withdraw from the WHO, both of which the new president accomplished with letters to Antonio Guterres, the UN secretary-general.

Recipient countries: donor darlings and donor orphans

So far, we have said little about the recipient countries. This is no coincidence. Development cooperation did not arise at the request of the developing countries. It was Belgium, for example, that offered a 'friendship treaty' to the young nation of Congo in 1960, in the form of technical aid coupled with the protection of Belgian economic and political interests in Congo (Van Bilsen, 1993). For a long time, technical cooperation dominated development aid, even when the transition was made to project or programme aid. Western experts 'gave' our development expertise to the 'recipient' countries or partner NGOs. Only in the last twenty years or so have cooperation workers received a new job description: they are now seen instead as 'intermediaries', 'facilitators' or 'colleagues'.

The partners in the recipient countries – governments and local organisations – still have no full control over the development aid they receive. They even play only a minor role in setting the goals for aid or determining working methods. This is done in the headquarters of agencies in London, Washington, Berlin, Stockholm or Beijing. The partners in recipient countries rarely if ever evaluate our efforts. At best, they are associated with the outcome or impact evaluations initiated by the donors who invariably set the terms of reference for these evaluations. As Figure 12 shows, local governments control only 53% of the official aid they receive to conduct their own policies; the 'country programmable aid' we have already mentioned.

Figure 12: Bilateral ODA composition: all DAC countries, 2014

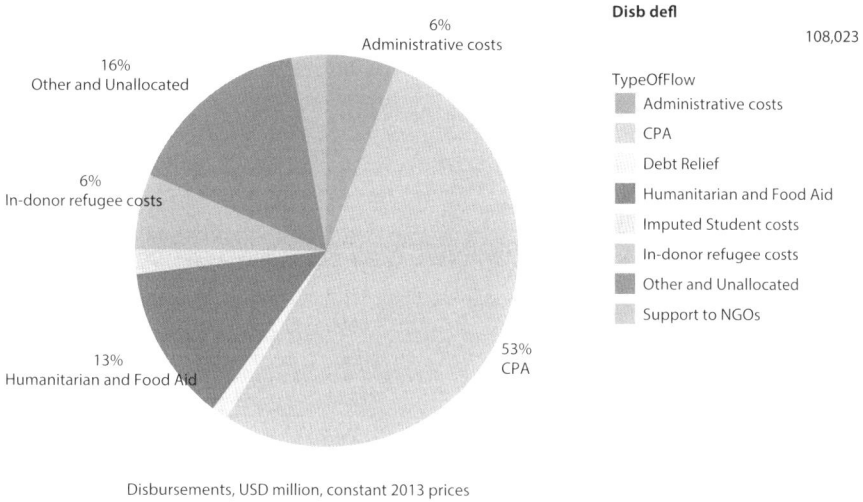

Disbursements, USD million, constant 2013 prices

Source: OECD-DAC, Country Programmable Aid, 2014[23]

Despite the slight progress that has been made in comparison to 2005 (when only 47% of programmable aid was reported) and despite all the rhetoric about ownership, it is not the local partners but the international donors who shape development cooperation. The local partners are 'receptors' or 'filters' for development cooperation. They have to compete against the donors, who – as we have seen – have their own agendas and working methods. They are confronted with the contradictory preoccupations and interests of the numerous donors. Some actors clearly opt for maximum ownership by local partners, but many others are explicitly and exclusively interested in the 'flow-back': the benefits of cooperation for the home country.

A second set of questions needs to be asked in connection with this. How do we choose partners in the South? What profile do they have? Do they have the necessary capacity to achieve the goals that the donors have in mind? We can start by taking a look at the destination of aid.

Table 2 shows us the 10 countries that received the most aid in 2018. You would probably have expected the list to consist exclusively of African and LDCs. In fact, there are just three African and three LDCs. There are even two upper-middle-income countries on the list. Afghanistan, Iraq and Syria are rightly associated with the fight against international terror and Colombia with the fight against drug trafficking. But isn't India also a donor? It is indeed, but it still receives much more than it gives. Both parties to the transaction are happy: we give India aid assistance in order to gain a place in the economic miracle that is taking place there, and they are happy to receive as it gives them a bit of extra financial leeway. Does there then follow a long list of countries that also receive a lot? Yes, the list is still a long one; but no, the others do not receive much. The top 10 receive just about 15% of all the aid distributed by the rich countries.

Table 2: Top 10 ODA recipients (2018)

	Countries	**Development level**
1.	Afghanistan	LDC
2.	Syria	LMIC
3.	Bangladesh	LDC
4.	India	LMIC
5.	Ethiopia	LDC
6.	Jordan	LMIC
7.	Iraq	LMIC
8.	Nigeria	LMIC
9.	Colombia	UMIC
10.	Kenya	LMIC

LDC, least developed country; LMIC, lower-middle-income country; UMIC, upper-middle-income country.
Source: Development Aid[24]

But how dependent are these recipient countries on aid? In fact, a country is considered to be dependent on development aid if that aid represents more than 10% of the economy's own output. Presently (2018), 26 countries are thus aid dependent. Only Afghanistan is on the list of the most receiving and aid-dependent countries. The most aid-dependent country in the world is Somalia, with ODA representing more than 33% of its GNI. And do not forget, with ODA we only look at what OECD-DAC members are giving; it does not include whatever Somalia gets from non-DAC members such as China or Turkey. Other very dependent countries are the Central African Republic, Liberia, Malawi, South Sudan and the Gambia. So, except for Afghanistan as we mentioned earlier on, all are African low-income countries. For many of these countries, their dependency has dropped significantly over the last decade. In many cases, this has more than halved. However, what is unknown by many is that small island developing countries are very dependent on aid as well. Islands such as Tuvalu and Palau are almost as dependent on aid as Somalia. Moreover, we should underline that as a group, the lower-income countries are not 'aid dependent' since 'only' 9% of their collective GNI is represented by ODA. For the lower-middle-income countries and middle-income countries, which receive the bulk of the ODA, aid plays an even smaller role: its injection is less than 1% of the GNI.

Why does aid not simply go to the poorest, most vulnerable countries which need it the most? Are there deserving poor countries and people on the one hand and undeserving on the other?

Several factors play a significant role. In Table 2, what is striking is the prominent place occupied by countries directly involved in the 'war on terror'. During the last 15 years, Afghanistan, Iraq and Syria have received a great deal of extra support not just from the USA but from many other donors too. Stephen Brown (2016), a scholar of the University of Ottawa, argues in an article that in the case of Canada under the conservative Harper government (2006–2015), this was part of a strategy to instrumentalise development aid for foreign and security policy reasons to the detriment of poverty reduction abroad. A significant amount of aid given to Afghanistan was spent on projects aimed at winning local hearts and minds: in other words, to garner support for the presence of Canadian troops. For instance, aid was used to try to win villagers' support by building them a school or a clinic, theoretically making them less likely to support the Taliban. Remarkably, Afghanistan is still the most important recipient of Canadian bilateral ODA, despite the fact that all Canadian soldiers left the country in 2014. This is called path dependency in the sociological literature; the past never fades away immediately.

Commercial and other economic interests certainly continue to play a role, too. This is a very contested issue for public opinion, NGDOs, politicians and academics alike, and is increasingly so with the emergence of the new paradigm that claims to reconcile altruism with mutual interests. 'Non-traditional' donors, often depicted as 'rogue donors', are not alone in promising African countries large amounts of development aid, concessional ODA-like and less-concessional 'other official flows', in order to facilitate their commercial relationship with these countries. Interestingly Dreher et al. (2018a) found that China, for example, uses its ODA-like projects primarily for foreign policy purposes (e.g., voting support in the UN) and its less-concessional loans to serve its economic interests. Martinez-Zarzoso et al. (2014), who looked at the 1988 to 2007 period, found an average positive effect of bilateral aid on exports from the donor country, especially when donors substantially tied their aid. But they also discovered an important evolution; they suggest that the recommendations given by the OECD-DAC concerning the untying of aid and aid allocation have been followed by the donors and led to declining impacts on their exports. The question will be whether this will continue to hold true when the new paradigm of mutual interests comes to full fruition.

Spending pressure is not a negligible factor. Many developing countries have weak institutions, poor governance and little development capacity. Donors, therefore, prefer to 'switch' a substantial proportion of their aid via somewhat better-run governments or countries that give donors plenty of space and freedom to get their aid to the population either directly or through local NGOs. The result is favoured countries, who get the epithet 'donor darling', where a horde of donors competes for attention and projects, and the less fortunate 'donor orphans' on whom nobody is prepared to spend much.

Donors want to be able to operate conveniently and efficiently. This is why countries where English is spoken receive more aid than others: there are more donors with officials and experts at home who know English than who have mastered French, Spanish or Portuguese. But donors do not just look for countries with which a common language can easily be spoken. There also needs to be common ground ideologically. Thus, for years, Sweden opted for countries run by politicians with a social democratic vision.

Having a presence in a country does not just ensure experience and a certain tradition of providing aid in that particular context, it also means that lobby groups are created (diaspora, experts, mixed marriages, businesses, tourism sector, NGDOs) which want cooperation with that country to continue for years to come, for a variety of reasons. This is most likely to be seen when one considers the aid that is given to former colonies. Table 3 shows that all ex-colonial powers still show a preference for their former colonies although this is significantly declining.

Table 3: The colonial preference (2007–2017)

Donor	Number of colonies in donor's top 10 (2007 → 2017)	ODA to colonies/total net ODA (%) (2007 → 2017)
Portugal	6 → 7	80% → 32%
The UK	9 → 5	56% → 8%
France	6 → 4	39% → 11%
Spain	5 → 5	35% → 7%
Belgium	3 → 3	27% → 9%
Germany	1 → 0	7% → 0%
Italy	1 → 0	3% → 0%
The Netherlands	1 → 0	5% → 0%

Source: OECD, Aid Statistics: Donor Aid Charts (2007–2017)

This brings us to geopolitics. Axel Dreher and his colleagues (2018b) have found that countries that serve on the UN Security Council get financial favours and attract surges in aid from traditional donors. They receive more US aid and loans from international institutions in which the US commands a powerful voice, including the IMF, the World Bank and UN aid agencies. These countries also receive softer IMF conditionality during their two years of temporary membership. Using data on voting behaviour in the Security Council, these scholars estimate that countries that voted with the US in the Security Council got an increase in US aid of about 40%. This, however, only applied to allies. Non-allies voting with the US received an increase in IMF loans of about 50%. In their paper on the determinants of aid from China to Africa, Dreher et al. (2018a) hypothesise that China punishes recipients of Western aid with reductions in its own aid due to their provision of foreign policy favours to the West. In any case, it is commonly known that countries that keep diplomatic ties with Taiwan are negatively sanctioned by Beijing.

So is no consideration given to combating poverty and vulnerability?

The consequence of the interplay of all the determinants of aid allocation that we just saw is that the poorest countries – and hence Africa – are less central to development cooperation than the public imagines. The LDCs have been promised for years that they will receive 0.15% of the rich countries' wealth. In 2017–2018, less than a quarter of ODA was allocated to the LDCs. This means that the LDCs could only count on less than half of what has been pledged time and again. Only a handful of the traditional donor countries kept that promise in the period 2017–2018 (being Denmark, Ireland, Luxembourg, Norway, Sweden and the UK).

Box 17. Why Burundi receives less aid than Rwanda

One of the interesting and intriguing questions is why countries in quite similar positions get more or less aid. Is it because of donor preferences or is it because recipient power relations and diplomatic skills also matter? Let us look at Burundi and Rwanda, for example. Burundi received around USD 50 per citizen in aid in the period 2016–2018, while Rwanda's population benefited from double that. Still, the two countries are very similar. They were both independent kingdoms in precolonial times. They were colonised by the Germans. This coloniser used the indirect rule system and thus governed via the agency of the monarchs in both territories. Both Urundi (later Burundi) and Rwanda became mandate territories under Belgian rule after World War I. Their populations are composed of the same communities (Hutu majority, Tutsi minority and Batwa, a tiny group of pygmies). They speak similar languages, have the same culture and the same history. Both became independent in 1962. Their size is approximately the same, as well as their population density. Both Burundi (1993) and Rwanda (1994) saw massive genocides caused by and amplifying existing social cleavages. Still, we call them 'false twins'. Rwanda, in precolonial times, had a more centralised system. Burundi's monarch relied more on local political forces. In Rwanda, the majority Hutu population mastered the postcolonial political landscape until the genocide of 1994, whereas the minority Tutsi elite dominated until then in Burundi.

Almost 30 years later, both have a different track record. Rwanda is attempting to build a service-led development state inspired by Singapore. It shows success compared to its Great Lake neighbours, with a GNI of USD 2200 per capita; it is also second of the 54 African countries in the ease of doing business ranking and in the top 10 of the Mo Ibrahim governance score in Africa. Burundi, on the other hand, is performing poorly. Its GNI per capita is the lowest in the world (USD 750) and both in terms of the business environment and governance it has a bleak situation. And then comes in the aid factor. Rwanda has always been an *enfant chéri*, a donor-darling, for the international aid community. Burundi is often called an example of a donor-orphan. As Marie Bamutese (2020) has shown, donors do play a role in this. Belgium, for example, has chosen to give as much aid to Burundi as to Rwanda. But some scholars say that we attribute the general preference for certain recipients too much to the preferences of donors. Donors, as we have seen, prefer anglophone countries and Rwanda has, after the genocide and the political advancement of the returned English-speaking Batutsi from Uganda, become an anglophone country. But Rwanda also received more aid under the Bahutu and francophone regime of Habyarimana before the genocide. So it remains a puzzle.

We should look more closely at local agency. Development cooperation agencies and aid policies do not shape local policies as much as we think. They do not even shape the development aid they give. Donors, inevitably, have to squeeze themselves through the filter the recipients provide and control.

As Deven Curtis wrote in 2015, in Rwanda, the ruling and very centrally led Rwandan Patriotic Front, and especially its leader, President Kagame, has largely maintained its image as an effective moderniser in the eyes of many donors, consistently emphasising the country's accomplishments as an alternative (African) source of internal legitimacy. The more fractured Burundian state and party scene, dominated by the more disintegrated CNDD-FDD, has had less leverage *vis-à-vis* donors. But things evolve. As much as before the genocide of 1994, Rwanda remains a donor-darling even if critics point to human rights abuses, the growing inequalities in the country, urban-rural divides and the party capitalist strangulation by regime-related companies. On the Burundian side, the European Council concluded consultations with its Rwandan neighbour under Article 96 of the EU-ACP partnership agreement (Cotonou Agreement) because it was violating human and political rights and norms and did not show good governance. Since then, the EU has suspended direct financial support to the Burundian administration, including budget support, while maintaining both its financial support to the population and its humanitarian assistance. This was a major blow for the Burundian state since the EU was Burundi's primary technical and financial partner, financing half of the country's budget.

Yes, things change, locally and internationally. In June 2019, during the China-Africa summit, Chinese President Xi Jinping promised to finance Burundi's 10-year (2018–2027) development plan with about €9.5 billion. This is more than what Europe was giving under the Cotonou Agreement, but it is not clear yet if it would be grants or (soft) loans. In any case, Burundi's political and economic elite are in this way forging intense and maybe enduring links with their Chinese partners who are so much interested in the precious metals, like columbium, tantalum and tine ore the Burundian soil contains.

It is also often said and written that numerous developing countries lack the real capacity to devise a policy, mobilise and manage government resources, and boost growth and development. The World Bank developed an interesting tool to gauge the governance and development capacity of a country: the world governance index. The institution looks at six dimensions: voice and accountability, political stability and the absence of violence, government effectiveness, regulatory quality, the rule of law and the control of corruption. Low-income countries, who should receive a fair share of development aid, systematically have a low score for these variables, while 70–75% of non-low-income countries perform better. Moreover, the index was launched in 2008 and shows little or no progress regarding governance in low-income countries.

When we go back to the 10 top receivers of Western ODA we do, however, see that they are amongst the worst performers and that for most of them, they were backsliding in terms of government effectiveness and regulatory quality. Progress in the other fields, if at all present, was mostly very scant. Perhaps we can still conclude that the Western donor community is not avoiding extremely difficult and even hazardous political environments altogether and is thus public spirited.

This also means that there is work to do and that it is no easy matter to work in these countries because the government is often more of a hindrance than a help. But it is not just the government that grapples with capacity problems: the same is also true of many local non-governmental organisations and other non-profit-making institutions such as universities. Because taxpayers and private donors in the rich countries also want resources to be used properly, many donors are inclined to stand in for the local institutions or be constantly looking over the shoulders of local ministers or officials. It has now been realised that this does not really help: it is very expensive to have everything done or monitored by international personnel, and it means that the local partners never assume responsibility and do not get a chance to learn and grow in their roles. So what capacity do governments and other actors in developing countries need?

It is first necessary to look at the *institutional capacity* of the government agency or local NGO in question. By this, we mean its capacity to play a role in the overall socio-institutional system. This implies that the government agency or local institution is in a position and capable of defining its own role, is able to develop positive patterns of interaction with other actors who are also active in the field, can mobilise resources (money, competent employees, relationships) that make it possible to fulfil its role.

Moving on from this last point, there is secondly a need for *organisational capacity*. In other words, the government department or local institution needs to be structured in such a way that it can achieve its goals in a purposeful, efficient and effective manner. Appropriate internal structures and working methods, therefore, need to be in place.

Finally, only when these institutional and organisational foundations have been laid can there be *development capacity*. This means that the actor who already has the right institutional and organisational features also has the skills needed to achieve the development goals. To put it another way, the actor needs to have the right talent at its disposal to reach the poor, boost economic growth, develop social services and create a favourable environment for sustainable development.

Box 18. When cultures meet...

Everybody who has worked in development cooperation knows it: local civil servants and local NGO staff are incentivised to supplement their often meagre and volatile wages with *per diems*, or daily and travel allowances, when they are taking part in capacity building exercises (Tostensen et al., 2016). It took us some time to discover that in the Democratic Republic of Congo a per diem is called a 'motivation'. So if people – peasants participating in a workshop, for example – are saying that they are not motivated or do not have enough motivation – they are expressing their dissatisfaction with the absence of a daily allowance or the meagre level of the per diem foreseen. Shomba Kinyamba's (2009) book on the popular locutions in Kinshasa sheds a fascinating light on how a 'mundele' (a white 'model' from North America or Europe or a 'Chinois' from anywhere in Asia) can get entangled in local semantic slips. 'Ba coopérant' does not refer to development cooperation professionals but to street vendors because they are willing to make deals. 'Coop' in Kinshasa's popular slang is an informal arrangement whereby several parties

cleverly override legal conventions. 'Deuropa' are secondhand goods mainly coming from Europe but increasingly also from other donor countries. 'Diasadiasa' is
the mockery name given to the disconnected Congolese diaspora, which is called
upon to help to rebuild the nation. 'Djicain' is a shortcut for 'Belgicain' and the nick-
name for a Congolese who comes from Belgium. 'First call for children' (*les enfants
d'abord*) – the 1990 UNICEF-led convention on children's rights that had to convince
the international community that children should get priority – had a completely
different meaning in the Congo: with that expression, university students in Kinshasa denounce the favouritism the children of professors benefit from.

Two crucial problems arise when one wants to 'strengthen capacities'. Firstly,
there is a problem of 'sequencing'. The simplest way to achieve a development
goal consists of finding an experienced local partner institution that already
has the requisite institutional, organisational and development capacities.
The problem is that such a partner is hardly ever found in countries with
a low level of development. This implies that development agencies do not
just need to keep in mind their ultimate development goal: they must also
invest in the path that leads towards it. In other words, development cooperation must also contribute to the partners' institutional, organisational and
development skills. It also means that a quick fix is not possible. Impatience
is thus out of place.

A second problem also arises. Technical assistance, development aid,
development cooperation or international cooperation is always an interactive process. The quality of the relationships between the parties concerned
is a variable that to a significant degree determines the outcome. To give an
example, the negative chemistry that arose between donor countries' interests and business interests on the one hand and the interests of a political
and business elite in the partner countries on the other hand was the cause
of the numerous shortcomings identified in development aid in the 1990s.
Concrete examples here are the projects that donors financed with grants
and concessional loans and which generally came to be regarded as white
elephants.

It needs indeed two to tango, and it needs two skilled dancers interpret-
ing the music in the same way to perform well.

The first pillar:
official bilateral cooperation

Official bilateral cooperation is actually the hub of international cooperation. It still represents two-thirds of all aid flows. It is on the basis of this bilateral cooperation that relationships with recipient governments arise, that a donor country acquires experience in the field and that ideas grow up about possible strategies for dealing with the numerous obstacles and problems encountered on a daily basis in development cooperation. Experience of bilateral cooperation also predisposes a donor country to deal in a certain way with its own national NGDO sector and increasingly with its domestic fourth pillar organisations, and determines the amount of resources and the importance it attaches to multilateral institutions.

Bilateral development cooperation is a rapidly changing scene. Half of DAC members updated their development cooperation policies and strategies between 2017 and 2020. New policies and strategies identify how they will contribute to achieving the SDGs in developing countries – both directly and by addressing global challenges – while also serving their national interests in areas such as trade and security (OECD, 2019a).

Many small players and institutional pluralism

However, most bilateral donors are small players. Europe is the biggest donor: around 55% of all ODA comes from the Old World. The collective ODA from the EU and its member states amounted to €75.2 billion in 2019. This represents 0.46% of EU GNI, significantly above the 0.21% average of the non-EU members of the OECD-DAC. The fact that Europe stands out in this way today is not just to do with the growth in the aid portfolio of virtually every European country but also with the accession of generous and slightly less generous member states (Sweden, Finland and Austria in 1995; Central and Eastern European countries in 2004). However, individually, the 27 member states contribute relatively limited resources. Only Germany is responsible for more than 15% of global ODA. The UK – until the end of 2020 an EU member state, contributes around 12% and France around 8%. Some countries, such as Luxembourg, the Czech Republic and Hungary, represent less than 0.3% of global ODA. Others, such as Romania, Lithuania and Latvia, represent even less than 0.1%. The biggest donor, the USA, provides 22%, while for all its wealth, Japan contributes only 9%.

However, not only do the donors contribute individual fractions of ODA but the landscape is also highly fragmented. The traditional donor countries all set up specialist development agencies or ministries in the 1960s and 1970s to carry out and/or coordinate aid actions. There has been constant institutional tinkering, but one or more institutions has always taken a leading role at any given time. In the USA, for example, the United States Agency for International Development (USAID) took firm control of development policy, while the Overseas Development Administration did the same in the UK. USAID quickly became the largest (and most powerful) bilateral aid institution in the world, but since the Bush administration, many other ministries and state agencies have competed with or overshadowed it. Meanwhile, the successor to the British Overseas Development Administration, DFID, became the trendsetter and leading bilateral donor under the Blair government (Morrissey, 2005). However, in 2020, DFID lost its standalone position and merged with the Foreign and Commonwealth Office to became part of the Foreign, Commonwealth and Development Office. Other key agencies that appeared on the aid scene and still play a prominent role are the Japan International Cooperation Agency (JICA) and the German Federal Ministry for Economic Cooperation and Development.

But in every donor country, we can see a growing trend towards institutional pluralism. Other ministries and government departments (such as national banks and parastatal agencies) are also entering the aid sector. The DAC and specialist aid institutions are very concerned about this fragmentation of cooperation, which is assuming ever more substantial proportions in a number of countries, as Table 4 makes clear.

In 16 of the 31 donor countries that reported to the OECD (2019a), the largest government institution providing ODA controlled less than 60% of the country's development aid. In a number of countries, an attempt has been made to gain coherence in the multiplicity of official development initiatives. There are good reasons for this. The ministries of employment, public health, the environment, security, finance, economic affairs, trade and foreign affairs have their own reasons for engaging in development cooperation, but these are not necessarily compatible with, for example, the SDGs. They also have their own approaches and again, these do not automatically coincide with the approach suggested by the Paris Declaration. Things become problematic when the policies of certain ministries are harmful to developing countries or when the opportunity is neglected to make national policy development friendly in numerous other fields.

Table 4: Fragmentation of aid

Country	Number of government departments involved	Most important department(s)	% ODA controlled by most important departments in 2009 → 2019
USA	50	USAID	56.7 → 56.3%
Sweden	4	Sida	77.5 → 49.3%
Germany	15	GIZ	57.7 → 40.7%
Canada	9	Global Affairs Canada	73.9 → 73.4%
Belgium	Nearly all ministries	DGD	69.1 → 55.1%
France	14	Secrétariat d'Etat à la Coopération	85.9 → 48.6%
Ireland	6	DCD Irish Aid	85.0 → 66.8%
Switzerland	5	SDC and SECO	71.2 → 67.3%
The Netherlands	8	Minbuza	99.2 → 98.8%

Source: Budget4Change; OECD-DAC, DAC Country Peer review Reports

Box 19. Leveraging: the new buzzword

In 2017, USD 33.9 billion of private sector financing directed to economic development and investment in developing countries was leveraged by a variety of mechanisms put in place by multilateral and bilateral aid agencies. The idea is that more private-sector money has to flow to developing countries if we want to reach the SDGs, but that it is hard to seduce the private sector to 'spontaneously' get excited about investments in countries with poor governance, limited resources and neglected infrastructures. So, aid agencies are experimenting with numerous attractive systems to de-risk and help rich countries' private sector actors become interested and to crowd them in. Many donor countries now have agencies that show the way and directly invest in private companies in developing countries so that private investors feel more comfortable about following suit. They also set up special-purpose vehicles, underwrite syndicated loans, buy shares in collective investment vehicles, provide guarantees and develop co-financing arrangements. Leveraging seems to be a tough job. At less than a quarter of ODA in 2017, financing mobilised from the private sector is modest. However, for a number of donor countries, investments leveraged have become increasingly important. In this way, in the USA, over USD 5 billion was leveraged in 2017; over USD 2 billion in France and USD 758 million in Germany. The volume of private 'development' investments not only remain relatively modest but questions also arise as to their destination. Since they generally have a better investment climate, it is no surprise that most of these private investments are being done in upper- and lower-middle-income

117

developing countries. Furthermore, foreign direct investment in developing countries fell by USD 70 billion, or 11%, between 2015 and 2016 (OECD, 2019a). This shows that there is more at stake than just investing in 'a good cause'.

Since the adoption of the SDGs in 2015, more than 25 Western donor countries have written new legislation, white papers, guidelines, masterplans or strategies to adjust their development cooperation policies and practices to the new international consensus and reposition their country in the international development cooperation community, arena and market. Some carry lyrical and telling titles that succinctly express the donor's ambitions. Take Finland's 'One World – Common Future' (2016), Norway's 'Common Responsibility for Common Future' (2016), Canada's 'Feminist International Assistance Policy' (2017), Denmark's 'The World 2030' (2017), Germany's 'Charter for the Future' (2017), Luxembourg's 'The Road to 2030' (2018) or Ireland's 'A Better World' (2019). These all point to the choice for principled international development cooperation. This was also the case for the 2017 New European Consensus on Development.

Others, though, explicitly refer to the return on investment that donors increasingly are looking for. The UK was the first to do so in 2015, with its strategy 'Tackling Global Challenges in the National Interest'. The Netherlands followed in 2018 with a new development and trade policy titled 'Investing in Global Prospects: For the World; for the Netherlands'. The USA, on its side, believes that aid can be replaced by other mechanisms of international cooperation as its aid agency, USAID, launched its guiding policy framework and document 'Ending the Need for Foreign Assistance' in 2019.

Donor countries also developed these kinds of all-encompassing policy documents to find more coherence and consistency in an ever more pluralistic first pillar scene of development activity. The first country to launch such a whole-of-government approach was Sweden. In 2003, the then-social democratic government launched a Policy for Global Development, which stipulated that all ministries had to contribute to fair and sustainable development.

In the meantime, various other donor countries have also looked for methods for deploying aid resources in a more uniform, coordinated fashion. In the USA, the position of the Director of US Foreign Assistance was created in 2005. This person has coordination powers over the numerous aid programmes created in government departments and agencies and the first coordinator introduced a series of measures to streamline American aid. In the Netherlands, finally, a so-called Homogeneous Budget for International Cooperation (HGIS) was created to ensure alignment between the many ministries involved in international cooperation and their international programmes. As a result, the Netherlands has an instrument for ensuring more consistency in the use of approximately €5.9 billion for international cooperation, of which €4.5 billion qualifies as ODA (2020 figures). The HGIS explicitly aims to reconcile multiple objectives: reducing international instability, fighting poverty in developing countries, promoting sustainable economic development, effective global climate action and strengthening Dutch international earning power.

In search of an institutional foundation for development cooperation

As can be seen, the policy field of development cooperation in fact has a completely contradictory relationship with other, conventional policy fields. On the one hand, those within development cooperation realise that they cannot do the job on their own. They want to act as a lever, ensuring that other ministries (with more power) also help to achieve the goals of development cooperation. Most of them would, for example, argue that debt cancellation is an essential precondition for creating a development-friendly context in developing countries. This is a task in which the ministry of finance also has a role to play. The ministries of foreign affairs, trade, employment and work, healthcare, the environment and agriculture can implement policies that have either a positive or negative impact on developing countries, and which may even undermine efforts at development cooperation. Some, therefore, even argue that development cooperation should become a 'horizontal or transversal role', which is not only carried out by a specialist department but constitutes an integral element of the other government services. Hence the plea for a whole-of-government approach.

On the other hand, according to many experts, the goals and working methods of development cooperation are beyond question. Concessions to economic, trade or diplomatic objectives and interests on the part of the donor country are unwelcome to the development sector. Furthermore, the department must always ensure that its portfolio and activities are not 'colonised', 'contaminated' or 'exploited' by other departments. Thus, an argument is put forward in favour of far-reaching autonomy in determining the goals and policy of development cooperation.

This difficult position has led to a quest in many countries for an ideal political and institutional foundation for development cooperation. Since the final decade of the last century, many Western donor countries have worked on the policy toolkit of official development cooperation. According to Cox, Healey and Koning (1997), the formal organisational structure of development cooperation in donor countries differs on three important points.

Firstly, there is the degree of integration or fragmentation of the cooperation apparatus. This has consequences for the coordination and coherence of the range of aid offered. As we have seen, Canada and the Netherlands, for example, have government agencies that manage virtually all aid instruments and devise policy for them. By contrast, the American and French models are particularly fragmented.

Secondly, there is the degree of autonomy that the specialised ministry or agency has in defining its development policy. In the large majority of OECD countries, the organisations responsible for development cooperation are formally integrated into the ministry for foreign affairs. This means that the minister responsible for development cooperation is continually compelled to find a compromise between their own goals and the specific political and sometimes commercial objectives of the more powerful ministry for foreign affairs. In a number of countries, an attempt has been made to safeguard the specific character and autonomy of development policy by creating a separate department or legally determining the goals and policy, governance, management and control mechanisms. It would be interesting to know to what extent this relative autonomy has a positive effect on the choice in favour of combating poverty and the distribution of resources for the benefit of the poorest countries and population groups.

Thirdly, there is the degree of freedom involved in the implementation of an autonomous development policy. This is related to the extent to which the development ministry or agency is subject to interference from the higher political echelons in the execution of its tasks. From the 1990s onwards, we see an attempt being made in various countries to limit such interference by increasingly entrusting the implementation of development programmes to autonomous or semi-autonomous agencies. This is the case with Expertise France, Lux-Development in Luxembourg, the Agencia Española de Cooperación Internacional para el Desarollo in Spain, Enabel in Belgium and Slovak Aid, as well as with numerous executive agencies in the UK (the Commonwealth Development Corporation, the Natural Resources Institute, the British Council etc.). Another solution consists of decentralising the executive role to field offices which gain considerable room for manoeuvre. Sweden's Sida and, until recently, USAID are examples of this.

Box 20. The European Practitioners' Network for European Development Cooperation

The Practitioners' Network has 17 members. All of them are non-profit national bodies of European donor countries with a public service mission and which directly implement bilateral or European development assistance. Their names are telling: France Expertise, Enabel, LuxDev, RoAid, CzechAid… The European Commission has an observer status in this informal network, which was established in 2007. The platform seeks to create opportunities for cooperation and synergies at the implementation level, and make links with, for example, European and other international development banks. It is one mechanism to get bilateral cooperation agencies out of their silos, stimulate joint implementation and look for more coherence in Europe's development efforts. At the same time, the consortium is a way to defend the interests of agencies that do not primarily listen to the demands of domestic stakeholders and taxpayers but to those of constituents in recipient countries.

Decentralisation: to reach the SDGs or also for other reasons?

It has become clear by now that other, non-specialist, government departments are writing a significant part of the development cooperation story. That story would still be a straightforward one if it were only the ministerial department for development cooperation and the other national government departments that were involved. In fact, the trend towards localisation means that plenty of other actors are also showing up to take on or even take over part of the official aid commitment.

Since 2009, the European Commission and the European Committee of the Regions have organised a Forum for Cities and Regions for Development Cooperation, gathering hundreds of local and regional authorities, their associations, city networks and practitioners from both Europe and partner countries. The initiative departs from the Paris Declaration, the Accra Agenda for Action and the SDGs as leading frameworks that strongly suggest a decentralisation and localisation of development cooperation, as well as cooperation amongst peers. The 2030 agenda is, indeed, first and foremost a local agenda: the OECD (2019b) estimates that almost 60% of SDG targets can only be achieved by subnational governments providing essential public services in health, education, emergency preparedness, water, energy, housing etc. But the think tank hastens to add that only USD

Figure 13: Trends in decentralised development cooperation

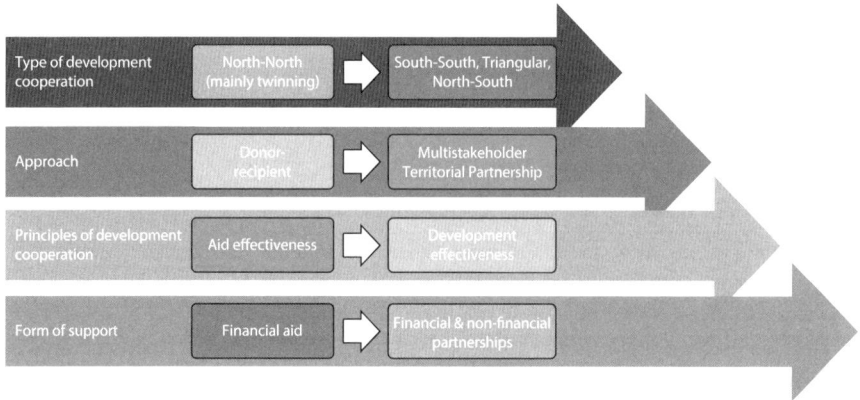

Type of development cooperation	North-North (mainly twinning)	→	South-South, Triangular, North-South
Approach	Donor-recipient	→	Multistakeholder Territorial Partnership
Principles of development cooperation	Aid effectiveness	→	Development effectiveness
Form of support	Financial aid	→	Financial & non-financial partnerships

Source: OECD-DAC (2019)

1.87 billion, or 1.3% of total bilateral ODA, is provided in support of cities and regions in developing countries.

As Figure 13 of the 2019 edition of the Forum shows, the decentralised development cooperation movement is also heading towards a new paradigm and new practices.

The total volume of decentralised development cooperation has increased by 12% over the period 2005–2015, reaching USD 1.9 billion in 2015 (Figure 14). The relative volume of this aid remained stable at 4–6% of total bilateral ODA.

At present, there is considerable debate in various Western countries about the role that regions, sub-states, *Bundesländer* or provinces can play in development cooperation. In a number of countries, including the USA, Germany, Switzerland, France, Canada, Austria, Spain, Italy and Belgium, there is, in fact, a fairly long tradition of involvement on the part of subnational authorities in development cooperation. Particularly in the last three of these countries, this debate has at times been fairly fierce and reflects the emotional upheavals concerning the organisation of the state. The sub-states or regions have their own approaches in these three countries, whereas the other countries have or are seeking more central control.

With USD 1.5–2 billion of total ODA from DAC-member countries currently deriving from subnational authorities, this kind of aid still remains very modest. This is also related to the fact that in many countries, sub-national authorities do not want to increase their own efforts but rather opt for

Figure 14: Trends in official decentralised development cooperation (DDC) financing, net disbursements, USD million, constant 2015 prices

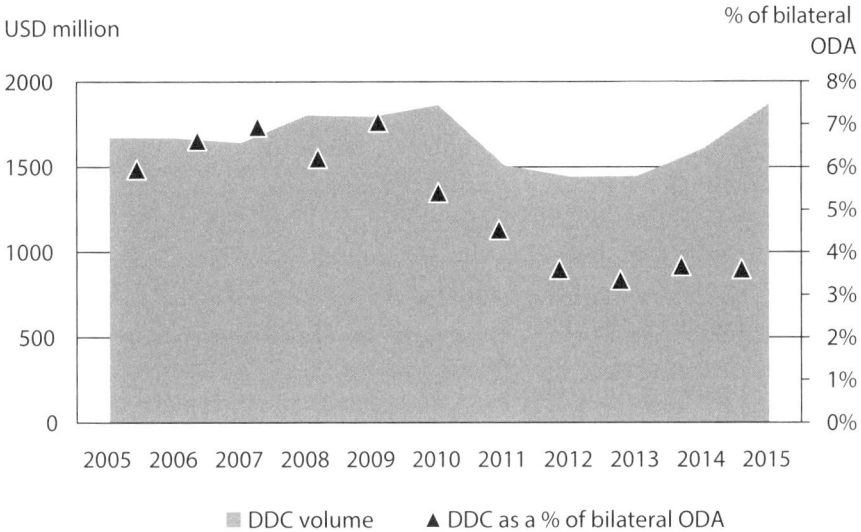

Source: OECD-DAC (2019)

a system whereby the national tax and financial authorities provide them with the necessary funds to engage in development cooperation.

In 2015, the top providers of decentralised development cooperation were Germany (7% of its bilateral ODA), Canada (9% of ODA), Spain (59% of ODA), and Austria (22% of ODA). It seems that Austria, Switzerland, Italy and Belgium have seen their decentralised aid increase most (European Commission and OECD, 2019).

Development cooperation by subnational authorities in most countries encompasses a very broad range of activities, but a number of trends can be distinguished (OECD, 2019b). For example, they prefer investments in education and healthcare, and frequently collaborate with the NGDOs and other private initiatives from the region in question. The fact that nearly 100% of Swiss and 80% of Spanish decentralised aid is channelled through NGDOs is a case in point (Pérez, 2018). The aid resources of subnational authorities are distributed among a large number of countries and a very large number of projects, which receive small budgets. On average, Spanish decentralised authorities invest €60.000 per intervention (Pérez, 2018).

The arguments for sharing out competence

Those in favour of giving greater powers in the area of development coop-eration to sub-states or other subnational authorities straddle party lines in most countries.

Defenders of decentralised development cooperation often advance con-stitutional arguments. The *foro interno, foro externo* principle, for example, in some countries[25] stipulates that the federated entities are responsible for the international aspects of their competences.

Some advocates argue that communities and regions can develop much broader and more solid support for this area than the federal government. They are closer to the general public, it is said, and are able to elicit much more support from the public for the problems in the developing world, which are currently regarded as rather remote. This was confirmed by the discovery by Janssen (2008) that confidence in ODA was higher in a num-ber of the countries with a high degree of decentralisation (Germany, Bel-gium and Austria) than elsewhere. However, he added that this equally had to do with the fact that the subnational governments in these countries also invest a lot of money in development education.

Subnational governments often argue that they can collaborate effectively with other subnational governments in developing countries. The OECD-DAC also takes this position for granted. France even has an explicit national policy of supporting such *coopération décentralisée* and encourages regions and large cities to join with local businesses, schools and civil society in forging links (*jumélage*) with a region or large city in the South.

A last argument has to do with transaction costs. Pérez (2018) found, for example, that the administrative costs of Spanish decentralised cooperation were substantially lower (6% of total project costs) than those of the central government (17%).

The arguments for closing ranks

Opponents also have a whole range of arguments, however. They point to the historic steps that the development community has just taken with the 2005 Paris Declaration and the SDGs. The new aid architecture is predicated on greater coordination and harmonisation, not greater fragmentation and vying for attention.

Development cooperation, opponents also argue, is an integrated area. Most projects and programmes include activities that relate to different pol-icy fields at the same time, such as agriculture, healthcare and education. It is undesirable, indeed impossible, to separate these components out and organise programmes in accordance with the division of powers and institutional set-up of the donor country.

Development cooperation should be based on the needs of the recipient countries, opponents add. If sub-states get involved, there is a danger that they will be far more focused on what they themselves can or would like to do than on what is needed in the countries themselves. This is not the way to get good development cooperation; what you end up doing is turning the principle of 'think global, act local' on its head. The result is 'think local, act global'.

Moreover, in the countries in question, there is invariably a very uneven commitment to development cooperation. Some regions are not even prepared to act globally. Sub-states which do get involved mainly push the aid money in the direction of their own NGDOs, schools, universities and consultants. They resist any move towards coordination at the national level.

These opponents also point out that development cooperation is increasingly being coordinated at the international level. When European member states come together in Benin to align their programmes with one another, the sub-states are not invited, the reasoning goes. Another example is that the World Bank is unlikely to invite German Bavaria or Spanish Andalusia to a donors' meeting about boosting the recovery and economic development of South Sudan. In any case, the ODA will still need to be added up by a federal authority that is recognised by the OECD-DAC.

Moreover, the opponents emphasise that the recipient countries are certainly not asking for more involvement by sub-states, as this would mean having to engage in discussions with even more institutions about even smaller sums of money. If every region were to start providing development aid autonomously in each of the aforementioned countries – which is not yet the case – this would add over a hundred donors, each with its own priorities, procedures and rules.

The second pillar: multilateral cooperation

By definition, development cooperation is always largely a multilateral affair. We have already seen how the national aid culture and patterns in each donor country have been inspired to a significant degree by what other actors and institutions have said or done. It could be argued that all development cooperation is increasingly taking on collective, multilateral characteristics. This is certainly very visibly the case since the MDGs were adopted in September 2000, and even more so since the SDGs were signed by all UN Member States in 2015. But, as Figure 15 shows, the interconnectivity of the worlds' people, nations and states intensified tremendously long before. By way of looking at the number of international governmental organisations (IGO) in the world, the figure demonstrates that since the 1900s, the group of IGOs has grown significantly. It is clear that the independence of an ever-increasing number countries has pushed for an even more dense international community, as has the collective feeling that we are one interdependent world since the last decades of the previous century.

Figure 15: IGOs in the world system, 1816–2014

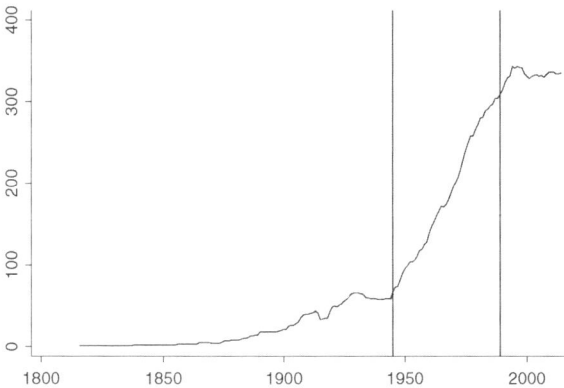

Source: adapted from Pevehouse et al. (2020)

In this chapter, we will zoom in on this amazing world of international organisations. We cannot, of course, deal with all of them. We will, therefore, focus on two prominent groupings, namely the EU and the UN.

127

Europe's development cooperation patchwork

European development cooperation is the nearest supranational level for European bilateral donors and belongs to the second, international, pillar of the development cooperation sector. The influence between the levels is asymmetrical in nature: national development cooperation is more influenced by European cooperation than vice versa. As we mentioned earlier, the EU member states together, taking both their national efforts and those of the European Commission into account, are the largest donor group: they provide around 55% of global ODA.

Europe is a major donor not just by volume but also by working method and content. As we will see, Europe has always been a trendsetter and an important laboratory for innovation in the sector. When national ministers in charge of development cooperation or high-level public servants meet in the EU Headquarters in Brussels, development policy ideas, practices and experiences are exchanged. New proposals are picked up, trends are sounded out and people gain important information. But the member states to a large extent decide on and shape European development policy.

Europe also has a long tradition of co-managing its policies and programmes with recipient or partner countries. Important are, for example, the ACP-EU Council of Ministers and other bodies established by the Lomé Convention and later by the Cotonou Agreement, as these make it possible for the EU member states and the ACP countries to manage their development programme jointly. However, as we will see, this co-management culture is suffering from some erosion under the new post-Cotonou agreement.

In addition, the members of the European Parliament raise the concerns of their countries and constituencies for discussion in various commissions, working groups and plenary sessions.

Thus, the European development aid system is crucial, but also highly complex.

The complexity is closely related to the political development of Europe itself and the associated history of European development cooperation, and to the awkward complementarity between the development aid of the Commission and the Union on the one hand and of the member states on the other hand.

In order to understand trends in Europe and European development policy, some academics rely on a liberal, intergovernmental explanatory model. To put it simply, they argue that the European decision-making process is determined by the member states. One good example of this can be found in the late 1950s, when France and Belgium wanted the market position of their colonies and former colonies to be safeguarded in a burgeoning European environment and, therefore, ensured that development relations also became a European concern. The intergovernmental deal that was needed became a reality in the first Yaoundé Convention, an association agreement signed in 1963, involving the European Economic Community and 18 African ex-colonies.

Supranational actors such as the European Commission itself also undoubtedly play a not-to-be underestimated role in European development policy. It offers a platform for exchange between member states and thus is the only one to have an elevated birds-eye view of the EU politics and concrete efforts in development cooperation. Since the signing of the Maastricht Treaty in 1993, the Commission has acquired the status of an additional European actor in development cooperation and can thus exercise its own competences alongside the member states.[26] According to neo-functionalist scholars, there is more going on. They refer to the spill-over effect from policy sectors and decisions. The reforms of the Lomé Convention and the development of a Common Foreign and Security Policy at the end of the last century have certainly affected each other. The successive Yaoundé, Lomé and Cotonou framework agreements with the group of ACP countries have largely determined how the EU deals with the rest of the developing countries. Moreover, the new 'post-Cotonou' agreement is repositioning the EU and its member states in the new international ballgame and especially the one played out in Africa.

Another illuminating explanatory model is provided by the narrative of multilevel governance. This is based on the premise that national authorities have to take account of and are influenced by both supranational institutions and non-state actors. This offers us a better understanding of how, for example, the member states are supposed to take account of the guidelines set out by the European Commission for each ACP country in the framework of the Cotonou Agreement when designing their own strategy papers and indicative programmes. Moreover, the national indicative plans that are drawn up by the Commission in conjunction with local governments are themselves influenced by local and international non-governmental organisations.

Seeking identity and complementarity
These different, fairly complementary explanatory schemes help us understand how a complex multi-layered system of international aid got a foothold in Europe. First of all, a broad range of instruments for development cooperation arose, which were managed within the Commission and its various directorates. At the same time, the individual European member states, while subscribing to a coordinated European-level approach to

development cooperation, did not and still do not refrain from developing their national aid policies and, because of the lack of real sanction mechanisms, without always seeking coherence and coordination with efforts at the European level.

Since the early 1990s, continuous debates have been conducted regarding the complex European aid mechanism, its role and its impact. The culminating point was reached with the New Consensus on Development, a 2017 agreement between the European Council (on behalf of the 28 Member States)[27], the European Parliament (on behalf of the European citizens), the European Commission and the European External Action Service.

The New Consensus reaffirms that poverty eradication remains the primary objective of European development policy. It fully integrates the economic, social and environmental dimensions of sustainable development and in doing so, aligns European development action with the 2030 Agenda for Sustainable Development, which is also a cross-cutting dimension for the EU Global Strategy. With the Consensus, European leaders committed to three areas that confirm their adherence to the emerging new paradigm on international cooperation. Firstly, they recognise the strong interlinkages between development, peace and security, migration, the environment and climate change. Secondly, they plead for a more comprehensive approach to the means of implementation, combining traditional development aid with other resources. For the latter they want to engage in more innovative forms of development financing, leveraging private sector investments through blended financing mechanisms and mobilising additional domestic resources for development. Lastly, the EU and its member states showed their will to create better-tailored partnerships with a broad range of stakeholders, including the partner countries, civil society, the private sector, foundations, think tanks and universities. A whole-of-society approach is thus indeed in the making.

Probably the most influential development cooperation deal: EU-ACP

As we have seen, cooperation between Europe and the developing countries dates back to the infancy of the European construction itself. But in the early 1960s, many colonies gained their independence. The way Europe dealt with its former colonies has set the trend for international development cooperation in general; Europe, in its rapport with those countries, launched new ideas, experimented with novel approaches, created the atmosphere for the many mood swings the international cooperation community went through. The political and economic ties between the former colonies and the then-European member states[28] were first continued via the Yaoundé

Convention (1963–1969). That association agreement was signed by the six European Economic Community member states and 18 Associated African States and Madagascar. Trade liberalisation was accelerated, and more aid was made available, partly in the form of loans.

In the late 1960s, international relations underwent fundamental changes. Politically, Africa was very unstable. Export income fell and economic growth stalled. The Group of 77, at that time the most powerful intergovernmental organisation of developing countries, called for a global and structural approach to development problems: the New International Economic Order. The recipe prescribed by the Second Yaoundé Convention (1969–1975) was, however, the same: the development of the social and economic infrastructure in former colonies, economic cooperation and reciprocal preferences. The one difference was that still more money was earmarked for financial aid.

In 1973, the UK joined the European project and brought with it a group of 20 independent states in Africa, the Caribbean and the Pacific region. The same year also saw the signing of the Georgetown Agreement in connection with negotiations for a new treaty. The ACP Group was formally established: the African, Caribbean and Pacific Group of States.[29]

The agreement entered into in Lomé in 1975 between nine European countries and 46 ACP countries no longer referred to an 'association' but instead to a "unilateral system of preferences with the ACP countries". The Lomé Convention was constructed around two main principles: preferential status for the ACP countries' export products (no customs duties and a reserved market share) and development aid. In addition, trade protocols were established for sugar, bananas, rum and pork. Thirteen basic products also became eligible for the Stabex Fund, a stabilisation fund to counteract the losses suffered by ACP countries due to price fluctuations, for example in the international coffee or cocoa market.

The first Lomé Convention attached great importance to support, via development aid and soft loans, for the ACP countries' industrial development. The Second Lomé Convention (1980–1985)[30] continued along the same lines, but more of an emphasis was placed on the food issue in the ACP countries. The Third Lomé Convention (1985–1990) paid even more attention to the food situation and agricultural problems in the ACP countries, as well as to employment, the protection of private investments, aid effectiveness and the burden of debt. Respect for human rights was referred to in the preamble only. This convention was more of an aid treaty than its predecessor. The focus shifted from project to programme aid and the aid budget was significantly increased.

The last Lomé Convention (1990–2000) again introduced a number of new features. The convention was for a term of 10 years. Human rights were incorporated as a fundamental element of the treaty. The environment, gender, the private sector and decentralised development got particular attention.

The revision of Lomé Convention IV in 1994–1995 was even more influenced by the new international order following the fall of the Berlin Wall in 1989. Respect for human rights, democratic principles and the rule of law were incorporated as essential elements. This meant that infringements could lead to the partial or total suspension of aid. It was the first development agreement to contain such a standard. In addition, in the field of trade cooperation, there was a slight expansion of the preferential access for ACP agricultural produce to the European market. Finally, the first form of phased programming was introduced with respect to development financing. This meant that only 70% of the promised aid was made available on the signing of the National Indicative Programme. The remaining 30% was allocated only after a performance evaluation during the first phase.

Strenghts and weaknesses of the ACP-EU partnership exposed

The successive Lomé Conventions formed the world's most extensive financial and political framework for North-South cooperation. A number of original features served as a model for many other development agreements.[31]

Dialogue and partnership on an equal footing was a sheer innovation in the field of development aid. The ACP countries were given a key function in the management of the programme. However, it was clear that the so-called 'Lomé culture' was coming under pressure in the final years. Programming and implementation were increasingly controlled by the EU, and many ACP actors had neither the desire nor the capacity to act as equal partners.

In each new convention, the parties gave a contractual undertaking to observe a number of principles and achieve certain goals. The most groundbreaking of these were the human rights clause and the structural adjustment goals. The European countries undertook to grant the ACP countries a combination of aid and trade benefits (on a non-reciprocal basis) for the duration of the convention. Each country was allocated a national budget which it could claim and that was predictable. Nonetheless, this principle gradually came under pressure following the introduction of the system of phased programming.

From the 1990s, the Lomé system came under considerable scrutiny. Various internal papers exposed the system's weaknesses, the macroeconomic environment and political context altered drastically and, worst of all, results were not forthcoming. The debate in the 1990s largely shaped the new Cotonou approach.

When the first Lomé Convention was signed, there were still very close historical and psychological links between the European and ACP countries. By the 1990s, the latter was no longer the case. Moreover, the preferential trade regime enjoyed by the ACP countries was inconsistent with the principle of non-discrimination which became a cornerstone of the international trade system. It was also uncertain if the Lomé mechanisms had any positive effect. The results in terms of ACP access to the European markets were pitiful. The ACP countries' share of the EU market fell from 6.7% in 1976 to 3% in 1998. The diversification of the ACP countries' production and trade was another goal that was not achieved; by the late 1990s, 60% of total exports from the ACP countries still consisted of just 10 products.

The Cotonou Agreement: an attempt to refresh EU-ACP cooperation
At the end of the last century, the EU wanted to fundamentally recalibrate its cooperation efforts to make them compatible with the new rapport between the EU and its member states, as well as with the new consensus on development cooperation as primarily a tool for poverty reduction. The ACP countries wished to maintain the unique and privileged relationship that had developed through the Lomé Conventions but expressed their desire to have it modernised and adapted to the new rules of the game in a liberalised and globalising world. So both parties were convinced that a refreshment, an *aggiornamiento,* was urgently needed. A consensus was found in 2000 between the 15 EU member states and the ACP countries.

The redefined partnership, the Cotonou Agreement, was established for 20 years. The agreement was much more of a political agreement than the Lomé Conventions had been. It was agreed that the parties, by means of political dialogue, could discuss any subjects of common interest. It was also accepted that a number of core values would form the basis of the partnership. They were called the 'essential elements': respect for human rights, principles of democracy and the rule of law. Their infringement could lead to aid being suspended. Because ACP countries feared arbitrary and unilateral sanctions, the principle of good governance was included in the agreement as a 'fundamental' rather than an 'essential' element. Thus, breaching the principle of good governance, for example due to a lack of institutional capacity in an ACP country or autocratic stubbornness, could not in itself lead to the adjournment of cooperation; on the other hand, serious cases of corruption, such as bribery, could do so.

Dialogue, aid and trade remained the three most important pillars of ACP-EU cooperation. Financial cooperation consisted of grants for the development programmes of individual ACP countries, and ACP regions were eligible for financial and technical support for the implementation of their regional programmes.

Box 21. Between policy and practice: What evaluations reveal

The think tank the European Centre for Development Policy Management (ECDPM) in conjunction with the German Development Institute (DIE) conducted an ambitious study on the EU's development cooperation with Sub-Saharan Africa in the period 2013–2018 (Jones et al., 2020). They concluded that policy priorities are not swiftly translated into spending patterns. Policy priorities that emerged in the period under review – the EU was moving from a poverty-reduction approach to a more interest-driven and sustainability agenda – hardly influenced the budgetary allocations made in the same period. They observed an important time lag between the formulation of (new) policy priorities and their translation into actual aid disbursements. This, they discovered, was mainly due to the lengthy EU decision-making process. Jones and his colleagues, who delved into 55 evaluation reports, found confirmation of the relevance of the EU's choices and approaches when it comes to development cooperation in Sub-Saharan Africa, as well as positive results that had been accomplished, but their findings are much more nuanced when it comes to the sustainability of these results. Moreover, they found that although gender equality is a cross-cutting priority in EU development policy, it was under-evaluated during the review period. Only one of the 55 evaluation reports focused specifically on gender equality, while others provided only patchy findings on gender. Budget support, strengthening recipient governments through direct contributions to the national budget, remains an essential aspect of EU development cooperation and one where the EU has confirmed added value. At the same time, there has been a stronger use of other aid modalities and delivery channels, including project-type interventions, centrally managed trust funds and blended finance. The EU has also increasingly channelled its aid through various intermediaries. These include international organisations and EU member states' implementing agencies.

The part of the agreement relating to trade underwent radical revision. Economic Partnership Agreements (EPAs) were proposed. These were intended to create a free-trade area between the EU and the ACP group. To be tailor made, the negotiations for the EPAs were carried out by region; in this way, six different groups were formed. The EPAs follow five principles: they are defined as development instruments, serve to promote regional integration and must safeguard the so-called *acquis*, or what has been reached and agreed upon so far; in other words, the ACP countries must be able to retain equal access to the European market. In addition, the EPAs must be compatible with the rules of the World Trade Organization (WTO), and only the LDCs can claim exceptions.

Box 22. Six economic partnership agreements, most of them under negotiation

1. *West Africa:* the 16 member states of the Economic Commission of West African States plus Mauritania. The regional EPA has been signed by all of the states concerned except Nigeria.
2. *Central Africa:* the six member states of the Economic and Monetary Community of Central Africa plus the Democratic Republic of Congo and Sao Tomé and Principe. Only signed by Cameroon.
3. *Eastern and Southern Africa*: negotiations proceed separately with the East African Community, successfully concluded in 2014, and the East and Southern African Countries.
4. *Southern Africa:* the Southern African Development Community; came into force in 2016.
5. *The Caribbean*: all Caribbean states (since 2008).
6. *The Pacific*: the Pacific islands; Papua New Guinea, Fiji and Samoa acceded.

Non-governmental organisations have campaigned vigorously against the EPAs. Several members of the European Parliament, academics and much of the political elite in the ACP countries were and are also still very critical of the negotiation process and the resulting outcomes of the EPAs. The catastrophic social and political consequences of trade liberalisation in the 1990s are still seared in the collective memory. It is said that the whole EPA process is (some say intentionally) locking in a neoliberal development approach and paralysing attempts for more autonomous or state-led development strategies. In addition, the negotiations were and are seen as asymmetrical political bargains between strong and united EU forces on the one hand and vulnerable, highly divided and competing ACP groups of countries on the other. To put it in perspective, the GNI of all the countries in the Caribbean region is equivalent to the capital of a medium-sized European bank. In order to maintain levels of trade and aid, the highly dependent ACP countries are willing to sacrifice their regulatory autonomy and much-needed import levies, the critics argue. While protagonists of the EPAs hail the advantages of regional integrated markets, the critical antagonists point to the fact that the regional entities being forged are artificially composed of countries that did not choose to be together, and especially not at the speed of geo-economic and geopolitical conglomeration that was imposed upon them. The price to be paid might be mistrust among neighbouring countries, competition and even tensions.

A genuine Africa-EU Alliance?

In his last State of the European Union address in September 2018, the President of the European Commission, Jean-Claude Juncker, launched a new Africa-EU Alliance for Sustainable Investments and Jobs. When Ursula von der Leyen succeeded him at the end of 2019, she immediately visited her counterpart in the AU in Addis Ababa, Ethiopia. At the end of February 2020, just before the coronavirus crisis would dominate everything, she took 21 European commissioners to Addis Ababa for a 'College-to-College meeting' with the commissioners from both sides. Within the first 100 days of the new Commission, a 'comprehensive strategy with Africa' was formulated. The strategy identifies five key areas for deepened cooperation between the twin continents: green transition and energy access, digital transformation, sustainable growth and jobs, peace and governance and, finally, migration and mobility. Is this an avenue for a genuine Africa-EU Alliance involving equal partners?[32]

Box 23. What Juncker literally said: a snippet

"To speak of the future, one must speak of Africa – Europe's twin continent.

"Africa is the future: By 2050, Africa's population will number 2.5 billion. One in four people on earth will be African. We need to invest more in our relationship with the nations of this great and noble continent. And we have to stop seeing this relationship through the sole prism of development aid. Such an approach is beyond inadequate, humiliatingly so. Africa does not need charity; it needs true and fair partnerships. And Europe needs this partnership just as much. In preparing my speech today, I spoke to my African friends, notably Paul Kagame, the Chairperson of the AU. We agreed that donor-recipient relations are a thing of the past. We agreed that reciprocal commitments are the way forward. We want to build a new partnership with Africa. Today, we are proposing a new Alliance for Sustainable Investment and Jobs between Europe and Africa. This Alliance – as we envision it – would help create up to 10 million jobs in Africa in the next five years alone. We want to create a framework that brings more private investment to Africa. We are not starting from scratch: our External Investment Plan, launched two years ago, will mobilise over €44 billion in both public and private investment. Alone, the projects already in the pipeline will unlock €24 billion. We want to focus our invest-ment where it matters the most. By 2020, the EU will have supported 35,000 African students and researchers with our Erasmus programme. By 2027, this figure should reach 105,000. Trade between Africa and Europe is not insignificant. 36% of Africa's trade is with the EU. This compares to 16% for China and 6% for the USA. But this is not enough. I believe we should develop the numerous European-African trade agreements into a continent-to-continent free trade agreement, as an economic partnership between equals." (Juncker, 2018)

Why this move?

While the migration wave and consequent crisis, starting in 2014, was mainly caused by exacerbating tensions in the war zones of Syria, Iraq and Afghanistan, European public opinion associated the influx of new migrants and refugees with Africa. The European Commission's own Joint Research Centre (2018) wrote in 2018 that "the number of African migrants settling legally in the EU Member States has dropped significantly in the past decade. In counterpart, irregular migration flows across the Mediter-ranean has increased". The ensuing crisis opened the eyes of many citizens and politicians to the harsh situation in Africa. The demographic explo-sion in Africa generated Malthusian fear. In 2100, the African population could be eight to 10 times bigger than that of Europe. Africa is becoming the youngest continent, with a fast-growing and highly mobile middle class and elite. This was the backdrop for a discourse that claimed to have the ingredients to 'tackle the root causes of migration'. Development aid and investments in the African economies were to be efficient and effective tools to keep Africans in Africa. Also on the drawing table were the fight against irregular migration and human trafficking, more performant border con-trol, stimuli for repatriation, take-back obligations and projects for legal and circular migration. Critics of this overlapping of development and migra-tion policies often referred to the 'migration hump theory' that basically claims that a country with a higher income or human development level will 'produce' more emigration. Only when the country's income reaches USD 7000–13,000 per capita will there be a decline in emigration. Hence the hump. Benček and Schneiderheinze (2019) recently debunked this very popular thesis. Using 35 years of migration flow data from 198 countries of origin to OECD destinations, they show that when a country's income increases, migration to rich countries drops. They add that many other fac-tors, such as the geographical position and the political regime of a country,

Figure 16: Step by step towards an Africa-EU alliance

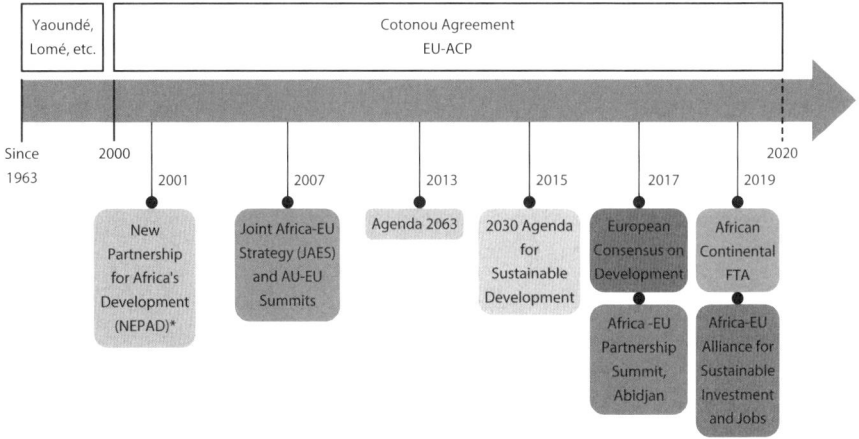

Overview of past African-European frameworks for partnership;
and of African, European, African-European, and United Nations initiatives.
Source EPSC.
* Renamed in 2018 to African Union Development Agency (AUDA)

are also at play in migration patterns. They hasten to add that this does not give much empirical artillery to those who want to tackle the root causes of migration. They write, "Yet, given the reasonably small size of the effect and the struggle of development cooperation to sustainably increase economic growth, the scope to affect migration through this channel remains limited".

We referred to geography. The distance between Europe and Africa is about 14 kilometres, which explains the fear of many Europeans that Europe will be engulfed with Africans. But this also gives ground to the worries that Africa will become a Chinese colony and lose ties with Europe. Europe is still Africa's most generous donor and biggest trade and investment partner. In 2018, Europe was responsible for 45% of all aid to Africa, while 32% of all African trade in goods was with Europe.[33] The stock of European foreign direct investment (FDI) is more than €200 billion and thus five times the volume of FDI from the USA and China. But the aid volumes of new players, like China, as well as trade and investments, are increasing rapidly. FDI flows from China into African economies are surpassing European FDI flows; add to that the high visibility of Chinese, Turkish, Russian and Arab presence in Africa. Hence the fear of Europe 'missing out' (Karkare et al., 2020). The Alliance is presented as a logical and political consequence of the partnership the EU developed with the African continent over the past 60 years, incorporating and relying on the Cotonou culture, the joint strategies elaborated and executed *en cours de route* and the collective commitments at the global level, such as the SDG agenda and the Paris climate agreement (Figure 16).

Figure 17: Africa and Europe: a unique and unparalleled strategic proximity

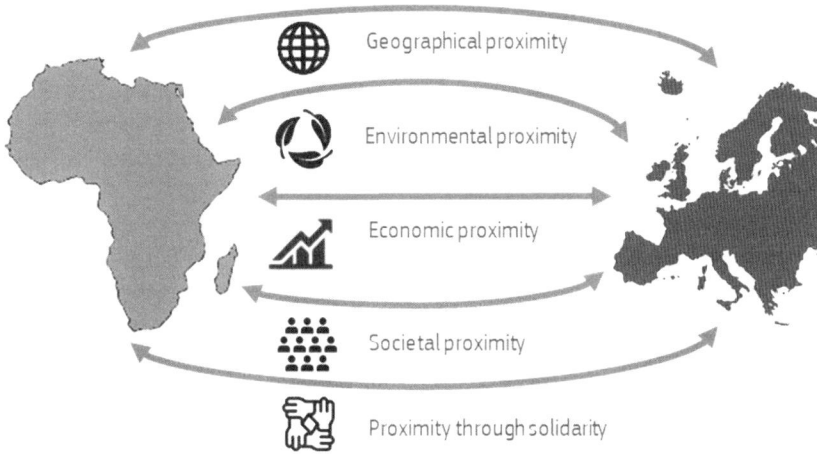

Geographical proximity

Environmental proximity

Economic proximity

Societal proximity

Proximity through solidarity

Source: Develtere, 2019

Juncker was the first European political leader to call Africa and Europe twin continents; they are partners in fate, he said. Europe's prosperity heavily depends on Africa's. This is not the case for the USA or China. The current dominant idea is that Europe has a completely different rapport with Africa than other countries or continents. Europe and Africa have a unique and unparalleled strategic proximity because of their geographic closeness, their historic and linguistic connectivity and the strong articulation of their economies and societies (Figure 17).

The logical consequence is the creation of a common platform for a shared future. Echoing the narrative of Juncker, the High Representative and Vice-President in the Von der Leyen Commission, Josep Borrell (2020), insisted that this means a radical departure from a previously unilateral North-South rapport characterising the EU approach to Africa: "The time is over when we said 'we have a strategy for Africa', now we say 'we share a common strategy, the Africans and the European, all together'".

The reasoning also goes that because of this proximity, Africa-EU collaboration inevitably has to be long term and strategic. To put it negatively, to invest, to trade and to aid cannot be quick and dirty if the partners do not want it to backfire one day. Moreover, the cooperation between Europe and Africa is of a broader nature than the one between other countries and continents and Africa. At least in theory, a whole-of-society approach is prevailing, involving not only government agencies but also the private sector and civil society on the part of both regions.

Some significant ingredients of the new approach

Europe has a strong tradition of working with the northern African neighbours in a separate way than with Sub-Saharan Africa. The new generation of cooperation is supposed to be with Africa as a whole. This implies that the AU and its Commission will play a more central role in the new framework that will run for at least 20 years. This will also impact the post-Cotonou agreement. Apart from the 'common foundation', which sets out the values and principles that bring the EU and the member states of the Organisation of African, Caribbean and Pacific States (OACPS)[34] together, Europe also has a specific, tailor-made and action-oriented partnership with Africa.

Europe's new Neighbourhood, Development and International Cooperation Instrument earmarks more than 60% of its funds for cooperation with Africa. Increasingly, these resources are considered to be a vehicle to leverage private funds and investments. The EU External Investment Plan, launched in 2017, foresees more than €4.5 billion to de-risk, give guarantees, provide technical advice to 'bankable projects' to better the investment climate in Africa and other neighbouring countries. This is supposed to leverage over €40 billion in extra sustainable investments.

As a consequence of Europe's development cooperation tradition, trade has a central role in its relationship with Africa. This implies technical, financial and political support to the African Continental Free Trade Area agreement that was signed by 54 of the 55 AU member states[35] and is to become the largest free trade area in the world. Many dream that this will finally result in an Africa-Europe continent-to-continent free trade area.

The internal working methods in Europe are also under revision. A 'whole-of-agency' approach is in the making. Specialised services such as the Directorate General Development Cooperation, renamed the Directorate General for International Partnerships in early 2021, and the European External Action Service take the lead, but all other services are called upon to contribute to the progressive intertwining of the twin continents. Similarly, a 'whole-of-Europe' approach is beginning to take shape. The Maastricht Treaty of 1993 and the subsequent Amsterdam Treaty have already put forward the principles of coherence, coordination, complementarity and consistency to harness the relationship between the EU and its member states. The von der Leyen Commission pushes this further with its Team Europe Initiatives; with these initiatives, the Commission, the member states and Europe's development banks claim to show their readiness to intensify, in a coordinated way, the political outreach to African countries and partners in other continents. The global Team Europe response to COVID-19 is advanced as a clear example as nearly €7 billion is going to Africa. Other examples are the work Team Europe has done on vaccine initiatives and the G20 Paris Club Debt Service Suspension Initiative (Urpilainen, 2020). The European institutions and member states also join forces to promote decentralised programmes such as a cultural entrepreneurship project in Timor-Leste and a cocoa sector initiative in Ivory Coast. All of them follow a problem-driven iterative approach to identify root causes of the problem and step-by-step solutions involving national and European stakeholders.

Europe is often accused of repackaging and relabelling old wine in new bottles, but the migration crisis and the arrival of new actors challenge Europe to fundamentally review its approach to Africa. Just like the new actors, Europe has ambitions to be a player and not just a payer. Trump's Prosper Africa initiative and the 'mutual prosperity policy' of the Johnson administration in the UK are equally a move to counter initiatives such as the Africa Growing Together Fund, a facility that China launched in 2014 with the African Development Bank.

The proof of the pudding will be in the eating, but already a number of critical voices are heard. Many observers applaud the attempts of the Juncker Commission to forge an alliance with Europe's twin continent, as well as the 'geopolitical ambitions' of the von der Leyen Commission. Their policies, it is said, contain ingredients that could be instrumental in the strengthening of the position of the EU as a leader in the multilateral space, for a more overt defence of European interests and the consolidation and mobilisation of the partnerships it already has, including with the AU and its member states. Initially, Johannes Trimmel, the President of CONCORD, the European umbrella body of some 2600 NGOs involved in development cooperation, welcomed the commitment to a new relationship with Europe's neighbours in Africa, but he warned that his support base does not agree with invest-ments that put commercial opportunities for EU companies, rather than people's needs, at the centre. Moreover, in his opinion, "approaches that say you'll only get aid if you stop your people from coming to Europe are not worthy of the proud values of our continent or likely to endear us to our neighbours" (Trimmel, 2018). For a think tank like the European Centre for Development Policy Management, "the case for a genuine interest-driven partnership is clear. The way forward is not. Both EU and AU member states may be tempted to continue business as usual, leading to aspirational state-ments with limited follow-through. A more useful way forward would look not just for areas of common interests but would also recognise diverging views where they exist. This means confronting the difficult issues rather than papering over the cracks with statements about equal partnership that lack any credibility" (Medinilla & Teevan, 2020).

In a special issue of the *Journal of Contemporary European Research*, Furness et al. (2020) observe that the evolution of European development policy is driven by the tension between its *raison d'être* as a concrete expression of global solidarity and international cooperation, and its increasing instrumentalisation in the service of European economic and security interests. They also refer to the long-term challenge of policy coherence, both in terms of managing the so-called 'nexuses' between EU-level policies including agriculture, trade, foreign/security policy and development, as well as clear incoherencies with member state policies, such as migration, tax and fiscal regimes, or arms sales.

In the same volume of the journal, Holden (2020) writes that the stress on new modalities of aid opens windows for development aid to be used in more egregiously self-interested ways. Blended finance instruments, for example, are 'dual use' in that they can be used for more flexible development policies but also to support EU businesses more directly. Essentially, the goal is to better harness the latent economic power of Europe; as European Commission Vice-President Jyrki Katainen put it: to "enhance the financial firepower of EU external action".

The long-term efforts for strategic cooperation, built on a pragmatic but consensual policy-making approach, lead more than ever to concerted European action in this rapprochement with the African continent. This eclipses and overpowers the divided, tension-ridden and often contradictory positions of the African counterparts; add to that the capacity of the European governmental stakeholders to rally extending segments of their financial sector, their business communities and their CSOs behind this new paradigm, while many governments on the African continent still insist on their state monopoly when it comes to international relations. This, as well as the change in the geographic profile of Africa's trade, with the dominance of the North-African economies, a decline of Europe-Africa trade and a reorientation of trade towards Asia, brings many observers to question the capacity of the African continent to gain from this new ballgame. For Hurt (2020), for example, it remains to be seen whether the new Europe-Africa Alliance will increase the prospects for African agency. The Alliance seems to be very much an EU-led initiative with tacit support from the AU.

Box 24. A preferential relationship becomes a reciprocal, interest-driven partnership

At the end of 2020, negotiations for a post-Cotonou agreement between the EU and the ACP states were concluded. The new treaty builds on the Lomé and Cotonou frameworks and experience, keeps the same geographical coverage, maintains the joint institutions[36] and continues to combine political dialogue with trade and aid. However, it also embodies radical changes in the rapports between the parties involved.

The global sustainability agenda comes much more to the fore. Take, for example, the priority given to climate change and the environment. However, the midterm review of the 20-year agreement is foreseen in 2030, at a time when the SDGs should be reached.

The new treaty has been regionalised. It consists of a 'foundation' part pertaining to the entire ACP membership, followed by three regional protocols dealing respectively with Africa, the Caribbean and the Pacific.

Partnership is the new leitmotif. 'Partnership dialogue' is the new terminology, together with 'equality of the partners', 'reciprocity', 'mutual respect', 'mutual accountability' and 'shared ownership'.

Economic development (and especially the role of the private sector) seems to take precedence over human development and also when it comes to financial and technical cooperation. Importantly, as the financial means necessary for the realisation of the agreement will be incorporated into the global EU budget in the future, the ACP countries will have less say over their volume, programming, allocation and management. Budgets will become less predictable. In line with current thinking, all parties are looking to diversify sources of financing and believe that remittances, private investment flows, blending arrangements and domestic fiscal revenues will help to do the job.

Trade relations are handled through the economic partnership agreements (EPA). Trade-related elements such as phytosanitary aspects, public procurement, and environmental and social standards will be subject to intensified dialogue.

The new agreement seeks to reconcile the wish of the ACP countries (and the OACPS) to remain united, the growing ambitions of the AU and Europe's desire to work towards a mutually beneficial continent-to-continent strategy with Africa, and all parties are convinced that it gives them a favourable position on the international geopolitical and geo-economic chessboards.

Jean-Claude Boidin, a former EU ambassador who was for more than 30 years actively involved in EU-ACP cooperation, concludes that since Cotonou, the preferential dimension of the Lomé conventions has been gradually eroded. For him, the relationship between Europe and the ACP lost its 'uniqueness': the ACP-EU trade regime was profoundly overhauled to comply with free-trade rules and with the end of joint management, aid is no longer at the heart of the partnership. "In many respects, the treatment granted to ACP countries is no different from that applied to other developing regions. The ACP-EU relation, which has long been a model, finds itself practically 'normalised'." (Boidin, 2020)

Multilateral cooperation: the UN galaxy fans out further

What we wrote earlier about the strengths and dynamics that have shaped European development cooperation is even more applicable to the multilateral institutions of the UN. The UN and the conglomerate of its organisations belong to the second pillar of the development cooperation sector but are more than development institutions. Only a few UN organisations, such as the UNDP and the World Food Programme (WFP), are exclusively concerned with this area. Most UN institutions pay special attention to particular development issues to the extent that they are directly relevant to their mandate and area of competence. Thus, the Food and Agriculture Organisation (FAO) was not established to tackle famine in developing countries but to ensure food security worldwide. When the FAO establishes international food standards in its *Codex Alimentarius*, this has implications for both developed and less developed countries. Again, when the WHO publishes its annual World Health Statistics Report, it compiles data from all its 194 member states. With the coronavirus crisis of 2020, we have seen that this UN organisation is a worldwide undertaking, not just a North-South one.

As is the case with the European institutions, the structures, activities and approaches of the UN institutions are more than the result of interactions between countries. Supranational institutions have a dynamic of their own and their own room for manoeuvre. Like the European institutions again, they have become important institutions and nodal points for multilevel governance. Member states and, increasingly, non-state actors (employers' and workers' organisations, businesses, NGDOs, rich philanthropists and wealthy foundations) take part in the decision-making process in these organisations. That then filters down into national decision-making, legislation and government practice in individual countries. This is why we so often hear our national politicians say that our country needs to do something in connection with the 2015 Paris Agreement on Climate Change or the negotiations at the WTO.

The UN and development cooperation
Where development cooperation is concerned, however, we need to understand the UN organisations in a different light from the European institutions and programmes. The UN institutions are, in the first place, consensus-seeking and normative organisations. A recent example of broad-based consensus-building and norm-setting are the SDGs. The SDGs commit the whole UN community, member states and many non-UN-affiliated institutions. However, not all agreements reach such an extended

span. Every UN organisation has its own, more focused and thematic discussions with its own members about dozens or even hundreds of items all the time. Each time, consensus and norms need to be established through dialogue between those who contribute a lot and receive little (directly) and those who contribute little and receive a lot. Thus, in this sense, the UN is a development actor whenever it can develop a consensus or a norm that is beneficial to the developing countries. A second pillar of UN development cooperation is technical assistance. The UN institutions all have countless teams whose task it is to help member states with technical issues. These may relate to irrigation, ICT, meteorological technology, transport, customs management, social legislation, public health and so on. With its technical assistance, the UN seeks to fill specific gaps in knowledge or technology. A third pillar is loans and (to a lesser extent) grants for projects and programmes. Most UN funds and banks that give loans do so on a concessional basis. Many UN organisations are working hard on their fourth function: giving policy advice to national governments or institutions.

International institutions adhere to a doctrine of neutrality and technicity. Development is regarded as addressing something that is lacking; what is lacking can be identified in a rational, neutral manner. The proposed functional and technical solutions always serve the general interest. The UN continues to adopt such an approach because it must always find a consensus between viewpoints, which may be diametrically opposed. All themes are therefore depoliticised and neutralised. However, this also makes it possible to approach issues which may be highly sensitive: for example, 'good governance' or human rights. By dealing with them as technical items and placing more emphasis on management aspects than on the underlying conflicts and malpractices which lie behind mismanagement, an artificial consensus can be created about the subject, and interventions can be carried out via UN programmes (Boas & McNeill, 2003).

There is considerable rivalry between the different UN institutions, relating to areas of competence, resources and, increasingly, knowledge. Each institution claims to have the best pool of knowledge and competence in its own domain but also systematically goes outside its field so as to be able to put forward a more holistic or interdisciplinary approach. Mission creep is thus one of the major flaws in the UN system, intended to strengthen a particular organisation by browsing adjacent, often relevant, fields. By doing this, not only is the system as a whole weakened but the organisation concerned does not always reap the benefits of its expansionist venture in the long run. Child labour is about children (UNICEF) and labour (the ILO), while reproductive health (the WHO) is primarily of concern to women

145

Figure 18: The UN system

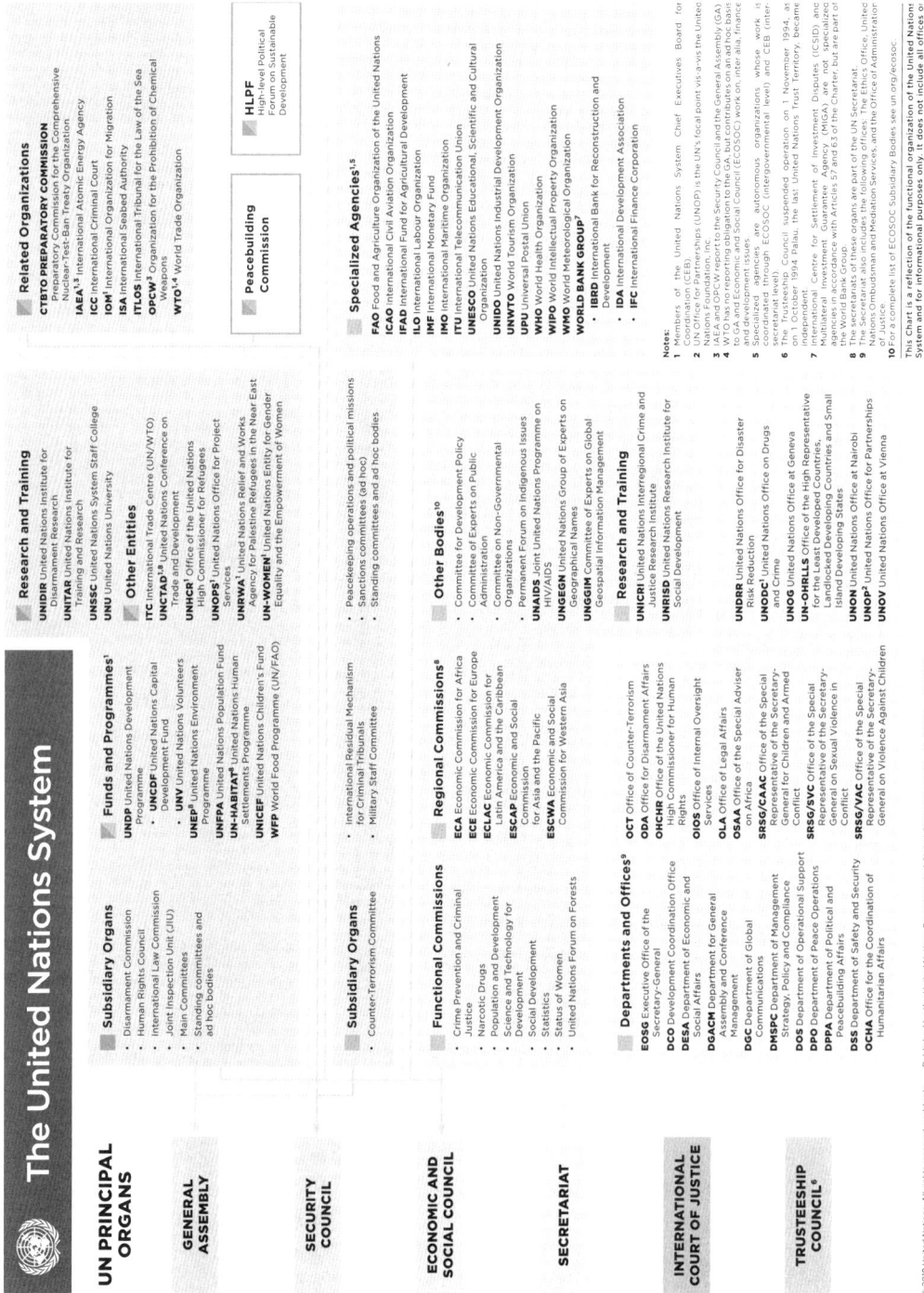

The United Nations System

UN PRINCIPAL ORGANS

GENERAL ASSEMBLY

Subsidiary Organs
- Disarmament Commission
- Human Rights Council
- International Law Commission
- Joint Inspection Unit (JIU)
- Main Committees
- Standing committees and ad hoc bodies

Funds and Programmes[1]
- **UNDP** United Nations Development Programme
  - **UNCDF** United Nations Capital Development Fund
  - **UNV** United Nations Volunteers
- **UNEP** United Nations Environment Programme
- **UNFPA** United Nations Population Fund
- **UN-HABITAT**[8] United Nations Human Settlements Programme
- **UNICEF** United Nations Children's Fund
- **WFP** World Food Programme (UN/FAO)

Research and Training
- **UNIDIR** United Nations Institute for Disarmament Research
- **UNITAR** United Nations Institute for Training and Research
- **UNSSC** United Nations System Staff College
- **UNU** United Nations University

Other Entities
- **ITC** International Trade Centre (UN/WTO)
- **UNCTAD**[1,8] United Nations Conference on Trade and Development
- **UNHCR**[1] Office of the United Nations High Commissioner for Refugees
- **UNOPS** United Nations Office for Project Services
- **UNRWA**[1] United Nations Relief and Works Agency for Palestine Refugees in the Near East
- **UN-WOMEN**[1] United Nations Entity for Gender Equality and the Empowerment of Women

SECURITY COUNCIL

Subsidiary Organs
- Counter-Terrorism Committee
- International Residual Mechanism for Criminal Tribunals
- Military Staff Committee
- Peacekeeping operations and political missions
- Sanctions committees (ad hoc)
- Standing committees and ad hoc bodies

ECONOMIC AND SOCIAL COUNCIL

Functional Commissions
- Crime Prevention and Criminal Justice
- Narcotic Drugs
- Population and Development
- Science and Technology for Development
- Social Development
- Statistics
- Status of Women
- United Nations Forum on Forests

Regional Commissions[8]
- **ECA** Economic Commission for Africa
- **ECE** Economic Commission for Europe
- **ECLAC** Economic Commission for Latin America and the Caribbean
- **ESCAP** Economic and Social Commission for Asia and the Pacific
- **ESCWA** Economic and Social Commission for Western Asia

Other Bodies[10]
- Committee for Development Policy
- Committee of Experts on Public Administration
- Committee on Non-Governmental Organizations
- Permanent Forum on Indigenous Issues
- **UNAIDS** Joint United Nations Programme on HIV/AIDS
- **UNGEGN** United Nations Group of Experts on Geographical Names
- **UNGGIM** Committee of Experts on Global Geospatial Information Management

Research and Training
- **UNICRI** United Nations Interregional Crime and Justice Research Institute
- **UNRISD** United Nations Research Institute for Social Development

SECRETARIAT

Departments and Offices[9]
- **EOSG** Executive Office of the Secretary-General
- **DCO** Development Coordination Office
- **DESA** Department of Economic and Social Affairs
- **DGACM** Department for General Assembly and Conference Management
- **DGC** Department of Global Communications
- **DMSPC** Department of Management Strategy, Policy and Compliance
- **DOS** Department of Operational Support
- **DPO** Department of Peace Operations
- **DPPA** Department of Political and Peacebuilding Affairs
- **DSS** Department of Safety and Security
- **OCHA** Office for the Coordination of Humanitarian Affairs
- **OCT** Office of Counter-Terrorism
- **ODA** Office for Disarmament Affairs
- **OHCHR** Office of the United Nations High Commissioner for Human Rights
- **OIOS** Office of Internal Oversight Services
- **OLA** Office of Legal Affairs
- **OSAA** Office of the Special Adviser on Africa
- **SRSG/CAAC** Office of the Special Representative of the Secretary-General for Children and Armed Conflict
- **SRSG/SVC** Office of the Special Representative of the Secretary-General on Sexual Violence in Conflict
- **SRSG/VAC** Office of the Special Representative of the Secretary-General on Violence Against Children
- **UNDRR** United Nations Office for Disaster Risk Reduction
- **UNODC** United Nations Office on Drugs and Crime
- **UNOG** United Nations Office at Geneva
- **UN-OHRLLS** Office of the High Representative for the Least Developed Countries, Landlocked Developing Countries and Small Island Developing States
- **UNON** United Nations Office at Nairobi
- **UNOP**[2] United Nations Office for Partnerships
- **UNOV** United Nations Office at Vienna

INTERNATIONAL COURT OF JUSTICE

TRUSTEESHIP COUNCIL[6]

Related Organizations

- **CTBTO PREPARATORY COMMISSION** Preparatory Commission for the Comprehensive Nuclear-Test-Ban Treaty Organization
- **IAEA**[1,3] International Atomic Energy Agency
- **ICC** International Criminal Court
- **IOM**[1] International Organization for Migration
- **ISA** International Seabed Authority
- **ITLOS** International Tribunal for the Law of the Sea
- **OPCW**[3] Organization for the Prohibition of Chemical Weapons
- **WTO**[1,4] World Trade Organization

Peacebuilding Commission

HLPF
High-level Political Forum on Sustainable Development

Specialized Agencies[1,5]
- **FAO** Food and Agriculture Organization of the United Nations
- **ICAO** International Civil Aviation Organization
- **IFAD** International Fund for Agricultural Development
- **ILO** International Labour Organization
- **IMF** International Monetary Fund
- **IMO** International Maritime Organization
- **ITU** International Telecommunication Union
- **UNESCO** United Nations Educational, Scientific and Cultural Organization
- **UNIDO** United Nations Industrial Development Organization
- **UNWTO** World Tourism Organization
- **UPU** Universal Postal Union
- **WHO** World Health Organization
- **WIPO** World Intellectual Property Organization
- **WMO** World Meteorological Organization
- **WORLD BANK GROUP[7]**
  - **IBRD** International Bank for Reconstruction and Development
  - **IDA** International Development Association
  - **IFC** International Finance Corporation

Notes:

1 Members of the United Nations System Chief Executives Board for Coordination (CEB).

2 UN Office for Partnerships (UNOP) is the UN's focal point vis-à-vis the United Nations Foundation, Inc.

3 IAEA and OPCW report to the Security Council and the General Assembly (GA).

4 WTO has no reporting obligation to the GA, but contributes on an ad hoc basis to GA and Economic and Social Council (ECOSOC) work on, inter alia, finance and development issues.

5 Specialized agencies are autonomous organizations whose work is coordinated through ECOSOC (intergovernmental level) and CEB (inter-secretariat level).

6 The Trusteeship Council suspended operation on 1 November 1994, as on 1 October 1994 Palau, the last United Nations Trust Territory, became independent.

7 International Centre for Settlement of Investment Disputes (ICSID) and Multilateral Investment Guarantee Agency (MIGA) are not specialized agencies in accordance with Articles 57 and 63 of the Charter but are part of the World Bank Group.

8 The secretariats of these organs are part of the UN Secretariat.

9 The Secretariat also includes the following offices: The Ethics Office, United Nations Ombudsman and Mediation Services, and the Office of Administration of Justice.

10 For a complete list of ECOSOC Subsidiary Bodies see un.org/ecosoc.

This Chart is a reflection of the functional organization of the United Nations System and for informational purposes only. It does not include all offices or entities of the United Nations System.

© 2019 United Nations. All rights reserved worldwide.
Published by the United Nations Department of Global Communications, 19-00073 — July 2019

(UNIFEM). And who is not concerned with the consequences of globalisation? The World Bank, UNCTAD, the WTO, the ILO... Similarly, do a search on their websites and you will see that not only the WHO but all UN agencies are helping to tackle the consequences of the COVID-19 emergency: the UNDP, the World Bank Group, UNAIDS, WFP, UNICEF, even the Office of the High Commissioner for Human Rights and the Universal Postal Union.

Thus, there is a lot of overlapping and competition within the UN family, as Box 25 shows. In the healthcare sector in particular, large numbers of international organisations and funds contend for a place, large or small. As a result, over a hundred bilateral and multilateral development institutions are currently active in the field of healthcare (as well as hundreds more NGDOs).

Box 25. Overlap and competition in the UN family

Healthcare: WHO, UNICEF, UNAIDS, World Bank, Global Fund for Aids, TB and Malaria, Gavi…

Education: UNICEF, UNESCO, World Bank, UNFPA, ILO, Education for All/Fast Track Initiative…

Agriculture: FAO, IFAD, WFP, World Bank, ILO…

The environment: UNEP, GEF, Montreal Protocol, Forest Carbon Partnership Facility, World Bank…

Good governance and democratisation: UNDP, World Bank, IMF, ILO…

Civil society: UNDP, World Bank, ILO, FAO…

Emergency aid: OCHA, UNHCR, World Bank, UNICEF, WFP, UNFPA, UNRWA…

It is telling that in the crowded global architecture of cooperation on health, the WHO is receiving only one-third of the ODA allocated to the Global Fund (OECD, 2018). This cannot just be brought back to the inability of the WHO to deal with all matters relating to its mandate but also has to be explained by the adroitness of some of its peer competitors in luring private and public donors who always want to put their eggs in more than one basket.

This 'mission creep' is not just informed by the internal drive of every institution to address as many issues as possible but is also encouraged by national donors and increasingly by large foundations too. These have their own agendas and for diplomatic, political or strategic reasons, may put their resources into a specific international organisation. For these donors, the question of whether the programme that is proposed and financed belongs to the core business of the recipient international organisation is derisory. Obviously, this increasing earmarking of the support given by national donors and foundations to international institutions jeopardises the latter's neutrality. This is why it is sometimes called 'Trojan multilateralism' because, in a covert way, it injects and imposes bilateral and private sector goals into international organisations. In 2017, the core share of voluntary funding for development-related activities – which UN agencies could use as they wish without the prior approval of the donor – was just less than 20% (UN, 2019); Earmarked funding reached USD 21 billion in 2016, double its 2007 level (OECD, 2018). Some international organisations, especially UN Funds and Programmes and, to a lesser extent, World Bank Group institutions, are becoming very dependent on designated or predestined funds. A loose but influential association of donor governments, known as the Utstein Group is trying to turn around things and bend the 'bilateralisation' of multilateralism. It prefers more coordinated, effective and efficient multilateral funding that is less earmarked and more predictable. These objectives have become the focus of the 2019 UN Funding Compact, which aims to make the UN system more efficient and effective with regards to implementing Agenda 2030 and the SDGs. In this context, soft earmarking, whereby the donor makes suggestions but does not decide where its funding goes, was put forward as a third means of high-quality funding. Some international organisations and donors have expressed their will to expand core funding with the concept of soft earmarking.

The funding landscape of multilateral organisations is evolving at rapid speed (OECD, 2018). DAC countries remain the main source of financial support in the multilateral development system, towards which they allocate a stable share of ODA: 41% in 2016, or USD 63 billion. As we have seen with bilateral aid, we also observe increasing pluralisation of the national agencies that contribute to and thus participate in the UN system. For the DAC members, on average five national agencies do core funding to UN agencies and six participate in non-core projects and programmes. At the same time, however, financial contributions are increasingly coming from other sources, such as the emerging economies (China in particular),[38] corporations, foundations, philanthropists and other generous 'world citizens'. The WHO, to which the Bill and Melinda Gates Foundation is the second biggest donor, and the World Intellectual Property Right Organisation, which relies almost entirely on private financing, lead the way. Some, like the World Bank's International Development Association and the Asian Development Bank, record major transformational boosts of resources through the capital market. Some UN agencies, such as UNICEF and UNHCR, have a long tradition of calling for individual contributions from rich philanthropists from the North and South, as well as from concerned individual citizens; 30% of UNICEF's and 7% of UNHCR's revenues are donations from individuals who themselves benefit from tax-deduction systems in many countries. For some years, the 2020 Nobel Prize awardee World Food Programme, has also invested in individual giving as a proven and scalable revenue stream and for this, uses novel mechanisms such as the *ShareTheMeal* app and new Facebook fundraising tools.

It goes without saying that the diversification of revenue sources in international organisations brings about major shifts in the power relations within the multilateral development cooperation system in favour of those organisations that are capable of attracting more new bilateral, private sector, individual and market sources than others. Inevitably, this also affects the internal workings of individual international organisations, whose staff are becoming increasingly sensitive to market signals to the detriment of the original ideational mission and the specific mandate of the organisation in question. The forces behind the new sources might have slightly or radically different interpretations of what the beneficiary organisations' immediate task-setting should be and, in many cases, will be less fanatic adepts of the neutrality and impartiality principles underpinning traditional policies and operations of international organisations.

Money is not the only power tool deployed by international organisations. It is generally accepted that the Washington-based World Bank is best equipped to attract, adapt, integrate and spread ideas and knowledge on a very wide range of themes. The *World Development Reports,* which have been published since 1978, are highly influential. They deal with themes that you would not immediately associate with a bank and that often lie within the scope of a sister organisation. Examples include the recent World Bank reports on such disparate topics as 'Learning to Realise Education's Promise' (a 2018 report on the core business of the Paris-based UNESCO), 'The Changing Nature of Work' (a 2019 report which one would expect to come from the Geneva-based ILO) and 'Trading for Development in the Age of Global Value Chains' (a 2020 report that could also have been written by the WTO).

The only serious intellectual competition comes from the New York-based UNDP, which has issued the *Human Development Reports* since 1990. In them, support is given to the multidimensional paradigm of human development as an alternative to the narrower neoliberal paradigm of the World Bank.

Figure 19: Resources beyond ODA funds from DAC countries account for between 12% (for the Global Fund) and 60% (for the International Development Association [IDA])

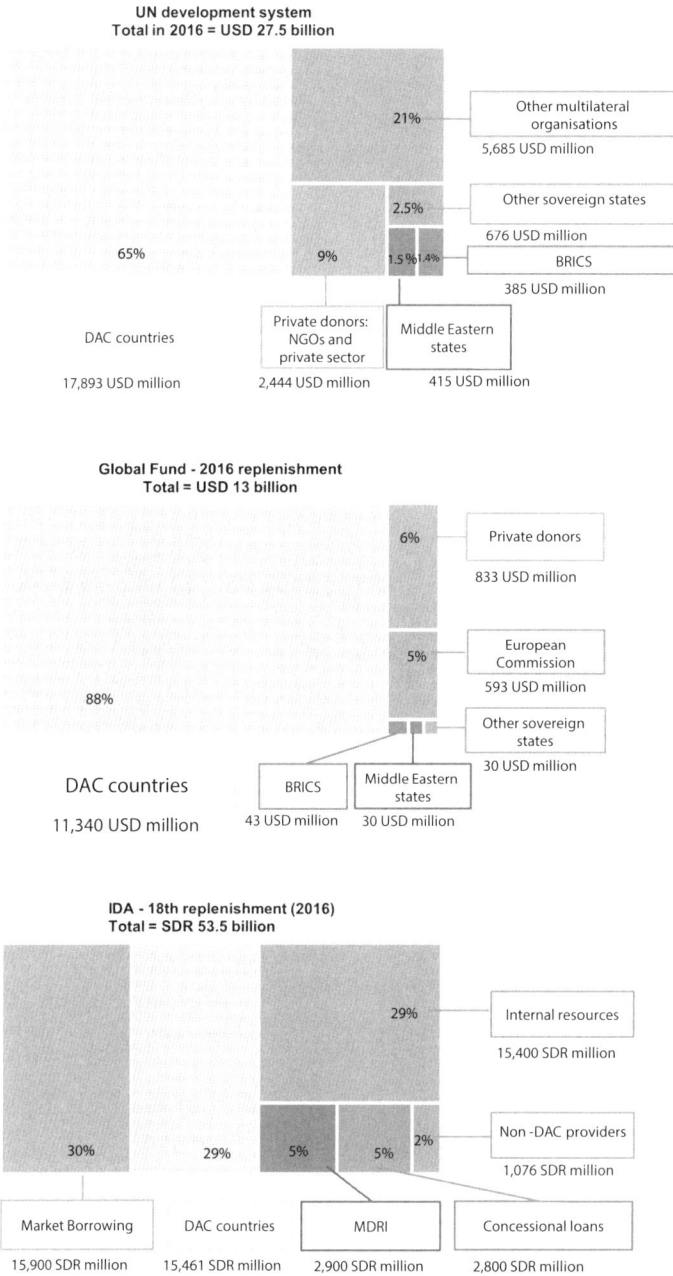

UN development system
Total in 2016 = USD 27.5 billion

21% — Other multilateral organisations — 5,685 USD million

2.5% — Other sovereign states — 676 USD million

1.5% 1.4% — BRICS — 385 USD million

65% — DAC countries — 17,893 USD million

9% — Private donors: NGOs and private sector — 2,444 USD million

Middle Eastern states — 415 USD million

Global Fund - 2016 replenishment
Total = USD 13 billion

6% — Private donors — 833 USD million

5% — European Commission — 593 USD million

Other sovereign states — 30 USD million

88% — DAC countries — 11,340 USD million

BRICS — 43 USD million

Middle Eastern states — 30 USD million

IDA - 18th replenishment (2016)
Total = SDR 53.5 billion

29% — Internal resources — 15,400 SDR million

2% — Non-DAC providers — 1,076 SDR million

30% — Market Borrowing — 15,900 SDR million

29% — DAC countries — 15,461 SDR million

5% — MDRI — 2,900 SDR million

5% — Concessional loans — 2,800 SDR million

Source: OECD-DAC (2018)[39]

Figure 20: Non-ODAble contributions make for a large part of financing to the United Nations Development system

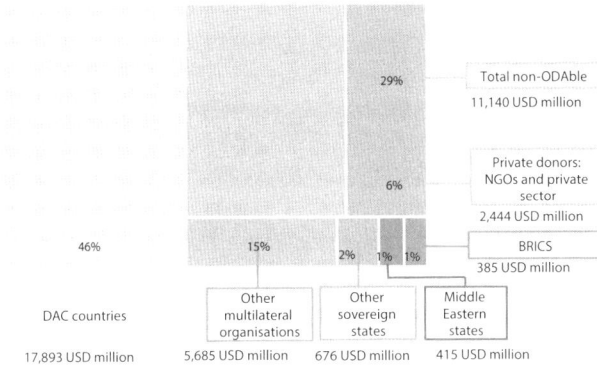

29%

Total non-ODAble

11,140 USD million

6%

Private donors:
NGOs and private
sector

2,444 USD million

BRICS

385 USD million

46%

15%

2%   1%   1%

DAC countries

Other
multilateral
organisations

Other
sovereign
states

Middle
Eastern
states

17,893 USD million

5,685 USD million

676 USD million

415 USD million

Source: OECD-DAC (2018)

Between 2004 and 2008, the UN family received approximately 10% of all ODA (Figures 19-20). In 2016, this had increased to 27% and even 41%, if you also take into consideration non-core funding and so-called multi-bi funding, used when a multilateral agency is contracted to deliver a project or programme on behalf of a donor. In 2016, the EU accounted for almost 10% of all funding to the UN development system (OECD, 2018). For years, the World Bank's International Development Association was the largest multilateral donor institution. More recently, the European Commission has held that position.

New donors reshape the international scene

As we have seen, a large proportion – the majority, for some – of the new donors' aid is channelled bilaterally rather than through international organisations. In addition, the institutions chosen to channel multilateral aid escape the traditional 'Western' multilateral system, suggesting an institutional rebalancing away from Western-dominated institutions. This rebalancing is also illustrated, on the 'demand side', by the wide membership of 'new' development institutions. For instance, Egypt and Ethiopia are members of the Asian Infrastructure Investment Bank, and Sudan, Libya, Algeria, Morocco and others are observers. Algeria, Egypt and Libya are major shareholders of the Islamic Development Bank, and many other African countries are members in their own right. South Africa is a full member of the BRICS'New Development Bank, an alternative to the World Bank. Whereas the Asian Infrastructure Investment Bank has only a limited number of projects in Africa, the Islamic Development Bank lists both Sub-Saharan Africa and the Middle East and North Africa region as two of its four 'core regions' of activity and boasts hundreds of projects on the African continent.[40]

Table 5: New donors' development cooperation agencies and their multilateral aid

Country	National authority responsible for development aid	Estimated multilateral aid as % of total aid	Preferred institutions as channels of multilateral aid *(non-Western institutions in bold)*
China	International Development Cooperation Agency	36%	**Asian Infrastructure Investment Bank (80%, founding member)**
India	Development Partnership Administration	20%	**Asian Infrastructure Development Bank (82%)**
Russia	MFA, Ministry of Finance, *Rossotrudnichestvo*	39%	**Asian Infrastructure Development Bank (46%),** UN (30%), World Bank (18%)
Brazil	Brazilian Cooperation Agency	66%	UN (67%), Inter-American Development Bank (33%)
Indonesia	Ministries of National Development Planning, of Foreign Affairs, of Finance, State Secretariat	88%	**Asian Infrastructure Development Bank (89%)**
Thailand	MFA, Department of International Organisations	68%	**Asian Infrastructure Development Bank (86%),** World Bank (3%)
South Africa	Department of International Relations and Cooperation	67%	**African Development Bank (33%), African Union (18%)**
Turkey	Turkish Cooperation and Coordination Agency	4%	**Asian Infrastructure Development Bank (71%),** UN (14%)
United Arab Emirates	Ministry for Foreign Affairs and International Cooperation	2%	**Islamic Development Bank (43%),** UN Agencies (24%), World Bank (19%)
Qatar	MFA, Qatar Development Fund	Unknown	**Islamic Development Bank (61%),** UN (39%)
Kuwait	Kuwait Fund for Arab Economic Development, Prime Minister	3%	World Bank (70%), **Arab Gulf Programme for Development (15%)**

Source: authors' own calculations

The World Bank: not a cooperative

The World Bank Group is the most important 'supplier' of development assistance in the UN family. The group consists of various closely interconnected institutions. The term 'World Bank' relates specifically to the International Bank for Reconstruction and Development (IBRD; established in 1945) and the International Development Association (IDA; 1960). The group also includes the International Finance Corporation (IFC; 1956) and the Multilateral Investment Guarantee Agency (MIGA; 1988). The IMF is often mentioned in the same breath as the World Bank; unlike the World Bank, however, the IMF is not a true development organisation. Its mission is far more restricted. The Fund only gives loans to member states that do not have enough foreign currency to pay for purchases made in other countries. It is no coincidence that the World Bank and the IMF have become associated with each other. Physically, they are quasi neighbours in the White House area of Washington DC; their philosophy on development never diverges greatly; they are often involved in joint strategies, such as the structural adjustment programmes in the 1980s and 1990s, the Multilateral Debt Relief Initiative launched in 2006 and, more recently, the Debt Service Suspension Initiative granting debt-service suspension to the poorest countries to help them manage the severe impact of the COVID-19 pandemic. Countries often have to obtain the agreement of the World Bank-IMF joint staff before any of these organisations will provide support. This staff has many times been accused of seeking one-size-fits-all solutions for all developing countries and having little or no feeling for the LDCs. The bank has large offices in over 130 locations and is present in every middle-income country but has no representatives at all in Djibouti and Eritrea, for example.

All the banks and funds of these Bretton Woods institutions (named after the place where they were created in 1944) almost exclusively give loans. The World Bank is able to offer cheap loans to poorer countries because the Bank itself has a very high credit rating and is thus able to borrow cheaply on the capital market. These loans often go hand in hand with technical advice. Only recently have grants occasionally been given.

The goal of the IBRD is to reduce poverty in middle-income countries and creditworthy poor countries. To this end, it provides loans, policy advice and technical assistance to the governments of these countries. It obtains its funds from private and institutional investors in North America, Europe and Asia.

The IDA gives interest-free loans to the 79 poorest countries. These are 'soft loans': they have a repayment period of 35 to 40 years, with a grace period of 10 years. Only the administrative costs are charged.

The task of the IFC is to provide financing for private companies in the South, in order to stimulate the development of the countries concerned. The IFC promotes the introduction of capital from within and outside the country for these companies.

MIGA encourages foreign investments in developing countries by offering foreign investors guarantees against political risks such as war or civil unrest.

Box 26. The influence of development agencies' staff

The World Bank funds and supervises tens of thousands of projects all over the world. Some are successful in the sense that they reach their goals and have a real impact, while others' scores are less impressive or they fail bluntly. Scholars have focused on recipient country factors that influence the performance of development projects. Authors have provided evidence for the role of liberal economic policies, liberal democracy and economic (in)stability. However, just focusing on the borrower country does not tell the whole story. Heinzel (2020), for example, has looked at the role of the World Bank's main staff members in charge of more than 3000 World Bank projects between 1995 and 2015. Three findings stand out. First, while the staff's relevant country and policy experiences do not correlate with project performance by themselves, when staff combine both, performance increases significantly. Second, this positive association is observable in the performance of the World Bank, the output of the project and the degree to which a project fulfilled the expectations set out at the start; i.e., the impact of the project. Third, when staff possess both relevant country and policy experience, increasing the number of projects individual staff members run in a country further helps the performance of projects. The same is not true of increasing policy experience. Therefore, there seem to be clear benefits to letting staff build up expertise and accumulate soft and private information in a particular country, and prioritising said expertise over mobility across countries. The latter is interesting because most international organisations and bilateral agencies opt for the regular mobility of their staff so as to avoid them getting too entangled in local political and other power networks.

Senior officials at the World Bank like to present their institution as a cooperative, oriented towards resolving social and economic problems, with member countries having a say in decisions. But the World Bank's capital comes from governments, not from private sources. Capitalisation takes the form of a more limited share of paid-in capital and a larger share of guaranteed or callable capital. Each member of the World Bank's organisations receives votes consisting of share votes: one vote for each share of the organisations' capital stock held by the member. Thus, the cooperative principle of equal voting rights for all members, 'one member, one vote' in the cooperative jargon, does not apply. Table 6 gives the most recent voting power division of the main World Bank Group institutions: the IBRD, the IFC, the IDA and MIGA.

Table 6: Voting weightings in the World Bank Group (2020)

	% votes IBRD	% votes IFC	% votes IDA	% votes MIGA
EU (27)	22.86	28.57	26.14	23.09
USA	15.76	20.93	10.19	15.03
Japan	7.66	5.99	8.38	4.22
UK	3.89	4.47	6.69	4.03
India	3.03	3.81	2.90	2.56
China	4.72	2.30	2.29	2.64
Russia	2.66	3.80	0.31	2.64
South Africa	0.74	0.67	0.26	0.86
Laos	0.04	0.04	0.17	0.13

Source: World Bank, Voting Powers, 2020

As Table 6 shows, Europe, not the USA, is the biggest player in the World Bank Group. But here too, we find that Europe has not yet succeeded in speaking with one voice.

The US influence on the World Bank (and the IMF) is disproportionate to its voting rights. Research shows that countries that align their voting behaviour within the UN with that of the USA are more likely to receive a loan. Larger loans are earmarked for countries where US banks have a significant stake and whose regimes are regarded as allies of the USA. But other big World Bank and IMF shareholders, such as Germany, France and the UK, also disproportionately influence the amount of money a country receives and the number and stringency of the conditional ties to the loans it gets. Jordan has, on several occasions, experienced at first hand the fact that the World Bank (and the IMF) is not immune to pressure from large shareholders. When that country refused to support the USA in the Gulf War of 1990–1991, not only was development aid from the USA discontinued but the World Bank and the IMF also temporarily stopped paying out their loans. When Jordan later began publicly criticising Saddam Hussein's regime, the taps were turned on again. And just three months after the signing of the historic peace accord with Israel in 1994, the country received approval for a large agricultural loan (Harrigan et al., 2006). More recently, Jordan was rewarded with additional financial assistance packages for its role in taking up hundreds of thousands of refugees in the wake of the Syrian war.

As Heinzel et al. (2020) write in a recent article, the institutional structure gives the most powerful shareholders, chief among them the USA, a greater influence on operations than other states. Both the IMF and the World Bank headquarters are located with eerily geographical proximity to the heart of American power. Their leadership is determined by an informal power-sharing agreement between Americans and Europeans, and the distribution of formal voting shares favours the powerful members. However, these scholars argue that international organisations' effectiveness and legitimacy anticipate grave consequences for those international organisations that are not able to convey to national stakeholders that they are sufficiently impartial. They, therefore, conducted a global survey in 2016, covering more than 100 countries, to determine whether key interlocutors in national governments perceive the international financial institutions as impartial executors of policy or biased actors who do the bidding of powerful member states. They found that the impartiality perception of high-level civil servants varied across different policy areas. In banking regulation, the two Washington-based institutions are perceived as least impartial, in monetary as most. The World Bank was evaluated as slightly less impartial than the IMF. Heinzel and his colleagues conclude that shared policy paradigms influence perceptions of impartiality, for example, whether national officials have studied at an economics department in the USA.

Regional development banks

Like the World Bank, the African, American, Caribbean and Asian development banks give loans from funds which they themselves raise on the international capital market. The members of these banks are both developing countries from the region and donor countries (from inside or outside the region). Although non-regional donor countries come up with most of the capital (paid-up and guaranteed), they do not command a majority of the votes in the regional development banks. However, their votes are weighted according to the amount of subscribed capital.

The African Development Bank Group is itself composed of the African Development Bank, the African Development Fund and the Nigeria Trust Fund. It is the only regional bank that originally tried to get off the ground without donor support. Only in 1982 were non-regional partners admitted. Since then, various traditional donor countries have become major underwriters of the African Development Bank. The USA, after Nigeria, has most voting power at the bank. The new donors have also sought to enter the African continent via the bank. The bank group currently has 28 non-regional members. India joined in 1982 and China in 1985. Turkey became a non-regional member only in 2013: it explicitly sees the bank as a lever to help involve Turkish businesses in large infrastructure projects on the continent (Özkan, 2008).

The United Nations Development Programme

The UNDP was established in 1965 through the merger of a number of existing UN institutions. It was designed to be the hub and driving force of the UN's development efforts. Following the 2019 reforms of the UN system, the UN Resident Coordinators, who are funded and managed by the UNDP, lead UN country teams in some 130 countries and are the designated representatives of the Secretary-General for development operations. Resident Coordinators are, from now on, supposed to be the engine of the UN development system on the ground. Ultimately, the new system has to provide full-time leadership at the country level and is empowered to lead UN coordination, strategic policy, partnerships and investments around the SDGs. It has to strengthen accountability for results and provide greater incentives for integrated action. The UNDP functions in more or less the same way as a non-profit-making organisation. In formal terms, voting rights within the organisation do not depend on the financial contribution of the member state concerned. Contributions to the UNDP are voluntary and core resources are spent in accordance with the UNDP's own priorities and programmes. Non-core resources are subject to agreements with the donors. In this way, donors can impart their own emphases and preferences.

The UNDP has become increasingly dependent on a small group of countries (the Scandinavian countries, Canada and the Netherlands). Due to financial problems, it has thoroughly altered its approach by placing less emphasis on technical assistance programmes (which are more expensive) and more on policy advice.

The rise of new vertical programmes and other transnational governance initiatives

We mentioned earlier the rise of parallel or vertical programmes, also called special-purpose trust funds. These are usually attached to a so-called lead agency within the UN but bundle together the resources and strengths of various different institutions. They also explicitly seek additional resources from national donors and private companies and foundations. The share of ODA financing to 'other multilateral organisations' has obviously increased a lot, reaching 19% in 2016 (OECD, 2018). Most of these programmes work in parallel with the UN's existing bureaucracies, steer clear of the various coordination mechanisms operated by the donors and recipient countries, and take an action-oriented approach. They go for 'quick results and quick wins'. In many countries, their dynamism enables these programmes to carry governments and other actors with them. The best-known example is the Global Fund, which works to combat Aids, TB and malaria. By 2020, the Fund, which is a unique collaborative venture involving various UN institutions, bilateral donors, multinational businesses, foundations and civil organisations, had disbursed over USD 45 billion since its inception in 2002. According to the Fund, it helped 18.9 million people receive antiretroviral therapy for HIV in 2018, treated 5.3 million people with TB and distributed 131 million mosquito nets to prevent malaria. At the very start of the coronavirus crisis, the fund earmarked USD 1 billion to help countries fight COVID-19 and mitigate the impacts on its HIV, TB and malaria programmes. The Fund's activities are heavily focused on outputs (reaching people in need) and only to a lesser extent on outcomes (having a long-term effect on the lives of the beneficiaries and taking a policy-driven approach to the problem). Ironically, though, the large quantity of resources used to combat these three diseases sometimes undermines the capacity of local health services to deal with other diseases. They stimulate a vertical, top-down approach to healthcare delivery to the detriment of a horizontal and comprehensive public health approach. Local health workers prefer to work for these programmes because they are paid better, are more prestigious and receive better supervision (Shomba & Develtere, 2020).

The Education For All (EFA) Fast Track Initiative was started in 2002 by the World Bank and a number of partners, including UNESCO, teachers' associations and foundations, to help low-income countries achieve the MDG for education. The ambition was that by 2015, children everywhere, boys and girls alike, would be able to complete a full course of primary schooling. The EFA Fast Track Initiative acts as a consultation platform at the global and national level. On the financial side, two funds are important: the Catalytic Fund and the Education Program Development Fund. Via these two funds, donors can make contributions to the EFA Fast Track Initiative. However, the EFA initiative has not proven to be on track at all. UNESCO, on its website, admits that the world failed on its promise for all children to go to primary school by 2015. The new education goal, SDG 4, has set the level of ambition a step higher, calling for all young people to complete secondary school by 2030. "To achieve this, all children of school starting age should have begun school in 2018, but in reality, only 70% did so in low-income countries for instance. Around one in sixty children, most of them in low-income countries, will never go to school", UNESCO concludes.[41]

Westerwinter (2019) has developed a dataset to capture these vertical programmes. But he goes further and broader, counting transnational governance initiatives (TGIs), which include vertical funds and other initiatives in which states and/or intergovernmental organisations cooperate with busi-

Figure 21: TGI growth 1955–2018

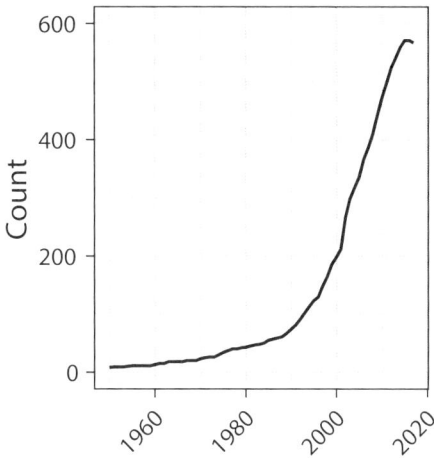

Source: Westerwinter (2019)

ness and civil society actors to govern transnational problems. He comes to the same conclusion: TGIs and vertical funds and programmes have flourished since the late 1990s (Figure 21). Today, they govern a broad range of global policy domains, including environmental protection, human rights, health, trade, finance and security.

Some TGIs are among the most important governors in their issue area. The global governance of 'conflict or blood diamonds' depends, for example, on the Kimberley Process in which states, the diamond industry and NGOs set, monitor and enforce standards for the import and export of rough diamonds. By far the largest initiative in his sample, the UN Global Compact has more than 15,000 participants. The Compact, launched by Secretary-General Kofi Annan in 2000, is a non-binding UN pact to encourage businesses worldwide to adopt sustainable and socially responsible policies and report on their implementation. For companies joining the Compact, it is a platform for dialogue amongst businesses but also with international organisations, workers' organisations, civil society and academics.

As these examples indicate, TGIs are a central part of global governance in many issue areas of world politics. They often possess the authority to make and enforce decisions that change the behaviour of governments, international organisations and corporations, and they affect the lives of millions of people around the globe. The World Bank, the EU and the WHO are key participants in many TGIs.

Westerwinter defines TGIs as institutions that involve at least one state and/or IGO, one business actor and one civil society actor; are transnational in terms of their participants and scope of activities; perform tasks that are related to governing transnational problems; and are institutionalised to the extent that they provide a basis for regular interactions among their participants.

Searching 13 source databases including the Global Solution Network database and the UN Partnerships for the SDGs database, Westerwinter listed a total of 636 TGIs in his dataset.

He found that knowledge creation and information sharing (62%) and capacity-building (48%) are the most common functions of TGIs. However, a large proportion of TGIs are also involved in service provision (42%), agenda-setting (36%) and funding (21%). Over half of the TGIs have a secretariat, but he still concludes that weak institutionalisation is common among these transnational public-private partnerships.

'Deliver as one': seeking cooperation on the market

Since the creation of the UN, an average of three or four new international institutions or programmes have been established every year. Many in the UN are concerned about the chaos that has resulted from this. The UN labyrinth or spaghetti bowl is becoming interwoven and inextricable through overlaps, competition, high transaction costs and coordination problems. Moreover, the 'out-of-system' channels, such as the vertical programmes and the emerging donors, are bringing in new actors, new working methods and a different mentality. At the same time, people are beginning to realise that the opaque structure that the UN has become is unable to cope with global problems. It is for this reason that in September 2005, former UN Secretary-General Kofi Annan set up a 'high-level panel' to devise proposals to enable the UN to act with greater unity and effectiveness.

The core idea that the panel put forward was that there should be extensive collaboration between the institutions in each country. In order to 'deliver as one', four 'ones' were suggested: one UN leader should be appointed in each country, one programme drawn up, one budget arranged and, where possible, one single building used. Certain donors supported the idea immediately and promised additional money for the countries where this happened. The delivering as one approach was tried out in eight countries. Again, though, there were power struggles. Certain countries, such as Rwanda, adopted the idea eagerly and sought to focus the support they got from the UN agencies on healthcare and education. Certain agencies that were not active in these sectors felt excluded as a result and saw finance bypassing them. Others preferred not to be housed in the single UN building but wanted to take up residence in the line ministry formally responsible for healthcare or education.

A 2012 evaluation learned that the methodology of alignment of UN agencies and rapprochement to the national government led to more coherent programmes and strengthened collaboration with the government. The latter benefited from lower transaction costs while those of the UN agencies increased significantly (Develtere, Huyse & Van Ongevalle, 2012).

Secretary-General Ban Ki-Moon and his successor Antonio Gutierrez kept their foot on the pedal to achieve cultural as well as structural changes in the working of the UN system. In 2020, the UN, on the occasion of its 75th anniversary, launched a 'Decade of Action' to deliver the SDGs by 2030. The idea is not only to unlock financing needed to reach the goals but also to open dialogue and discussion on new areas as varied as the global labour market, disinformation, cybercrime and the fight of pandemics. The UN Sustainable Development Cooperation Framework, hammered out during the Deliver as One exercise and fine-tuned with the SDGs, is now the primary instrument for the planning and implementation of UN development activities at the country level. The Management and Accountability Framework of the UN Development and Resident Coordinator System has to further help the many UN agencies keep their noses in the same direction. Lastly, a common Business Innovation Group has to maximise programmatic gains through better back-office operations and bring about change in the culture of UN corporate business operations from risk-averse compliance to risk-informed service.

The foot is on the pedal, but it has to be seen whose foot will be on the brake as not all countries are committed to supporting a more powerful, effective and impactful UN. Will the coalition of the willing be able to gather more strength than the alliance of the unwilling obstructers? In any case, the UN itself called the shots.

The third pillar:
non-governmental development organisations

Box 27. NGO or CSO: what's in a name?

While civil society organisations (CSOs) operating in the development sector have, for a considerable time, been equated with non-governmental organisations (NGOs), this has shifted over the last decade. Scholars and norm-setting organisations such as OECD-DAC have gradually changed their terminology from NGO to CSO. Why does this matter? This chapter will show that this debate is a reflection of changing views of what civil society is and should be. At the same time, to the general public, NGOs are still the best-known part of civil society in the development sector. This chapter will also show that they are still by far the preferred partner and beneficiary for governmental funding. NGOs in the development sector (NGDOs) cover all possible positions in the triangle of government-business-civil society, with some mimicking businesses, others closely tied to government and others purely run by and for communities. This enormous diversity has also led to creative abbreviations:

BINGOs: Big international NGOs
BONGOs: Business-organised NGOs
CBOs: Community-based organisations
DONGOs: Donor-oriented/organised NGOs
GONGOs: Government-oriented/organised NGOs
GRINGOs: Government-run/inspired NGOs
QUANGOs: Quasi-NGOs

In the 1980s and 1990s, NGDOs – the third pillar of development cooperation – occupied an increasingly centre-stage position. This led a former secretary-general of the UN, Kofi Annan, to describe organised civil society as the 'new super-Power'[42]: a force for the good with true global power. Over the last two decades, NGDOs have lost some of their standing and are no longer necessarily seen as the golden bullet solution for development problems of all kinds. There has been a pushback from different corners and with different agendas. This chapter describes how we got there.

NGOs have found their way into the media and became an important source of information on development issues. Governments and UN organisations are earmarking money to subsidise their activities and engage in dialogue with the organisations' experts. Other organised social action groups – trade unions and environmental and peace movements – which constitute the driving force behind what is generally known as the 'global justice movement', have forged alliances with the key players in the NGDO sector. Together with other civil organisations, they stand for a value-driven, rights-based form of development which is regarded as morally superior by the international community. Witness the fact that since 1997, 10 Nobel Peace Prizes have been awarded to NGDOs or leading figures in civil society, both in the Global North and the Global South.

Historically, the NGDO sector has presented itself in many Western countries as a new social movement, distinguishing itself from more traditional social movements, such as the trade union movement. At the same time, as illustrated in the introduction, NGDOs span a broad spectrum of organisational forms and agendas, which complicates efforts to categorise them as a distinct group in civil society. Sociological research into the phenomenon agrees that it is a strongly structured and organised part of civil society, also described as a 'tamed' social movement.

NGDOs have been a historical forerunner of the network movements that have sprung up everywhere since the latest wave of globalisation. While social movements (including the new ones) are characterised by the continuous striving for unity of ideology, praxis and organisation, network movements are characterised by a rather different architecture and approach. Unlike the traditional social movements, they thematise an issue without seeking to achieve a coherent and consistent ideology or vision. Participation is less streamlined, less orchestrated and less permanent than with traditional social movements. Mobilisation is often virtual and does not take place in a fixed context. As well as organisations specialising in a given field, all kinds of other actors can be involved: research institutes, media groups and so on. In such cases, some researchers have even dropped the term 'social movement', preferring terms such as 'mixed actor coalitions', 'alliances' or simply 'networks' (Develtere & Huybrechts, 2008).

A movement with many faces, roles, visions and strategies

The NGDO sector highly integrated into only a few Western countries. More commonly, there are dozens or even hundreds of private development organisations that are recognised by their governments as NGDOs. All of them taken together constitute the Northern NGDOs (which also include NGDOs from

Australia and New Zealand!): a very comprehensive and wide-ranging sector. But the NGDO archipelago has just a few major players and tens of thousands of minor ones. This becomes apparent when one views Table 7 in perspective.

Table 7: The six largest NGDOs in the US

NGO	2019 revenue (USD)
Direct Relief	1,235,283,489
World Vision	1,055,102,715
Catholic Relief Services	1,009,233,176
Compassion International	890,299,730
Save the Children International	829,948,062
Care USA	606,808,858

Source: The Non-profit Times: The NPT Top 100 (2019)

The world's largest American NGDOs (Direct Relief, World Vision, and Catholic Relief Services) have budgets similar to or even larger than those of many official donors, including Austria, Finland, Portugal and Greece.

But we need to look beyond the NGDOs, as they are not the only specialist private organisations in Western countries occupied with the Global South. In most countries, there are also country committees or country working groups (such as a Myanmar Committee), working groups (for issues such as female circumcision), coalitions (the Clean Clothes Campaign, for example), foundations and funds, press agencies (such as the Inter Press Service), cooperative partnerships (such as Oikocredit), think tanks (such as the Center for Global Development), fair trade shops (in most Western countries), fair trade cafés (in countries such as Austria, Italy and Belgium) and interactive web-based platforms.

The NGDO sector is also very much intertwined with a large number of other CSOs for which development cooperation is a subsidiary agenda. In many Western countries, as we will see, the trade union movement and cooperatives are highly active in development cooperation. In the USA, the same is also true of foundations and student organisations.

As well as having many faces, the NGDO sector has also taken on many roles. The sector and its actors present themselves as idealistic workers for a good cause, zealous entrepreneurs in development projects, watchdogs or advocates, awkward or ugly customers, and as transformational partners to their partners in the Global South. How to balance all these roles is a constant source of friction.

An idealistic, altruistic image is consciously cultivated in order to develop and maintain support for fundraising. The message is that there is a need that can be alleviated, and the best way to do that is through individuals taking responsibility by contributing to the NGDO in question (financially, through voluntary work, etc.). Volunteering – the giving of time and money of one's own free will – is the existential core of every NGDO. In English-speaking countries, the terms NGO and 'private voluntary organisation' are interchangeable. NGDOs seek to give a place to this voluntary participation through campaigns. In recent years, this has been packaged with increasing professionalism. Many NGDOs have become large, professionally run concerns with hundreds of members of staff, marketers, lobbyists, in-house research departments, planners and project implementation managers. They dispense action-inspiring idealism to their militant campaigners and generosity-inspiring emotionalism and altruism to their financial supporters. As activists and financial supporters constitute overlapping segments in every NGDO, they need to strike an optimal balance between the two spheres.

NGDOs have also taken on the role of zealous entrepreneurs in development projects. Their preferred sectors are education and training, healthcare and rural development. The collective message here is that NGDOs are efficient and effective actors in the development process itself. This has gone hand in hand with growing attention to professionalisation and, several scholars would argue, also bureaucratisation. However, NGDOs have succeeded over time in gaining active support, not just among a broad swathe of public opinion but among governments and businesses too. Moreover, in many donor countries, the funds that NGDOs receive from governments have risen dramatically since the introduction of subsidy systems in the 1970s, although unevenly and at a decreasing rate in the last decade.

Most of the money raised by CSOs, however, comes from the general public: an estimated USD 42 billion per year or more than twice the amount received through OECD governments. This really is an estimate, as only the figures that NGDOs report to their governments and then reported by the governments to the OECD are known. It is even harder to calculate the contributions in kind made by people via NGDOs.

According to Riddell (2008), who performed calculations on the basis of data available in the USA, private donors give USD 1.5 billion worth of goods (clothes, school equipment, etc.) to the NGDO community every year.

NGDOs in most Western countries also receive government subsidies to finance their projects. OECD figures (2019)[43] demonstrate that since 2014, the total ODA funding to CSOs has gradually stagnated at around USD 20

Figure 22: ODA to and through CSOs, 2010–18 (USD million, disbursements, constant 2018 prices)

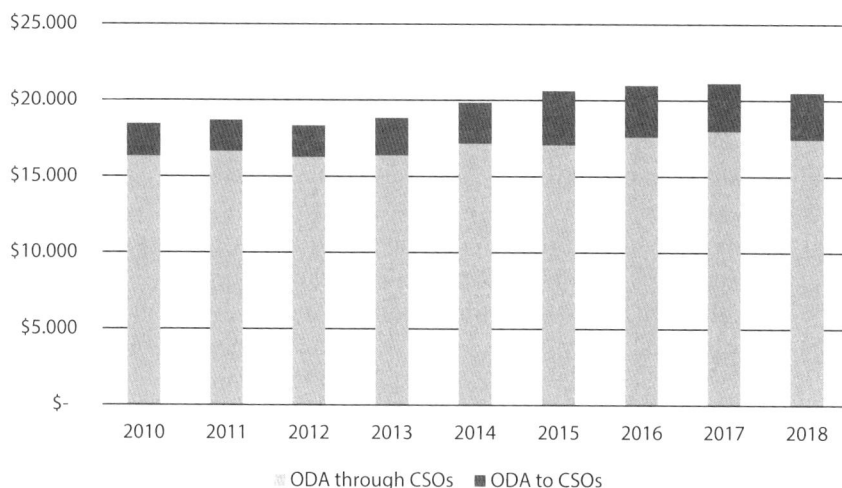

Source: OECD, Development Assistance Committee Members and Civil Society, 2019

billion (see Figure 22). In this period, CSO funding constituted around 15% of the total ODA spent by OECD countries. While the CSO label covers all the different types of CSOs, only an estimated 7% goes directly to developing country-based CSOs. The majority of CSO funding (93%) goes to donor country-based and international CSOs, which mainly consist of NGDOs.

The NGDOs' degree of dependence on government funding varies from country to country and from NGDO to NGDO but can be very high. Since the late 1980s, donor governments have also discovered NGDOs to be comparatively inexpensive implementers of their own bilateral projects. They have asked competent NGDOs to run hospitals, build schools, and even give training to local officials. Figure 22 illustrates that a large majority of the funding to CSOs is *through* CSOs, which refers to situations where CSOs are acting as an implementing agency for projects and programmes initiated and defined by governmental donors. For only 15% of CSO funding, CSOs are supported as independent development actors ('*to* CSOs') that do their own thematic and geographic agenda-setting.[44] This is an illustration of changing donor government views about the role of NGDOs. The extent to which NGDOs should allow themselves to be used by the government as subcontractors and consequently alienated from their own supporters is the subject of heated debate in many donor countries. At what point do they get too close for comfort? At what point do they become alienated from their own private supporters?

This close interrelationship with the government agenda does not sit well with the other guise that the NGDO sector likes to assume, namely that of watchdog, advocate, militant and awkward or ugly customer. During the first 20 years of its existence, the sector was a lobbying group that opposed governmental or official development cooperation and insisted on its non-governmental profile. Later, a broader critique of the prevailing international model was formulated, and other societal and economic institutions and actors, multinationals, financial institutions and international monetary institutions were also challenged with regard to their role in the North-South divide. The NGDOs developed this role professionally, making use of their field experience, research departments and media-supported campaigns. They mobilised and still mobilise public opinion through constantly demanding more responsible political behaviour and policies, and by naming and blaming policymakers who do not follow their suggestions. It is undoubtedly the case that the NGDO sector has considerable influence in many countries with respect to difficult political issues such as the relationship between the UK and the Zimbabwe regime, investments by Western companies in low-income countries and the availability of COVID-19 vaccines in low-income countries. Some critical stakeholders have been arguing for years that NGDOs should prioritise this kind of advocacy and lobby action in favour of structural changes to the imperfect system over the myriad of concrete projects that offer only short-term relief to a minority of the population in the South.

For about three decades, NGDOs have also been trying to put pressure on business actors. Multinationals involved in the banana industry, soft drinks, the clothing sector, construction, dredging, the financial sector, the extraction of raw materials, etc. know what we are talking about. NGDOs know to find their Achilles' heel, to expose whatever it is that is bad that they are doing in developing countries, as well as globally, and to picture them as real culprits. By means of activities such as the Clean Clothes Campaign, exposing the bad working conditions in the clothing industry, they have demonstrated that purchasing power can be converted into social power. Increasingly, NGDOs are advocating for mandatory regulation that would hold companies to account when they contribute to negative human rights impacts through their own operations, through subsidiaries in third countries or through other business relationships.

Since the NGDO sector's early days, NGDOs have also, at regular intervals, played the role of actual or potential troublemakers. Governments and the business community in both donor and recipient countries are often ill at ease with these well-funded and very vocal activists. Cambodia, Ethiopia, Uganda, Niger and the Philippines are among the countries that have recently tightened their grip on the NGDO community. But it is not just the usual suspects who are doing so; in an increasing number of recipient countries, human rights activists connected to NGDOs are monitored, harassed and even jailed, as Civicus, a global alliance dedicated to strengthening citizen action and civil society around the world, regularly reports in its civic space monitor. Mandatory, burdensome registration and broad government discretion to restrict, control and shut down NGDOs are common practice in many recipient countries. Organisations in Ethiopia, for example, must notify regulatory authorities within seven days of a general assembly meeting. In Tanzania, an international NGDO must "refrain from doing any act which is likely to cause misunderstanding" in local civil society.

But NGDOs are not always the ones who make waves. They are also highly effective at riding the crest of the wave and attacking specific aberrations in society and the economy. Examples include successful campaigns in which NGDOs have entered into shifting coalitions with trade unions, consumer organisations, peace activists and the media; for instance, in order to impose codes of practice on producers of baby milk powder, to get landmines banned and to get mega-dam projects postponed or cancelled. Large organisations have magnanimously admitted that they have been forced to yield to NGDO pressure or have had their eyes opened by NGDOs. Thus, the World Bank acknowledges that it has revised its structural adjustment approach of the 1990s on the basis of research material and arguments which largely derived from NGDO circles.

Finally, NGDOs from the Global North do not only want to be recognised as professional implementers of projects but they also aim to develop transformational partnerships with their counterparts in the Global South which transcend those individual projects. In this role, NGDOs need to be adaptive to quickly changing contexts, be responsive to learning needs in the partnership, build ownership for the change process among partners in the Global South, and contribute to long-term, structural change. Several scholars (e.g., Kamstra, 2017) have described the tensions between a managerial, donor-driven approach (professional implementers of projects) on the one hand and an approach geared towards social transformation on the other.

Several generations of NGDOs

The NGDO sector is often publicly perceived as an amalgam of different non-governmental initiatives. Some of these emphasise charitable and humanitarian interventions, others structural measures in favour of the

Global South, and others still the need to transfer know-how. This diversity is based on the five periods or trends which have led to the creation of a succession of new non-governmental development initiatives.

The first generation consisted of the colonial pioneers. In the context of community development initiatives in the colonies and mandated territories – mainly supported by the Catholic and Protestant churches – lay volunteers were activated. Volunteers were also involved in structures such as education, administration and healthcare. Specialist organisations such as the Damien Foundation were established for the purpose.

As early as the inter-war period, the basis was laid for the second generation of NGDOs. Both the churches and the labour movement set up NGOs to address the needs of the victims of the war in Europe and subsequently turned their attention towards the developing countries.

From 1940 to 1960 several trends and movements can be seen emerging within the NGDO community, each of which influences the others.

Firstly, several humanitarian and Christian NG(D)Os were started, which sought to provide aid to victims of the Second World War, the Korean War and poverty in Africa. Oxfam (originally the Oxford Committee for Famine Relief) originated out of protests against the British government's refusal to give any help to hundreds of thousands of starving Greeks during the war. Within both Protestant communities and the Catholic churches in the north, NGDOs were founded which could rely on a very broad and committed body of supporters among religious and laypeople alike. Some of the biggest NGDOs originated in this way: Caritas Internationalis, World Vision (USA), Center for Concern (USA), Christian Aid (UK), CAFOD (UK), Manos Unidas (Spain), Misereor (Germany) and many member organisations of the World Council of Churches.

In addition, NGDOs were established to give further support to the institutions and organisations that had been created during the colonial period. Many of these were of church origin. The task of these NGDOs was to maintain links with the Catholic parishes and Protestant congregations in developing countries, but they also needed to further expand and finance the network of social services associated with these Christian institutions. Other social movements such as the trade union movement and the cooperative movement also set up their own NGDOs to support their colleagues in the South.

At the same time, there were very widespread calls to not just give money for the poor countries but actually to work for them, and a number of the largest organisations for volunteers were created, such as UK Voluntary Service Overseas in 1958, the US Peace Corps in 1961 and the Dutch organisation SNV in 1963. These volunteers, who received a modest government salary, were expected to engage in the local culture, live with the people and gradually bring about change and improvement through processes of 'inculturation'.

On the other hand, a pro-Third-World school of thought developed, which aimed to carry out a far more radical project. Inspired by the Latin American *dependencia theorists*, proponents of these views argued that there was a clear link between the underdevelopment of Third World countries and speedy development of Western capitalism. Such views emerged at universities and were responsible for numerous new non-governmental initiatives. NGDOs sought to provoke debate about the international system and North-South relations, and support the emancipatory initiatives of the working classes in the Third World. These NGDOs had much sympathy for the non-aligned nationalist countries such as Cuba, Chile, Tanzania, Algeria and India.

Midway through the 1980s, debate arose in France about the fundamentals and implications of the pro-Third-World ideology (Brauman, 1986). Particularly in charity circles, and more specifically in the recently established Médecins sans Frontières (Doctors without borders; 1980), a new vision of non-governmental development action was launched. The emphasis was placed on humanitarian law, which legitimises emergency aid interventions even when governments invoke their sovereign right of self-determination. Moreover, this vision led to criticisms of the dysfunctionality of many Third World states. Blame for the development problem was no longer attributed to the international system, as it had been by the 'pro-Third-Worlders', but to actors and institutions in the Third World countries. Development organisations themselves were maintaining inefficient, bureaucratic and even corrupt and oppressive regimes, it was argued.

Box 28. Southern NGOs become NGDOs

So far, most NGDOs have come from OECD countries. They specialise in defending the interests of CSOs in recipient countries and giving them financial and other support. For some years, certain domestic CSOs that were set up to solve local problems have branched out into other developing countries. In this way, we see the Bengali micro-finance organisations BRAC and Grameen Bank experimenting with micro-finance in Afghanistan or Africa. Indian dairy cooperatives give support to Kenyan dairy cooperatives. 'Un Techo para mi País', a local NGO promoting decent housing in Chile, has ventured out into 19 Latin American countries. It would be interesting to know if these Southern NGOs that become NGDOs in other developing countries differ from the Northern NGDOs in terms of their vision and approach, or the impact of their work.

Not only did the vision of development change profoundly but preference also began to be given to different types of intervention. This generation of organisations stood back from supposedly emancipatory projects, preferring technical interventions for which specific know-how was required. In this sense, they were 'technicians without borders'. Dozens of specialist organisations were created, following the example of Médecins sans Frontières: there are now 'without borders' organisations of vets, journalists, pilots, lawyers, architects, engineers and teachers. Moreover, organisations specialising in water supply, sanitary facilities, entrepreneurship, microfinance, rural electrification, the marketing of agricultural produce and environmental conservation opted to provide local communities with new development instruments via an appropriate technical and technological approach without much regard for the flaws in the policy environment in which they operated.

Over the last decades, a new generation of NGDOs has emerged, which mimic business in various ways. Some are adopting business models by integrating social entrepreneurship principles into their projects. Others integrate management practices from the business sector into their own operations by commodifying their ways of working into modules that can be branded and commercialised, or by promoting development strategies that have the best value for money. Another group builds close partnerships or coalitions with business actors to tackle shared development problems related to clean water, quality education or agricultural productivity. The growing orientation towards business is not constrained to those new NGDOs. Our own research with NGDOs in Belgium in fact showed that over the last decade a large majority had plans to improve their engagement with business actors. This latest wave in the NGDO landscape reflects the growing attention for the role of the private sector in development cooperation (Vaes & Huyse, 2015). Different drivers have triggered this development, amongst which are the growing critiques of the lack of tangible impact of traditional forms of development cooperation and the search for additional funding sources in times of austerity.

A sector with many different visions and strategies

As our brief historical outline shows, the NGDO sector is a colourful collection of organisations and movements with highly diverse backgrounds and rationales. This partly explains the diversity of analyses, ideologies and visions within the NGDO sector, which certainly cannot be described as subject to an ideological monoculture. Depending on when they were created, NGDOs may focus on making voluntary work possible, alleviating acute needs, giving support to 'partners', bringing about changes in North-South relations and supporting emancipatory projects, or carrying out humanitarian or technical interventions.

In most countries, the national NGDO sector has, so far, not come up with a consistent common vision or joint strategy. Few countries have strong umbrella organisations or federations. InterAction, the largest American NGO coalition, is arguably one well-known exception to this. It has 188 members, which together run three-quarters of all private NGDO funds in the USA. It employs a mere 50 or so professionals, but its 30-strong board of directors includes several of the world's largest NGDOs. The organisation takes a highly critical line on the USA's official development policy and lobbies effectively using 'evidence-based policy alternatives'. Standards are imposed on its own members in terms of integrity, quality and effectiveness. Each member has to report on these areas every year.

The difficulty for most national NGDO communities is that – unlike the 'old' social movements – they lack fixed democratic and participatory working methods for arriving at a joint, crystallised decision about their vision and developing their own strategies on the basis of that vision. There are no NGDO congresses, colloquia or conferences meeting at regular intervals and following procedures enshrined in statutes to present the organisations' collective vision and joint actions for the discussion and approval of supporters or members. This difference with old social movements can be explained by the different nature of their membership. In trade unions or the women's movement, for example, leaders are elected by the membership to represent their interests (respectively workers and women). Northern NGDOs defend or support the interests of specific groups (workers, farmers, women, disabled, orphans, girls…) in low-income countries, but this is not through a formal mandate from these groups. The membership of NGDOs is different from the target groups they support. As volunteers, they wish to contribute to the good cause of the NGDO.

Figure 23 is a schematic attempt to situate the divergent visions on development and strategies within the NGDO sector.

The vertical axis reflects the fact that some organisations argue that the problems in recipient countries can only be resolved by wealth creation in these countries, while others see reducing the inequality between countries or within countries as the solution. Over the last decade, the topics of climate change and biodiversity loss have gained prominence on the agenda of CSOs, so the objective of wealth creation will often be accompanied by

Figure 23: Four types of NGDO strategies to address global challenges

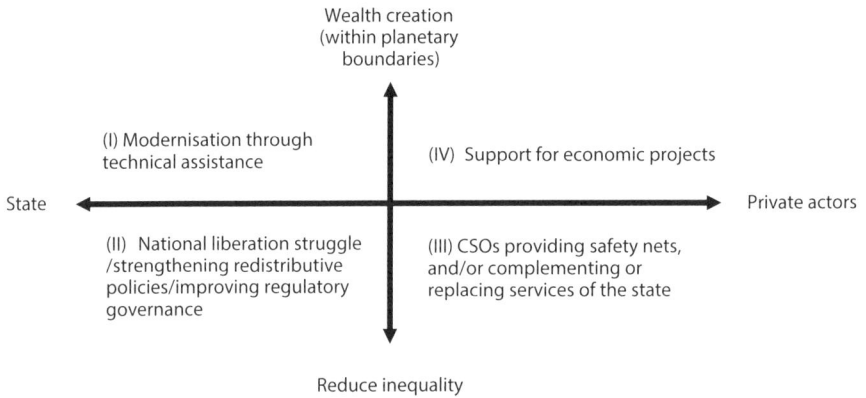

Wealth creation
(within planetary
boundaries)

(I) Modernisation through
technical assistance

(IV) Support for economic projects

State ← → Private actors

(II) National liberation struggle
/strengthening redistributive
policies/improving regulatory
governance

(III) CSOs providing safety nets,
and/or complementing or
replacing services of the state

Reduce inequality

Source: Authors

an objective that refers to the planetary boundaries. The horizontal axis in Figure 23 indicates the various actors who can and must play a key role in carrying out the development agenda. There is the state in the developing world, but private actors can be an alternative. The resultant matrix yields four different strategies.

The first strategy (Quadrant I), which is advocated by one wing of the NGDO sector, aims to increase the wealth of developing countries by promoting a modernisation process. The state is assigned a central role in this. This strategy was especially popular during the first and second UN Development Decades (1960–1970 and 1970–1980) and coincided with attempts by developing countries to modernise their own production apparatus through a strategy of import-substitution industrialisation, create their own markets and build up a state-run network of social welfare institutions. NGDOs supported these efforts, mainly by sending out technical personnel (health workers, teachers, agricultural experts, irrigation specialists, engineers, etc.) and providing financial support for the construction of health centres and schools, the building of roads, water supply and the establishment of marketing institutions such as agricultural cooperatives. More recently, the technical NGDOs operating in this quadrant have started paying attention to climate change and biodiversity. So, while wealth creation is still the central objective, they will promote technologies and solutions that do not contribute to climate change or the further loss of biodiversity.

The radicalisation of the NGDO sector in the 1960s, which was mentioned earlier, coincided with a more general paradigm shift in thinking about development and underdevelopment (Quadrant II). This was partly influenced by the *dependencia* thinkers, who pointed to the unequal exchange relations between developed and underdeveloped countries, and to the dependence relationships between central and peripheral countries. According to this school of thought, radical action was needed to bring national and above all international inequalities to an end. Countries from the Third World needed to detach themselves from the international system and steer an independent course. In many countries, they argued, the national elite acted as a bridgehead, helping maintain the international capitalist system, thus independence could be achieved only by means of a national liberation struggle, followed by a state-led emancipatory strategy.

Many NGDOs, therefore, opted to give financial and technical support to national liberation movements. In countries with a conservative dictatorship, support went to the opposition, which in some cases had to operate clandestinely. In countries where a liberation movement had succeeded in gaining power, there was cooperation with the local authorities, with social organisations associated with the national unity party and specific government departments. In this way, a significant element of the NGDO sector became allied to nationalist and populist regimes which were trying out a 'third way'. Well-known examples are the support given to the African socialism of Julius Nyerere (Tanzania), the left-wing experiment of Salvador Allende (Chile), the Sandinista regime (Nicaragua) and Fidel Castro's communist Cuba. The failure of these regimes did not bring this trend within the NGDO community to an end. A contemporary version of the 'third way' is found in the global justice movement, which opposes the neoliberal model and again argues in favour of a more central role for the state in the development process. A growing group of NGDOs offers developing country governments both intellectual and practical support in the defence of their interests in international forums such as the WTO and the World Bank. This quadrant also covers the actions of NGDOs that do not necessarily tie their actions to specific ideological or political models but do advocate for redistributive policies, for example in the area of social protection or taxation. Along the same lines, NGDOs are increasingly advocating for stronger regulation (regulatory governance) of the international operations of companies, in order to improve working conditions and/or avoid tax evasion.

The collapse of the one-party states and the subsequent democratisation movement in many Southern countries from the mid-1980s onwards also created political circumstances in which new civil actors could emerge and operate (Quadrant III). This 'associative revolution' was, to a large extent, indebted to support from the Western non-governmental world. In the first phase, certain Western NGDOs initiated non-governmental structures, mainly acting alone. In doing so, they worked as social engineers, deliberately recalibrating the local social and associative fabric.

Box 29. The difficult task of NGDOs

More than ten years ago, Riddell (2008) estimated that more than 600 million people in the developing world came into some form of contact with NGDO projects and programmes. Because of the expansion of the sector and its increased financial strength, we can assume that NGDOs currently reach even more people. Most NGDOs explicitly target the poorer sections of the population. Evaluations suggest that a majority of NGDO projects succeed in achieving their immediate goals: the school works, the well is used, the bush radio reaches the farmers, the coffee gets onto the international market. But NGDOs do more than that: they also give people self-confidence and bring them into contact with the outside world.

Yet there are also serious challenges to face.

NGDOs often say and think that they work with the poor. But few check whether this is actually the case, and numerous studies have shown that it is particularly difficult to reach the poorest of the poor (Develtere & Huybrechts, 2005). Those living in extreme poverty rarely have a fixed dwelling, are hard to get in touch with and are excluded by other poor and not-so-poor people. Communities in poverty and extreme poverty are riven by conflict and intrigue. In their subsistence economies, the risks are high and the margins between success and failure slight. Poor people, therefore, play it safe or focus on what is convenient to them. *Nakei kobeta coop!* ('I'll try to do a deal') is a sentiment expressed every day by millions of Kinois (inhabitants of Kinshasa). People are prepared to take on even things that are physically impossible or morally unthinkable to keep going for another day (Olela, 2007. Setting up an *ONG-bidon* (false NGO) or *ONG-de-serviette* (aid-lobbying NGO) is a tried-and-tested method. For them, development cooperation is a market in which a deal can be struck. In return for payment, savvy intermediaries, also known as *courtiers du développement* or 'aid-brokers', give advice to these local 'survival NGOs' so that they can use the right words ('gender', 'participation', 'sustainable', etc.) and make the right symbolic gestures (producing a leaflet and website, setting up a small savings fund, etc.) to get the foreign development worker to come up with the goods. But even for the more substantial local NGOs with a respectable track record, the development sector is a complex market environment. They are approached by countless Northern NGDOs and also by the World Bank or USAID, with requests to reach the poor together. They may be rewarded handsomely for doing so but in exchange, must ask the impossible of the poor: to voluntarily help build a clinic or school, to take the time to devise a poverty plan for the village, to collect money for repairs to the well, even to save the natural environment and solve the local unemployment problem. If the SDGs are not achieved, will NGDOs and the poor then be to blame?

At times, fairly interventionist methods have been and still are used to create 'a civil society' in the Global South, which primarily hark back to the associative models from Europe and North America or are inspired by a limited number of highly successful initiatives (for example, the microfinancing system of BRAC and the Grameen Bank in Bangladesh). At times, more participatory methods have been used, which take a local needs analysis and civil traditions as their starting point. Later, many NGDOs adapted their role somewhat, often presenting themselves as facilitators for and partners to local civil society.

Although Western NGDOs and their local partners set great store by the 'partnership idea' and working on an equal footing, their relationship remains rather ambiguous and asymmetrical. Increasingly, Western NGDOs are professionally organised and have a clear agenda for which they have or seek support from Western private and public sponsors. Southern civil organisations are often fragile structures, which are highly dependent on Western financial and technical support, and to a great extent derive their legitimacy from their capacity to channel funds to the district or members in question. Critics also deplore the tendency to address everything via local NGDOs, calling it 'NGO-isation'. NGOs take over the role of governments in healthcare, education and many other fields, and through their emphasis on service provision and their focus on financial solutions for every problem, they tend to quash the militant spirit of social movements, such as trade union movements, farmers' organisations and other emancipation movements, which would have been capable of fighting for structural solutions on their own (Jad, 2007).

The final strategy (Quadrant IV) – the most recent one – returns to the idea that the role of development organisations is to increase the target group's income through wealth creation rather than redistribution. According to this school of thought, development agencies, including NGDOs, should primarily create opportunities for local private actors. This can be done by setting up or improving local institutions, such as property rights or marketing mechanisms, or by giving support to local entrepreneurs. Many NGDOs have adapted their approach along these lines and invest in 'income-generating projects'. The supporters of the social movement approach prefer collective action and promote cooperative entrepreneurship or initiatives in the social economy. A second group opts for private entrepreneurship, with some organisations giving support to 'micro-entrepreneurs' (usually one-person or family businesses) and others preferring medium-sized companies. Similar to the NGDOs operating in Quadrant I, NGDOs in Quadrant IV have become more sensitive to the side effects of strategies that are exclusively oriented towards economic growth. Many will favour economic sectors that contribute to sustainability (renewable energy, recycling, etc) or sectors that at least do not contribute substantially to global warming or loss of diversity.

Across these four quadrants, NGDOs in the Global North have struggled with similar challenges in how to achieve social, economic and environmental change. Initially, cooperation models in the 1970s and 1980s were focused on sending Northern volunteers and professionals to execute development projects in the Global South. After growing critiques that they were actually filling up permanent local positions (teachers, doctors, engineers, agricultural experts etc.) which could continue indefinitely, there was a switch to a project- and programme-based approach, increasingly working through local partner organisations. Other critiques revolved around the donor-driven character of much of the NGDO support. This explains the focus on alternative project-management practices. For this purpose, special project and programme instruments were developed, such as the participatory rural/rapid appraisal,[45] objective-oriented intervention planning[46] and outcome mapping.

Box 30. Local actors in the driving seat of development

In response to the humanitarian crisis as a result of the war in Syria, the international NGDO Save the Children implemented a programme in support of adolescents and their caregivers in the Middle East region, financially supported by the Swedish government (2018–2020). The ultimate goal of the project was to see that adolescents affected by crisis would be more resilient and act as agents of change in their societies, including by improved access to education.

In order to contribute to positive changes in adolescents' lives that could be sustained beyond the timespan of the programme, Save the Children decided to work through local intermediaries rather than directly with the adolescents. To manage the collaboration with local actors, an outcome mapping methodology was used instead of traditional project management instruments. Outcome mapping allowed Save the Children and its partner organisations to identify the local actors ('boundary partners' in outcome mapping jargon) who could play a key role in achieving the programme's goal. The municipalities, for example, were identified as one of those key actors that were instrumental in facilitating access to safe spaces for adolescents. Outcome mapping also promotes forms of planning, monitoring and evaluation processes that are deeply participatory. By asking local actors and beneficiaries to determine how their own practices, behaviours or even policies would need to change in order to achieve a sustained improvement in the lives of adolescents and their caregivers, outcome mapping builds ownership and institutional sustainability beyond the lifetime of the programme.

This approach represented a major shift in the practice of Save the Children, as the programme's performance is not only measured by the direct benefits received by adolescents and caregivers but also by the level at which these benefits can be sustained beyond the programme. At the same time, Save the Children and its partners learned that trying to influence local actors, such as municipalities or religious leaders, is a much trickier endeavour than direct service delivery and needs continuous trial and error and real-time learning and adaptation.

However, while the project-based approach continues up to today, it has been accompanied by intensive debates about the exact roles of NGDOs. Previous classifications of the roles of NGDOs would typically distinguish between service delivery, capacity development and watchdog (lobby and advocacy), also called the 'change triangle'. Over time, the service delivery role gained more criticism as it was seen to lead to projects in which the role of the state was replaced. Several scholars and donor agencies that fund NGDOs started to push for a stronger focus on the capacity development and watchdog roles. However, in reality, the picture has become more complex. On the one hand, new roles have emerged. The widening set of development goals that are now on the international agenda, for example in the area of climate change, globalised trade and value chains, migration and security, has set in motion new thinking about the roles that NGDOs can and should play, such as the role of broker in multi-stakeholder processes, linking local challenges to global developments and organising civil society at the regional and international level. Secondly, with the important role of the private sector acknowledged and pushed by the donor community, NGDOs are increasingly expected to partner with business to scale-up and innovate, and/or act as social entrepreneurs. The growing attention for the role of the private sector also leads to calls for a greater focus on the watchdog role to counterbalance the growing power of the private sector. On the other hand, there are new drivers that push the service delivery role back on the table. The strong orientation towards achieving tangible and measurable development results and the setting of ambitious development targets by leading donors such as the UK and the EU have contributed to this. This issue remains unresolved.

Discussions about what exactly is good NGDO development cooperation is ongoing. In addition, with the growing capacity of NGDOs in the Global South, settling the question about what exactly should be the role of Northern NGDOs becomes more relevant and urgent. A number of new platforms have tried to capture the principles for an alternative approach to development, such as the Doing Development Differently initiative,[47] and thinking and working politically[48]. These approaches emphasise "the importance of understanding and working with the grain of local context, and a project cycle which replaces 'The Plan' with a messy process of trying, failing, learning and adapting (and trying again)".

Along similar lines, the London School of Economics (Howell, 2012) came up with a specific set of operational principles for the strengthening of civil society in developing countries. These are based on the extensive evaluation research of CSO programmes funded by AusAID in the period 2011–2012. Howell's research reveals the importance of a set of operating principles for the effective working of civil society, including the importance of uncovering local cultural 'norms' about democratisation, poverty and accountability, and the importance of placing donor engagement within a political debate about the relative roles of civil society, the state and the marketplace in providing for global security – not just for donors but also for partner countries, where the very idea of civil society might be perceived as threatening. Howell also warns about the tendency to give precedence to NGOs at the expense of other pivotal civil organisations such as faith groups and trade unions, and points to the significance of the local context, including the history of state-civil relations and competing visions of civil society. Since it was written some 10 years ago, it was no surprise that the Howell paper made mention of the significance of the 'War on Terror' in decisions about development aid and the danger of CSOs being drawn into security agendas, either as possible suspects or potential anti-radicalisation agents. The research was picked up by AusAID and has been integrated as guiding principles into their work with CSOs since 2012.

A movement with a plural support base

The Northern NGOs have a fairly ambiguous relationship with their support base. Yet along with the work they do to improve the standard of living in the developing world, their support base is the most important source of legitimacy for NGDOs. It consists of adherents, constituents and supporters. No NGDOs have members.

'Adherents' agree with the decisions that NGDOs (or a specific NGDO) have made. They have a more or less emotional and ideological connection with the sector as a whole or with a specific NGDO. For example, they may also be in favour of increased public support for development cooperation, share the conviction that education is the most important vector for social development or accept the idea of a Tobin tax, as proposed by some NGDOs. Adherents can be individuals but also associations or businesses. Increasingly large organisations such as trade unions or businesses explicitly support the mission of (some sectors of) the NGDO community. There are few contacts between the adherents and the NGDOs; NGDOs do not even know how many adherents they have. Only surveys can tell them that. Longitudinal research in Belgium, for example, shows that only a minority of people know what the term 'NGDO' stands for; few know what NGDOs really do in the donor and recipient country. Even so, there is still a great deal of trust in NGOs: they are popular, yet little understood (Pollet, 2010).

'Constituents' are adherents who do not confine their backing to theoretical advocacy but also contribute financial, material and human resources that make the projects of the NGDOs or a particular NGDO possible. Again, these constituents can be individuals, associations or businesses. However, this support is on a voluntary basis and on their own initiative; they provide their support without the NGDO even asking for it. Examples include people who contact an NGDO's local campaign coordinator to help raise funds, take the initiative to set up a new fair-trade shop in a given location, or create an Internet community linked to an NGDO project, for example via Facebook. Enterprises making a link to a particular NGDO on their website are also constituents of the NGDO sector.

Finally, the 'supporters' consist of those adherents and constituents who can be mobilised. When called upon to do so, they are ready to provide extra financial, material and human resources. You can expect them to be the warmest adherents and the most active constituents. NGDOs go to great lengths to extend and activate their support base. They are primarily interested in loyal supporters who can themselves recruit new adherents and constituents. The supporters organise training activities, immersion trips, debate series, petitions and fund-raising campaigns. From this group, volunteers are co-opted to represent the voice of the social base at the NGDOs' board and general assemblies.

The NGDOs expect adherents, constituents and especially supporters to provide financial support for their actions.

In the UK, for example, the growing importance of individual giving for NGDOs has been documented in detail in two recent studies, showing that larger NGDOs capture the largest slice of governmental funding, while smaller NGDOs are finding new ways to tap into public giving. A 2018 study by Bond (2018), the umbrella organisation for development NGDOs in the UK, analysed the income sources of 305 of its 393 members. In the period 2006–2016, the overall income of this group of NGDOs went up from GBP 2.5 billion to almost GBP 4 billion. From this, government funding represented the most important source of income (around 33%), followed by individual giving (31%). However, the increased funding volumes had been almost fully absorbed by a small group of large NGDOs (with annual budgets of over GBP 40 million). Two-thirds of the income is going to only 25 NGDOs. According to the same report, medium-size and smaller NGDOs were losing out and did not or hardly benefit from higher governmental funding levels. Another study (Brockington & Banks, 2017) analysed the income sources of 898 development NGOs, including many smaller organisations that are not Bond members. The picture that emerges from their study is more positive for medium-sized and smaller NGDOs: the development sector is thriving, with both the number of organisations and overall expenditure on the rise. The most important source of funding for the NGDOs included in this study is not government funding but income from the public, which accounts for roughly 40% of all income. At the same time, this report confirms the high concentration of income, with 8% of organisations controlling 88% of total expenditure.

The sector breaks free from the NGDOs

As specialised organisations, NGDOs attempt to channel and shape social support for development cooperation as much as possible. Yet they have only partially succeeded in doing so.

Research shows that a growing group of people give support to people or organisations in the Global South without a Northern NGDO being involved. This probably also points to the large number of other channels through which people have direct or indirect contact with people and groups in the Global South. These certainly include the support groups of missionaries and development workers but also the possibilities for remitting money in favour of international and foreign organisations, and the financial adoption of a project or person via specialist websites.

Moreover, we should also mention the increasing number of alternative forms of involvement and participation that have arisen thanks to greater individual mobility and modern information technology. The NGDOs are themselves great promoters of such forms of *engagement distancié*, long-distance engagement or solidarity (Ion, 1997), by which individuals are called upon via demonstrations, marches, the Internet and other IT channels to join in and help shape public opinion on a specific issue, in order to bring social and political pressure to bear, often across national borders.

Analysis of the Movement for the Abolition of Child Labour, which made its voice heard internationally in the mid-1990s, shows that NGDOs played an important but not exclusive role. Trade unions, women's organisations, youth movements and numerous non-organised individuals took part in demonstrations, circulated petitions and engaged in discussion with policymakers at home and in international organisations. Many did so in an international setting. The fact that the Worst Forms of Child Labour Convention of 1999 was ratified by 132 countries in less than three years shows that such a transnational network movement is capable of applying a great deal of political pressure (Develtere & Huybrechts, 2008).

This last example shows that NGDOs have not gained a monopoly over representing and shaping public opinion on development challenges in the Global South. Increasingly, we are seeing new players who also have a 'Third World-friendly agenda'. In other words, the issue is currently in the process of being mainstreamed – partly thanks to the NGDOs themselves. Important new actors in the field are the media, local authorities, certain segments of the business world, schools, youth and student organisations, trade unions and all kinds of foundations. Many new actors do not just develop a discourse about North-South issues but actually travel out to the Global South. This generally happens through cooperation with fellow institutions in a low-income country and is known in some European countries as 'decentralised cooperation'. Such 'twinnings' between local authorities, trade unions and student organisations in the North and South do not just mean a multiplication of financial flows from North to South: they also lead to an exponential increase in contacts, relationships and exchanges between individuals, groups and institutions.

As a consequence, the relationship between the non-governmental development sector and government is also changing. Since the introduction of the subsidy systems in the 1970s, the NGDOs in most countries have had an exclusive relationship with the government. Recognised and registered NGDOs have been regarded as the most important non-state stakeholders on development policy and the only potential recipients of subsidies for project work, awareness-raising campaigns and posting cooperation workers. In most OECD-DAC countries, the home-based NGDO community had almost exclusive access to domestic ODA sources until a decade ago. The situation is gradually evolving; this is also illustrated, for example, in the changing terminology used, with a growing number of OECD-DAC donors using the term CSO instead of NGDO. The expanding views of donors with whom they want to partner relate to the type of actors, the nature of the cooperation and the role of intermediaries. In an earlier study (Huyse & De

Bruyn, 2015) we observed that for five out of the nine OECD-DAC donors in the study, there was a deliberate strategy to widen the group of CSO beneficiaries beyond the traditional home-based NGDOs, including in the UK, the EU, the Netherlands, Denmark and Sweden. However, as described earlier, recent OECD-DAC figures show that up to now, home-based NGDOs still take the lion's share of governmental funding.

Is the new social movement becoming an established network movement?

The NGDO sector has developed over the last four decades into an important actor in the area of development cooperation and North-South relations. It has thematised global development as a public and collective challenge, and has succeeded in creating a fairly broad basis of support for the issue and its own work. While doing so, many NGDOs have evolved from what was initially described by scholars as new social movements to professionally run organisations, described by some as tamed social movements. However, we question in this book whether analysing NGDOs through a strict organisational lens blinds us from structural changes that have emerged over the last decades in the third pillar ecosystem: a system that increasingly acts as a multitude of networks, including with external actors.

Box 31. Recommendation of the Global Coalition for Social Protection Floors

In the absence of strong global institutions, multi-actor coalitions and networks with non-state actors can pioneer and overcome institutional deficits in the architecture of global governance. In a way, these governance deficits at the global level open up spaces for different types of non-state actors and new movements to air their grievances (Marchetti, 2016; Reed et al., 2013). Different CSO advocacy networks and trade unions find new avenues to introduce their concerns to international policy agendas, and new social movements emerge, which confront the powerful finance institutions with their claims (Gereffi & Lee, 2016). While the role of organised civil society is well recognised, many studies have shown a bias towards the role played by 'Anglo-European' parts of global civil society. Bob Deacon (2013) uses the example of the 2012 ILO Recommendation on Social Protection Floors to highlight the important role played by Latin American and African states and civil society through, amongst others, the Global Coalition on Social Protection Floors. "Members of the policy advocacy coalition for the global social protection floor used their relative autonomy within the ILO Secretariat and worked within the framework of complex multilateralism to win support from the global workers' organization in alliance with a series of progressive governments to achieve the policy change" (Deacon & Stubbs, 2013, p.18).

With regard to the praxis or involvement of the supporters too, the image that arises is that of a network. With the exception of a very limited group, the specialised organisations in this new social movement do not have close ties with their activists. Rather, we see a fairly large group of individuals who are broadly sympathetic to the approach taken by the NGDOs but limit their contribution in terms of time and extent. Individuals circulate freely within the sector. They put together their own menu of participation. These developments also illustrate shifts in how citizens translate their engagement for societal causes into practice. Scholars (Piot & Heylen, 2017) have observed that volunteers and financial supporters tend to develop more loose connections with individual organisations and rather support specific causes or campaigns they find relevant, switching more regularly between organisations, individual initiatives and networks. Other networks offer them the opportunity to get involved with the NGDOs yet retain a far greater distance. Examples of this are chequebook activism and Internet militantism, both of which are made possible by financial and digital networks.

Finally, the organisational dimension of the NGDO sector likewise has a network character. The organisational bases are profoundly heterogeneous and multiple. The sector has never generated an organisational model that can be used by all newcomers in the field. Rather, all actors try to develop their own model. As a result, domain-specific organisations include registered and unregistered non-profit-making organisations, foundations, cooperatives and social entrepreneurs.

In addition, many other non-specialised organisations are also active in the sector's field of action. We refer here to a whole host of civil and social organisations, businesses, school communities and local authorities that are also helping to 'make waves' on sustainable development issues. We will look more closely at those challengers when we discuss the emergence and rapid development of a fourth pillar in development cooperation.

That is partly also the case for the international networks with which the NGDO sector has become inextricably linked. In the first place, branches of large international NGO concerns (World Vision, Plan International, Tear Fund International, Save the Children International, Oxfam International) can be seen emerging in both the North and South. Usually, they are not homegrown but bring a mission, philosophy, organisational form and working method with them from the USA or UK. Secondly, we are seeing the tentative integration of national NGDOs into broader international contexts such as the European NGO Confederation for Relief and Development (Concord) and hundreds of international NGO networks. But in each of these cases, the national branch still has a great deal of freedom to develop its own organisation, set its agenda and seek out a support base.

It seems, thus, that the third pillar of development cooperation, as much as the first and second, is becoming increasingly heterogeneous under pressure from local dynamics as well as international ones.

Box 32. The Banco Nacional de Bolivia's support of World Vision

BNB (Banco Nacional de Bolivia) is one of the main banks in Bolivia. Joining the UN Global Compact, BNB expressed it care for corporate social responsibility in 2006. The bank has set different goals in several fields of development based on the SDGs. BNB has programmes around health, the environment, housing, access to water and the right to education for disabled children. Most of these programmes are executed in cooperation with other development institutions. One of these is the biggest NGDO in the world: World Vision International. With the local branch of this multinational NGDO, the bank has ventured, for example, into the field of access to water. Through its programme 'BNB Agua – Valoramos La Vida' (BNB water – we value life), the bank provides funds and promotes the voluntary engagement of its staff for a World Vision-executed project that is supporting water supply in 15 remote villages in the country.

The fourth pillar:
towards a whole-of-society approach

Complementary to official bilateral development cooperation (the first pillar), international institutions (the second pillar) and NGDOs (the third pillar), a fourth pillar is rapidly developing and expanding. The mainstreaming and localisation of development cooperation represent an unstoppable sociological process. A succession of individuals, CSOs, media actors, companies, healthcare institutions and many other novel and non-conventional development workers are taking short-term or more institutionalised initiatives, which they themselves regard as development aid. This might surprise many in the development community because these newcomers are not recognized as legitimate development actors, they are not socialized by the development cooperation system and they do not know the ins and outs of the values and norms of the development community nor the nitty-gritty of the established standards, rules and regulations governing the sector (Develtere, 2008; Develtere & De Bruyn, 2009; Develtere, Huyse & Van Ongevalle, 2012; De Bruyn, 2013).

Such novel and unconventional international cooperation can assume many forms. Professional groups set up their own 'without borders' organisations (Architects without Borders, Journalists without Borders, Lawyers without Borders etc.) or 'without holidays' organisations (Medics without Vacation, Pilots without Vacation etc.). Students and alumni, such as national branches of Academics for Development, get together for joint projects. Researchers set up collaborative research and development initiatives with colleagues from around the globe. Schools and colleges network over the web with schools in developing countries or organise exchanges. Businesses and businesspeople venture into their own development projects. Western service clubs, such as the Lions Club, liaise with service clubs in Africa, Asia or Latin America. Northern youth organisations, like the World Scouting movement, interact with Southern youth movements. Feminist organisations mobilise support against women-unfriendly or degrading practices such as female circumcision or *purdah* (the isolation of women), present in both the South and North. International transgender alliances in the North and South are inspired by the South Asian third gender *hijras*. International networks of organisations and individuals, such as the MenEngage Alliance, challenge patriarchal systems and promote female empowerment and gender equality. Individual migrants and diaspora organisations link up with families, communities and regions of their country of origin. Celebrities, from the American singer Madonna to Swiss tennis idol Federer set up foundations to give away part of their immense financial resources. Trade union federations invite unionists from the developing world and work together within multinationals to enhance the working conditions of the employees throughout their value chain. Environmental NGOs buy up tropical forests in order to protect natural fauna and flora. National and international federations of sports clubs, even individual sports clubs, the most famous of which is FC Barcelona,[49] engage in intercontinental collaborations with their colleagues to promote sport as a tool for development with the ambition of generating social development through the use of sport and even overcoming conflicts and its effects.

Box 33. Novel, unconventional actors in international development

Many development practitioners, international institutions and academics have reflected on the origins and consequences of the remarkable expansion of the number of actors in the international development cooperation field. In this book, we suggest looking at this from an institutional lens of four different pillars. Another way of handling this conundrum is preferred by the OECD-DAC; this normative institution uses the concept of CSOs. By focusing on all CSOs that receive funds from donor countries, the OECD-DAC amalgamates NGDOs (what we call the third pillar) with parts of what we label fourth pillar organisations, but only those that do not refuse government funding. An advantage of this is that it can weigh the importance donors attach to civil society engagement in development cooperation. In 2018, CSOs received above USD 20 billion of government aid or on average 15% of donors' ODA. The fact that 85% of these subsidies are channelled through domestic CSOs is a compelling argument for calling them a forceful lobby. In France, it is common to use the terminology *cooperation décentralisée* (decentralised cooperation) and *réseaux régionaux multi-acteurs* (regional networks of multiple actors) since regional authorities often take the lead in promoting international twinning arrangements. On the one hand, this vocabulary reflects well the ambition of the centralised, Jacobin French state to involve as many state and non-state actors as possible in international cooperation. On the other hand, it has to be said, this creates some confusion since the term 'decentralised cooperation' is also used by the European Commission and the OECD but exclusively for the participation of cities and regions in international development cooperation.

Next to bilateral, multilateral and civilateral – meaning stemming from civil society – development cooperation, Dutch scholars Kinsbergen, Schulpen and Ruben (2017) point to an onrush of alternative development actors in the Netherlands, which they group together under a fourth channel they call the philanteral aid channel or private development initiatives (PDIs), which are, by definition, voluntary and self-funded organisations. As we shall see, these are consequently very small-scale 'do-it-yourself' type development organisations. These PDIs are proliferating in most donor countries and become a social movement *an sich*, which justifies a special focus and, at the same time, their inclusion in what we call the fourth pillar of international cooperation.

We will look now at the fourth pillar from different angles, assuming that all these projects, programmes, activities and novel ventures are harbingers of a fundamental overhaul of the traditional paradigm that has inspired and underpinned development aid and development cooperation since its inception. In other words, they metamorphose the old idea that there is a rich North that has to help a poor South into a proposition that advocates that there is one single world where international interaction matters for everybody.

The term 'fourth pillar', which we apply to this highly heterogeneous group of initiatives, suggests that this is a kind of left-over category or at least an alternative form of aid. We can regard it as a fourth grouping which is positioned alongside the three traditional pillars we already studied, namely the bilateral cooperation channel, multilateral agencies and specialised NGDOs. After reviewing the most visible fourth pillar types, we will add to that institutional prism three more dimensions: generational, domain-specific and methodological dimensions.

This will make it clear that there is more going on: development cooperation is being pluralised, mainstreamed and de-specialised. At lightning speed.

The key players of the fourth pillar

In order to gain recognition from one of the three traditional pillars of development cooperation, one needs the fiat of one's peers. For example, the OECD-DAC determines what counts as 'official aid'. In fact, though, the official development agencies regard only their own work as development cooperation and attempt to dismiss much of the international work of their colleagues at the ministry of employment or health as 'not proper', 'not as good' or 'not as correct' aid. We see a similar situation among international organisations and NGDOs. Some newcomers are admitted to the community; others are viewed askance. However, there are not many means of keeping specific institutions outside the club. All you can do is use gentle compulsion to, for example, encourage foundations to provide information on their development work to the OECD-DAC or propose national governments to give subsidies only to NGDOs and CSOs that meet certain criteria.

Thus, one of the basic tenets of this book is that we are seeing a significant increase in the number of institutions, within governments, the UN, the business community and civil society, that are not regarded as belonging to the club of development specialists but are engaging in projects and programmes in a development cooperation fashion. Some of them do not even want to belong to the traditional club. They do not want to be development workers: rather, they want to do some good in the South because it 'works for them' and is, at the same time, beneficial to certain people in the South. Yet this new, fourth pillar has injected considerable dynamism and has made the development cooperation world a real melting pot. We will take a look at the big nine: the faith-based organisations, the private development initiatives, the trade unions, the farmers' organisations, the health funds, the businesses, the cooperatives, the migrants' communities and, finally, the foundations and philanthropists.

Faith-based organisations: the fourth pillar 'avant la lettre'

Until a few years ago, there was neither cooperation between the secular donor organisations, such as the World Bank, the European Commission and NGDOs, and faith-based organisations (FBOs) nor any meaningful research on such cooperation (Awiah & De Tavernier, 2020). Broader, more comprehensive conceptualisations of human development that take into account diverse aspects of quality of life, including spirituality and faith, have paved the way for a more collaborative atmosphere between secular and faith-based development organisations. While some in the development community still warn of the dangers of the proselytes' zeal of many FBOs as an unsurmountable hindrance to working with them, others refer to their strengths, notably their embeddedness in local communities and capacity to mobilise on a grand scale in societies where religion shapes almost every facet of life.

According to research from the Alliance of Religions and Conservation (ARC), major faith groups run half of the world's schools, a quarter of its colleges and universities, and a third of its hospitals. Collectively, they feed people half a billion meals per day, own a tenth of the world's forests and control 14% of the world's investment portfolio – in sum, trillions of dollars (ARC, 2016). These Baha'i, Buddhist, Christian, Daoist, Hindu, Islamic and

Jewish FBOs have not waited for a broader fourth pillar movement to see light to develop a worldwide network and financially support the expansion of their rank and file in the North and South. Since time immemorial, they have forged close intercontinental contacts, permanent collaborations and interactions between individual believers, local faith groups, churches, parishes and congregations. Importantly, faith-based organisations give a higher premium to why they do something than to what they do. For this, they refer to their own idiosyncratic interpretation of the universe, its genesis, the place and role of man in it, the relations between humans, classes and communities, as well as the thereafter. Each faith's belief frame, value set and normative code have profound effects on and percolate through the cooperation patterns that span several countries or continents. FBOs are extremely diverse and as institutions, they cannot be reduced to the formal doctrinal authorities such as the Vatican, the Church of England, the Sangha in Buddhism or the Shari'a Law Courts in Islam. As the 2016 ARC paper rightly reports, "their creativity lies in countless movements, youth organisations, voluntary bodies, education projects and so forth" (ARC, 2016).

As Pollet, Steegen and Goddeeris (2020) advance, a wide range of virtues are attributed to faith-based actors. While not holding the monopoly on specific strengths, FBOs are applauded for, among other things, their attention to holistic development, incorporating moral and spiritual aspects of well-being; their capacity to engender trust, legitimacy and commitment, and to motivate and mobilise donors, volunteers, staff and communities; and their cultural proximity and responsiveness to poor communities. In their own empirical research on religion, meaning and spirituality in Belgian NGDOs in particular, religion does not seem to be a 'development strategy' or, even worse, some form of 'window-dressing' but an intrinsically meaningful part of their identity and functioning.

Examples can shed a light on the heterogeneity but at the same time the commonalities of these faith-based organisations. Look at the domestic workers' movement in India, initiated by a Belgian catholic nun and supported by Belgian catholic parishes and social movements (Hendrickx, 2019). Compare this to the funds gathered by the 'brothers and sisters' of the Christian Ministry of Spiritual Combat in the diaspora in Belgium, France or Canada to finance their social, educational, health and other projects in the Democratic Republic of Congo (Shomba, 1999). The New Psalmist Baptist Church of Baltimore, USA, has a network of some 2000 churches in East Africa. Its Foreign Outreach Ministry heavily invests in water, sanitation and hygiene in schools around the world. The Sarvodaya Shramadana Movement, the largest non-governmental and Buddhist organisation in Sri

Lanka, interacts and interlinks with adherents from all over the world. They help the movement with projects as diverse as chronic kidney disease prevention and disaster relief efforts. Characteristically for fourth pillar organisations, they also foster concrete interactions between stakeholders through volunteering and internship opportunities. The Parsi Panchayats, who manage the community funds for Parsi and Zoroastrian communities around the world, have similarly, for centuries, invested in housing, education and healthcare.

The major institutional faiths are also amongst the largest investors in the world. In recent years, this financial power has been used in a number of ways, including disinvestment in tobacco, oil and weapon industries, proactive ethical investment in forestation and renewable energy projects, as well as impact investing. One of the pioneers of social impact investment is the worldwide cooperative Oikocredit. This ethical investment channel is embedded in Christian communities around the globe and provides financial and technical support to more than 800 partner organisations in over 60 countries.

FBOs are increasingly recognised as important actors in development and international development cooperation.

Box 34. Humanitarian *jihad*

In 2013, Huffington Post UK published an article titled 'Muslims 'give most to charity'' (Huffington, 2013). According to a poll of 4000 British citizens carried out by ICM, a public opinion research company in conjunction with JustGiving, seven in 10 Muslims, Catholics and other Christians donated, as did six in 10 of the Jews interviewed. Muslims, however, topped the poll and gave significantly more.

Since the 1980s, we have seen a proliferation of Islamic non-governmental organisations and networks which energetically offer support to poor fellow-Muslims in Central Asia, West Africa and even the Caribbean. Some have ties with the radical Muslim brotherhoods. They are disenchanted with political Islam, which has not succeeded in creating an Islamic society, and they now want to Islamicise society from the bottom up, starting from within the mosques. Ghandour (2002) conducted a sociological study on humanitarian *jihad*. A number of large Islamic private organisations, such as the International Organization for Relief, Welfare and Development, formerly known as the International Islamic Relief Organization, play a leading role and have been involved in many joint programmes with UN agencies and international non-governmental organisations. Some of these Muslim organisations are based in Western countries. Islamic Relief Worldwide, which has its headquarters in Birmingham, UK, works in more than 40 countries and has a reputation for delivering aid to some of the world's most hard-to-operate-in conflict zones, including Palestine, Yemen and Somalia. Through the religious command-ment to engage in *zakat* ('purifying one's possessions'), mosques and associations can raise millions for aid actions of all kinds. In various Islamic countries, there are special *zakat* funds and *zakat* foundations to collect alms from the faithful. It is not uncommon for a Muslim pilgrim from Mali who returns from Mecca as a *hajj* to be able to build a new mosque as well as a clinic and school in his village thanks to the generosity of his fellow-pilgrims. In an in-depth ethnographic study on Islamic charity in Egypt, Amira Mittermaier convincingly shows that giving in the Islamic world is giving to God in the first place: "It is neither about economic growth nor about compassion toward, or the deservingness of the poor. It is not even about human rights. It is to and from and because of God" (Mittermaier, 2019, p.181).

Little is known about the volume of funds faith-based organisations transfer to developing countries. According to the Index of Global Philanthropy (Adelman et al., 2016), in 2013–2014, religious organisations in the USA donated USD 6 billion of development aid, equivalent to around 30% of the American government's aid budget. A substantial proportion of these religious communities' funds is still handed over to large Christian NGDOs such as World Vision, but a previous index (Center for Global Prosperity, 2010) refers to a study that demonstrates that a growing proportion is used by congregations to give support to sister churches and associated social and development projects.

Personal development initiatives: looking at the man rather than the plan

In the preface, we presented the – real – story of the faraway Senegalese village of Toubacouta that attracted and still attracts actors belonging to *all* pillars of development cooperation. Many do-it-yourself aid workers, well-off individuals and small groups of individuals who want to do good and assist less well-off individuals and small communities in Africa, Asia or Latin America are piloting and supporting socioeconomic initiatives in this remote village and other places. These long-distance forms of solidarity and engagement have been termed 'small NGOs' in the UK, 'grassroots international non-governmental organisations' (or GINGOs) by some scholars (Appe & Telch, 2020) and 'private development initiatives' (PDIs) by others (Kinsbergen & Schulpen, 2013). For Kinsbergen and Schulpen, they are the non-institutional section of what they baptised the philanteral aid channel.[50] We consider them as part and parcel of the fourth pillar group of development cooperation.

Kinsbergen and Schulpen (2013) define a PDI as a group of people who directly give support to 'partners' in one or more developing countries. A

PDI offers structural support to organisations, communities or groups of people, rather than one-off, individual support to, for example, a footless beggar whom a tourist encounters at the *Place de l'Indépendance* in Dakar, Senegal's capital. Private development initiatives do not receive direct funds from their national government. Importantly, the voluntary engagement of their support base is prominent and they are small in scale, which means that they have fewer than 20 regular paid and non-paid staff or an annual budget of less than €1 million. Estimates of the number of PDIs in the Netherlands vary widely between 6400 (Bouzoubaa & Brok, 2005) to 15,000 (Voorst, 2005) in a population of 17 million. Using a similar, but not identical, definition, our own HIVA surveys (Develtere & Stessens, 2007; Huyse & De Bruyn, 2009) counted over 1100 non-temporary, institutionalised, small-scale initiatives in Flanders, the Dutch-speaking region of Belgium, in 2007 and between 2500 and slightly over 6000 in 2009: this in a population of roughly six million. At present, over 800 of these small PDIs in Flanders are registered on a joint platform.[51] A total of between 25,000 and 60,000 people are thought to be active in these Flemish initiatives. Moreover, the amount of money that these initiatives collect through fundraising from the general public is equivalent to the funds mobilised by the traditional NGDOs (Develtere & Stessens, 2007). This phenomenon is not part of some kind of exceptionalism of the so-called low countries. Clifford (2016) reports that there were over 10,000 charities operating internationally in England and Wales in 2014, up from 2300 in 1995. Schnable (2015) who looks at how foreign aid is "voluntarizing", tells us that 60% of the 11,000 registered American relief and development organisations have an annual budget of less than USD 25,000 and hence presumably rely heavily on volunteers. And this does not report how many are not registered and operate under the radar.

The most important triggers for people to start a development cooperation venture are ignited during a concrete confrontation with the realities, suffering and needs of people in a resource-poor context. As Kinsbergen and Schulpen (2013) write about these sprawling personalised fourth pillar initiatives, their 'own project' or their collaboration with an existing local organisation or institution often stems from a coincidental encounter; in many cases, there is no preconceived plan to start a PDI in the first place.

The emotional and altruistic build-up this results in drives the people concerned to reflect on what they themselves could do to help. This usually happens during holidays, professional stays, short-term voluntary work, internships and exchange programmes of students in a development context.

Box 35. Who gets most out of it?

For many, tourism used to be about beaches and beer. But for over several decades now, we have seen an alternative but expanding tourism industry: voluntourism. For Kumaran and Pappas (2012), voluntourism bridges traditional volunteering with traditional tourism, with volunteers providing their services to needy communities in destinations to which they travel. However, they hasten to add that due to the merger of these two major fields, it is not easy to narrowly define voluntourism, especially because other nomenclatures are also used, such as moral tourism, charity tourism, ethical vacation, social tourism, goodwill tourism and leisure travel philanthropy.

Voluntourism options can range in duration from about one or two weeks to multiple months and involve projects ranging from building a school somewhere in rural Guatemala before backpacking the Ruta Maya to caring for a handful of *talibé*, very young Koran students and street-beggars rummaging Mali's capital, back from a trip to the cliffs of Bandiangara and encounters with the Dogon people. Medical voluntourism is widespread among health professionals globally, and many an eye-surgeon has combined a few weeks of cataract operations in Nepal with a trip on Mount Everest. Motivations to take up a volunteer vacation are varied. Since most voluntourists are youngsters from affluent backgrounds, for some it is a give-back operation. It figures well on their resumés and might boost their careers. For other do-gooders, it is also a way to immerse themselves in an unknown culture and perfect their command of a local language, or a post-modern and explicit rejection of today's mass tourism.

Voluntourism has become a multi-billion-dollar business involving specialised tour operators, travel agencies, social enterprises, non-profit organisations, NGDOs and university campuses. It is clearly a fertile breeding ground for new PDIs and other fourth pillar organisations.

Research, both in the Netherlands and Belgium, indicates that most activities taken up by PDIs are geared towards the improvement of the living conditions of a particular group of people: a well-defined community such as the inhabitants of a slum area, street children, orphans, young girls or illiterate women. In this, they take another angle than traditional development workers who make unabated efforts and systematic claims to make structural changes for many, if not all; thus, they are life improvers versus world improvers. The intervention methodology of many small development organisations is iterative and development practice is discovered *on cours de route*: step by step. There is no preconceived plan. This is more often than not an explicit choice. The 'man' is central in the philosophy of the vast majority of PDIs, not the 'plan', which is the favoured reference and pivot for conventional development workers.

As Appe and Telch (2020) conclude, it is the personal not the professional that drives private development aid, while conventional agencies and individual development workers pat themselves on the back specifically because of their experience and professionalism. Small, fourth pillar organisations have an explicit preference for visible, concrete quick wins that show immediate results. They build schools, orphanages and clinics, dig wells, install solar energy panels, deliver teaching materials, and provide medicines and medical equipment. They are output focused, rather than outcome or impact oriented, much to the irritation of the conventional actors who, for some time now, are convinced of the need for an impact-oriented approach.

When one engages in a discussion on fourth pillar organisations, and especially PDIs, with conventional development professionals or adherents of traditional development cooperation, the debate indeed soon becomes very snappy, even heated and emotional. Revealingly, the discussions revolve around issues that have always been present in the development cooperation community and arena.

We can distinguish at least two sets of problems signalled by the traditional players: one relating to the legitimacy of these Lilliputian newcomers, another concerning the rapport between recipient and donor.

The first criticism fired in the direction of PDIs concerns the legitimacy of the intervention and the intervening agency. They are not (yet) part of the development cooperation community, so they do not know what the values, norms and standards are of this well-established community, and their set of beliefs and frame of reference may be incongruent with those of the conventional development community. For example, as we have seen, they often neglect the structural causes of poverty and are – allegedly – putting a plaster on a wooden leg. Their projects even hinder domestic and international social, economic and political changes that otherwise could fundamentally alter the oppressive power relations that generate poverty. So, what right do they have to step in? Development cooperation in essence means cooperation, but PDIs excel in working in splendid isolation. In addition, to what extent are their practices regulatorily acceptable? Do they conform to regulatory institutions, rules and laws? Do they work in close collaboration with local authorities: something you would expect looking at their social service portfolio? Kinsbergen (2019), who interviewed local government officials in Kwale County in Kenya, found that, in general, these civil servants concluded that from a normative and pragmatic point of view, the Dutch PDIs operating in the county can be considered legitimate players because of the huge and diverse demands in the region. However, aligning their operations with the priorities and policies of the local authorities might be a problem.

Remember the Paris Agreement on Aid Effectiveness and how traditional donors still struggle with the same challenge.

The 2005 Paris Agreement was, first and foremost, about turning the tide: to get rid of the despised and ineffective culture of donorship and allow for the more politically correct, effective and genuine option of ownership. The recipient country or partner organisation, following the Paris recipe, is in the driving seat, writes the overall script, determines its own development strategy and invites development partners to make a contribution. This is considered demand-driven development cooperation. Private development initiatives are accused of introducing a renewed culture of donorship in which the Northern philanthropist takes the lead, determines the goals of the operation, and the mode and practice of implementation. In addition, in the community of small fourth pillar organisations, concrete experience in the North is considered valid and becomes a 'me and us' story instead of a 'them and them' story. They talk, at the same time, about 'my project' and 'our project' (Develtere & Stessens, 2007). Critics would argue that the discourse on co-ownerships hides an asymmetric *rapport de force* in favour of the donor, while at the same time creating perpetual dependency and, thus, limited prospects for the financial and operational sustainability of the activities undertaken. Here, we come close to the founder syndrome, the known phenomenon that an activity, project or organisation does not survive the departure of the initiator. But did we not see before that conventional donors are also increasingly seeking to become players again and not just payers? Are they not tempted to again set the agenda and take the initiative in the policies, projects and programmes they temporarily agree to financially support?

Box 36. The saviour complex

'White saviour complex' is a term encapsulating the cultural practice of people travelling to foreign areas as aid workers, or making a donation, for that matter, with the conviction that they can and will save entire communities from all problems, even those with which they themselves are unfamiliar. There might be good intentions behind such endeavours but, as Li (2018) asserts, we must ask ourselves: at what cost are we doing this, and for whose benefit? Which stereotypes are we promoting? What narrative are we playing into?

Already in 2012, the famous writer Teju Cole (2012), in a sharp and controversial article in *The Atlantic*, warned of the white saviour industrial complex, saying we should act with "awareness of what else is involved. If we are going to interfere in the lives of others, a little due diligence is a minimum requirement".

The saviour complex, though, is not a prerogative of Westerners who believe in helping people who cannot help themselves. Yang (2019) undertook a critical dissection of China's 'civilising project', which includes a series of attempts by the majority and dominant Chinese Han group to bring the benefits and responsibilities of their purportedly superior civilisation to the inferior Tibetan people. For example, since 2015, China has established a programme of 'Group Form of Educational Aid for Tibet' to dispatch ethnic Han majority teachers from inland cities to teach in Tibetan schools for a short period of time. Through the programme, the state aims to offer the gift of educational development to this highland area with a concentrated Tibetan minority population. Yang's analyses on the narratives of the aid-Tibet teachers revealed a multi-layered 'saviour complex' parallel to the 'white saviour complex' in Western societies: the superior aids the inferior, the advanced aids the backward.

The dangers of the saviour complex are profound. The recipient of 'help' can internalise the idea that they, and the community they are part of, are less civilized, incapable and in need of rescue and perpetual support. In the longer run, the saviour complex contributes to epistemological monoculture and epistemicide, destroying local knowledge systems by imposing other ones.

The trade unions: a win-win situation for employees

When talking to older trade unionists about development cooperation, many will remind you that international solidarity was an important component of the trade union movement, long before development cooperation emerged. In its early years, organised labour had already internalised the 'politics of connectivity' – seeking change in one particular spatial scale by taking action in another (Vlaminck & Huyse, 2021). However, for a long time, ODA played only a small role in the international solidarity of trade unions, as most donors had a preference for NGDOs as international do-gooders over their 'radical' counterparts (Edwards, 2014).

The situation started changing from the 1990s onwards, due to a mix of drivers (Vlaminck & Huyse, 2021). First, the dwindling membership of trade unions in developing countries after years of neoliberal market policies increased the pressure for unions to look for alternative sources of funding. Secondly, in the same period, several donors in Western Europe gradually started opening up their ODA channels for trade unions after a number of high-level events called for the systematic incorporation of working conditions into the development agenda, further strengthened by the ILO's decent work agenda. Finally, the donor hype around the role of the private sector in development also triggered fresh calls for trade unions to play a significant role in ensuring economic growth would be inclusive and redistributive. The increased attention to decent work is also visible in the SDGs, specifically SDG 8, which underscores the importance of the decent work agenda.

A great deal of support for the union movement in the South has traditionally come from the Scandinavian countries, the USA, Germany, the Netherlands, the UK and Belgium.

Trade union development cooperation is based on a number of dimensions. Some forms can be regarded as development cooperation in the strict sense, while others are better labelled as international cooperation, with an important international economic and political significance. Although this is not often associated with development cooperation, we will take a brief look at it, as it constitutes the framework within which the trade unions organise their development cooperation.

One important lever for trade union development cooperation is the large international umbrella organisation, the International Trade Union Confederation (ITUC), and the 11 global unions which bring together national trade unions from different sectors and occupational groups. The ITUC, the product of a merger between the International Confederation of Free Trade Unions and the World Confederation of Labour in 2006, represents more than 200 million workers in 163 countries and territories. The endorsement of a development cooperation agenda as an important component of ITUC's international operations was gradual: only in 2006 were development cooperation and capacity building ranked among the political priorities, calling for "new trade union internationalism".[52] At the same Congress, the ITUC also created new working methods and structures to strengthen its work in this area. It called on "the ITUC to adopt working methods and practices which will put it in the best position to confront the challenges facing trade unions worldwide and to implement this programme of work". In 2008, the Trade Union Development Cooperation Network (TUDCN) was created. The network has "an open and inclusive structure, based on voluntary commitments of the cooperating organizations. It is composed of organizations active in development cooperation both in the Global North and South. The mandate of TUDCN is based on two interlinked dimensions: support the trade unions positions and views in development cooperation policies; and, secondly, enhancing trade union development cooperation effectiveness, bringing greater 'coordination of trade union development cooperation'" (TUDCN, 2011).

Modern, international network trade unionism brings national trade unions into constant contact with colleagues in the Third World and the social problems they face. Together, they conduct campaigns such as 'Decent

Work, Decent Life', 'Fair Play at the Olympics' and 'Decisions for life: What working women want'. The ITUC has its own solidarity fund to help trade unions suffering from repression, but most support for trade unions in the Global South is still provided bilaterally.

Box 37. International framework agreements

Trades unions have instruments other than money and technical advice at their disposal with which to address social and labour problems in the South. International framework agreements are one example. By 2018, 115 such agreements had been signed by multinational companies and the international trade union movement (Hadwiger, 2018). As a result, millions of workers are, in theory, better protected because their employers have agreed to respect fundamental labour rights in every country where the company operates. However, studies have shown that there is still a long way to go. Workers in developing countries rarely know that their companies have entered into such an agreement, subcontractors often fall outside its scope, it is not easy to process complaints and monitoring compliance is time consuming and complex, and not a priority for many multinationals.

The ITUC has advisory status to the UN's Economic and Social Council and specialised institutions such as UNESCO and the FAO. In recent years, it has also maintained frequent contact with the World Bank, the IMF and the WTO, but the most important lever for the trade unionists' international strategy is the ILO. Every year, trade unions take part in the International Labour Conference. During the conference, which is attended by representatives of each member state's government and employers' and workers' organisations, international conventions and recommendations on trade union freedom and social rights are always on the agenda. The ILO decided a few years ago to promote eight 'core labour standards': freedom of association, the right to organise, collective bargaining, the elimination of forced and compulsory labour, minimum age, the abolition of the worst forms of child labour, equal remuneration and the elimination of discrimination in the workplace.

Box 38. Trade unions and NGDOs

In many countries, mutual interest between trade unions and NGDOs is growing. Until recently, the relationship was much tenser. In a special issue of *Development in Practice* devoted to the subject, Deborah Eade (2004) stated that relations between trade unions and NGDOs had long been characterised (and often still are) by ignorance, mistrust, rivalry and, at times, open hostility. There are various reasons for this. Trade unions have a sociological or class basis that is different from that of NGDOs, which means that they have a different organisational culture. Trade unions are mandated organisations on which members and grassroots activists have a significant impact. NGDOs often have little contact with their grassroots and, as a result, are able to speak out more quickly and freely. Trade unions defend a number of general social principles but do so by standing for private interests, whereas NGDOs usually stand for public interests.

Although the two groups have drawn closer, tensions remain. Thus, the international trade union movement believes that it gets few opportunities to participate fully in international development programmes and initiatives, unlike NGDOs. Trade unions are also disturbed when NGDOs implement projects or set up advocacy campaigns in core areas of the labour movement, without involving organised labour. Multistakeholder initiatives between business and NGDOs can be a typical area of friction, especially when NGDOs speak on behalf of workers in a sector or negotiate with business on workers' issues.

The increased encapsulation of international trade union solidarity work into development cooperation brings its own challenges in those cases where genuine trade union work is replaced by donor-driven agendas, managerialism and projects with short timelines (leading to stop-and-go dynamics). The trade union movement is confronted with the challenge of moving beyond projects driven by resource- and capacity-building logics, in order to achieve the true transformative potential of trade union development cooperation (Vlaminck & Huyse, 2021).

The farmers' movement: the call and challenges of globalisation

Traditional development cooperation actors, especially NGDOs, are deeply sceptical of the Western farmers' movement. There is a firmly rooted idea that the Western farmers' movement has corporatist instincts which are partly responsible for creating the global crisis on the food market and the lack of food security and sovereignty in developing countries. The NGDOs' strategy has long consisted of exposing and complaining about the dysfunctionalities and perverse effects of the world food market. European and American agricultural policy is lambasted because it does not give farmers from the developing world the opportunity to bring their produce onto their own home markets and export it to the Western market at reasonable prices. The same farmers' organisations and, by extension, the entire Western food sector, is accused of dumping subsidised food on unprotected markets in the South, suffocating small local farmers unable to compete with international big business. However, many NGDOs started supporting farmers' unions and organisations in developing countries in the 1990s.

The new respect for the farmers' organisations in the last 10 to 15 years is related to a structural trend. The agricultural agreement that came into effect with the establishment of the WTO in 1995 definitively changed the position of the farmers' unions. Europe shifted its policy from price support to direct subsidies (e.g., per hectare, per pig) and recently to a 'farm to fork strategy' "for a fair, healthy and environmentally-friendly food system". Farmers' organisations have become enmeshed in an intricate tangle of conflicts of interest between North and South, between the USA and Europe, between farmers and the food industry, between national food companies (including farmers' cooperatives) and multinational companies, between the call for good but safe food and the protection of farmers' social status and income, between environmentally sustainable development and sustainable business for farmers, between the farmers' trade union movement and the NGDO sector and so on.

At the same time, the international farmers' movement repositioned itself as a united global movement. In 2003, AgriCord, a cooperative venture between farmers' organisations and their international cooperation branches ('agri-agencies') from Europe, North America, Asia and Africa, was set up to promote mutual support between farmers' organisations. Since then, and with the financial backing of different bilateral and multilateral aid agencies, AgriCord has stimulated exchanges between farmers' organisations on rural development strategies, promoted expertise sharing amongst its members on, for example, farmer-to-farmer extension work, set up training seminars for agricultural leaders from the North and South, supported efforts to develop value chains, advanced the idea of long-lasting twinning arrangements between farmers' organisations and deployed joint lobby and advocacy initiatives that defend the interests of farmers worldwide.

The fundamentals of this type of international collective action are, of course, very much shaped by the evolving nature of globalisation. One of the characteristics of the current wave of globalisation is the blurring of the boundaries between different types of actors, such as local public agencies, (cooperative) enterprises, NGOs and social movements, that operate both locally and transnationally. These players, once firmly embedded or even locked into their own category, now increasingly borrow narratives, vocabulary, organisational principles and action models from other kinds of organisations they previously rejected. This even leads to hybrid forms of organisations that do not want to be reduced to one of the traditional categories. In many countries, we see the emergence and vocal position-ing of NGOs, for example, that distance themselves from the once-despised professional-based and money-oriented NGO community and that present themselves as an activists-based and ideals-oriented 'people's movement' (T. Brown, 2014). This is why Donatella Della Porta (2020), a world-famous scholar on social movements and civil society, advances the idea that next to the NGO-isation of social movements, the known fact that established social movements borrow characteristics and strategies from NGOs, atten-tion should also be given to the inspiration NGOs get from social move-ments organisations, which she calls the SMO-isation of civil society. At the international level, this blurring of boundaries translates into ever-more ad hoc and permanent international collective action and coalitions involving different types of CSOs, hybrid forms of organisations and engaged individ-uals linked to public authorities and the media. This challenges the interna-tional farmers' movement that still adheres to a rather strict member-based movement model and often radically criticisies and rejects the NGO-model and heterogeneous coalitions.

Box 39. For the dignity of small farmers

Deogratias Niyonkuru (2018), who lived with peasants in the Congo, Cameroon and Burundi for over 30 years and founded the association Appui au Développement Intégral et à la Solidarité sur les Collines in Burundi, is one of those outspoken, char-ismatic leaders who defend the dignity of the small farmers in Africa and sees local NGOs, associations and cooperatives as powerful vehicles for endogenous peasant social movements. In his book *Pour la dignité paysanne*, he concludes: "The best way, at the same time simple and difficult, is to take back self-confidence, to value one's own culture, one's potential and the opportunities offered by one's environ-ment, to refuse to let money be the engine of development. Let us give primacy to spirituality and human values. Let us refuse a civilisation that is founded on the frantic enrichment of the few and leads to the irreversible degradation of natural resources. Let us demand public policies that are favourable to development and peace at the same time. Let us stop believing that others are responsible for our miseries or salvation, and let us resolutely work towards transforming our lives with the divine message: 'Get up and walk'. Get up, African peasant!"

Modern-day globalisation is indisputably affected and stimulated by the decentralising effects of social and other media. In this new world, pur-poseful and flexible, but equally haphazard, interactions take precedence over hierarchical and systemically organised patters of relations. This again challenges the international farmers' movement, as much as other CSOs, as we see time and again in this book, with its desire to form a well-organised, respected, unified and coherent actor. The international farmers' movement creates its own reactions to this galloping process of decentralisation and hyper-interaction. The opportunities AgriCord and other platforms create for farmers and related organisations to meet, exchange, reflect together and experiment with innovative ways of working together lead to new initiatives that often remain close to but escape the social control mechanisms of the established movement. In this way, Access Agriculture, for example, presents itself as an international and expanding "group of passionate people devoted to promoting effective agricultural training videos for the benefit of farmers and rural businesses" worldwide. This not-for-profit venture collaborates with more than 200 communications professionals across the globe and claims that from 2013 to 2018, over three million farmers watched Access Agriculture videos during screenings, on DVD or on their mobiles. With 44 TV stations across the South broadcasting their videos, over 60 million watched some of the programmes on TV and many more listened to radio broadcasts.

Future research has to show how many new collaborations, North and South, and within the South, have grown out of these virtual interactions and thus further given stimulus to the expanding fourth pillar.

Box 40. The OVOP movement: One Village One Product

In 1979, the One Village One Product movement was launched under the charismatic leadership of the then-governor of the Oita prefecture in Japan. The movement encourages people to select one product in their rural village or region that will then be promoted nationally and globally. The core ideas of this movement are 'think global, act local', self-help and creativity, and human development. The movement has now broken through at the international level and taken root in numerous developing countries: first in Asia, later in Africa and Latin America. With support from the Japanese development agency JICA, tens of thousands of people from developing countries have now attended courses in Oita. Experts with hands-on experience from the OVOP movement give on-the-spot advice to villages in far-flung corners of the Philippines or Lesotho and look at how 'local treasures' such as dried fish, porcelain, soap and jam can be turned into internationally valued products.

Evaluations of the 'export' of the Japanese prototype OVOP model show mixed results. Claymone (2011) attributes the failure of the introduction of the model in

Thailand to a top-down and government-led policy that focused on productivity rather than strengthening the communities involved. Hoang et al. (2018) were much more positive and conclude that three years of piloting the adoption of the OVOP strategy in the Quang Ninh province in Vietnam led not only to poverty reduction but also to local creativity, capacity enhancement and an increase in social capital.

Health insurance operators: ensuring access to healthcare

For a number of years now, an international network movement that promotes access to healthcare for the world's poor has arisen. As a network movement, it is a loose coalition of stakeholders that take on different positions in civil society, political circles, national and international agencies and business. Forging alternating collaborative arrangements between themselves, their projects and programmes, experiments, conferences and seminars, advocacy and lobby work and other collective forms of mobilisation demonstrate that there is a tremendous injustice done to the world's majority poor due to the lack of access to affordable and qualitative healthcare. At the same time, they argue and provide evidence that there are effective and impactful ways to remedy the situation. The main protagonists of this movement are European and North American CSOs such as mutual not-for-profit insurance organisations, health maintenance organisations, NGOs, big insurance corporations, research centres, microfinance institutions, official development agencies and international organisations. National policymakers and homegrown organisations, such as federations of mutual health insurance organisations, micro-insurance institutions, healthcare providers and healthcare rights activists in many developing countries have joined the ranks of this international network.

Their interest in the accessibility of healthcare services in Africa, Asia and Latin America was provoked by a number of developments in the health sector in the developing world and the explicit demand from development actors for support and expertise. In the late 1980s, important international organisations such as the World Bank, the WHO and UNICEF reformulated their policies with regard to the health sector. They dropped the idea that a welfare state based on the Western model was possible; the resource-poor developing countries were regarded as incapable of offering free high-quality healthcare to all classes of the population. The Bamako initiative launched by the WHO and UNICEF in 1987 meant, among other things, that patients had to contribute to healthcare costs themselves via so-called 'users' fees', representatives of local communities had to participate in the running of local health centres ('primary healthcare') and preference was to be given to generic and basic drugs.

In many cases, access to healthcare grew worse. Patients were not in a position to pay for the services and drugs needed, let alone able to make the additional illicit under-the-counter payments demanded by underpaid health workers. Use of health services continued to decline because of the substandard quality of the services offered.

With the technical and financial support of Western mutual healthcare organisations, NGDOs and national and international agencies (such as the ILO and the WHO), projects and programmes were launched to experiment with different forms of member-based and not-for-profit social insurance mechanisms. This happened simultaneously in Africa, Asia and Latin America and they were given various names, the most popular of which were 'community health insurance', 'mutual health insurance' and 'health micro-insurance' (Soors et al., 2010).

In 1999, the ILO launched the global programme Strategies and Tools against Social Exclusion and Poverty in close collaboration with the mutual health insurance sector in Europe and NGDOs. For more than a decade, it was one of the most important programmes for the promotion of 'micro-insurance initiatives in healthcare'.

The American development institute PHR, the German GTZ, the Association Internationale de la Mutualité and the French health mutualist movement have also launched support programmes for emerging solidarity-based insurance initiatives in the healthcare sector in developing countries.

With failing states and healthcare systems aggravated by the complete absence of social protection mechanisms in many developing countries, there were and still are particularly high expectations that private solidarity-based and more market-based insurance systems could provide a solution. The variety of models that have been introduced and experimented with is immensely broad. In many cases, aid agencies' traditions and experiences in their own country determine the preferred model. There are mutualistic or participatory models, provider-managed models, prepayment models and micro-credit schemes that include insurance packages for healthcare costs coverage. Mutualist methodologies based on member-based and member-run social insurance enterprises that trigger solidarity mechanisms when a member has to pay for healthcare services are promoted by European mutual insurers, who often act as donors or partners providing training to start-up mutual insurance initiatives in the developing countries and/or invest with initial kick-off or revolving funds. Provider-run and prepayment models are, in many cases, inspired by or even promoted by existing health maintenance organisations (HMO) as they exist, for example, in the USA. As an insurer, an HMO covers care rendered by medical professionals who treat patients as agreed by contract and in exchange for a steady stream of clients. In recent years, a number of large American HMOs have discovered the rapidly expanding demand for quality healthcare in emerging markets and established themselves in countries such as Nigeria. Nonetheless, some remain under national control. This is the case, for example, of the Brazilian UNIMED, a medical work cooperative and health insurance operator, which has more than 100,000 affiliated doctors and more than 15 million beneficiaries. The Bangladesh micro-finance bank, Grameen Bank, works with a health insurance plan for the banks' borrowers and offers community-based health centres and satellite clinics to ensure quality services. Through the Grameen Foundation, the Grameen Bank has become a world-known advocate of this model, combining microfinance, micro-insurance and healthcare services in many countries. Both in Bangladesh and abroad, it is also active in and experiments with innovative uses of information technology. Member-customers who have a mobile phone receive healthy lifestyle messages and healthcare workers get reminders about patients' schedules to help them better manage their caseloads.

The micro-insurance landscape has evolved enormously in recent years. Micro-insurance has become a recognised business model that regards poor people not only as bankable (Dowla & Barua, 2006) but also insurable. Many schemes are market driven, rely on brokers and agents or are run by mobile network operators. But microfinance institutions and cooperative, community-based and mutual insurance organisations also play a very important role in micro-insurance set-up and distribution (Merry, 2019).

Most observers have noted steady though not spectacular growth in the sector (Churchill, 2006). Still, the World Map of Microinsurance of the German Munich Re Foundation[53] shows that micro-insurance for health is making significant inroads in countries such as Ghana, Ecuador and Mauritius.

Box 41. More than micro for the masses

The international network movement promoting access to healthcare has been branching out and grown more ambitious. The lobby and advocacy work of the constituents of this movement, in coalition with anti-poverty and social rights movements, has been instrumental in bringing the right to social protection high on the international agenda. The 2030 SDGs include reference to social protection in no less than five goals. This broader movement relies on adherents and active constituents from the trade union movement, women's movement, child rights movement, social solidarity economy movement, NGDOs and many others. Strategies and tactics are deployed at the national, regional and international level. In the Dominican Republic, for example, the national network has managed to introduce minimum security standards into law. In Nepal, the network is the co-author of the new social security law, which extends social security coverage to workers in the informal economy. In Africa, the continental network is a recognised interlocutor of the AU and the West African Economic and Monetary Union.

Companies: money, markets and morals

The business sector has always had a very ambiguous relationship with development cooperation. On the one hand, it is interested in development cooperation as a market and seeks to appropriate part of its turnover. Official cooperation, NGDOs and multilateral actors have no alternative but to turn to the business sector for the supply of goods and services such as medicines, vehicles and logistical support. In doing so, the traditional development cooperation players accept that business is motivated by profit-seeking, not altruism. Moreover, they want the relationship to be conducted under market conditions as much as possible so that they can procure goods and services cheaply.

On the other hand, the business sector also presents itself as a lever, catalyst or even driver of development and development cooperation. As an analogy to economic and social development in mature market economies, reference is made to the essential and central role of businesses in initiating and injecting dynamism into the economy in developing countries. Who has better credentials in this area than businesses in the rich countries, which made the whole thing happen? Why should the business sector itself and the government not dedicate resources to ensuring that businesses can achieve development goals? So go the arguments.

The traditional development cooperation actors view this ambivalent position on the part of the business sector with suspicion. Profit and development goals are incompatible, they argue. When it comes down to it, the development objective is subordinate to the profit objective. Some NGDO circles have become so sensitive to the development-impeding role of businesses that they have evolved into non-business organisations.

The business sector has undeniably redefined its position and role in development cooperation. In connection with this, a number of causes and trends can be identified.

The business world's image took a severe knock in the mid-1990s when it became clear that quite a lot of development cooperation money was being invested on the basis not of the needs in partner countries but of the short-term interests of specific companies headquartered in rich countries. This gave rise to a process of 'untying' development cooperation in various donor countries. Strategies for this gradual un-coupling of development aid from commercial interests in the donor countries were devised within the OECD-DAC and World Bank circles.

Vulture funds 'preyed' on private and sovereign debtors facing financial problems and purchased their distressed debts much below their nominal value on a secondary market to later resell them at great profit. This tarnished the image of the private financial sector during the sovereign debt crisis of the 1980s and 1990s because it clashed with the efforts of the international community to reduce the debt burden of poor countries at the expense of the donor countries.

It was not only the perverse or even pernicious role of business in development cooperation that was exposed in this period. A fairly broad-based, media-driven movement also arose, which pilloried the role of companies (especially Western and multinational companies) in developing countries. Campaigns such as the Rugmark, Nike, Clean Clothes and 'End the Vulture Culture' campaigns demonstrated that NGDOs had found the weak spot in big companies' and private sector image-building. The new rallying cry became 'consumer power is social power' and NGDOs developed – often alongside other actors such as the consumer or trade union movement – a 'corpwatch' practice, as a result of which businesses could continually feel them breathing down their necks.

Box 42. Philip Morris International: the smoke screen of corporate social responsibility

Despite being over 170 years old, Philip Morris International (PMI), best known for its Marlboro brand, only became involved in development in 2011, when the multinational company launched its Agricultural Labour Practices programme. PMI decided to progressively eliminate child labour practices and all types of labour abuse on its tobacco farms, while also promoting better living conditions in communities where the tobacco for its products was grown. Later, in 2015, PMI joined the UN Global Compact and committed itself to the UN SDGs. At the same time, PMI somehow paradoxically pledged to work for global human health, thus lowering cigarette sales and instead shifting to smoke-free products. This is currently the main mission PMI portrays: delivering a "smoke-free future" by developing vaporisers and systems that heat tobacco instead of burning it like traditional cigarettes.

In 2017, PMI also created the Foundation for a Smoke-free World. Recently, PMI became a member of the Society for International Development (Igoe, 2019).

PMI focuses its development efforts on education, women's empowerment, economic opportunities, deforestation and disaster relief. All of these initiatives are part of the multinational's corporate social responsibility strategy. This boils down to the idea that helping communities you are involved in will, in the short term, strengthen your position as a company: thus, a win-win. Critics from NGDOs, civil society activists, the media and academics often point to the inherently selfish corporate reaction this can generate.

In China, the largest producer and consumer of tobacco products worldwide, for example, PMI has a partnership with the state-controlled China National Tobacco Company. The schools that were built in rural areas, which this Chinese company and PMI invested in, have become the subject of much controversy. Tobacco control activists have concluded that the schools serve as sources of indirect pro-tobacco propaganda aimed at children (Fang, Wan & Yang, 2018). Many of these schools have the companies' logos on their walls and one is even called the Sichuan Tobacco Hope Primary School. This results in the general population having positive views towards tobacco products and being blind to their harmful effects. "Tobacco schools built by the tobacco industry go as far as using slogans promoting smoking, such as: 'genius is from hard work; tobacco helps you excel'" (Fang, 2019).

However, as several observers have argued (Heap, 2000; Jamali & Keshishian, 2009, Darko, 2014), not all NGDOs have developed an antagonistic relationship with the business sector; some sharply critical at first have since attenuated their confrontational and adversarial style, and some exhibit a more favourable collaborative inclination since the adoption of the corporate social responsibility principles by many businesses. Some NGDOs have opted for a 'neutral' strategy; for example, by looking for routes towards a more positive contribution from businesses in the framework of government-run and multi-stakeholder-monitored programmes. Another category prefers 'cooperative' collaboration with business and attempts to change corporate policy and practices from within. Thus, NGDOs may attempt to raise funds within one or more businesses and try to involve those businesses, their managers or their personnel in selecting, carrying out and monitoring the supported projects.

Influenced by the trend towards corporate social responsibility, a number of businesses have not waited to be prompted by the NGDO sector to redefine their position and role with regard to development cooperation. Many companies have set up business foundations to plough part of their profits back into society, among other things by supporting projects or programmes in developing countries. Some do this directly. Business philanthropy can go even further; certain businesses have found their way into cause-related marketing or emotional marketing. They adopt public standpoints on controversial themes (the arms trade, sustainable development etc.) or present themselves as ethical, environmentally friendly or developing country-friendly businesses. Others launch 'personnel volunteer programmes', in which employees' efforts on behalf of a good cause (often a development project) are rewarded by, for example, funding the ticket for a project visit or paying an employee's salary during a month of voluntary work in Malawi.

In the last decades, most bilateral donor institutions have also developed instruments to encourage the private sector to play a role in development cooperation. Many have set up special agencies to promote private sector involvement in development work. Schulpen and Gibbon (2002) discovered similar strategies on the part of most donors, which also raised similar questions. The link between the private sector's goals with regard to development cooperation and the goal of other development cooperation actors (i.e., poverty alleviation) is highly abstract and theoretical. But the incoherence they found was not just confined to the content of the work. The free-standing status of the agencies that are supposed to carry out development work from within the private sector ensures idiosyncratic procedures and working methods which do not always coincide with those of the rest of the development cooperation sector. This makes coordination and harmonisation difficult. The instruments and methods used mean that countries from the middle-income group are the main ones to benefit because they have the best starting positions for private sector investments. Moreover, it tends to be the businesses in those countries that are already relatively effective which are able to attract investment and support. The amounts involved are often fairly large (for the sector). Finally, most programmes opt for a series of standard inputs, which are presumed to be relevant in every developing country. The starting point is not the strengths and weaknesses of the private sector in the chosen poor countries, but the instrument available for use.

The UN likewise encourages the business sector to express its responsibility towards the developing world not just by putting part of its profits back into society but also by making its business policies and profit-seeking socially responsible.

For example, the Global Compact initiative of former UN Secretary-General Kofi Annan seeks to involve businesses in the challenges of globalisation. Thousands of companies all over the world are now engaging in the initiative on a purely voluntary basis – the engagement does not involve any legally binding measures. Global Compact simply asks businesses to respect and implement certain values in the areas of human rights, labour rights, the environment and tackling corruption. In this way, the private sector can help build a more sustainable and inclusive global economy. In recent years, the idea has also been circulating in UN corridors that the four billion poor possess a huge amount of 'dormant capital' (de Soto, 2000) and that at the bottom of the pyramid are numerous creative entrepreneurs and value-conscious consumers with whom business can profitably be done (Prahalad, 2006). In a report, the UNDP (2008) uses numerous case studies to demonstrate that the private sector can work step by step to overcome the many obstacles to doing business with the poor. Private businesses need to collaborate with governments, donors, NGDOs and philanthropists in order to do so. For example, the products and services that are provided need to be adapted to the poor. The government has to be persuaded that poor people need legal ownership of their land and homes before they are able to take risks. For example, poor people cannot get a loan from the bank if they are unable to provide evidence that they have a legally recognised dwelling-place. Moreover, poor people have a good knowledge of the local market and brilliant ideas. Who else but poor people in Mauritania would have imagined that there is a market for camel's milk and derivative products?

Cooperatives: working together for social justice

The cooperative movement claims to be one of the oldest social movements in the world, having roots in the British consumer cooperatives, the so-called Rochdale tradition that got off the ground in the mid-19th century, the German rural savings cooperatives, the Raiffeisen tradition that first spread in mainland Europe in the same period, and the credit unions that started the successful penetration of North America a few decades later. Already during colonial times, cooperatives and similar social and member-based enterprises were considered appropriate vehicles for the economic and social uplifting of the rural and urban poor and other sections of the population in Africa, Asia and Latin America (Develtere, Pollet & Wanyama, 2008). After independence, support for a cooperative alternative did not wane. On the contrary. The result is a broad movement representing over three million cooperative enterprises worldwide with a membership base of more than 10% of the world's population (World Cooperative Monitor, 2020).

Up to today, the promotion of cooperative enterprises has been taken very seriously both by NGDOs and many bilateral and multilateral organisations. In 2002, the ILO adopted a Recommendation on the Promotion of Cooperatives (No. 193) at its annual conference. In it, the ILO called, among other things, for more collaboration on the part of cooperatives from the North with their counterparts from the South. The UN had also declared 2012 to be the 'International Year of Cooperatives', stressing the unique contributions of cooperatives to socioeconomic development. Time and again, the UN has reiterated its recognition of the role of cooperatives, most recently in the realisation of the 2030 Agenda for Sustainable Development. Every year, on the first Saturday of July, the world cooperative movement celebrates the International Day for Cooperatives.

In various countries, the cooperative movement itself in fact has a long tradition of international cooperation. There are the great pioneering examples from the USA, such as Land O'Lakes and the National Cooperative Business Association, but in countries such as Sweden, Germany, Italy, Great Britain, Spain, Canada and Japan, cooperatives have likewise been working for years to build up a cooperative sector in developing countries. The nature of their contributions has varied hugely and is largely influenced by the fact that they themselves are businesses, albeit ones with a social and participatory tradition, and thus have corporate social responsibility in their DNA. Although the Northern cooperatives also give technical assistance to their partners in the South, such assistance tends to lay more stress on business aspects than it does with other actors (such as government or NGDOs). The Canadian cooperative bank Desjardin, for example, has a worldwide reputation for its support for the development of cooperative banking institutions.

Box 43. From cooperating out of poverty to #coops4dev

In the 1970s and 1980s, the cooperatives in Africa were particularly strongly supported. Their governments firmly believed that cooperatives were better adapted to the local culture. Donors – and especially the World Bank and the Scandinavian countries – invested massively in the cooperative sector, with generous loans and a lot of technical advice.

Then, the structural adjustment programmes came along and turned everything upside down. The cooperatives in Africa, the World Bank concluded, were not genuine cooperatives. They resembled too much the state enterprises, which were inefficient and politicised. So, support for cooperatives or anything that smacked of government management was withdrawn.

Surprisingly, it turned out that 10 to 15 years later, there was still a dynamic cooperative movement in many African countries (Develtere, Pollet & Wanyama, 2008). Was the neglect an unexpected blessing? There were certainly no fewer cooperative enterprises active on the African continent than there were during the high days of their international popularity.

In 2007, the ILO launched a Cooperative Facility for Africa: CoopAfrica. As the discourse and dominant paradigm of the time dictated, the focus was on poverty reduction: COOP stood for 'cooperating out of poverty'. The programme, again, gave legitimacy to the cooperative model, provided much-needed access to seed money and suggested changes in the legislative environment. Ten years later, the successor programme differs in a number of significant ways from the previous approaches. The new programme, #coops4dev, is not run by an external agency but by the international umbrella body of the cooperative movement, the International Cooperative Alliance (ICA). The programme, supported by the European Commission and ICA members, aims to strengthen the global cooperative movement, North and South, East and West, as a key actor, and cooperatives as a tried-and-tested model in international development. The programme stimulates national and cross-border business cooperation among cooperatives, tries to find out what cooperatives can do to reach younger generations, supports the accelerated uptake of ICT in cooperatives and engages with national and international authorities in the development of appropriate legal and regulatory frameworks. This kind of programme is an attempt to push cooperatives to internationalise in a context of further globalisation and global networking. At the same time, it relies heavily on the assumption that locally rooted cooperatives are needed to foster the stability of local communities facing the negative effects of neoliberal globalisation on local development. This agenda is also pleaded for by several scholars sympathetic to the global cooperative movement and global civil society (e.g., Bretos & Marcuello, 2017).

Many cooperative organisations also have a somewhat different approach from that of other actors when it comes to giving financial support. The Dutch Rabobank, a "triple-A cooperative bank", gives guarantees to financial institutions in developing countries that give loans to farmers and cooperatives that put their coffee, tea, cocoa, fruit or cotton onto the international market via fair trade circuits. From within the international Rabo group, Rabo International Advisory Services also give technical advice to cooperatives and rural banks in developing countries.

One feature that is typical of cooperatives is the attention they pay to the legislative and regulatory framework in developing countries. For example, the German agricultural cooperatives are working to make legislation and government action in a number of Latin American countries more business- and cooperative-friendly. The existence of cooperative shops in some countries also offers numerous possibilities. In the UK, as in Italy and Switzerland, the Co-op shops have become significant vendors of fair-trade products. Co-op is the largest consumer cooperative in the UK, unique in the supermarket sector, with more than 4.5 million active customer members. It is the country's largest convenience seller of fair-trade products. Its bananas are 100% fair trade; the Co-op's own-brand chocolate and sugar range is also 100% fair trade; tea, coffee, wine and flowers are sourced from cooperatives in the South respecting fair-trade principles.

Box 44. Fair trade: an exploitation barometer?

In 2001, a definition of fair trade was adopted by the international fair-trade movement: "Fair trade is a trading partnership, based on dialogue, transparency and respect, that seeks greater equity in international trade. It contributes to sustainable development by offering better trading conditions to, and securing the rights of, marginalized producers and workers, especially in the South."

There are two main fair-trade movements: one in Europe and one in North America. Both are active in the World Fair Trade Organization.

The European Fair Trade Association consists of 11 organisations that import fair trade products into nine European countries. About 50% of the products are sold via traditional fair-trade shops, often known as 'Oxfam shops', but supermarkets are also becoming important channels via which fair-trade products are finding their way to consumers. A sizeable market share has successfully been achieved with certain products such as bananas, coffee and tea.

The Fair Trade Federation is a trading association for North American fair-trade organisations. Presently, there are approximately 250 Federation members, of which a large majority is profit-making.

Whether fair trade can, theoretically, and does, in practice, achieve its intended goals has been hotly debated in academic circles. Dragusanu, Giovannucci and Nunn (2014) conclude on the basis of the existing empirical evidence that fair trade does achieve many of its intended goals, although on a comparatively modest scale relative to the size of national economies. Fair-trade farmers do, on average, receive higher prices, have greater access to credit, perceive their economic environment as being more stable and are more likely to engage in environmentally friendly farming practices.

Research by Anna Milford (2009 has shown that fair trade has rippling effects on the local economy and society. Fair trade destabilises the local cartels that often have power over the farmers because the latter become much more aware of how the market works and of alternative prices and purchasers. Thus, non-members also benefit when wholesalers are obliged to behave more correctly. For these non-members, fair trade functions as an 'exploitation barometer'.

Migrants' remittances: not foreign money

The relationship between migration, development and development cooperation has attracted considerable interest for more than two decades now. This is not surprising when one realises how strong the links are between emigrants and their country of origin, and how much money these migrant communities send home every year. According to the World Bank Remittances Dataset, transfers[54] to low- and middle-income countries reached a record USD 547 billion in 2019, overtaking FDI, up from USD 304 billion 10 years before and, with USD 65 billion 20 years earlier, an eightfold increase in two decades.[55] Many observers believe that the COVID-19 crisis will have a medium- and long-term negative effect on remittances due to declining incomes of migrants. However, this drop might not be as significant as the drop in FDI.

The top five remittance recipient countries are India, China, Mexico, the Philippines and Egypt. All five are middle-income countries. At first sight, the remittances do not look particularly significant. The more than USD 80 billion sent home by the 30 million or so non-resident Indians and other people of Indian origin living all over the world represents just a tiny fraction of the more than USD 10 trillion in GDP generated by the fifth largest economy in the world. Yet it links Indian communities worldwide and opens the door to new cultures, networks and opportunities to millions of people. That USD 80 billion is more than double the FDI inflow and 25 times more than the ODA that India receives. Although poor countries receive far less support from their emigrants, this financial injection can be very significant. Take Haiti and South Sudan, two of the poorest countries in the world. They belong also to the list of the five countries receiving most financial and in-kind transfers as a share of their GDP: 37% and 34%, respectively. They are very aid-dependent countries but are even more remittance dependent. Haiti receives three times more remittances than it gets aid (ODA); South Sudan twice as much.

There is no disputing the fact that migrant communities are much more generous, give to good causes in their host country (De Bruyn & Develtere, 2008) and still send far more money back to their country of origin than is registered. There are many informal networks that make it possible to get funds to the family via travelling relatives and friends, intermediaries and institutions. Reliable data on the volume of these informal transfers do not exist, but studies show that in many countries, informal transactions are far more extensive than formal ones. The advantages for the sending and receiving parties are the speed of transfer, cheapness and simplicity of the deal, avoidance of foreign exchange transactions and efficiency. Most informal systems rely on personal connections, trust, multiple intermediaries or brokers and, increasingly, digital systems. They might offset the drop in the formal remittances observed in the wake of the coronavirus crisis. During the crisis, international remittances increased significantly in Pakistan, for example. Does this have anything to do with the drop in expenses, and thus increased savings, during the Eid-al-Adha (sacrificial feast) or on the occasion of the Haj in a COVID-19 context? Similarly, many African migrants see the COVID-19-crisis as a reason to delve deeper into their pockets to help their families back home; this time through popular but unregistered digital services.

It is almost invariably assumed that migrants and migration have a positive effect on the home country's development chances. However, it is generally accepted in the debate that there can also be negative aspects for the home country. It is usually the more dynamic and better-educated members of the workforce who leave. Before their departure, their own societies have already invested a great deal in them, and they thus leave behind them a deficit in human capital (the brain drain). The vast majority of these emigrants are graduates. A study by the International Organization for Migration (IOM, 2014) showed that medical students already develop strategies to go abroad while being trained at home and it is often the young, with new knowledge, who move. Given that the possibility of migration is so prominent in the collective consciousness, young people prefer training that is suitable for the foreign labour market (health worker, footballer, fashion model or programmer) to any that is useful locally (lawyer, accountant or weaver). Moreover, those who return home, the *remigrants*, have apparently acquired few if any new skills in the host country. Even so, the benefits of migration are believed to outweigh the costs.

Migrant communities maintain preferential ties with their countries, regions and families of origin. Philippine health workers, for example, remit somewhere between 40–50% of their salaries to their home country (IOM, 2014). In their host country, they come into contact with a 'modern' culture in which entrepreneurship and ideas such as human rights are taken seriously. They expand the networks on which the country of origin and the home base can rely to attract investments, acquire knowledge and technology, and tap sources of finance. As well as an emotional link and strong motivation, they also have a long-term commitment, language skills and transcultural baggage – all key elements for sustainable and effective cooperation. But could it be that migrants bear a certain resemblance to Janus, the Roman god with two faces? For example, Devesh Kapur (2007) warns against turning a blind eye to the 'long-distance nationalism' of many migrant communities and their tendency to finance extremist groups in their country of origin.

Thus, there is much discussion in the literature about the pros and cons of remittances. Virtually the only thing that anyone agrees on is that they have a positive effect on the recipient country's balance of payments. But are they not primarily used for private consumption purposes rather than for investment? On the other hand, is that necessarily a problem? After all, increased consumption is a lever for development. But is it not the case that remittances mainly go to well-off families in well-off communities in countries that are not particularly poor?

Box 45. Three-for-one in Mexico

Capital transfers from migrant communities can also have far-reaching political consequences for the home country. Take Mexico: on average, every Mexican receives more than USD 300 per year from abroad. Most of this is received directly from family in the USA. Its political effect should not be underestimated; this support from abroad makes many Mexicans far less dependent on the political bosses who seek to bribe them for votes.

For a number of years, so-called Mexican Hometown Associations have been springing up rapidly across the USA. There are now hundreds of such clubs, financing more than one-fifth of infrastructure work in the Mexican towns concerned. The Mexican government is encouraging this formula via the three-for-for programme (*Iniciativa Ciudadana 3 por 1*). For every dollar that comes from a Hometown Association, the federal authority, as well as state and city authorities, each contributes one themselves. This transnational matching-grant programme does not only add supplementary funds but also makes the infrastructure programmes more transparent and inclusive.

During the last 10 to 20 years, both remittance-receiving countries and development organisations have been trying to optimise and streamline the phenomenon of migrant solidarity (De Bruyn, 2017). With varying success, a number of countries are trying to get migrants, including undocumented migrants, to use official channels for their transactions. Some receiving countries are offering their migrants concessional rates of duty on imports of machinery and equipment, or business training for returning migrants. Several international institutions have supported microfinance organisations and postal services, which are particularly accessible to remittance senders and receivers living in remote areas or which deal with small amounts of money, to enter the remittance market. The International Fund for Agricultural Development's Financing Facility for Remittances, for example, gets subsidies from different donors to support such innovate projects.

Development actors of the first, second and third pillars have drawn attention to the migrant community, and the same applies in reverse. However, it is far from easy to reconcile the two sectors' cultures, goals and methods. This has been discovered by countries such as the Netherlands and France, which have been experimenting for a number of years with formulas for involving the migrant community in development programmes run by the other pillars.

Foundations: the philanthropic revolution

Take a few of the major problems with which developing countries contend and you will find that important foundations are working on them. This has been the case for several decades (Scott, 2003). The Green Revolution, which by introducing new cereal variants ensured an enormous increase in agricultural productivity in India in the 1960s and 1970s, was made possible by research financed by the Rockefeller Foundation (USA). Research into solutions for parasitical and viral diseases such as HIV-Aids, Ebola, hookworm, malaria and yellow fever is largely financed by large foundations such as the Gates Foundation (USA), the Nuffield Foundation (UK) and the Wellcome Trust (UK). Foundations such as the Ford Foundation and the Carter Centre (USA), the Friedrich Ebert Stiftung and the Konrad Adenauer Stiftung (Germany) run and finance democratisation programmes and lobbying by civil organisations such as NGOs, farmers' organisations and trade unions in the South. In 2018, around USD 8 billion was disbursed by the foundation sector, most of it by the 33 largest philanthropic foundations (OECD, 2018; OECD, 2020). In 2019, a total of USD 5 billion, or about half of total foundation development aid, was granted by the Bill and Melinda Gates Foundation. This makes it by far the biggest and most powerful philanthropic provider in the world. It is disbursing more money for development than many mid-sized countries that are members of the DAC (OECD, 2019). The Gates Foundation is followed by the BBVA Microfinance Foundation, the United Postcode Lotteries, the Mastercard Foundation and the Wellcome Trust as the biggest philanthropic organisations in the world.

Foundations are almost always set up by a wealthy individual or by private companies. They usually operate with a starting capital (a gift or bequest), but in many cases, they start fund-raising from the general public or the government after a while. Because of the huge and acute needs brought about by the COVID-19 crisis, some foundations, such as the Ford Foundation, announced that they would borrow in order to increase their capacity to provide grants. Africa remains the most targeted region for foundations. Significantly, almost a quarter of foundation funds are allocated to just five middle-income countries. Ethiopia, Tanzania, Uganda and the Democratic Republic of Congo seem to be the only darlings of the foundations belonging to the LDCs.

The number of foundations is also increasing exponentially in the developing world itself. They reflect changing patterns of globalisation. In countries such as India, Bangladesh, China, Indonesia, South Africa, Kenya and Brazil, foundations have been established to raise funds among the traditional elite, the *nouveau riche*, the burgeoning middle classes, local businesses and branches of multinational companies. As in the USA, philanthropy is increasingly becoming an essential dimension of elite behaviour everywhere. In countries where there is no or just the skeleton of a welfare system, philanthropy cannot just be equated with spontaneous generosity or the desire to help. Philanthropy is a social duty associated with the privileged position of the upper class. Looking for prestige or access to certain social circles is also a factor. Most foundations and charities in developing countries do not engage in cross-border philanthropy but focus on domestic giving. That does not make them small players *per se*. Take the Azim Premji Foundation, which has become the largest philanthropic institution in India. It is named after the tsar of the Indian IT industry, Azim Hashim Premji: the mastermind behind the diversification strategy, from soap to software, of the Indian giant Wipro. From him, the foundation received a gargantuan endowment of over USD 20 billion to invest in the Indian primary education system.

While focusing on the needs of his own country, Premji still became an important trendsetter in international giving. He signed up for The Giving Pledge, a campaign launched in 2010 by mega-donors Bill Gates and Warren Buffet, to encourage high-net-worth individuals all over the world to make a commitment to give away most of their wealth to good causes.

In recent years, we see more and more Southern foundations and philanthropists going international. The One Foundation, formally known as the Shenzhen One Charity Fund, was established in 2011 and focuses on child welfare and the training of welfare professionals, mostly in Asia. The Tata Trust, linked to the Indian Tata multinational conglomerate, has, in recent years, intentionally metamorphosed from a traditional and modest grant giver to an important vector of change in fields such as healthcare, nutrition and digital transformation. The Senegalese singer Youssou N'Dour has put his weight behind open-source software technologies for health workers in

Africa and supports UNICEF as an ambassador. The retired great NBA star Dikembe Mutambo financed a hypermodern hospital in a poverty-striking district near Ndjili in his country of origin, the Democratic Republic of Congo. The Sudanese-British businessman Mohammed Ibrahim through his Mo Ibrahim Foundation has been the standard-setter on the quality of governance in Africa since 2006. The Argentinian football star Diego Maradona established his own foundation in 2012 to galvanise his charitable activities in sports, arts, education and social action.

Box 46. The power of philanthrocapitalism

"It's kind of the best of capitalism", Bill Gates said about the Giving Pledge (Albrecht, 2020). But criticism is mounting because charitable giving is made possible by inequalities and other social injustices maintained under the pressure of the same powerful class that is showing off its generosity. The presumed largesse and unselfishness are accompanied by generous tax deductions in many countries. The wealth and stature of big foundations make them part of the system that must be changed if real progress on some of the world's greatest challenges is to be made, some argue (Levine, 2020).

Philanthrocapitalism, some scholars and other critics state, is not only the expression or by-product of a liberal market economy gone astray; the argument goes that it also perverts the international mechanisms that deal with it. This has been most documented in the sway of foundations over the agenda and *modus operandi* of global health. Birn (2014), for example, illustrates how the Rockefeller Foundation was already the *de facto* international health leader before World War II and later imposed its techno-biological paradigm on the WHO.

We have seen earlier how foundations such as the Gates Foundation have become the second-most important financier of the WHO. This foundation and many other ones are also vital financial and ideological supporters of a wide array of disease- and therapy-specific programmes, such as the Global Fund to Fight Aids, TB and Malaria and Gavi or the Vaccine Alliance. Although they more recently embrace the idea of health system strengthening, these programmes have been criticized for having negative impacts on already strained country health systems (Storeng, 2014). While they focus on targeted technical solutions with clear, measurable outcomes, they are said to impose techno-managerial approaches, disrupt the policy and planning processes of recipient countries, syphon off human and other local resources that were earmarked for a more holistic and appropriate public health policy and, thus, hinder or debilitate poor countries' healthcare systems.

The case is not closed, it seems. It is, by now, acknowledged that new actors, and especially financially well-endowed foundations, have a considerable effect on the rest of the sector and even alter the field of development cooperation altogether.

Nonetheless, others look at the flipside and discover that penetrating a field like development cooperation with a strong set of norms and principles also has a homogenising effect on all concerned: the conventional actors as well as the new ones. Fejerskov (2015), for example, argues that the Bill and Melinda Gates Foundation has progressed from a state of intentional isolation to one of actively engaging in and adhering to the field's norm and principle-setting.

Across the board, foundations show a preference for investing in 'soft' areas such as healthcare and education. By doing so in pretty much a collective way and letting their group be led by prestigious foundations, such as the Bill and Melinda Gates Foundation in the healthcare sector, philanthropists have become forces to be reckoned with when international organisations, national governments and CSOs set out their policies. There is yet another phenomenon that makes charities puissant players in the development cooperation field; they more often than not do not have their own boots on the ground, are not working themselves at the operational level and thus do not live through the daily confrontation of their ideas and projects with the concrete doggedness of day-to-day realities. They prefer to work via NGOs, CSOs, universities and international organisations. These 'intermediaries' have become increasingly dependent on these private donors and have to listen to and speak their masters' voices. While priding themselves on having accumulated their wealth through private investments and entrepreneurship, few foundations venture into working with the private for-profit sector. Only one-fifth of the disbursements of the 33 biggest foundations goes to profit seeking partners, according to OECD (2020) calculations, and a meagre 16% is invested through non-grant vehicles such as equity instruments (shares, for example) or debt instruments (such as loans).

Box 47. The Aga Khan Development Network

The Aga Khan Development Network (AKDN) was founded in 1957 by Aga Khan IV, who is still its current chairman. Aga Khan IV belongs to the Ismaili Muslim community, which is a minority sect in Shia Islam. He is the 49th hereditary Imam, or spiritual leader, of about 15 million Shia Imami Ismaili Muslims worldwide. Being a royal, he is referred to as 'His Highness'. The Shia Imami Ismaili Muslim community has for a long time been focused on charity work. Besides, the ethical tradition in Islam states that religious leaders should help improve the quality of life in the community and society in general; therefore, the AKDN is underpinned by the ethical principles of Islam. However, it does not limit its development work to a particular community, country or region. The network consists of multiple institutions, amongst which a fund for economic development, an agency for microfinance, a foundation, several universities, a trust for culture, health and education services, and a trust for habitat.

There are 16 areas in which the AKDN is active, ranging from agriculture and food security to tourism promotion. Geographically, the AKDN constituents run programmes in over 30 countries, employing almost 100,000 people. They focus mainly on poor areas of the developing world, such as South and Central Asia, Eastern and Western Africa, as well as the Middle East. However, they also have programmes in North America and Europe. Their budget for development activities is around USD 925 million each year. The Network is funded by the Aga Khan and his followers, as well as donor partners, among which are governments and international organisations. The Aga Khan himself is investing considerable amounts of money as well. The associated agencies branch out in different fields. The Aga Khan Academies agency, for instance, is building 18 residential campuses in Africa, the Middle East and Asia; the Aga Khan Habitat agency is constructing safe drinking water and sanitation facilities for the rural and urban poor; and the Aga Khan Fund for Economic Development generates electricity for over 10 million people. Furthermore, it had a revenue in 2019 of USD 4.5 billion, which was reinvested in other development activities.

The fourth pillar: the children of globalisation challenge the children of the North-South

We have now studied at some length the fourth pillar as a separate category of aid workers that functions *alongside* the conventional specialist pillars; i.e., the first (governmental) pillar, the second (international) pillar and the third (non-governmental) development sector. In fact, we looked at the most visible and most vocal challengers of the development sector as we have known it since its inception, such as the faith-based organisations, the trade and farmers' unions, the cooperative organisations, the corporations and the foundations, but also the thousands of individuals and small groups that show genuine interest in liaising with other individuals and small groups thousands of kilometres away. Without explicitly opposing or being at odds with the traditional development specialists, the newcomers have the guts to go their own way, to interrupt and shake the consensus and equilibrium in the relatively closed circuit of international development aid. They are also the ones who, after imposing themselves *de facto* concretely and on the field with their own rationale and modus operandi, have received some recognition by the conventional 'guardians' of the development cooperation field, its conventional occupants, and the 'custodians' such as the Development Aid Committee of the DAC and some of the foremost authorities of the sector such as the UNDP, the World Bank, the European Commission and national official funding agencies. The OECD-DAC invites foundations and other CSOs to report on their aid allocations, and the World Bank and other international organisations engage with the faith-based organisations to realise the SDGs. Several traditional donor agencies are opening windows to financially support trade unions, cooperatives, farmers' organisations and private enterprises, and even small 'citizen initiatives', in their efforts to 'do development work'. At a time when globalisation is replacing the North-South divide as the main prism and driving force, their non-specialist interventionism, alleged amateurism or dilettantism is no longer seen as an obstacle but as an advantage.

A second way of approaching the new trends in development cooperation and the emergence of a fourth and distinctive pillar is thus to consider change over time and the forces that propel these changes. Inspired by conscious organisational strategies to confront global challenges in favour of the interest groups they represent, we see plenty of trade unions, farmers' organisations, cooperatives and healthcare institutions from the North liaising with their counterparts in the South. The international federations or platforms, such as the ITUC, the World Farmers' Organisation and the International Association of Mutual Benefit Societies (Agence Internationale de la Mutualité), operate as open-door contact centres: centripetal mechanisms that bring similar organisations and soulmates together in a common comfort and battle zone. At the same time, they function as broker clubs that incite social organisations from all over the globe to develop concrete and enduring working relations. For these erstwhile locally and nationally oriented social movements, the international forums they belong to are nodes in the open, global, information technology-driven networks that have come to dominate and drive the new global social morphology. These meeting points are like marketplaces; they do not imply a top-down, orchestrated and strict matching process but rather a bottom-up, decentralised and impulsive dynamic that is constantly transforming the topology of the global network society. Seemingly contradictory, the centripetal function of these international organisations or platforms results in a multiplicity of stop-and-go as well as more permanent interactions between the parties involved. The same can be seen in the world of business and foundations where exchange is sought through chambers of commerce, national and international business associations or elite clubs that create a community of purpose between those that believe in the importance and force of entrepreneurship but also function as powerful accelerators and amplifiers of relations between parties that seek beneficial cross border transactions.

The emergence of new players is partly connected with or the result of the broader social development of globalisation and the multiplication of contacts with other cultures and countries. Relatively recent communication technologies such as the Internet and related connectors, including Facebook, Twitter or WhatsApp, and increased mobility have opened up access for individuals to other parts of the world. The world has become a network society, as prophesised by Castells (1996). The world is flat, argues Thomas Friedman (2005). A new global architecture and mode of participation have arisen. With the information age, the world and society are constantly de-structured and restructured.

Globalisation has also changed the way in which the South and its people are perceived and how the latter perceive themselves. Instead of people and organisations being regarded as passive 'incapable others', in need of aid and happy to be rescued by white saviours, they are now seen and want to be seen as equal partners with talents, expertise, experience and knowledge from which lessons can be learnt in the North. The new players, therefore, often act out of a genuine interest in the people of a specific region, rather than for ideological reasons or with a view to changing the world. The ambition of the modern do-gooder is to save people, enhance their lives and alter their living conditions, not to save the world, nor to improve it or alter its course. At the same time, the goal is to seize the opportunities that cross-border operation offer to both sides.

Even so, changing the world can still be a motive for action. Awareness-raising campaigns, education about the North-South issue and the message that 'changing the world starts with yourself' have inevitably had an impact. The focus on the development issue has become an everyday concern: it is not something that is pushed only during short, temporary media campaigns by large NGDOs, as used to be the case. Citizens and organisations have discovered or created their own ways of getting involved in development cooperation on a more permanent basis. The traditional development cooperation organisations offered few forms of action and involvement other than donating or raising money. Organisations and citizens have developed their own initiatives and set up their own projects, sometimes on their own, but more often with direct contacts in the South and via the international professional or social networks to which they belong.

The other three pillars arose in order to find a solution to the North-South divide; by contrast, the new generation of fourth-pillar initiatives represents a response to globalisation, a challenge to everyone to be a global citizen, global business or global organisation – one which shows solidarity. It is no longer the world that people want to change but the lives of the friends whom they have got to know and value on the other side of the planet.

They are children and parents of a new world, a new society (Castells, 1998).

Starting from a different field

The new trends in development cooperation can also be considered in light of the fields from which initiatives are started.

The traditional development cooperation actors share a common jargon, have developed ways and patterns of interacting, use their proper methodologies and instruments, and legitimise everything they pretend to stand for and do by their own values and standards. They regard themselves, and are regarded by a large section of the public, as specialists in development cooperation. After all, most institutions and organisations in the first, second and third pillars were created specifically to focus on development cooperation. For them, 'doing development cooperation' is not something for amateurs, an odd job or side business; it is a profession that requires a profound knowledge of the field in which you operate, a correct and appropriate attitude and behaviour, the accumulation of experience and adherence to the norms of the sector.

The new players' story is different: in numerous cases, they were not set up for the purpose of development cooperation or in order to change North-South relations but already existed in their country as professional experts in their own field, which was not necessarily related to development cooperation. On the basis of their experiences within their sector or of everyday life, they started to work with people in the South. For example, this may be because they wanted to share their expertise with colleagues grappling with the same problems. Businesses exchange experiences and municipalities, hospitals and schools establish cooperation links with similar institutions in the South and exchange experiences. The trade unions join forces and together set about improving working conditions in both the North and South, instead of specifically focusing on the conventional poverty alleviation programmes. In a globalising society, it is preferable if the cobbler does not stick to his last: rather, he should try to collaborate with other shoemakers.

In this way, new needs and possibilities are also being discovered – in the North as well as the South. The traditional development institutions are not blind to this trend and are starting to adapt their approach to specific projects accordingly. In this way, they are contributing to the ongoing de-specialisation and mainstreaming of development cooperation. Thus, in the Netherlands, the NGDO Oxfam-Novib is supporting migrants' organisations that want to work with microfinance institutions in the South. In the 1990s, the Belgian NGDO WSM, the Christian Mutual Health Fund of Belgium and the ILO had already published a manual on micro-insurance in healthcare. Together with German, American and French bilateral development organisations, health insurance funds and NGDOs, they have since promoted solidarity-based health insurance in Africa.

But bilateral donors are also trying to streamline this trend. The American USAID has set up an Office of Global Development Alliances for this purpose. The multistakeholder alliances that it is encouraging in this way are based on the idea of private-public cooperation. Several thousand such alliances had been created by USAID and billions of dollars in combined private and public resources were generated. The Sustainable Forest Products Global Alliance, for example, seeks to promote sustainable logging practices. USAID gives this alliance basic financing. The World Wildlife Fund manages the Global Forest and Trade Network, a network of more than 360 businesses from over 30 countries which wish to practise 'responsible forest management'. Metafore – a programme of the NGO GreenBlue – promotes, together with American businesses, the responsible purchase and use of wood and paper. The forestry department of the US Ministry of Agriculture gives it technical assistance. A private company, Home Depot, contributes funding and its purchasing model.

From a level 'telling' field to joint action

As has already been said, the development cooperation community solemnly believes in a number of principles. One of these is that a fair relationship with partners in the South must be incompatible with acting out of self-interest. The argument goes that the inequality between North and South is so great (both financially and in terms of capacity) that the South can never catch up unless it receives absolutely all the benefits of cooperation. In other words, investment in development cooperation must not yield any profit for the donor. You have to operate *à fonds perdus* (invest 'sunk capital'); you literally have to give away without expecting a return.

The new generation of fourth-pillar initiatives seems to prefer other options. This is not surprising, as they start from their own working, living or travel experiences. They want to enrich this by working with people from the South. Thus, they seek a win-win situation, and it follows that they do not confine themselves to giving alone. They invest money, time, experience and so on, and look for a return on investment. Both parties stand to benefit.

Furthermore, the conventional development cooperation actors have, over the decades and through a process of trial and error, developed a methodology that is based on a 'planning logic', in which a long-term vision, processes, programmes and ownership are central. The Paris Declaration of March 2005, which has been signed by hundreds of development institutions and recipient countries, is a good summary of the consensus within the conventional development community. It states that development cooperation should be based on the following principles: national ownership, alignment with national priorities and procedures, harmonisation and coordination of development aid, results-oriented working and – finally – mutual accountability. Thus, the starting point is for institutions and people from the South to develop their own long-term strategies and associated plans and programmes, which they themselves control. Autonomous and adapted to local ways of working, they address the needs of the target group and build up rights.

By contrast, the new players do not depart from a belief in development-by-design but set out from an 'anthropo-logical' approach, in which faith in the qualities of people with specific talents is central, as is frequent personal interaction with partners from the South. In practice, work, therefore, focuses on concrete – often short-term – projects, in which people can use their talents optimally. Cooperation between organisations and enterprises from the North and South is often iterative, project after project and open ended. A level 'telling' field, as a common discourse and narrative, which spells out the shared analysis of reality, whether problematic or not, and the opportunities it offers for joint action to remodel it to the benefit of all parties involved, gradually takes shape. The common locus thus created is, from then on, seen through that shared lens using a mutual vocabulary. Contrary to the traditional aid community, in fourth pillar settings, this lexicon will not contain terms and expressions as 'your project, which we support', instead making room for 'our project, which we jointly realise'. The benefits of cooperation and exchange need not be reaped exclusively by the community or institution in the South: the actor in the North may also benefit, if possible. A win-win situation is sought – explicitly in some cases.

Box 48. Panorama or tunnel vision?

In their enthusiasm, many of the new actors have forgotten that development cooperation is a craft – and a particularly difficult one at that. After all, if it were easy, the situation in many developing countries would not be so wretched, would it? Or is the enduring misery in the developing world to be ascribed to incompetence or even a lack of desire to evolve and grow on the part of governments, businesses and civil society in those countries? Granted, many of the problems in the developing countries are related to the shortcomings of the local institutions, including universities and other education centres. In other words, their institutional, organisational and developmental capacity is underdeveloped. There is often a lack of institutional capacity: there is no vision and long-term strategy, no or limited impact on the environment and an absence of eagerness or willingness to learn or pick the brains of those who have proven that there is a way forward. The existing organisational capacity is also far from ideal in many cases. Decision-making bodies do not work properly, and human and financial resources are lacking or are not deployed appropriately. And, of course, this has implications for the development capacity of the institutions concerned. They are not really an effective lever for local development.

But let us be honest: do we not happily engage in pointing the finger of blame like this because it is a convenient way of disguising the fact that our voluntary efforts are not always (or perhaps that should be 'are rarely') efficient and effective? To what extent does our cooperation lead to capacity building? To what extent are we helping to reinforce the institutional, organisational and development capacity of our 'partners'?

The tunnel-vision approach with which we very often operate in development cooperation is one of the greatest obstacles here. We start from our own position and our own ambitions, just as we do when we drive into a tunnel. The boot of our car has our own luggage in it: the knowledge we have developed in our own society, the experiences we have accumulated in our part of the world, the things we have read at home and, above all, perhaps, the knowledge that we generated for our own society and economy. We also set out with our own individual driving skills, style and speed (which may include a tendency to 'step on it'!). Once we are in the tunnel, we simply look ahead. All our energy is put into reaching the light at the end of the tunnel. We do not need to look to the left or right, we reason, as there are only solid walls. Gradually, we start to suffer from narrowed vision and short-sightedness. In the dimly lit tunnel, we may even go colour-blind. The drive is monotonous. We think that we are driving, but really, we are being driven.

Yet the reality at home and abroad is far more colourful, more chequered and more varied than our tunnel vision allows us to perceive. The reality is a panorama. The road is bumpy, and there are unexpected bends, beautiful views, dangerous precipices and obstacles along the way. A panorama perspective makes development cooperation much more realistic: harder but also more fascinating. You gain a sense of what local people and institutions are really like. You discover that your car (and your luggage) may not be suitable for the terrain. They may not even be desirable – who knows? You realise that there is a long way to go, but you do not know the route in advance (there is no GPS!). You have to start by asking for directions – from those who live and work there. They may also need to hurry to your rescue if your car ends up in a ditch. If that happens, it is best to let them sit behind the wheel. The new development cooperation of the fourth pillar and that of the specialists: tunnel or panorama? "You pays your money and you takes your choice…"

The development of a concrete cooperation discourse in which individuals' expertise is applied enables the new players to focus on the South without needing to gain command of the specific jargon and working methods of the traditional development cooperation specialists.

The near and distant future of a whole-of-society approach

When we consider the recent trends in development cooperation in terms of the aspects described above, we see that there is more going on than just the arrival of new players on the development cooperation stage and the establishment of a fourth pillar. Thanks to the efforts (including awareness-raising campaigns and information provision) of the traditional development cooperation organisations and an increasingly globalised society, interest has arisen among wider sections of the population and a range of institutions and organisations in getting involved with development cooperation and forms of cooperation with like-minded and similar actors in the South.

Development cooperation is no longer the exclusive preserve of specialists: it is the business of the whole of society: theoretically, of everyone. The mainstreaming of development cooperation means that non-specialists can do their bit by donating money and resources to the traditional organisations but can also roll up their sleeves and design concrete projects, programmes and other collaborative arrangements.

The mainstreaming of development cooperation raises a number of questions. Firstly, there is discussion about the possible impact of fourth-pillar initiatives. On the one hand, some development specialists (active in the NGDO sector, government and the academic world) argue that most fourth-pillar initiatives have no structural impact on the countries, regions, organisations or people they are targeting, because their projects are small-scale, short-term and insufficiently embedded in the economic or social development policy of the major traditional development actors, disregarding the discourse, tools and methodologies that have been developed and used by the latter over the last few decades. As a result, the door is open to the repetition of mistakes made in the past by the traditional development actors but overcome by them because of years and years of experience. Others, including the fourth-pillar organisations themselves, argue that their projects do, in fact, have a positive impact on local people who take part in them. That impact may be small, but it is not to be underestimated. In addition, these initiatives make an important contribution to raising public awareness in the North (particularly among those who are involved in the project), for example about specific problems in the South. So far, however, the proponents of these views have lacked any data to support their position. There is virtually no research into fourth-pillar initiatives, and this means that there is very little reliable information available about their impact.

Closely linked to this is the question of whether fourth-pillar organisations communicate the big story behind North-South issues or the harmful consequences of globalisation for the population when they are promoting their activities. Traditional development organisations try to explain the structural causes of North-South problems to the general public, whereas, according to some development specialists, fourth-pillar initiatives focus more on a concrete problem without setting it in a broader context. A concrete story, for example the need for wells, is easier to sell than an intricate analysis of the underlying structural reasons for wells not being constructed by the government in a given area.

It remains to be seen what the consequences of the arrival of more and more players in the field of international cooperation will be. It could be that the newcomers will adopt the recipes of the conventional players. They would then turn into development specialists themselves, talking the same language and using the same methodologies as their predecessors. Some are forced to do so when they seek recognition from the sector in search of subsidies or partners. So, if they want to get the funds they request or if they want to benefit from a partnership, they have to accept, at a minimum, the terms of reference of the other party. Some, like the Bill and Melinda Gates Foundation, as we have seen, are also feeling the homogenising effects of the international cooperation sector and are copying many of its features (Fejerskov, 2015). This probably also has to do with the fact that foundations share many of the characteristics of NGDOs and other conventional actors of the sector of international development cooperation. Foundations are charities, primarily oriented towards the needs of others, mainly domestically but now increasingly on the other side of the globe. They are experienced in the 'art of giving away' and, at least theoretically, do not represent specific interests.

The other hypothesis is that the fourth pillar community as a whole will fundamentally alter the way we look at international development cooperation and make it more attuned to the present and future waves of globalisation. It is a view we share in this book. We see that the fourth pillar organisations are moving the sector in a new direction. They are pushing the dominant paradigm to change by bringing in logics from other fields. To put it simply: when a banker from Canada gets involved in a microfinance institution in Cape Verde, he will see things differently than when a Canadian NGDO worker is collaborating with the same microfinance institution. An expert from an official Spanish development agency, who has years of field experience, will give a different kind of advice to the government and social partners of Cambodia on how to organise collective bargaining systems than representatives of the Spanish social partners.

Along with the insights and experiences they gathered in their own country or field, the fourth pillar initiatives are also infusing the sector with new options that might even be in conflict with the dominant visions and practices. These can and will differ from sector to sector. But it is already evident that the desire to experiment, innovate, take risks and seek mutual benefits might become the most contentious issues brought to the table by the fourth pillar initiatives because they do not figure in the traditional recipes of the actors of development cooperation.

Humanitarian aid:
more dispersed or more networked?

Humanitarian aid is associated with disasters, crises and emergencies. These three terms are used interchangeably (Al-Dahash et al., 2016), probably because scholars, policymakers and the general public associate all three with the more-or-less sudden nature of and damage caused by a certain event or chain of events. Humanitarian aid is, therefore, a quick response instrument to bring first aid and start to heal the wounds inflicted. This is in contrast with rehabilitation aid, which is supposed to redress the *ex-ante* situation, and structural aid, which is designed to create a solid basis of long-term development and resilience. But while interconnected, the terms 'disaster', 'crisis' and 'emergency' do represent different aspects of a problematic humanitarian reality. Disasters are often defined as sudden, unforeseen, high-impact events with natural or technological causes that lead to destruction, loss and damage. A crisis is associated with an abrupt disruption threatening the foundations and core of a system, while an emergency is any natural or man-made situation bringing considerable harm to health, life, property or the environment.

The development sector has not been immune to the consequences of the increasingly frequent and complex calamities in the world. For example, over the past 25 years, the world population witnessed the genocide in Rwanda in 1994, which called for profound reflections on the failure of development cooperation but also for massive emergency and rehabilitation efforts; less noticed but no less deadly was and is the war in the Democratic Republic of Congo's great lake region since 1996, causing many to wonder how the humanitarian aid system can stem tensions in societies; there were the famines in the Horn of Africa in the early 2010s and in the Sahel region in 2020; the wars in Iraq and Afghanistan, both starting in the early years of the 21st century but continuing to cause considerable collateral damage and suffering among the local population; the earthquake in the Iranian city of Bam in 2003 and the Asian tsunami in 2004, resulting in unseen havoc; the plague of locusts in West Africa in 2004, and in 2019 and 2020 in East Africa, which were responsible for widespread harvest devastation; between 2003 and 2013, the war in the western region of Sudan led to the genocide of Darfuri; hurricanes ravage the Caribbean and Central America every year; the monsoon season from July to September causes recurrent flooding in Bangladesh; the 2020 Beirut port explosion left thousands of families shocked and homeless; over the last 25 years, earthquakes struck, amongst others, in China, Pakistan, Iran, India, Nepal, Indonesia, Chili, Mexico and Haiti; an unprecedented number of people around the world – over 70 million at the end of 2018 – have been forced from their homes by conflict and persecution; the COVID-19 outbreak was declared a pandemic by the WHO on 11 March 2020, at the time of writing causing over a million deaths and leaving healthcare systems around the world in disarray.

The number of reported disasters has increased significantly in recent decades. Over the last 20 years, 7348 disaster events were recorded worldwide by the Emergency Events Database, EM-DAT. In total, disasters claimed approximately 1.23 million lives, an average of 60,000 *per annum*, and affected over four billion people, many of them on more than one occasion. Additionally, disasters led to approximately USD 2.97 trillion in economic losses worldwide. These numbers represent a sharp increase in the number of recorded disaster events by comparison with the previous 20 years. Between 1980 and 1999, EM-DAT recorded 4212 disasters linked to natural hazards worldwide, which claimed approximately 1.19 million lives and affected over three billion people. Economic losses totalled USD 1.63 trillion. Much of all of this is due to a significant rise in the number of climate-related disasters. Between 2000 and 2019, there were 510,837 deaths and 3.9 billion people affected by 6681 climate-related shocks. It is thus clear that the impacts of climate change and global warming are being felt in the increased frequency of extreme weather events, including heatwaves, droughts, flooding, winter storms, hurricanes and wildfires. Unsurprisingly, the relative cost of these disasters is much higher for the low-income countries, especially the small economies, than for the high-income countries (CRED & UNDRR, 2020).

Naturally, the cost of all these disasters is thus very high: several hundreds of billions of dollars per year. However, cost calculations should be interpreted with due caution. The financial value ascribed to infrastructure in industrialised countries is many times higher than that in developing countries. There is also much underreporting of the costs incurred by governments, the private sector and families in developing countries. In addition, we should bear in mind that, by definition, a disaster lacks any short-term solution. If, in 2020, your cornfield somewhere in the north of Kenya was destroyed by locusts, or you lost a leg in a landmine explosion in Cambodia, your only cow died in a drought in Myanmar or your hut was plundered by passing militiamen in the east of the Democratic Republic of Congo, you would be very unlikely to have recovered from this personal disaster by 2025 – even if you received a lot of aid.

In the context of increasingly common disasters and protracted crises, it is not surprising that emergency and post-conflict aid has increased substantially. An estimated 216 million people needed humanitarian assistance in 69 countries in 2019: an increase of almost 10 million from the year before (Global Humanitarian Assistance, 2020). The families of the victims, their neighbours and their communities were, in almost all cases, the first to render support, financially and practically. In many instances, the local authorities, as well as regional and national governments, also came to the rescue. International aid, mostly, came a bit later.

International humanitarian assistance in 2019 totalled approximately USD 30 billion, almost double what was spent 10 years earlier (Global Humanitarian Assistance, 2020). The bulk of this, just over USD 23 billion, came from governments, DAC members and multilateral organisations, which take money from their reserves when disasters occur. Private sources, which mobilised USD 6.4 billion for humanitarian aid, are as diverse: compatriots and families living abroad, generous individuals, philanthropists, private corporations and NGOs regularly find quick ways to show their solidarity. Global Humanitarian Assistance, a respected observer of the world of humanitarian aid, arrived at this figure by including 'humanitarian' aid that is not directly classified as such by the DAC but still represents assistance for those who have been the victims of a disaster. Examples include clearing landmines or taking possession of light weapons.

The fact that Yemen, Syria and Iraq are outspokenly the biggest receivers of humanitarian support raises many eyebrows since these are countries that are caught in international wars in which donors are actively involved. On the other hand, UN appeals for humanitarian contributions for crises in the Democratic Republic of Congo, Burundi, Pakistan, North Korea, Haiti, Venezuela, South Soudan, Cameroon and Nigeria could not mobilise half of the financial support requested. Is this because they are lesser geopolitical hotspots?

Providing and targeting humanitarian assistance has become more difficult over the years. One of the reasons for this is, of course, the increase in the incidence of disasters worldwide. But another is the prevalence of protracted crises. Prolonged crises confront local people and communities with a long, drawn-out series of interconnected, hazardous situations such as civil war, natural disasters, outbreaks of epidemics and massive displacements. These structurally vulnerable people and communities often live in long-term destitute situations. They live in an acute survival mode, hand to mouth, and have limited prospects for seeing their living conditions getting any better soon. Over one billion people, in a global population of 7.8 billion, live in countries experiencing protracted and multifaceted crises. They are home to half of the world's population living in extreme poverty (Global Humanitarian Assistance, 2020).

To deal with the increased complexity of crises, disasters and emergency situations, the UN and prominent NGOs, such as the Red Cross and Red Crescent Movement, have developed strategic approaches to better coordinate the planning, funding, implementation and monitoring of humanitarian interventions. In their toolbox, they have, for example, consolidated appeals and Common Humanitarian Action Plans. The consolidated appeals, which identify humanitarian needs in major crises and the desired, early assistance to be provided in a coordinated way by UN agencies and NGOs, are growing year after year and reached an all-time high in 2019 with over USD 30 billion requested in this way. Never has the international community responded as generously to these appeals by the UN; 64% of the demand for funding was pledged in 2019.

For a long time now, the three largest donors of international humanitarian assistance have remained the US, Germany and the UK, but the European Institutions, Saudi Arabia and Sweden also have a tradition of humanitarian aid. In recent years, these and other bilateral and multilateral donors have committed a growing share of their ODA to so-called Disaster Risk Reduction Initiatives, which aim to diminish the vulnerabilities, mitigate the consequences of the hazards and strengthen the resilience of recipient countries and communities that face protracted crises. Funding from private sources for humanitarian aid has remained relatively constant over the past decade. Individuals, trusts and foundations, companies and corporations, and national Red Cross and Red Crescent societies contribute about one-fifth to one-quarter of humanitarian aid funds. Funding for humanitarian purposes from non-DAC countries is still negligible. However, humanitarian aid by China, for example, while welcomed by recipient countries, as has been witnessed during the coronavirus crisis, has already been criticised on motivational and technical grounds, and is surrounded by intensifying political scrutiny. China's humanitarian aid is looked at sceptically by those who fear it will disrupt the new consensus on good humanitarian aid because it follows reactive, *ad hoc* and case-by-case approaches. In addition, the involvement of Chinese charities, such as the Jack Ma Foundation and Chinese diasporas, make it very opaque (Renwick, 2020).

Box 49. Not an island: Cuban health internationalism

Cuban health internationalism started shortly after the country's revolution of 1959. It was a key part of its support for anti-colonial struggles. In 1963, a Cuban medical mission was sent to Algeria during its War of Independence. Shortly after, Cuba also sent medical teams to Guinea Bissau and Angola. From then on, Cuban brigades went on disaster relief missions and also longer-term assignments to offer routine health services. Inspiration for this came and still comes from Cuba's successful prevention-oriented, community-based domestic healthcare system. Since their inception, Cuban health missions in over 100 countries have involved more than 150,000 Cuban health *brigadistas*: mainly doctors but also nurses, psychologists and logistics staff.

Although Cuban engagement in international health security is not very visible, it is known that the Cuban government was one of the first to respond to the 2014 Ebola outbreak in West Africa. For Wenham and Kittelsen (2020), this stands in contrast to the criticism that the global community as a whole has faced for its delayed and inadequate response to the crisis.

A critical role in Cuba's health internationalism is played by the Escuela Latino Americana de Medicina (the Latin American Medical School) in Havana. Students from Cuba and around the world receive government-sponsored medical training in this school as well as an immersion in the Cuban official international healthcare approach. The basic tenets of this are long-term collaboration, human care for those in need, contextualisation; transdisciplinarity (with a major role for psychologists), respect for the local collective historical memory and an ethical stance in favour of accessible and equally distributed care (Castro, Melluish & Lorenzo, 2014). The island's involvement in the international healthcare scene has also received some criticism. Protest often comes from local medical professional federations that petition their governments because of Cuban medical staff being underpaid and so putting pressure on their own salaries (Walker & Kirk, 2017). The country was also lambasted when, in the early 2000s, it made an 'oil for doctors' deal with the socialist Chavez regime of Venezuela, sending tens of thousands of medical personnel in exchange for oil[56] and provided thousands of healthcare workers to middle-income countries such as Brazil through quasi-commercial contracts. More recently, eyebrows were raised by some when, as an income-generating programme, it started to sell its high-quality and highly sophisticated medical services to rich countries, for example in the Middle East.

The inroads made by humanitarian aid, also in terms of emergency responses, reconstruction, relief and rehabilitation, disaster prevention and preparedness, into the available development budgets of the donor community have been expanding steadily for years. In 1980, scarcely 1.3% of all

ODA was used for interventions in disasters. For over a decade now, this proportion hangs at around 10%.

The above figures show that the general public's generous support for emergency aid funds goes beyond what it pays in national taxes. Disaster appeals motivate many people to give money to NGDOs, the Red Cross and the Red Crescent or UN institutions such as UNICEF. A number of very large NGDOs have specialised in emergency aid operations, although most opt for an integrated approach consisting of structural development programmes, rehabilitation projects and emergency aid. The largest emergency aid organisations include Caritas Internationalis, Catholic Relief Services, the Red Cross and Red Crescent Movement, Save the Children, Oxfam and Médecins sans Frontières/Doctors without Borders.

What place for emergency aid?

In most donor countries, the twofold trend towards more humanitarian aid and more 'politicised' emergency aid has proceeded unchecked. Despite its far-reaching implications, this trend has never been the subject of serious public debate.

Until the 1980s, emergency aid was invariably a mere palliative. It served short-term goals (such as food distribution during famines) and was largely arranged in cooperation with the governments in developing countries, which were still regarded as legitimate and sovereign actors. Humanitarian aid was supposedly politically neutral and not partisan. But in a couple of decades, a humanitarian system or space has emerged which has assumed completely different dimensions. Because many disasters are directly attributable to mismanagement, a lack of development capacity and corruption in the state, or to civil and inter-state conflicts, humanitarian intervention is regarded as a duty of the international community: as a contribution to the universal application of the rights of all humans to the basic necessities of life and freedom of movement, organisation and opinion. No government has the right to stand in the way of these things.

Humanitarian action is increasingly being linked to new political goals and the political reaction of donors to complex aid situations. For many donors, emergency aid has become an integral part of their strategy for transforming conflicts, stemming violence and making liberal development strategies possible (Curtis, 2001). Examples of the politicisation of humanitarian aid are seen in the international response to complex crises in countries such as Afghanistan, Iraq, Somalia, Syria and Sudan. Thus, techniques such as compulsory repatriation are used, and conflict resolution is coupled with humanitarian aid, the blocking of food aid and even the incorporation of emergency aid in military structures and operations. In this way, emergency aid becomes detached from the two other components of cooperation: rehabilitation and structural aid. It becomes an instrument of (global) foreign policy rather than of development policy. This politicisation of humanitarian aid has been criticised and resisted time and again by many aid agencies (Bristol, 2006) because it jeopardises the very essence of humanitarian interventions as being consistent with the humanitarian principles of humanity, impartiality, neutrality and independence.

This trend is diametrically opposed to the conclusions of international NGDOs and development agencies about the pitfalls of traditional emergency aid and the new approaches they have adopted. 'Active and localised humanitarian aid' and 'network humanitarianism' are the names often given to the new visions. The new approaches proceed from a long-term strategy (which starts with prevention and early-warning and ends with structural interventions), which is *ad maximum* based on local capacities and is organised in a coordinated, decentralised and networked fashion. This way of handling crises is not politically neutral, but – unlike the dominant strategy mentioned earlier – it is not an instrument of foreign policy nor is it the prerogative of the funder to impose new ways of approaching the local ecosystem. A disaster, in this modern vision, is seen through the lens of the local population, which has sufficient sociological insights to understand the social, cultural and economic consequences of a crisis, the structural tensions in the local community it rests on and the potential conflicts it might generate. They are capable of transcending their position as mere passive victims. They have the ability to make a diagnosis and set action priorities. They resist short-term solutions imposed by outsiders who have only limited insight into the local dynamics, and they see short- and medium-term interventions as stepping stones for long-term and structural solutions. Local civil society, which is more than the sum of individual local organisations, and authorities are their preferred pacemakers, not the external agencies. The same goes for the resources needed to rebuild the economy and infrastructure. Local resources, known to the local population, get precedence. The *status-quo-ante* is not the desired option; rather, the crisis is seen as an opportunity to develop new structures and solutions to structural problems. Passive waiting for a new disaster to happen is rejected as an unhelpful attitude, in favour of the search for lasting solutions.

International humanitarian actors who adopt these new concepts acknowledge two things. First, they accept that they are largely out of touch.

Most of the time, they have, at best, superficial knowledge of local socioeconomic and political circumstances, let alone a deeply engrained cultural and emotional attachment. In most cases, they have never operated in the region concerned, and if they had previously been active, it was most probably as emergency aid interveners who left 'the field' once the funds dedicated to the disaster situation were emptied and thus their operations terminated. Secondly, they realise that their resources and capacities account for only a small part of the response to crises. Often, even before international agencies set foot on the ground, the local population, local authorities, social organisations, benefactors and volunteers have already got into action. The contribution of the international aid agencies is thus complementary. If the latter want to be efficient and effective, they need to start their local operations with a wide consultation that includes the affected communities and already active local aid providers (Bryant, 2019). The fact that localisation is a desirable end goal is being accepted by a growing group of actors in the humanitarian aid community. That in many cases, and for a variety of reasons, localisation can only partially be attained is well illustrated by Figure 24, which visualises Saferworld's localisation spectrum.

The international humanitarian system is confronted with yet another major challenge. On the one hand, there is a plethora and further expanding set of humanitarian actors, big and small alike. On the other hand, many victims of disasters and crises are never reached by any outside humanitarian organisation, although they are in distress. Tatham and Pettit (2010), for example, estimate that after the 2010 earthquake, the number of NGDOs operating in Haiti was between 3000 and 10,000, thus, theoretically, one NGDO per 300 to 1000 people. On the website of the UN Office for the

Figure 24: Saferworld's localisation spectrum

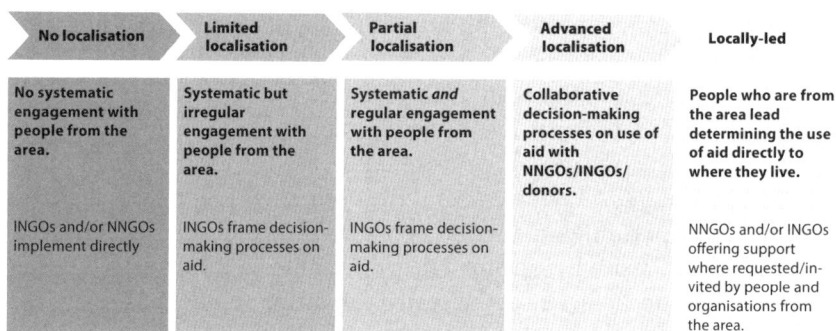

No localisation	Limited localisation	Partial localisation	Advanced localisation	Locally-led
No systematic engagement with people from the area.	Systematic but irregular engagement with people from the area.	Systematic *and* regular engagement with people from the area.	Collaborative decision-making processes on use of aid with NNGOs/INGOs/donors.	People who are from the area lead determining the use of aid directly to where they live.
INGOs and/or NNGOs implement directly	INGOs frame decision-making processes on aid.	INGOs frame decision-making processes on aid.		NNGOs and/or INGOs offering support where requested/invited by people and organisations from the area.

Source: Stephen and Martini (2020)

Coordination of Humanitarian Affairs, we can find reference to 1475 different organisations involved in humanitarian aid.

Indeed, many victims are still left behind. The World Disaster Report 2018 of the International Federation of Red Cross and Red Crescent Societies calculated that fewer than half of the population estimated to be in need were actually known to have been reached by internationally supported humanitarian assistance in 2017 (IFRC, 2018). The report identifies five fatal flaws that are allowing so many people to fall through the cracks: too many affected people are 1) out of sight, 2) out of reach, 3) left out of the loop, or find themselves in crises that are 4) out of money or deemed to be 5) out of scope because they are suffering in ways that are not seen as the responsibility of the humanitarian sector.

To remedy these ills of the system, many in the humanitarian aid community are calling for an adjustment to the dominant global network society in which we live. The humanitarian community has already created many network sub-systems and structures within the community to coordinate action, set norms and standards, exchange experiences etc. But for some critical observers, such as Currion (2018), humanitarian actors remain in a market mode, preferring a transactional prism when dealing with each other and outsiders. In other words, it is about the money, competition, market position, market control and turn-over. Network humanitarianism is seen as a potential alternative, stimulating networks, within the community but more importantly with the outside world, as responses. Network humanitarianism, which accepts the freedom of others to operate in the humanitarian field and facilitates technological capabilities to connect people and organisations, could be a better fit for the networked morphology of the global society in which we live.

Overcoming the humanitarian nemesis

The most fundamental principle that the humanitarian aid community seeks to observe is that the humanitarian response to a disaster must be based on need. Political or diplomatic motives are viewed askance. Cultural or ideological instincts should not play a part, either. Even the presence or absence of resources should not affect willingness to help. This 'humanitarian imperative' is enshrined in the so-called humanitarian charter, which was first drafted in 1997, and the Sphere project, which started in the wake of the Rwanda crisis of 1994. The more than 40 international, non-governmental and humanitarian organisations that subscribe to the charter and collaborate in the Sphere platform collectively affirm that action should be taken to prevent and alleviate human suffering arising out of disaster or conflict and that nothing should override this principle. Among the signatories, one finds the major humanitarian actors such as Care, Caritas, Inter-Action, Oxfam, Save the Children and World Vision.

Nevertheless, international humanitarian actors often find themselves between a rock and a hard place. The participants in the Sphere project recognise that this is one of their main challenges. In armed conflicts, their intervention potentially renders civilians more vulnerable to attacks or may, on occasion, bring unintended advantages to one or more of the parties in the conflict. This kind of unintended, adverse effect can become the humanitarian nemesis or arch-rival of the emergency sector. The nightmare of every aid worker or aid organisation is to worsen the situation it wants to heal, perpetuate crises or conflicts and bring them into spirals they can no longer stop, create new divisions and conflicts in communities in which they want to restore harmony and peace or make the position of the victims they are trying to rescue more precarious.

The humanitarian nemesis also produces nightmarish self-destructive effects when aid leaves a 'disaster after the disaster', an overflow of interveners annihilates the efforts of each or aid is mistargeted or not adjusted to the needs of local culture. It is, therefore, no surprise that the post-genocide humanitarian intervention in Rwanda and its neighbouring countries showed how much the aid community could become its own antagonist and called for due self-reflection. It was a traumatising experience for destitute people who became victims twice; they suffered both from the war and from ill-organised aid. And it inflicted a trauma upon an aid community that could not live up to its expectations.

Hundreds of organisations travelled out to help and turned Rwanda and the camps in east Zaire, Tanzania and Uganda into a chaotic and hypercompetitive environment, the like of which had never been seen before. Reading the catalogue of fiascos from that time still brings many emergency aid workers out in a cold sweat. Organisations – some of them huge, others one-man ventures – competed for money, influence in the camps, victims, media attention, competent local personnel and so on, as long as the cameras were focusing on the conflict and the human catastrophe it created. Local organisations that had taken root in the refugee camps were overlooked or, in some cases, jealously co-opted. Aid resources were traded by opportunistic dealers or driven off to other areas in army trucks. In the meantime, the war raged on, and to cap it all, considerable quantities of aid resources were seized by the ringleaders of the genocide and used in the conflict.

Box 50. Reacting to a biblical catastrophe: the 2019–2020 locust crisis

The 2019–2020 outbreak of desert locusts threatened food production and supply across regions of East Africa, the Arabian Peninsula and the Indian subcontinent. It took many by surprise, especially local farmers and villagers. This upsurge of locusts was the worst in 70 years in Kenya, and in 25 years in Ethiopia, Somalia and India. It also hit Eritrea, Djibouti, Uganda, Tanzania, Pakistan, Iran, Yemen, Oman and Saudi Arabia. Over 40 million people were reported to be living in severe acute food insecurity in the three regions affected by the crisis. Plagues of locusts have been reported since the Pharaonic times in ancient Egypt. Over the last century, desert locust plagues occurred in 1926–1934, 1940–1948, 1949–1963, 1967–1969 and 1986–1989. An invasion of locusts is unpredictable since they come without any warning. But when they invade, they descend and spread in their millions. The vicious predators settle on anything green, and within hours, any vegetation in their path is eaten and hectares of farmland and nature are destroyed. Locusts have a voracious appetite and eat the equivalent of their own weight daily. They quickly grow in number and travel over 100 kilometres a day. The insects are able to multiply 20-fold in three months and reach densities of 80 million per square kilometre. But how do these plagues come about? When cyclones in the Indian Ocean made landfall the year before, they may have created an attractive and fertile environment for locusts to swarm into the region from their nesting sites in the Middle East. Indeed, scientists note climate change as a main driver of the current outbreak. Severe weather conditions, including exceptional and prolonged heat, heavy storms and abundant rainfall, in the Arabian Peninsula created ideal conditions for adult populations to explode. The most destructive locust species is the one that, during the 2019-2020 crisis ravaged vast areas: the desert locust. Given their voracious appetite, combined, a relatively small swarm of one square kilometre, congregating up to 80 million locusts, can eat food equivalent to that consumed by 35,000 people a day.

The combined coronavirus and locust crisis made it even harder for local communities, governments and the international community to react efficiently and adequately. For one, the pandemic is disrupting the supply chains for pesticides and other equipment to control the spread of these migratory insects, so farmers and villagers had first to resort to other means to drive away the swarms. They used the metal tools they had to drum away the grasshoppers, lit fires and burned debris. Kids and women were instructed to scare the locusts away by screaming. When and where possible, farmers started manually spraying (harmful) chemical pesticides. Neighbouring villages hosted and fed people who fled their land and homes. Farmers who saw the opportunity started to invest in fruit and vegetables, and left behind their crops such as cowpeas, sorghum and maize, which are more vulnerable to locusts.

National government agencies, if they were equipped, commenced the aerial spraying of pesticides and, if available, fungal deterrents. They also mobilised their agricultural extension workers to give advice to the affected communities and farmers.

International non-governmental humanitarian agencies, such as the International Rescue Committee, arrived to train farmers and livestock herders in new resilient techniques. They also provided food help to the most vulnerable who faced an acute hunger crisis. Bilateral agencies, such as USAID, also stepped up efforts and got involved in pest control operations and the provision of protective equipment. The FAO of the UN made an international call for millions of US dollars to pay for pest control, surveillance and livelihood support. It directly quick-started a Locust Emergency Response Toolkit (eLERT), an online database to serve as a reference with critical information on such aspects as pesticides registered in the affected countries for locust control, technical specifications of recommended equipment, suppliers, standard contracts for aerial operators and consultants to reinforce the response capacities in the field etc. In May 2020, the World Bank Group approved a USD 500 million Emergency Locust Response Programme to provide flexible support to countries in African and the Middle East.

Only later will we know whether this reaction was timely, inspired by lessons learned from previous crises, efficient, effective and resulted in a sustainable impact.

Cash-and-carry on the market

For years, sending aid in kind, in the form of food, blankets, tents or drugs, has been the dominant approach to humanitarian aid provision. Recently, though, this view has been challenged by the idea that in some humanitarian crises, financial aid in the form of cash is a more appropriate response, although the advocates of humanitarian aid in cash state very clearly that this is only possible if the local market has the right conditions. Are the products that are needed sold on the local market? How competitive is that market and can it offer a response to a growing demand for certain products? How great is the risk of price increases? The debate between the two viewpoints is also known as the 'in cash or in kind' debate.

Opponents of the idea of giving financial humanitarian aid object for various reasons. They believe that humanitarian aid in this form is more susceptible to corruption. More than goods, money attracts those who do not really need it; thus, there is a real chance that financial aid will end up in the pockets of the elite. Moreover, local organisations can do what they like with the cash they have acquired. There is, therefore, a risk that in conflict regions, for example, the money will be used not for humanitarian aid but for buying weapons. This is a problem of fungibility. Opponents are also very concerned about the possibility that the cash will be used for antisocial purposes; for example, if men are the traditional money managers, there is a risk that they will use it to buy alcohol and not to feed their hungry children. Giving humanitarian aid in the form of banknotes also involves a considerable security risk, both to donor personnel and the recipients. The risk of theft and violent attacks increases.

Those in favour of financial humanitarian aid reject a number of these criticisms. They argue that the corruption and security risks associated with this kind of aid provision are not greater than, but fundamentally different from, those associated with traditional humanitarian aid. After all, cumbersome or valuable goods have to be stored in a secure location. In addition, the dangers involved in cash can be minimised by using banks, other financial institutions and modern telephone-based transactions. According to the proponents, the risk of antisocial purchases is also less significant than suggested. Evaluation reports show that in the overwhelming majority of cases, the money that is provided is used for the basic goods needed, such as food and soap. There is very little evidence of antisocial purchases. The proponents also argue that the security risks mainly relate to the transportation of the money, but that this can be addressed by making transportation less noticeable. Money that is transported less visibly may even involve less danger than voluminous consignments of goods. It is also argued that there are a number of inherent advantages associated with this type of humanitarian aid provision. The local population's ownership is respected. People can choose for themselves what to spend the money on, and will, therefore, meet their needs more effectively. The fact that they can make their own choices is also empowering. Moreover, this approach has a less disruptive impact on local markets. Yet while goods often have a demoralising effect on local commerce and production, financial humanitarian aid can contribute to inflation. As there is more money in circulation, there is a chance that the prices of the most coveted goods will rise.

Thus, both forms of humanitarian assistance have their advantages and their drawbacks. The goods-based approach remains dominant, but a gradual yet noticeable shift has taken place for about a decade now.

.

The unbearable lightness of the support for development cooperation

Policymakers and other players in development cooperation have a big problem: they do not know whether the public supports them in what they do. Yet they need its support; the government and other players operate with tax revenue, which is best used on things that the public actually supports. Similarly, NGDOs and other development organisations rack their brains about the best way to involve their supporters more, get the public to give more financial support and extend their support base.

The uneasy relationship with the support base

Talking about the support base is like discussing whether a glass is half full or half empty. The support base is always there, but it may be large or small, dormant or active, negative or positive… The same is true of support for anything: a new motorway, windmills in a densely populated area, extending working hours, a political party – and so too for an NGDO.

If the players in the development sector take such a keen interest in their support base, they have special reasons for doing so, and these are very much related to the sector's characteristics.

Take the government. Policymakers who work on international development cooperation seek support for their policy domain in general and their policy choices in particular. They want the views, attitudes and behaviour of the general public or particular groups that might be interested in the policy to be positive, or at least neutral. But such views, attitudes and behaviour are not very readily expressed in the case of development cooperation: the political support base is largely latent and not activated. Development cooperation is not a theme that really stirs high feelings in a nation's political and social sphere. It has too little connection with matters of immediate concern to do so. It relates to what Fowler (1992) refers to as long-distance obligations, which have little topicality in everyday social and political debate. Moreover, support for development cooperation is not based on people's direct and short-term interests.[57] Such support is less easily appealed to, less clearly defined, less readily mobilised and demonstrated collectively on fewer occasions. The marches, demonstrations or happenings associated with other issues, by which people nail their colours to the mast, are not effective tools for mobilisation here. The support base for development cooperation is thus far more diffuse, fragmented and vague than it is for many other social issues, which makes it far harder for policymakers in the development sector than it is for their counterparts working on other issues to gain a feel for, understanding of or handle on the support base, or to muster public support for what they do.

But there is another factor. The social and political support bases for development cooperation also have few links with each other. Development cooperation policy evolves without reference to public opinion and with little input from the majority of the organised support base. By contrast with many other domains, we can speak here of an advocacy void or a democratic deficit. Development cooperation policy lacks transparency, is developed without much consultation and is rarely subjected to the test of public opinion. The minister for development cooperation can easily act in isolation; they can seek out new partner countries, take up new themes and alter budgets, and expect little protest in cabinet, parliament, public opinion or even the sector. Like no other minister, they can make substantial changes *en cours de route*. Unlike fellow ministers responsible for education, healthcare, infrastructure or the armed forces, the minister for development cooperation has a (fairly large) budget at their disposal, which is free from any corresponding long-term spending commitments and is not examined with a fine-tooth comb by all kinds of interest groups.

Other players in the sector, the NGDOs for example, have a similarly ambiguous relationship with their support base. As we have seen, this consists of adherents, constituents and supporters. Few, if any, NGDOs have members. The supporters are changing all the time. People are quick to come forward if asked to do so but equally quick to step back again. Many of those who donate money shop around among the different NGDOs, giving money now to one, now to another. Many wait until there is a campaign and they are explicitly asked for support.

No (more) aid fatigue?

Table 8 shows a clear upward trend since 1983 in the percentage of Europeans who regard development aid as an important subject; this percentage stabilised at more than 80% between 2004 and 2019.

Moreover, attitudes towards development aid seem to be less elastic than we may imagine. This was observed by the Aid Attitudes Tracker, which

Table 8: Percentage of Europeans regarding development aid as an important issue

	% European population
1983	67%
1987	75%
1991	80%
1995	77%
1996	82%
1998	75%
2002	82%
2004	91%
2009	88%
2010	89%
2013	83%
2016	89%
2019	86%

Source: European Commission, Eurobarometer nos. 36, 44.1, 50.1, 58.2, 62.2, 79.4 and 405

surveyed 8000 people across the UK, France, Germany and the US every six months between 2013 and 2018 (University of Birmingham, 2020). The surveys show that support to aid in the UK has remained stable despite various austerity measures and strong criticism in the right-leaning press during the build-up to the 2015 bill on spending 0.7% of GNI on international development. Even specific incidents such as the Oxfam sexual abuse scandal in Haiti in 2018 or the influx of migrants in Germany in 2015 may have caused a temporary spike in opposition at the time, but overall support for development aid seems to have reverted back to the norm rather quickly. Similarly, in the USA, regardless of President Trump's critique and proposed budget cuts for foreign aid, polling shows that Americans' support towards US active engagement in the world has remained generally stable. According to recurrent waves of the Chicago Council survey on global affairs, the percentage of Americans in favour of taking an active part in world affairs remained relatively stable at 60–70% from the 1980s to 2020 (Smelts et al., 2020). At the same time, a majority of Americans agree with specific foreign aid policies, with 80% in support of humanitarian relief programmes and 65% in favour of "aid that helps needy countries develop their economies" (Wojtowicz & Hanania, 2017).

Popular, yet little understood

At the same time, surveys of public opinion towards development aid show that the public in donor countries knows relatively little about development issues and development cooperation. Our own HIVA research has shown that more than half of people of the Flemish region in Belgium know little or nothing about the situation in developing countries (Pollet, 2014). It was not just subjective knowledge that turned out to be limited: objective knowledge, measured using a number of quiz questions, was also poor. In particular, few people know which minister(s) are responsible for the development cooperation portfolio. The percentage of people who know that we spend less than 1% of our wealth on official development cooperation was only 24.5%. Similarly, in Germany, the share of development cooperation in the federal budget was overestimated by 80% of the respondents during a survey in 2018. Knowledge questions on combating poverty, child mortality and climate change were also answered incorrectly by a majority, and over 50% of the respondents had not yet heard about the SDGs (Schneider & Gleser, 2018). While an overestimation by the general public of their national government's budget for development cooperation applies across Europe, this is even more striking in North America. Research has shown that the average United States citizen thinks that the government gives five times more aid than is really the case (Wojtowicz & Hanania, 2017). Moreover, there is a huge discrepancy between what the sector actually does (technical assistance, budget support, working with civil society, lobbying and advocacy, etc.) and what people think it does (emergency aid, installing water pumps, building schools etc.) (Pollet, 2014).

Despite the limited subjective and objective knowledge, the level of appreciation for development work turns out to be quite high. The work of NGDOs is particularly well regarded. They are seen as best suited to taking on the difficult task of development work and are also considered to be the most effective performers. Most surveys also point to the high level of confidence and appreciation for the work of the UN institutions. People's own national governments are viewed with greater scepticism: they are regarded as less well-suited to the task, and there are doubts about their performance.

Public opinion regards development work as the business of specialists and those with appropriate credentials. Yet there is also a growing belief that businesses, cities and local authorities, trade unions and even individual citizens are fit to tackle development work. HIVA research in Belgium has shown that thinking in favour of these new actors has evolved very rapidly and positively over recent years (Pollet, 2014; Pollet et al., 2014). What is more, although public opinion is still somewhat doubtful about the value of these 'fourth-pillar players' for developing countries, private opinion about the role of my own business, my football club or my next-door neighbour who is working in Senegal is thoroughly positive. In the Netherlands, one-third of the working population believes that its own business or organisation should be working with a business or organisation in a developing country.

Something needs to be done: but by whom?

Most public opinion polls on development cooperation show that the vast majority of the population believe that the gap between the rich North and the poor South is unacceptably large. Blame is ascribed both to political leaders in developing countries, who keep their own people in poverty, and to Western countries, which recklessly deplete the third world's natural resources (Pollet, 2014). Various polls published by the Development Engagement Lab[58] show that economic crises, climate change, inequality, war and conflict, and migration are often ranked as the most important issues.

These views are coupled with quite pronounced pessimism. Only a minority thinks that poverty in Africa will decrease in the years ahead (Pollet, 2014) and believe that the SDGs will be achieved (Schneider & Gleser, 2018). A global survey carried out in 2016 by Glocalities showed that 87% of respondents think extreme poverty has either stayed the same or got worse over the past 20 years. Only 1% knew that it had actually decreased by 50% (Lampert & Panadongonas, 2016).

At the same time, there is a view among the public that various measures can be taken to support developing countries. Opening up markets to their products is regarded as having the most development potential, but efforts to promote democratisation in developing countries and the eradication of corruption are also widely backed.

Should taxes be increased to pay for such measures? A number of surveys, in the UK and elsewhere, suggest that there is little support for such an idea. According to a World Values Survey carried out in 2012, only 23% of Americans indicated they would support higher taxes to increase foreign aid, while the average of the surveyed countries was 39% (Doherty et al., 2020). Interestingly, earlier research showed that a majority of Americans would not object to additional taxes if it meant poverty could be eliminated from the world (Riddell, 2008). Of course, citizens can also take action themselves. In keeping with tradition, many citizens support national NGDOs or church organisations that are internationally active. However, donation behaviour is hard to measure. Can people accurately remember what and how much they have given over the past year? How do you add up what people have transferred out of their bank accounts to charities, what they have given to volunteers who come round collecting for charity with stickers or pencils and what they have put into the collection at church? Do people distinguish between a good cause in their own country and what they give for projects in developing countries? Surveys do point towards a decrease in the number of people donating money in support of organisations working in developing countries. In Belgium, the proportion of Belgians donating money decreased from 51.3% in 2010 to 25.7% in 2013 (Pollet, 2014). Similarly, from 2013 to 2020, the percentage of people donating in Germany fell from 29% to 16% and in the UK, from 37% to 17% (Hudson et al., 2020). This decrease in donations goes hand in hand with growing scepticism about the state of affairs in the world and the effectiveness of development cooperation. Furthermore, growing concerns about one's own economic situation and increased competition from fundraising initiatives that are not linked to traditional development organisations (see, for example, the Riot Games initiative in Box 51) contribute to this trend.

Box 51. Riot games

Riot Games is a US video game developer, publisher and e-sports tournament organiser based in west Los Angeles, California. The company was founded in September 2006 by University of Southern California students and roommates Brandon Beck and Marc Merrill (Kollar, 2016). The company's first and flagship product is 'League of Legends', a multiplayer online battle arena game which was released in 2009. By 2020, it was one of the most popular video games worldwide, with an estimated active player count of more than 100 million and an average daily active player count of eight million (LeagueFeed, 2021). Since 2011, Riot Games has been active in fundraising and charity causes, and has been collaborating with multiple NGOs in different fields, donating around USD 20 million over the past decade (Burrell, 2019). Money is raised through the release of in-game accessories (e.g., skins for characters) that can be purchased by players. During the 2017 World Championship of their game, they launched an in-game charity fundraiser to support three global organisations (BasicNeeds, Learning Equality, and the Raspberry Pi Foundation) (Riot Games, 2017). The results exceeded every expectation. By selling only one in-game item, they managed to collect USD 2.35 million for the three NGO's (Porter, 2017). In 2019, Riot Games went one step further by launching the Riot Games Social Impact Fund. By 2020, the fund had already collected and donated over USD 10 million on players' behalf to promote equal opportunities in education and global citizenship through partnerships with NGOs such as City Year, Cultural Heritage Administration and Active Minds (Burrell, 2020).

To a limited extent, citizens can also display solidarity with developing countries in their consumer behaviour. However, fair trade products are certainly not filling up shopping trolleys. In surveys in the Netherlands and Flanders, between one-quarter and one-third of people say that they regularly buy a fair-trade product. But the figures from the fair-trade circuit suggest that consumers will pay a supplement in order to give producers a 'fairer' price for their work for only a small fraction of their shopping costs.

In the USA, research has revealed that 88% of American consumers describe themselves as 'socially responsible' and 'conscious' shoppers. Despite this positive attitude, an Alter Eco Study of 2008 found that no more than six consumers out of 10 could spontaneously name a fair trade organisation and only 10% of the respondents declared that they had recently bought a fair-trade product (FTF, 2009).

Finally, involvement in fourth-pillar initiatives has been on the rise in the last few years. This may be an indication of a growing sense of self-responsibility. Limited research data from the Netherlands and Belgium indicate that considerable volunteering energy and financial resources are being devoted to this fourth pillar. In the case of the Flanders region of Belgium, this is equal to the time and money that the Flemish already devote to conventional NGDOs. Perhaps this will provide a shot of adrenaline, which will surge through the ageing veins of the development community and give it a fresh burst of vitality.

Time for a new narrative: from development education towards education for global citizenship

As early as the 1960s and together with the emergence of the development agenda, development education has been supported by governments, NGOs and educational bodies providing funding and resources for educational environments on development and global issues. The field of development education is a rather diverse and complex landscape of various programmes, actors and approaches that are known under an equally diverse array of definitions (Bourn, 2020). At the same time, the changing paradigms and practices in international development cooperation discussed in the previous chapters resonate with evolving trends in development education and its transition towards global citizenship education. These trends are closely linked to existing perceptions of development and development cooperation. Over several decades, there has been a gradual shift from a traditional aid perspective that places the aid system at the centre of development education (the charity perspective), over a more technical focus on economic development (the economic development perspective), to placing rights-based thinking at the core (the global justice perspective). These different paradigms have not started neatly the one after the other; they actually co-existed for many years, but there is a tangible shift in where the momentum is going: towards a global justice perspective and education for global citizenship.

The charity perspective: heroes helping victims

Within the charity perspective, it is assumed that social justice can be achieved by helping those in need through concrete, individual actions. This often involves remedying problems without surfacing or tackling their underlying and structural causes. These causes are also more likely to be searched for with individuals themselves and their immediate context rather than within social or societal structures. In development education, the charity perspective is often visible in all kinds of fundraising activities set up for the benefit of charitable causes in developing countries. This is particularly the case when such actions are aimed at arousing feelings of compassion by showing emergency situations and the circumstances of poverty. They are also often accompanied by an implicit or explicit message that the proposed problems can be solved through 'help' from richer countries. The underlying causes or contexts in which these problems occur are usually less extensively discussed.

There is growing criticism of the charity perspective because of the stereotyping depiction of people in developing countries as powerless and needy (the victim frame) and lack of deeper analysis and reflection on the structural causes of inequality (Vossen & Van Gorp, 2016). Research into public support for development cooperation has also shown that both the stereotypical image in the media and the sometimes-archaic messages in fundraising run the risk of contributing to a predominantly critical attitude among the general public towards some development cooperation actors, especially NGDOs (Pollet, 2013). In recent years, various initiatives have sprung up to question the uncritical use of the 'victim frame' in the communications of some development cooperation actors. A notable example is the 'Radi-Aid' awareness-raising campaign initiated by the Norwegian Students' and Academics' Assistance Fund.

Box 52. Radi-Aid Award: changing perceptions of poverty and development.

This initiative, which emerged from a satirical campaign and music video (Radi-Aid: Africa for Norway[59]) has been issuing the Radi-Aid Award for the best (rusty radiator) – and worst (golden radiator) – fundraising videos over the period 2013–2017. In 2017, the rusty radiator went to a Red Nose Day fundraising video shot in Liberia: 'Ed Sheeran meets little boy who lives on the streets'. At one point in the video, Ed Sheeran suggests bringing two street children to a hotel until they are 'sorted'. The verdict of the jury was not mild: "This video is about Ed Sheeran. It's literally poverty tourism. The video should be less about Ed shouldering the burden alone but rather appealing to the wider world to step in. Massive improvement in the end. But is Ed Sheeran willing to pay for the boy's housing forever? What an irresponsible thing to do, and for this video to glorify that is terrible." The golden radiator of 2017, on the other hand, went to the War Child UK video 'When Batman visited a refugee camp'. The video shows the superhero playing with a Syrian eight-year-old child in the setting of a refugee camp in Lebanon. The clip shows the two characters playing soccer, arm wrestling and flying a kite, while the song of the band Queen 'You're my best friend' plays in the background. At the end of the clip, Batman changes into the kid's father, who is carrying him as he walks through a desert-like area with smoking buildings and an attack helicopter in the background. The video that went viral on social media got the following verdict from the jury: "What a powerful video! Our heroes are never too far away from us. They give us strength, hope, peace and the drive to strive for the best. One thing this video did a really good job of was showing the kid as a kid. The children are dependent on their parents/guardians. Effective humanitarian crisis imagery."

The economic development perspective: teaching a man to fish

An economic development perspective is particularly visible from the 1960s onwards. Economic development, mainly based on a Western model, is seen as an important solution to the problems encountered in developing countries. In this context, greater and greater importance is attached to supporting local actors to take control of their own economic development. Such support is, admittedly, often based on the paternalistic view that the richer, industrialised countries should provide the necessary technical know-how. The proverb "give a man a fish and he has food for one day; teach a man to fish and he has food for life" to some extent illustrates this view (Mesa, 2011). Within development education, this approach can be found in interventions aimed at providing information about the projects of development actors and the local communities being supported. It is often associated with a fact-based approach, whereby global challenges are largely understood as the result of a lack of sufficient knowledge and can be addressed by accumulating scientific knowledge and technical know-how (Stein, 2020). It comes with a strong belief in economic growth as the best way to address material poverty. Instead of development aid, the focus is on development cooperation. There is also less use of stereotypical images, as was the case with the charity perspective. Strengthening the support base for development cooperation among the general public is not a primary objective but rather seen as a potential added value. Communication and representation are often done on the basis of a 'progress frame', which asserts that countries are poor because their economies, infrastructure, healthcare or education systems are not yet sufficiently developed. It is also portrayed that these shortcomings can be addressed if the necessary (technical) support is provided (Vossen & Van Gorp, 2016).

Development education from an economic development perspective has been critiqued for its presumption that 'true' (universal) knowledge moves in one direction: from the Global North to the Global South. At the same time, it is seen to perpetuate a 'server-served' dichotomy, with the one who knows being the expert and the one who is supported sitting at the receiving end of the relationship: the one who does not know or does not have (Bruce, 2013). At the same time, information on development and economic growth is often provided in an uncritical manner without addressing the underlying and structural causes of the problems. Critical scholars also question the naive belief in the benefits brought by modernity and continued economic growth. Stein et al. (2017) use the metaphor of 'the house that modernity has built' to argue that global challenges such as climate change, the growing numbers of refugees, economic crises… that are often perceived as external threats to the house are, in fact, a product of the 'violent and unsustainable' practices that are required in order to build and sustain the house itself.

Box 53. Reaching out for knowledge from the Global South

Critical scholars from the Global South and Global North have raised questions about an economic development perspective that presumes that true (universal) knowledge moves in one direction: from the Global North to the Global South. They argue that the interconnectedness of global challenges such as poverty, inequality and climate change, and the specific way these issues play out in particular locations, ask for solutions that are negotiated with different stakeholders, underpinned by different knowledge and value systems, and rooted in people's everyday experiences. Hence, stronger searching and reaching out for non-Western ideas, concepts and knowledge from the Global South are called for. It is argued that such knowledge can benefit educational outcomes in the Global North as well as in the Global South (Pieniazek, 2020). It is indicated, for example, that the philosophy of Ubuntu (from Southern Africa), which highlights the interconnectedness and unity between human beings, may support learners to develop a broader understanding of the world beyond their Western conceptualisations. It may also bring learners from the Global North into contact with authors from the Global South and help them to understand that their experiences, history and perspectives are merely one of many available forms of knowing the world. Some scholars also examine how the principles of Ubuntu can provide a framework for African philosophies of education, citizenship and democratic education, and inform educational policy and practice that is indigenously led and relevant (Waghid, 2014; Takyi-Amoako, 2018).

The global justice perspective: discovering co-responsibility

The global justice perspective opposes the traditional North-South contradiction and emphasises the interdependence between what happens at local and global levels and how daily activities can influence global challenges. It also puts more emphasis on the underlying causes of social and global problems and our personal role or responsibility in them. This is done by bringing the target groups of development education interventions into contact with the ideologies, political-economic systems and other structures that create and perpetuate global injustice, as well as the way in which they can be co-responsible for such injustice through their daily actions. In fact, a critical approach shifts the focus from the 'needy' or 'victims of social injustice' to the group that is privileged and, therefore, seldom, if ever, ends up in the position of, for instance, the person 'at risk' (Angus, 2012). There is, indeed, a risk that this 'privileged' position is experienced as self-evident and sometimes even inevitable. Social injustice then arises when individuals use their privileged position to the detriment of non-privileged individuals or groups to strengthen their position or avoid criticism (Juchtmans & Vandenbrouke, 2013). A critical approach to development education will try to make explicit the privileged position in which certain target groups find themselves in relation to disadvantaged persons. The aim of development education is then to make target groups aware of this position and its consequences on their convictions, actions and behaviour. In this way, the role of power relations in development education can be addressed. At the same time, deep-rooted views on how the world works can be questioned and alternative ways of looking upon the world can be explored.

Box 54. Changing minds through systemic thinking

"Hi Europe, n(r)ice to m-eat/eet you, Benin" was a joint initiative of the Belgian Hubi & Vinciane Foundation which organises projects on food and healthcare in Benin, and Djapo, an educational organisation concentrating on sustainable development education. Djapo encourages professionals who work with children and young people to engage in systemic thinking, creative thinking, philosophising and action-oriented thinking in the classroom. The first step in the project was to produce short documentaries and informative videos on food habits in the Parakou-N'dali region in Benin. The documentaries and videos formed the basis for an educational program targeted at primary school teachers and teacher students. The programme "supports teachers, teacher students and local governments in teaching children skills in critical and creative thinking. Systemic thinking in this project was explored by looking at differences and similarities in the dietary habits in Belgium. The experience of Djapo is that even with young children, it is possible to talk about systems like food chains". One example is looking at the journey that is taken by rice to end up on our plates. "Enabling people to think about 'systems', offers a more nuanced view on the world because it considers the different actors (farmers, buyers, supermarkets, consumers) and their views in a specific context. Making these connections in different situations enables people to make better choices. This kind of thinking can eventually help to make more conscious choices, for example, as (future) consumers or voters" (Frame, Voice, Report!, 2019).

Hence, communication within this approach often takes place through a 'social justice' frame, which draws attention to the problem of inequality, and a 'global village' frame, which points to shared responsibility in a globalising world (Vossen & Van Gorp, 2016). The growing impact of globalisation and the demand for more collective action to respond to global challenges such as climate change and growing inequality (as opposed to promoting individual action in other approaches) are important drivers behind this approach (Bourn, 2015).

Box 55. Film as a medium for global citizenship education

Audiovisual productions such as film are seen as a particularly suitable medium for global citizenship education interventions. In addition to their thematic flexibility and adaptability to viewers' different ages and backgrounds, they particularly have the potential to enable cross-cultural connectivity and convey a very complex reality in a more accessible way (that is to say, content density). Film's potential for cross-cultural connection concerns its ability to help learners place global issues or situations that initially may seem distant within their own frame of thought and link them to their own experience. In this way, their own mindset and personal experience can be broadened, which forms an important basis for the learning process (Kruesmann, 2014). Its potential for content density relates to the fact that film can address many different issues within a very compact range of images and sounds. As a result, film is able to present the often very complex issues raised within development education in an accessible and clear way.

While film is considered a suitable medium for global citizenship education, the literature also points to the importance of the learning process that is set up around such media. Viewers react differently and these reactions do not automatically lead to a deeper critical learning process. Productions with a hopeful ending, for example, can give viewers a feeling of relief that a solution to the problem is possible after all and that, as a well-intentioned citizen, they can also contribute to this, for instance by buying fair trade products or signing a petition. This may already be a step in the right direction, but from a critical point of view, it would become problematic if the learning process were to stop there and viewers were not further involved in critical reflection on their underlying assumptions about the causes of poverty and inequality.

A critical approach to global citizenship education can be confrontational and uncomfortable from an ethical, emotional and cognitive point of view, both for global citizenship education providers and learners. It can also lead to learning processes that raise more questions and uncertainties than answers. This helps to explain why a critical approach is less often part of 'mainstream' development education (Bryan, 2013). An additional explanation may be that a critical approach also requires a specific effort on the part of global citizenship education providers. After all, it involves a learning process in which learners need to be supported in dealing with different perspectives and processes of self-reflection. Such a learning process often requires active guidance. Many studies on immersion journeys, for example, point to an increased risk that participants' existing prejudices and perceptions may be reinforced if no pre- and post-learning path is linked to the immersion journey (Bourn, 2015).

Box 56. COVID-19: an unexpected window of opportunity for global citizenship education

With nationalism on the rise in many parts of the world linked to a growing discontent about the unequal distribution of benefits from globalisation and multilateralism, the COVID-19 pandemic has the potential to fuel such dynamics. Controlling borders, limiting international travel, competition among countries to purchase personal protective equipment or vaccines are all high on the political agenda and hotly covered in the media. Interestingly, the pandemic also confronts the general public and policymakers with some of the benefits of international migration, which may not have been broadly understood or realised. Many workers who are providing essential services during the pandemic such as doctors, nurses, farm workers, delivery drivers…, come from abroad. In a blog for the Brookings Community, the Director of the Overseas Development Institute points out that 30% of doctors and 27% of farm workers in the USA are foreign-born, while 54%of doctors and 35% of nurses in Australia are immigrants (Foresti, 2020). This realisation has already resulted in promising reforms of some stringent immigration policies. In Portugal, all migrants and asylum-seekers have been temporarily granted citizenship right, while in Italy and the USA, regularisation has been temporarily granted to workers in some sectors. Although these reforms are a step in the right direction, it has to be seen how they can be sustained after the pandemic. Experience with current immigration reforms during the pandemic shows that this will require locally led and politically smart solutions. The temporary reforms in Italy were, for example, supported by the Minister of Agriculture and the Minister of Local Development and Cohesion, not the Minister of Internal Affairs. From a global justice and global citizenship education perspective, COVID-19 provides an opportunity to approach the immigration issue not as a problem that needs to be solved for 'them' (migrants) but instead by working towards a 'collective' future while considering each other's (migrants and receiving society) aspirations, perspectives, skills and humanity.

Sixty years of international development cooperation: where has the bumpy road led us?

Between 1960 and 2020, the DAC countries spent over USD 4000 billion on ODA. Other official and private donors contributed an unknown amount of aid too. We estimate that aid from non-DAC countries such as China and Saudi Arabia, NGDOs, foundations and other private sources was well over USD 1000 billion in this 60-year period. Aid has represented a very important financial flow for developing countries for a long time. In real terms, the total ODA provided by the DAC members rose by around 48% between 1970 and 1980, and by a further 32% in the 1980s. From 1993 to 1997 there was a significant drop, and the increase in the total volume of aid resumed only in 1998. In 2018, just 20 years, later total ODA from DAC countries stood at USD 150 billion.

> **Box 57. Aid and self-reliance: two sides of the same coin?**
>
> India has refused to accept foreign aid for disasters since 2004, when a tsunami killed more than 10,000 people on its southeast coast and thousands became homeless. The government founded the Federal Emergency Management Agency in response to the tragedy and vowed to deal with disasters on its own. With the 'flood of the century' devastating the state of Kerala in 2018, India did not accept over the USD 100 million of offers in external help. This stubbornness stirred up a lot of debate in the Indian press and intensified tensions between the state government of Kerala and the central government in New Delhi. This is a speaking example of how recipient countries struggle with the dilemma of receiving aid, being dependent and showing dependency on the one hand, and the desire and political pressure to remain in control and stand on their own feet on the other. The Grand Ethiopian Renaissance Dam – a USD 5 billion project – is an analogue case. Ethiopia is financing the controversial dam without external support, and Ethiopian government officials and workers are contributing the equivalent of a month's salaries per year. Government-owned banks are giving loans. Refusing to beg for international aid for the project, the Ethiopian government is using money from local taxes and has issued special government bonds to finance this geopolitically sensitive project. Private companies and even other countries such as Djibouti are buying them. The dam is now showcased as proof of an innovative approach to project financing and also as an illustration of the wish of developing countries to become less aid dependent. They are now increasingly turning to new systems to collect domestic

taxes, dismantle tax havens and try to track and stop illicit financial flows. Overall, since 2000, the proportion of government spending that is given by foreign donors has decreased by one-third in the world's poorest countries (Stanford, 2015). Some will argue that this is due to pressure from … the donor community.

So if, in the opinion of many, desperately few developing countries are able to produce a good economic and social report despite all this aid and generosity, should we conclude that aid is an ineffective tool? Or is such a conclusion unwarranted?

To answer this particularly difficult question, we need to consider not less than six other questions. The first relates to the overall balance sheet: is it all that negative or have development efforts contributed to specific positive results in terms of economic growth and human development? Secondly, we need to examine whether or not we are on track and if we still have the right agenda. In other words, is our strategy and approach future-proof? A third interrogation concerns the extent of the input: has there really been as much development aid and cooperation as many people think? Then, we also have to look at the recipients: does the aid actually reach those countries and people most in need of it? The most polemic question is perhaps at the same time the most complicated question of all: how efficiently are the resources used? Are we achieving the right results, the ones that we want, with development cooperation? A final and sixth question concerns the capacity and willingness of the donor community to sort out the problems on its own doorstep.

Progress, but not for everyone

When we consider the situation in most countries in the South, we are entitled to ask what has been achieved in the 60 or so years that there has been something we all called development aid, technical assistance, development cooperation or international development cooperation.

Simply concluding that developing countries have not made any progress would demonstrate a lack of historical perspective. Over the past half-century, the international community has been guilty of much self-deception, put up plenty of smokescreens and made many unwise promises, but in a number of respects, progress has undeniably been made. It will never be possible to scientifically attribute these positive evolutions to development cooperation alone. But from the examples that we will see, we can only conclude that development cooperation has made a significant contribution, be it by setting the agenda, monetarily or otherwise. By 1977, smallpox had been successfully eradicated. The Global Hunger Index in 2000 stated that the worldwide situation concerning undernourishment was serious; in 2020, it was concluded that it was 'moderate' and less severe.[60] Since the early 1990s, the number of small children who died from diarrhoea has dropped by two-thirds (from over 1.5 million to about half a million). This was largely achieved by improving access to drinking water and distributing a simple sugar-salt solution (oral rehydration therapy). According to the WHO, 90% of the world's population now has access to clean drinking water. Moreover, the Polio Eradication Initiative indicates that all but two countries are now polio-free: only parts of Afghanistan and neighbouring Pakistan still see new cases of infantile paralysis. Globally, over 95% of all children survive the first 15 years of their life. Over the last 20 years, stunting prevalence in children under the age of five dropped significantly; in 2000, almost one in three children were significantly shorter than average for their age and thus suffered from stunting, as a consequence of poor nutrition or repeated infections. Now, this is one in five. UNICEF figures show that, worldwide, more than 90% of primary-school-age children have been enrolled in school. Around half of the countries and areas in the world have achieved or nearly achieved universal primary education – that is, the net enrolment rate or net attendance rate in these countries is more than 95%. The Lancet's (2020) special issue on the global burden of diseases, injuries, and risk factors demonstrates that the health of the world's population is steadily improving. Global life expectancy at birth increased from 67.2 years in 2000 to 73.5 years in 2019. Healthy life expectancy has increased in 202 of the 204 countries and territories under review. Half of the world's population now live in middle-class or wealthy households, spending USD 11–110 per day per person (2011 purchasing power parity) (Kharas & Hamel, 2018). Over 90% of people now have access to electricity, up from 78% twenty years ago, World Bank data indicate. Our World in Data shows that almost 60% of the world's population are active internet users. Over 60% owns a mobile phone. The IMF DataMapper teaches us that emerging and developing countries' share of the world's GDP rose from 43% in 2000 to 57% in 2020, in large part, of course, due to the impressive breakneck growth in China and India. At the end of the last century, 62% of all bilateral trade was between just rich countries – namely the USA, Canada and Europe. In 2019, that share was down to 47% as developing countries are becoming more prominent trading partners (Tartar & Sam, 2019).

Box 58. Evidence-based optimism

The world is in a much better state than most of us think. This was the mantra of Hans Rosling (1948–2017), a Swedish professor of international health and one of the founding fathers of the Gapminder Foundation. His TED talks and the book (2018) he wrote with Ola Rosling and Anna Rosling Rönnlund, *Factfulness: Ten Reasons We're Wrong About the World – And Why Things Are Better Than You Think*, became world famous.[61] The book starts with 13 fact-based questions, such as 'how many people in the world have some access to electricity?'. It seems that journalists, scientists, politicians and ordinary people suffer from massive and collective ignorance and an overdramatic worldview. Most people still believe, and want to believe, in an over-simplistic and outdated idea: the dichotomy of 'the West and the rest' or 'the developed world and the developing world'. The Roslings write and convincingly present graphs showing levels of income, tourism, democracy, access to education, healthcare and electricity. They "all tell the same story: that the world used to be divided into two but isn't any longer. Today, most people are in the middle. There is no gap between the West and the rest, between developed and developing, between rich and poor. And we should all stop using the simple pairs of categories that suggest there is".

In one sense, we can thus assess the past decades in relative terms in an optimistic light. When the emphasis is on the historical perspective, significant progress in social and economic, even political, development can indeed be observed.

At the same time, there is no getting around a number of persistent and pressing problems that make any triumphalism misplaced. First, there are trends we have to detect, and we have to take into account new developments and threats. A recent joint annual report of the FAO (2020) and four other UN Agencies on the state of food security and nutrition in the world, for example, warns that after decades of decline, hunger has increased every year since 2014. It is expected to spike even higher over the coming years due to the effects of COVID-19. There are many *bêtes noires* around the corner we do not see as yet but that menace progress. The 2017 and 2018 editions of this UN report showed that conflict and climate variability and extremes undermine efforts to end hunger, food insecurity and malnutrition. In 2019, the report showed that economic slowdowns and downturns also undercut these efforts. In 2020, the COVID-19 pandemic, as well as unprecedented desert locust outbreaks in East Africa and elsewhere, was obscuring economic prospects in ways no one had anticipated. In any case, the projections of this authoritative report show that the world is not on track to achieve

Zero Hunger by 2030. We already mentioned major improvements concerning access to safe drinking water, but it remains a fact that almost 800 million people still lack even a basic drinking-water service, including 144 million people who are dependent on untreated surface water from lakes, ponds, rivers and streams. The WHO (2019) estimates that by 2025, half of the world's population will be living in water-stressed areas because of climate change, increasing water scarcity, demographic changes, urbanisation and the strain these trends exert on water supply systems.

Thanks to massive and intensive vaccination campaigns, Nigeria has seen no wild poliovirus cases since 2016. However, as we noted, polio remains endemic in Afghanistan and Pakistan: two countries with weak health systems, mobile populations and many conflict zones. So, the world has to remain vigilant. Because the virus is so highly infectious, failure to eradicate polio from these last remaining strongholds could result in a resurgence of the disease in other vulnerable countries. On the other hand, if polio can be eliminated in these two wild polio bastions, the world will be able to list polio next to smallpox and rinderpest[62] on the coveted list of globally eradicated diseases.

The prevalence of malnutrition has diminished considerably over the last decades but remains alarming: nearly half of all deaths in children under the age of five are attributable to undernutrition leading to stunting (low height for age) and wasting (low weight for height). The alarm bells are sounding even louder because of the COVID-19 pandemic. Malnutrition, including stunting and wasting but also micronutrient deficiencies and overweight, are becoming more problematic. Food systems are impacted by disrupted production, food trade, transportation and the sale of affordable and nutritious food.

Then, of course, we have not dealt with the thorny issue of inequality as yet. While we saw that, in many respects, the world has made major advancements as a global community, this does not mean that each and every citizen has got a fair share of this so-called progress and benefited from it in the same way. At the same time, we cannot conclude at once that this is automatically accompanied by a narrowing of the disparities and unequal chances of the lucky and the not-so-fortunate, or the rich and the poor. It remains a fact that life expectancy in the Central African Republic and Chad is around 54 years: in Japan, it is 30 years longer.

Although it is a useful and easy-to-understand proxy for what individuals' chances are in life, life expectancy is not an indicator used by UNDP and the University of Oxford in their Global Multidimensional Poverty Index (OPHI & UNDP, 2020). This index measures the complexities of poor people's lives, individually and collectively. It does not pretend that the lives of better-resourced people are not difficult or complex but rather sheds light on the extra impediments and difficulties that extremely poor people simultaneously face beyond income. It identifies how people are being left behind across three key dimensions: health (for example, any under-18-year-old child that died in the family over the last five years), education (for example, looking at young household members not having completed six years of schooling) and standard of living (for example, when the household cooks with dung, wood, charcoal or coal). In their latest 2020 report, the researchers of UNDP and Oxford conclude that across 107 developing countries, 1.3 billion people, or 22%, live in multidimensional poverty. About 84% of them live in Sub-Saharan Africa and South Asia.

Is aid future-proof?

We cannot conclude our first look at the balance sheet of 60 years of development cooperation without taking into consideration some global evolutions such as the epidemiological transition and environmental changes we are going through. Here also, so-called rich and poor countries or donors and recipients of aid are in the same boat. This is, first of all, the case for the ravaging pandemic of non-communicable diseases (NCDs). Four major categories of diseases are taking the upper hand across the world: the group of cardiovascular diseases (such as heart attacks and strokes), diabetes, cancer and chronic respiratory diseases (such as asthma). NCDs kill more than 40 million people each year, equivalent to more than 70% of all deaths globally. Importantly, NCDs disproportionately affect people in low- and middle-income countries where more than three-quarters of global NCD deaths occur. They are activated by poor living and working conditions, while at the same time their exorbitant costs negatively affect the already limited resources of poor families.

Secondly, driven and accelerated by human activity, the Earth's ecosystem is undergoing drastic changes. Climate change is, of course, an often referred-to consequence of this, and also disproportionally affects countries, regions and populations in the South because of temperature anomalies, prolonged droughts, unpredictable weather storms and hurricanes, and so on. But the Earth is under more pressure. Look at the decline in biodiversity, the loss in tropical forest, the depletion of fisheries, sea-level rises, the acidification of the oceans and pollution. Because their social and economic systems are more nature-dependent and because they have fewer instruments

Figure 25: Sustainable Development Goals: distance to target

Goals

1: Eradicate poverty
2: Food
3: Health
4: Education
5: Gender equality
6: Water
7: Energy
8: Economy
9: Infrastructure
10: Reduce inequality
11: Cities
12: Sustainable production
13: Climate
14: Oceans
15: Biodiversity
16: Institutions
17: Implementation

— — Levels of achievement to be attained by 2030

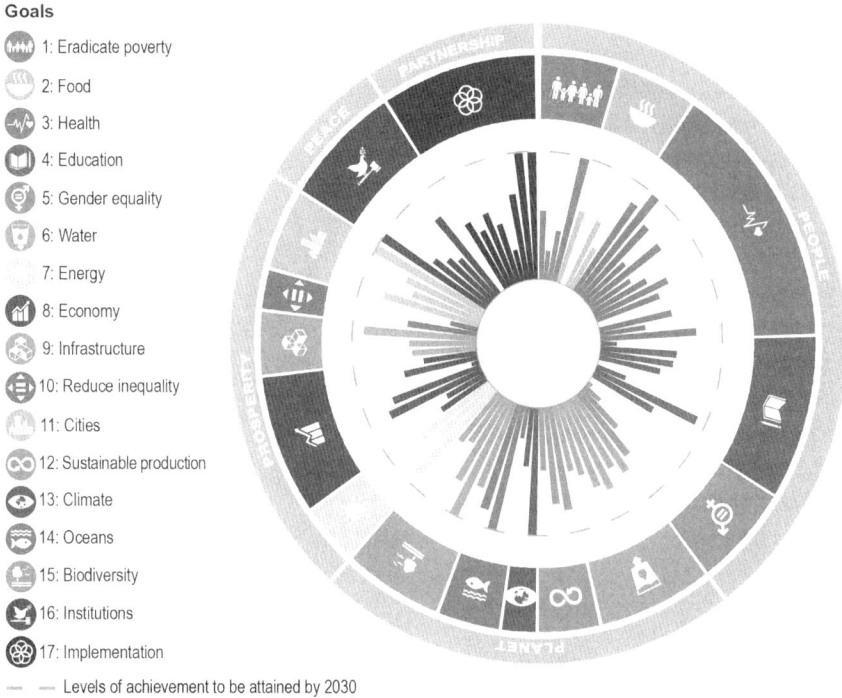

Note: The chart shows how far OECD countries (on average) are from achieving each target for which data are available. The longer the bars, the shorter the distance to be travelled by 2030; target levels are represented by the outer dotted circle. The inner circle (the starting point for the bars) represents a score of 3 or more standardised distances away from target, which most OECD countries have achieved on most targets. Targets are shown by goal, and goals are clustered by the '5Ps' of the 2030 Agenda.

Source: https://www.oecd.org/sdd/measuring-distance-to-the-sdg-targets-2019-a8caf3fa-en.htm.

to cope with the changes we are experiencing globally, developing countries are disproportionally affected by these environmental changes. Extreme weather triggers crop failure, migration, disease outbreaks and so on.

These epidemiological and environmental transitions were not on the radar when international development cooperation got out of the starting blocks some 60 years ago. But now they are. So, the international development cooperation sector has to deal with it. The aid sector, or industry, has to take these evolutions into account. It should mitigate the damage already incurred and make the global system future-proof. It has to make the shift from a focus on infectious diseases to one on non-communicable health conditions. It is called upon to help restore the pact between man and nature, even to move away from anthropocentric myopia. One way to evaluate if we are on track what this new, global mission is to have a look at whether or not progress has been made in realising the SDGs.

Are we really that generous?

We have repeatedly stressed that the volume of aid invested in developing countries since the 1960s is particularly volatile. Before the financial and economic crisis of 2008, aid budgets were on the increase and since the beginning of the new century, extra aid money had been promised and, in some cases, committed. As a result of the 2002 UN Financing for Development Conference in the Mexican city of Monterrey, donor countries promised a combined additional USD 16 billion per year. But only a few countries, such as Luxembourg, the Netherlands, Denmark, Ireland, Finland and the UK, effectively became more generous. Today, only Luxembourg, Sweden, Norway, Denmark and the UK meet the totemic commitment to dedicate 0.7% of their national wealth to ODA. Within the EU, various national ambitions to raise aid budgets were set out. In May 2015, the European Council reaffirmed its commitment to increase collective ODA to 0.7% of EU GNI before 2030. The UK did not wait to leave the EU to let drop its legally binding and emblematic engagement to reach the internationally set standard.

At present, the total aid given by the rich countries is about USD 150 billion. Yet we are not *so* generous.

In the rich countries, we give the average equivalent of one cup of coffee per person per week, in development aid – probably less than what we spend on food for our cat or dog. We have definitely not become more openhanded over the years. Through tax contributions, we now spend about three times more on ODA than we did in the early days of development aid, but we have also become three to four times richer. According to OECD figures, the support that the population of the rich countries gives to NGDOs has increased slightly, from 0.03% of our wealth in the early 1990s to 0.04%. Our collective sense of generosity distorts our perception of the capacity of development agencies to achieve real changes in the developing world with the 'ample' resources at their disposal. Many expect NGDOs – most of them with the income of a small or medium-sized enterprise – to be able to solve highly complex and varied problems in countries and regions that lack the basic prerequisites for such an outcome (properly functioning government, existing infrastructure, human capital and economic and social fabric).

We are also forced to conclude that we are not particularly generous because our priorities clearly lie closer to home. International spending, including on development aid, is dwarfed by domestic spending. Most donor countries spend less than 1% of their (central) government budgets on international aid. Compare this with OECD data indicating that its members expect to spend about one-third of their budgets on national social protection schemes, more than one-fifth on supporting their own economies, just less than 20% on their healthcare sectors and almost 10% on defence. The annual municipal budget of a city like Berlin, the capital of Germany, exceeds the yearly contribution Germany makes to international development cooperation by nearly 50%. This last example also sheds some light on the weak lever international development cooperation can be for tackling the immense problems faced by developing countries and their citizens. Many people consider the aid their country is allocating to developing countries to be a change-maker; for some, it is even a magic bullet: a generous instrument that helps recipient countries to radically better the lives of all their citizens. But beneficiary governments face much bigger and more difficult challenges than Berlin. How could a vast country like the Democratic Republic of Congo have changed the living conditions of the 84 million Congolese with the USD 30 that donors gave it per Congolese in 2018? Do we suppose that the Bolivian government can make a difference thanks to the USD 66 donors provided for each of its citizens? What can war-torn Mali do with the USD 78 it gets per citizen or Laos with USD 80? And, as we have seen, not all of that aid is quality aid. Not all of it gets into the hands of the local government or is country programmable aid that helps a recipient government to set out a long-term policy. Finally, not all of that aid reaches the final target group.

Who is receiving aid?

The next question is whether this limited amount of aid actually reaches the countries and people most in need of it.

There are international agreements regarding this. Since the early 1980s, the donor community has repeatedly undertaken to devote 0.15–0.20% of its GNI to aid for the LDCs. In 2001, a promise was also given that aid to the LDCs would be completely untied. Such targets have been reaffirmed in every Programme of Action for the LDCs since, as well as in the MDGs and 2030 Agenda for Sustainable Development in the context of the global partnership for development.

The current 47 LDCs, representing over one billion people, or 13.4% of the world's population, not only have a particularly low income (and in most cases, a significant part of the population living far below the international poverty line of USD 1.9 per day in purchasing power) but their human resource base is also very weak in terms of the health conditions of their population or their level of education and they are economically very vulnerable. This makes them more reliant on development aid than other countries. It can be concluded from Table 9 that the LDCs do receive 2.5 times more ODA per citizen than 30 years ago. The international pressure on donors to be more selective in their aid-giving behaviour in favour of countries most in need thus might have had some effect. However, it remains that only about 5% of their wealth, in terms of GNI, can be attributed to international aid from the traditional donors, down from around 20% 25 years ago. They have, therefore, become less dependent on international support for their economic and social prosperity and development.

Table 9: ODA by income category, 1990–2018

Region	ODA per head 1990	ODA per head 2008	ODA per head 2018
All developing countries	9.4	23.7	21.8
LDCs	19.5	38	53.2

Source: World Bank

Figure 26: Distribution of ODA by income group (2017–2018) in millions of USD

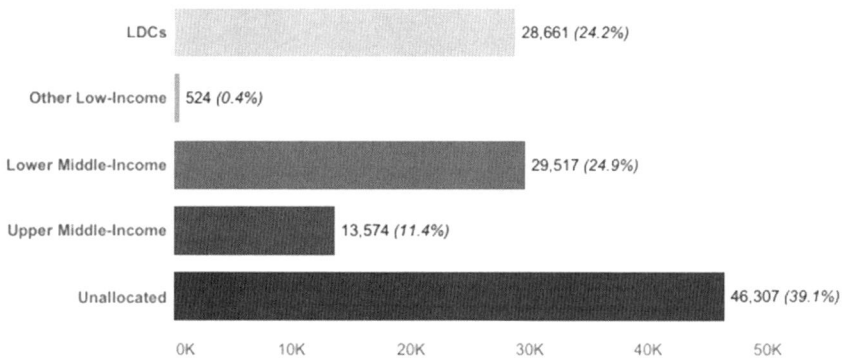

Source: OECD-DAC, Data Visualisations 2017–2018[63]

270

However, the DAC countries have not yet kept their promises. Rather than 0.15%, a mere 0.09% of collective GNI goes to the LDCs.

Moreover, as Figure 26 makes clear, the 12 other low-income countries receive almost as much aid as the 49 LDCs do. This is no surprise since the gluttons of aid, Pakistan and Nigeria, belong to the former group.

There is a popular notion that Africa in particular is given generous quantities of development aid. Yet since 1960, Asia has received over USD 40 billion more aid than Africa and received significantly more support than Africa up to the 1990s. It is true that the aid intensity is greater for Africa than for any other continent: per head of population, Africa has always received more aid, and relative to GNI, aid has always represented a more significant contribution there. Yet although several African countries derive a very large proportion of their income from development aid, it is revealing that not a single country has ever received as much support as South Korea (USD 170 per head and 20% of GNI) and Taiwan (USD 190 per head and 40% of GNI) in the 1950s.

The effectiveness and impact of development cooperation

This brings us to the hardest question: can development aid or cooperation contribute anything significant to the development process in developing countries? This question is particularly difficult to answer, if only because we are discussing an 'unguided missile' that is constantly changing direction.

Defenders of development cooperation are fond of pointing out that aid has been a very significant factor in the spectacular success of a number of countries – Indonesia and South Korea in the 1970s, Bolivia and Ghana in the 1980s, Uganda and Vietnam in the 1990s and Rwanda of late. International programmes supported the Green Revolution, measures to combat river blindness, immunisation campaigns against children's diseases, the fight against HIV/AIDS and, more recently, efforts to contain the spread of the coronavirus. We have dealt with this proven track record before.

A textbook example is Mozambique, which, thanks to large-scale international support in the early 1990s, has signed a peace treaty and been able to organise a process of national reconciliation. Initially, 80% of the government budget was provided by donors. Thanks to that support, two million refugees were repatriated, 96,000 soldiers from both sides of the conflict were disarmed, elections were organised, and social services reconstructed. The country recorded economic growth of over 5% per year during the last two decades. How it will structurally react to the headwinds of the cyclones in 2019, the swarms of desert locusts ravaging its agriculture in 2020 and the coronavirus crisis remains to be seen. This is a classic example of what can be achieved with aid. Since the start of development aid (the Marshall Plan, the World Bank, etc.) as an instrument for getting post-war Europe back on its feet, we have known that large-scale aid can be particularly effective and provide a substantial boost in post-conflict situations.

The aid sector has always been the subject of fierce controversy. Radical opponents of development aid were found in the early decades in both the so-called dependency school and the liberal school. The former group regarded development aid as an instrument of neo-colonial dominance that prevented the countries in the South, which they called under-developed countries, from developing. The liberal school emphasised that aid blocked economic development because it was in the interest of bureaucracies in both the donor and recipient countries to consolidate their inefficient, often corrupt aid industry and not create the conditions for sound (i.e., free-market-based) economic development. Peter Bauer, the leading advocate of the liberal school, bluntly stated that the concept of the Third World or the South and the policy of official aid are inseparable. They are two sides of the same coin. For him, the Third World is the creation of foreign aid: without foreign aid, there is no Third World (Bauer, 1981). Bauer has many successors, even today. The Ghanaian economist George Ayittey (2005), for example, has been speaking out for years against the 'vampire states' in Africa, which give their people no development opportunities, yet are kept in power by development aid. The Zambian-American economist Dambisa Moyo stirred up much controversy with her suggestion that the time has come to turn off the aid tap. In her much-discussed book, *Dead Aid* (2010), she sketches the way in which over-reliance on aid has trapped many African countries in a vicious circle of aid dependence, aid-induced corruption, market distortion and further poverty, leaving them with nothing but the 'need' for more aid.

Both schools argue in favour of 'trade, not aid'. However, as well as their motivation for scrapping aid, the alternatives they propose differ fundamentally. According to the dependency school, a new international economic order will solve all the problems; the liberal school believes that the free market will bring the solution.

In the 1990s, a kind of donor fatigue arose in most rich countries. One of the most widely cited causes for the erosion of public support for development aid was a lack of clarity about the positive impact of the support that had been given. However, what actually happened in many donor countries was that a set of arguments against aid was built up on the basis of negative cases. Expensive, presumptuous and otiose 'white elephant projects', called this because they are a rarity and anomaly in the local biotope, were held as proof that aid was not being spent efficiently and was also failing to deliver the expected effectiveness and impact. Critics claimed that aid money also distorted local price mechanisms in a way that was harmful to the country's development (through rising exchange rates, falling interest rates). Moreover, aid was said to make it possible for recipient governments to engage in unproductive spending, maintain the army and the apparatus of repression and keep local taxes low (including for the rich). Meanwhile, few examples were found of bilateral and multilateral aid projects that had actually succeeded in reaching the poor (Griffin & McKinley, 1996). It has since become clear that all this proves is that there were shortcomings with the aid apparatus. In other words, there were problems with the performance and efficiency of development aid.

Box 59. Evaluation trends

Within the conventional development cooperation sector, without any fanfare, an evaluation culture has emerged over the last 10 to 15 years. On the website of the DAC Evaluation Resource Centre, there are now several thousand evaluation reports contributed by around 30 bilateral and multilateral donors. The evaluations show that most development projects succeed in achieving the direct goals that have been set; for example, the construction of a clinic. Most donors claim to be doing well in more than 75% of their projects. Moreover, the proportion of successful projects is apparently rising. But a critical look at the many evaluations shows that the success rate is particularly high for projects with tangible, clearly delineated objectives, such as the construction of schools, the writing of textbooks or the provision of training. Projects with more complex social objectives such as institutional strengthening or changes in behaviour with regard to gender are definitely no less relevant – quite the reverse – but are harder to plan, more sensitive to all kinds of internal and external factors, and are often such that success cannot be expressed in hard figures.

In any case, it is often hard to ascribe success (or failure) to the project or programme itself, as numerous other factors are involved over which neither the donor nor the local actors have any control: macro-economic developments, political problems, natural disasters and so on. Moreover, a project usually has control only over the resources it invests and has to operate via all kinds of existing intermediary structures. Whether the final target groups ultimately change their behaviour or experience the benefits of a new service depends on far more than just the project. This is called the 'attribution problem'.

Because development organisations are under great pressure to prove that they are operating efficiently and effectively, and have a lasting impact on people's lives, many have set up meticulous monitoring and evaluation mechanisms. The jargon terms for these are 'project cycle management' and 'results-based management', and their best-known component is the logical framework, or 'logframe', so called because a fairly strict link is sought between a project's general goals (for example, reducing women's vulnerability), its direct goals (for example, giving access to small loans), activities (for example, establishing a microfinancing institution, training the women etc.) and budget (for example €100,000). There is now a general feeling in the sector that these tools oblige everyone to engage in highly sterile and bureaucratic procedures. They work well for predictable projects with easy-to-grasp outcomes but cannot cope with social change processes. What is more, if you put in the necessary effort you may gain an understanding of what has changed among the target groups – in our example, a reduction in women's vulnerability – but it is usually impossible to work out exactly why this is the case and what the project's contribution has been. The result is that you learn little from the process. Alternative approaches for planning, monitoring and evaluation have been suggested. 'Outcome mapping', for example, helps a programme track changes in the behaviour, practice or relationships of the people or actors with whom the programme directly works. These actors are called the programme's boundary partners. They are the local change agents who are supported by the programme and will continue their work, even after the end of the development programme. For example, students' clubs and curriculum development committees were boundary partners in an environmental education programme in Zimbabwe that implemented outcome mapping.

Regular monitoring cycles are a key feature in outcome mapping. These cycles are characterised by processes of self-assessment and collaborative learning, and help programme staff and the programme boundary partners learn about the programme results, the programme activities that may have contributed to these results and the programme team's own internal performance.

A vibrant global outcome mapping learning community[64] shows that more and more development organisations are developing an interest in outcome mapping and are starting to implement this alternative planning, monitoring and evaluation methodology.

During the same period, there was growing scientific interest in the subject, and various studies were carried out to try to examine the relationship between aid and goals in a more sophisticated manner. The persistent theme running through the findings is that under certain conditions, aid does have a favourable impact on a country's or community's economic and social development. Development aid ensures that poor countries, which lack sufficient savings of their own to finance investments, get the chance to do so anyway. Capital goods and technology are scarce in the poor countries themselves; development aid consists of hard currency with which these can be purchased on the international market. Moreover, aid can ensure that the recipient government, which can count on only limited tax revenue locally, is still able to deliver minimal services.

Museru, Toerien and Gossel (2014) investigated the effectiveness of aid as a contributor to economic growth for a panel of 26 Sub-Saharan African countries over the period 1992–2011. Their results indicated that aid contributed to growth in Sub-Saharan Africa over the time period covered, especially in the study period preceding the financial crisis (1992–2007).

However, it is clear that aid does not have a direct impact on economic growth, other than via certain transmission mechanisms: investments, imports, the fiscal regime and public policy (Gomanee, Girma & Morrissey, 2002). It is also assumed that aid has a positive and significant influence on public investments in the recipient countries. But aid is fungible and enables recipient countries to use their own resources, and governments their tax-revenues, for other purposes. Those 'other' purposes (such as investments in military equipment) are not necessarily compatible with the donor's objectives, which focus on economic growth and human development.

Gomanee, Girma and Morrissey (2002) calculated that investments that were financed with aid had the most effect on the economic growth of the African countries studied. Aid can serve as a lifebelt even for the very poorest. According to Collier (2007), aid to the then 58 poorest economies, where the poorest one billion people are trying to survive, has added around 1% of growth over the previous 30 to 40 years. When you bear in mind that growth in these countries was – at that time – far lower than 1%, it becomes clear that development aid has prevented these countries from completely collapsing.

Studies commissioned by the World Bank in the second half of the 1990s came to similar conclusions. Financial aid has a positive impact only if the recipient country applies the right policy measures. But there is a tendency for the recipient governments with poor policies to use the aid for government spending rather than growth-promoting investments. In countries with a sound economic policy, foreign aid does not replace private initiative. Instead, aid works as a magnet, attracting private investments. Every dollar of aid brings in nearly two dollars of investment, it is claimed. Aid is primarily efficient and effective if it reinforces local institutions and policies. If the latter receive financial support, coupled with knowledge transfer, they will be in a position to provide better services to the population and economic actors (Dollar & Pritchett, 1998; Burnside & Dollar, 2000).

Yet much uncertainty remains about the alleged causal and fruitful relationship between aid and good policy. Does aid encourage good policy, or does good policy attract aid? There are plenty of examples to illustrate the point that aid money has not accelerated the required reform and democratisation processes: rather, it has slowed them down.[65] In any case, it looks as though donors have a very limited influence on the policies of their partner countries. The local political environment and power relations have a far greater impact on the way in which governments manage state affairs than donors. Donors can often exert pressure to ensure that the government apparatus of the recipient country is adjusted on paper, but they have less control over actual changes. Moreover, psychology plays a role here. Governments and their populations do not like being dictated to by foreign countries. It elicits resistance – even to proposals that may be rational and sensible.

Sociologists, from their perspective of the emergence of a world society, hypothesise roles for aid – bilateral and multilateral – in the diffusion of various institutions, including stock exchanges, legislation, women's rights, population policies and environmental policies (Swiss, 2016). For them, international development cooperation helps facilitate the world society spreading norms and underpins institutional isomorphism among countries. It remains to be seen, however, if the creation of a ministry for decentralisation and democratisation, an agency for the promotion of gender equality or a programme for decent work and social protection in a recipient country, like Benin, Papua New Guinee or Belize, represents a genuine commitment to these agendas or gimmicks and mimics to please the donor community.

Box 60. Nobel Peace Prize laureates: international norm entrepreneurs

As we read on its website, the Nobel Peace Prize has been awarded 101 times to 135 Nobel laureates between 1901 and 2020: more specifically, to 107 individuals and 28 organizations. The International Committee of the Red Cross has been given the Nobel Peace Prize three times (in 1917, 1944 and 1963), and the Office of the UN High Commissioner for Refugees has received the award twice (in 1954 and 1981). In 2020 the World Food Programme received the Nobel Peace Prize "for its efforts to combat hunger, for its contribution to bettering conditions for peace in conflict-affected areas and for acting as a driving force in efforts to prevent the use of hunger as a weapon of war and conflict". With this gesture, the Nobel Prize Committee gives a clear signal that should shake the international community and particularly those forces that set the SDGs in train. The 2020 Global Hunger Index found that 51 countries have levels of hunger that are seriously alarming. The prevalence of undernourishment has stagnated since 2015, and the absolute number of people who are undernourished was nearly 690 million in 2020 (von Grebmer, 2020). Roger Alford (2008), who studied how laureates have served as agents in pursuit of the international rule of law, distinguishes different periods, during which the Prize originally put forward pacifists, later turned its focus to statesmen, humanitarians and human rights defenders and, in more recent times, has showcased promotors of democracy. Looking at the list of the awardees, it becomes clear that the 20th-century international norm entrepreneurs, as Alford calls them, are often highly visible, vocal and exceptionally courageous individuals from the South, such as Shirin Ebadi, an Iranian human rights activist (in 2003), Wangari Muta Maathai, the founder of the Kenyan green belt movement (in 2004), Mohamad Yunus, the initiator of the Grameen Bank in Bangladesh and one of the captains of the international micro-finance movement (in 2006), the Indian social reformer and children's rights campaigner Kailash Satyarthi and the Pakistani activist for female education Malala Yousafzai (both in 2014), and the Congolese Denis Mukwege, known as the doctor who treats raped women, together with the Iraqi Yazidi human rights activist Nadia Murad (both in 2018). These civil society representatives have undoubtedly helped facilitate the emergence, cascading and internationalising of norms that inspired and also legitimised the development community.

At one time, use was made of so-called *ex-ante* policy conditions: countries were required to promise reforms – no more and no less. And promise they did, time after time, without anything much coming of those commitments. When this was realised, donors began to link aid to the recipient governments' performance: a practice also known as *ex-post* or outcome conditionalities. A modest but clear shift was seen in favour of countries with better policies and against those with worse policies. This then led to a debate about the 'cost of neglect'. Turning off the tap to or reducing cooperation with weak states can mean that they completely disintegrate, their populations are left without assistance and civil war ensues. The Democratic Republic of Congo and Somalia are telling examples of this. Even the more recent process of governance conditionalities, in which the recipient government is required to enter into dialogue and cooperate with the private sector and civil society (trade unions, local NGOs, churches etc.), comes up against insurmountable problems in such countries. Why should an incumbent president have to soft-soap the *de facto* opposition and even give them a share of the aid pie? Do the donors want to undermine his position of power?

The debate about aid effectiveness and its effect on economic growth remains vigorous, mainly among academics. Doucouliagos and Paldam (2011) conducted a meta-analysis of 1217 estimates of aid effectiveness published in scientific papers and articles. Their analysis suggests that, on average, aggregate development aid flows are ineffective in generating growth. They show that the distribution of results is significantly asymmetrical in a way that reflects the reluctance of the research community to publish negative results. There is thus a publication bias, they conclude.

In a more recent paper, Doucouliagos and other colleagues (2020) suggest that the career situations and ambitions of researchers are at play as well. On the basis of data they collected on 190 authors, they found that on average, older, non-tenured researchers inflate research findings on aid effectiveness. One plausible explanation they have for this is the link between these authors and aid agencies.

In our foreword, we wrote that emotions are always present in discussions on human suffering, distress, poverty and the responsibility of outsiders to give a hand. Even in academia, the effect of metaphysical pathos cannot be excluded. In much that is written about development cooperation, the author's underlying mood of pessimism or optimism, of sympathy or bitterness is expressed in many analyses. As a consequence, in this kind of a polemic, the attention is focused on the differences between two extreme points of view, to the neglect of convergences, continuity or nuance. This is probably why Doucouliagos and Paldam, in their 2011 article, hastened to add that aid ineffectiveness does not mean that there are no individual countries and time periods where aid is effective. It can also not be concluded that aid is never effective. Food aid given for emergency relief and aid given to reduce debt do produce positive effects.

Box 61. Aid helps, but it is not the solution

Some local NGOs can boast excellent results in terms of the number of people that they reach, the services they deliver and the levers for development that they offer to their members or clients. Examples of this are the microcredit institutions Grameen Bank and BRAC in Bangladesh, the Self-Employed Women's Association in India, the farmers' organisation Groupement Naam in Burkina Faso, Hundee, an organisation in Ethiopia promoting seed banks, savings funds and women's participation among the Oromo people, the Movement of Landless Farmers in Brazil, the Confederación Autónoma Síndical Clasista, a broad-based trade union in the Dominican Republic, and the savings and credit cooperatives in Jamaica.

The following are some of the features that we invariably find in such organisations:
– their development strategy had already been defined before external aid was given;
– their policy choices and visions are very clearly formulated, and development aid has to fit in with them;

- they lay stress on social justice and redistribution;
- they develop their own systems and mechanisms to ensure local ownership;
- they encourage local participation within those institutions;
- they invest in the long term and adopt a programme approach rather than a project approach;
- they are expansive and growth oriented, and they seek a scale of operations that generates efficiencies;
- they involve very poor, less poor and not-so-rich people (target mix);
- they show great appetite for and interest in the ideas and experiences of others; and
- they pick up on external opportunities and integrate externally acquired knowledge into their own processes.

Development cooperation: a stumbling-block?

Studies referred to earlier sought to identify how recipient countries should behave. In recent years, there has also been growing interest in how donors should behave. After all, whether projects and programmes are designed and executed by official or non-governmental, bilateral or multilateral agencies, the institutions concerned always have their own philosophies and approaches, which can themselves be the cause of poor performance and, hence, a lack of effectiveness and impact for aid (Martens et al., 2002). They can push local governments and populations into erroneous ways of thinking and encourage attitudes and behaviour that are not conducive to self-reliance. In recent years, fierce debate has broken out. The protagonists are Jeffrey Sachs and William Easterly, two economists who look at the macro-level effects of development aid (Miller, 2011). Sachs, the Director of the Centre for Sustainable Development at Colombia University (USA), has declared that it is possible to eradicate poverty from the world within a single generation if the will to do so is there, along with the right plans and strategies (Sachs, 2005). Above all, he calls on donors to take a more generous and ingenious approach to development aid and to back the SDGs (Sachs, 2015). Easterly (2002) opposes the development planners who seek to adopt a strategic and centralist approach to poverty. He wants to replace them with 'seekers' who understand and accept the mechanisms of the market. According to him, the overconfident donor community is itself to blame for underdevelopment and poverty. Notwithstanding much rhetoric on international efforts to better aid effectiveness (remember the 2005 Paris Declaration roadmap) when assessing 51 aid agencies, Easterly finds only a modest improvement in transparency and more in moving away from ineffective channels such as tied aid, food aid and technical assistance. He did not find evidence of improvements in specialisation, fragmentation and selectivity (Easterly & Williamson, 2011).

In recent years, we have seen a growing body of research looking at the micro-level, analysing projects, programmes and policies on a case-by-case basis to determine what is effective aid (Miller, 2011). This is also what Nobel Prize-winning economists Banerjee and Duflo (2014) are doing with their Poverty Action Lab. Their premise is that ideology, ignorance, and inertia on the part of the expert, aid worker, or local policymaker often explain why policies fail and aid does not have the effect it should. Banerjee and Duflo are so-called *randomistas*; they use randomised control trials or experiments to find out what works and what does not. They provide evidence, for example, that directly investing in children's and pregnant women's nutrition produces tremendous social returns. They show how giving away fortified foods, deworming children and providing micronutrients or free nutritional supplements can do wonders in reducing undernutrition and poverty.

When we discuss the role of the aid apparatus itself, we are naturally primarily considering the coherence of donor countries' development cooperation and other policies. What is the point of reinforcing developing countries' export capacity if donors' trade policies maintain import barriers? Or of investing in the demobilisation of combatants and the promotion of peace in a country, while simultaneously exporting light weapons to the same region? And how can environmental policy be aligned with development cooperation policy?

As regards the development agencies themselves, one other significant criticism is that the bureaucratic structures and mechanisms they use are themselves dysfunctional or at least constitute obstacles to development.

Box 62. Financial donors and cultural nitwits

In his book *State of Denial*, Bob Woodward (2006) refers on several occasions to the cultural short-sightedness of the US army in Iraq. In March 2004, Condoleezza Rice sent Frank Millar, a senior director of the National Security Council, to Iraq. There, he accompanied a Humvee patrol as it drove through the notorious defiant Shia slum Sadr City, where he saw poverty of the kind that breeds the desire for vengeance. There was no drinkable water and the sewers were blocked. The people lived amid filth and simply dumped their rubbish and faeces in front of their houses. The American soldiers were being deployed more as engineers than as infantrymen, setting up water distribution systems and repairing roads. The money for these *ad hoc* projects came from the Commander's Emergency Response Program, a form of official American development aid. Millar concluded that these funds needed to increase and be made available more quickly. They were having a clear impact on the population. He was struck by the Iraqis' response: they seemed friendly and their attitude was certainly not hostile. Little children would greet the passing soldiers with big smiles and give them the thumbs-up. He noted that it was not their middle finger that they were sticking up, but what he failed to realise was that in Iraq sticking up your thumb is equivalent to the middle-finger gesture in the US!

American soldiers do not have a monopoly over such blunders. Even practised development workers constantly come up against intercultural obstacles in their relations with partners. How long does it take to realise that the friendly Tanzanian with his humble *ninaomba* ('I beseech you') expects just as much compliance from the donor as his Kenyan counterpart – sometimes felt to be aggressive – who instead says *ninataka* ('I want')? Again, many have been happy to give money to rescue Malinese *talibé*: children in Koran schools who have not seen their parents for years, have to live with a *marabout* and scour the streets, begging or picking pockets. But who exactly are they rescuing? Their parents, the *marabout* and the children themselves believe that they are saved, thanks to their religious classes. How do you approach 'development' in a society that attaches more importance to shame than honour? Bob Elsen et al. (2007) have developed a practical 'coconut model' for this, which is useful for anyone wishing to think about the cultural environment in which they wish to work. Just as with a coconut, you have to penetrate five layers to gain a better understanding of a culture. The outer skin is hard but instantly visible: the clothes, the etiquette, the language and the rituals. Then comes the pith. Here one finds the conventions and attitudes that are dominant and stubbornly ingrained in a culture. Next, one encounters the shell of the coconut seed – the symbols that every culture has and that are hard for outsiders to grasp. The coconut flesh lies even deeper and is also juicier: it consists of the foundations of a culture with its beliefs, norms and values, attitudes and ways of dealing with emotions or violence. Finally, one comes to the milk: the cultural patterns. Cultures differ fundamentally in the extent to which they are based on community or individualism, on democracy or justice, on status or skill, on rules or flexibility and so on.

Most development agencies work with fairly standardised set-ups, which leave little space for variations. Standardisation is used as a complexity-reducing mechanism that is supposed to ensure that the different actors (the legislative, executive and bureaucracy in both the donor and recipient country) back the institution's multiple goals and that the ways in which tasks are carried out by the various parties concerned (from the head office in the donor country to local personnel 6700 kilometres away) are compatible.

Some, as we already mentioned in the case of the EU, experiment with more flexible, iterative approaches to tackle very specific problems in a creative but coordinated way. The marching orders are to engage in the fight against corruption, the improvement of access of African cacao to the European market or the prevention of non-communicable diseases such as asthma but, also, to work together, form different alliances, experiment, invest, learn from experience and exchange evidence. In recent years, innovations have also been introduced in the management of the aid apparatus. Particularly worth noting is the decentralisation of the toolkit: part of the apparatus is deconcentrated and a number of powers are delegated. As a result, local departments of the bilateral donors are assigned a more important role and have more room for manoeuvre. Moreover, part of the task is outsourced to private actors such as NGDOs, consultancies or local companies. In some cases, a public-private partnership is sought with such private institutions.

Box 63. The Samaritan is trapped … and so is the person he has helped

Anyone who has ever been involved in a cooperation project knows how many complex relational elements, which are hard to discuss, are involved. Earlier, we referred to the tendency on the part of both parties (donor and recipient) to fudge the question of the material ownership of the thing that is given, whether it is a well or a computer. There is also the question of how much I should give. Is it sensible to give more than the amount of resources held by the partner themselves? Should I give cash so that my partner can decide for themselves what to use it for, or resources in kind so that I can be sure that they are used properly? Should I give 'cold money' (*argent froid*) without conditions or 'hot money' (*argent chaud*) that has to be repaid in some way? For how long should I give? Should I state from day one that I intend to cooperate over the long term, or should we get to know each other properly first? Do they have to put all their cards on the table if I prefer to keep some of mine back? Should I dissuade them, or even forbid them, from also working with other donors on the grounds that they are not following my strategy? Does it make sense to break off cooperation as soon as something goes wrong, or is that the moment to strengthen my resolve and get everything back on track again?

Essential though such questions are, they are rarely the subject of discussion in the sector and almost never the subject of research. Gibson (2005) has taken a somewhat more in-depth look at one specific issue from the viewpoint of collective action theory. He speaks of the Samaritan's dilemma, with a nod to the parable of the Good Samaritan in the New Testament. The Samaritan has a psychological need to help but would, of course, like the recipient to also make enough of an effort to get out of trouble. The recipient would, clearly, like the donor to continue with their efforts. They are thus likely to promise to make a big effort but fail to carry through with this in practice. The Samaritan, who wants their intervention to bring about the right results on a long-term basis, is forced to continue with their support…

The recipient might also be described as being in a 'Catch 22' situation. The expression is based on the situation of the insane military airman Orr, who, in Joseph Heller's satirical novel set in World War II, is unable to tell his superiors that he is crazy because that would be the sane thing to do, and he would then have to carry out more bombing raids. The recipient is in a similar no-win situation. If they wish to ignore stupid or irrelevant advice from the donor, they have to do so covertly, otherwise the aid will stop.

Another common dilemma in the development sector can be described as a 'double bind' situation. The position of aid recipients is dependent and less powerful. They are stumped by contradictory messages – even those implicit in the whole 'ownership discourse', which sound like 'do what I say but only because it is your own decision'. And do you think that your partner in the South does not know that you consider them to be disorganised, inefficient and lacking in pride in the project when it says on your website that you are cooperating with a dynamic self-help group, which is making a big difference in the local area?

But confidence in local governments and institutions – despite the fact that they are called 'partners' – continues to be very limited. Many still prefer project aid to the more flexible programme approach, and few dare shift to budget support, which enables the 'partner' to develop and implement their own agenda in accordance with their own pace, habits, procedures and methods. Usually, the preference is for a comfortable interventionist tunnel approach in which clear goals are set and pursued single-mindedly. The desire is to see results as soon as possible and to be able to show off those results to taxpayers or generous donors. This persists, despite the fact that it has been proven that development is a particularly complex and long-term process, which, above all, must empower local institutions, such as ministries, NGOs and private companies, to build up their own capacity and ability to render services to target groups. But do we have the patience to invest time and energy in a lot of capacity-building first, which will, after some time, most probably lead to institutional strengthening, which should, as we hope, after some time, make it possible for the local institution to deliver services, which will, after some time, we suppose, lead to poverty reduction?

Conclusion:
the past will not come back but is still there

The central thesis of this book is that the dichotomy of the North and the South is an outdated but also over-simplistic idea that still pervades the sector of international development cooperation. We are in times of globalisation. Are we in the first wave of globalisation, some will ask? Many scholars will protest vehemently and contest this suggestion. But are we undergoing the second wave, the third wave, the fourth wave, the fifth wave of globalisation? We do not know. And we do not think it matters much for what we are studying here. Globalisation is here. It is a social fact, as Durkheim would have said. It has been here since we were born and will remain here when we are gone. How much it affects us in our daily life, to what extent it even determines what we do, at what speed it propels us into the future, … we do not know as yet. In any case, for over 50 years, people involved in development aid, or call it international development cooperation, have ignored the profound consequences of globalisation. They (as we said in the preface: we) are children of the idea that there is a North which has much and a South which lacks much. And this is correct. They see a North which even has too much, which benefits excessively, or at least disproportionately from the economic, social, political and even cultural *rapports de force* in the world. This is also correct. So, the North should transfer some of what it has in excess or abundance to the under-resourced South, and even more importantly, start addressing the root causes that continue to create social, economic and environmental injustice across the globe. Financial transfers and coordinated actions to challenge existing power structures are, in this view, one of the ways to bring things back in balance. It is considered one way to do justice to humanity as a whole. Development aid, technical assistance, development cooperation and international cooperation are and were a variety of ways – and ever-better ways – to do this: on the one hand, to fill the gaps, make the bridges, provide for the finances that were lacking in the South, or the knowledge, know-how, experience or technology; on the other hand, to advocate for structural changes in the global economic system, to demand more inclusive forms of national and global governance and work towards a just green transition. While historical inbalances need to be addressed, both North and South should get and have its fair share. This respectable conviction also inspired the so-called alter-globalist movement which has mobilised many an NGDO militant, trade unionist and environmentalist since the 1990s. With this network movement, they wanted to act as a countervailing power to a globalisation wave that sharpened the inequalities and divisions between North and South even further and suggested that globalisation could take alternative, more equitable, forms. But globalisation is more than a flurry or a passing shock wave. It is determining the new social morphology of the world, the way we look at things, the manner in which we think, act and interact. So, it is also making for a sea change for the sector of development cooperation: a sector that was and still is to a great extent, but not entirely, linked to the past reality and old idea of a fundamental North-South divide.

For over 50 years, the people involved in the development cooperation sector, be they paid professionals or volunteers, were convinced and tried to convince others that they were needed, even essential as 'specialists', to bridge the gap between the North and South, even to fill that gap and remove all disparities between, let us say, the USA and the Philippines, France and the Central African Republic, the UK and the Gambia, Romania and Moldavia. But, as we have seen with the picture we took in our preface of the local reality of the small hamlet of Toubacouta in Senegal, these North-South specialists do not have the monopoly anymore. Others, many others, have entered the scene. Because of globalisation. We see an increasing, even exponential, number of actors involved in a complex web of interactions. Many of them are not entering the game because of development cooperation *per se*. They are not engaging in collaborations with people or organisations at the other end of the world because they want to do something to restore the balance between the North and South, in favour of the latter. We also see local actors in Africa, Asia and Latin America that do not wait for someone or an organisation somewhere in the North to show solidarity and willingness to transfer money, know-how or technology. 'Transfer' might have been, for quite some time, the main vector looked at as a solution to the North-South divide. 'Network, acquire and appropriate' is now the new motto, especially when there is some degree of level playing field. In more unequal or hostile environments, a wide variety of local, national and transnational civil society organisations try to challenge the status-quo and demand policy change. Again, it is globalisation that is shaping the environment that makes it possible for this change in attitude to take place both in the North and South. The people in the South are – for sure – no longer the 'incapable others' or 'victims' who have to be helped and assisted by the benevolent of the North.

The consequence of all of this is a fundamental change in the landscape of international development cooperation. Development cooperation is no longer the reserve of development aid specialists. In this book, we have looked at them and seen how they are themselves realising that they have to open up, that they are challenged by others who are entering 'their field', even that they might be sidelined by others who claim to be able to do a better job. We have categorised the aid specialists into separate 'pillars'. We saw the first pillar of government agencies, mainly in traditional donor countries, which set the standards and norms via authoritative platforms such as the OECD-DAC. The second pillar is crowded with an extremely large group of international agencies, which make it their mission to create a level playing field for their national member states, some of which are resource poor or not so resource poor and richly endowed. Specialist NGDOs from the third pillar represent the civil society concern in Northern, rich countries about the unwanted and unsustainable gaps between North and South. These three pillars have dominated the sector of international development cooperation for about five to six decades. But things are changing. As we have said: because states, individuals and organisations in the developing world are taking charge of their own destinies and seeking new alternatives. And also because of the advent of new actors, such as government agencies that do not have development cooperation as their main remit, and – of course – new donors such as China, the Arab countries, Turkey and Brazil. Both categories, the first coming from traditional donor countries, the second called emerging donors, are increasingly visible in recipient countries while undertaking development cooperation in a different, novel fashion. This challenges the identity, specificity and development cooperation narrative and paradigm so dear to the conventional aid specialists from the North. They make international development cooperation a truly global ballgame with a role for each, specialist or not. The traditional North-South demarcation of the sector of development cooperation has become more porous because of the forces of globalisation. Thousands and thousands of other actors, not claiming to be development cooperation specialists, are doing their part for development aid, development cooperation or technical assistance. We suggested calling this group of new kids on the block 'the fourth pillar' in development cooperation. Not because we have any reason to consider them best in class but – maybe – because they are more visible and we came across them in our own wanderings in the sector. We zoomed in on faith-based organisations, private development initiatives, the farmers' movement, trade unions, health insurance operators, companies, cooperatives, migrant communities and foundations. We could have added sports clubs, media, schools and universities, local authorities and others because their commonality is that they are only of late engaging in something they call development aid or development cooperation. In most cases, these fourth pillar organisations were not set up to become development cooperation specialists; they are only to a limited extent interested in the lessons learned by the first, second and third pillar specialists and do not adhere to the principles, values and norms that inspire the conventional actors. In other words, they *de facto* challenge the traditional actors and give food for thought for a new paradigm. These new donors and fourth pillar actors are transformative for the sector because they are numerous, highly visible, energetic, innovative and increasingly represent a political and financial force. They do, indeed, make the sector shake to its foundations and make everyone wonder if they themselves are fit for a further globalising world that shatters the North-South perspective into a million pieces.

Probably the most fundamental move the new actors have imposed relates to the concept of ownership. As we have seen, for good and justified reasons, the traditional development cooperation specialists have – at least in principle – opted for a more tacit, humble and subservient role. The recipient was supposed to take the lead. Ideally, the donor was just a payer. The newcomers, like China or the fourth pillar organisations, do not want to be only payers but to realise their own agenda. They want to be players because they are also interested parties. Parties, indeed, with their own interests. And these interests can be put openly on the table and do not have to be hidden behind a screen of altruism. The sector reacted timidly at first. Some coined the term 'co-ownership'; some like to express it more poetically by insisting that 'we are in this boat together'; or that 'we share the same destiny'. 'We are looking for mutual interests', some argue repeatedly.

Yet another often-used saying that illustrates the recent mood swing in the sector of international development cooperation is that 'we are looking for a win-win'. Both parties have to benefit: the recipient but also the donor. More ambitiously, some go for a triple win: a win-win-win proposition. The recipient, the donor and society at large have to see some kind of progress thanks to the cooperation efforts undertaken. This fits very well with the new, widely accepted grid presented by the SDGs. These SDGs echo the idea that there is one world, that we are all stakeholders in this world and that we all benefit from the efforts to reach them. In this way, the SDGs are a forceful catalyst for the new paradigm that is in the making. It legitimises a whole-of-society approach in which not only aid specialists and recipients are involved in development projects and programmes; all sections of society in the Global North and Global South are invited to play a role, forge alliances and cooperate. This, of course, leads to hyper-interaction and a myriad of projects, programmes, experiments and innovative collaborative initiatives which nobody can oversee, let alone steer.

In this book, we have tried to sketch this ever-expanding world of international development cooperation. We looked at the four pillars and the way in which they react to these developments and towards the new actors. We could, of course, not identify nor present all new actors. In any case, not everybody is involved as yet. But those that did make their first steps in the field of international development cooperation, notwithstanding unavoidable dilettantism and sometimes amateurism, can certainly be considered high-profile role models for many newcomers and inspiring challengers for the conventional actors. And, indeed, we see that others are following their example. The conventional development cooperation actors sometimes feel irritated because of the unrequested intrusion of the unconventional actors or flabbergasted by the bravado with which the latter operate without taking account of the rules of the game in 'their domain'.

But we have seen that initial opposition has been replaced by proposition. As we have said, it made no sense to exclude anybody from being involved in international collaboration and self-declared development aid. As long as there is no definition of development aid or development cooperation, let alone a definition of good development aid or good cooperation, everybody has a license to operate. The traditional actors propose a variety of ways to join forces and remain in the driving seat. We saw how the specialised bilateral, first pillar agencies experiment with so-called whole-of-government policies, which try to lead while accompanying other government agencies that are starting to work with their counterparts in developing countries. The emerging donors are invited to get involved in joint, triangular projects and programmes in an effort to teach the newcomers to 'do good development cooperation'. This is also the central objective whenever the new donors are invited to participate in the multitude of committees, workshops, conferences and other platforms that the sector has established to get noses pointing in the same direction. The international second pillar also has manoeuvres to keep some coherence and consistency in its field. The European Commission is experimenting with a whole-of-agency approach and 'team Europe projects' involving different departments and member states. The UN is trying to get its act together with its Delivering as One UN exercise and is pushing for One Leader, One Budget, One Programme and One Office in as many countries as possible. Its agencies are also setting up collaborative arrangements with foundations, corporations and donor countries through a variety of vertical programmes and special-purpose trust funds. The best known of these out-of-system channels is the Global Fund to Fight Aids, TB and Malaria. The NGDOs, the third pillar, are increasingly inviting other internationally ambitious actors to work together. Trade unions, businesses, farmers' organisations and diaspora organisations are attracted to participate in collaborative arrangements with NGDOs because they give opportunities to work with colleagues on the other side of the globe and access funding from government agencies and private donors.

Working with the novel actors has thus become a permanent game for the specialist agencies. It can be debated who is influencing whom and who is finally in charge. Are there homogenising effects? Is there a tendency towards isomorphism? Further research will have to tell. What we suggest is that these interactions make it possible for a radically alternative paradigm, a new development cooperation model, to ferment. This incipient paradigm no longer departs from a North-South perspective as its starting position. Globalisation is the new frame of reference; hence, the evolution from a vertical and unidirectional approach that seeks to fill the gaps and restore the deficits in the South by a generous and well-equipped North to a horizontal and reciprocal model that eagerly looks for opportunities and, at the same time, challenges structural inequalities when needed. Thus, the old-school donor-recipient scheme gives way to a *modus operandi* that allows the partners involved to realise (part of) their own agenda and happily discover that looking for mutual interests can let all parties get something out of the collaboration. The sequencing of the collaboration process is no longer nailed down in an elaborate and stringent plan; instead, it is becoming iterative. The new art is to create a cooperation pattern that allows for the achievement of quick wins and intermediate objectives. Dropping or reducing the processes inherent in planning means, of course, that a culture of (and even a desire for) risk-taking emerges and the joint project becomes open ended. Aid, with its traditional ingredients of money and assistance, is not the pivot of the new style of international development cooperation. It still plays a significant role but solely as a vector or facilitator of other, sometimes more potent levers for change or transformation: interaction, exchange, joint-ventures or trade, and joint lobby and advocacy for policy change.

This is where the challenges lie for the specialist development cooperation community. In a world that is rapidly changing, where resources are unequally distributed, where some are more vulnerable than others and where power relations are asymmetric, there is no guarantee that the new forms of international development cooperation will automatically result in balanced win-win situations, let alone that they will be guided by public-spiritedness and a drive to create a better future for those who have less perspective on it. This is why principled international development cooperation is still needed.

Sixty years of experience and the lessons learned from it can be a good guide for this. The past will not come back but is still there. This is always the case with a conceptual revolution and evolution towards a new paradigm.

Notes

1 Until 2005, there was also a second list of 'new developing countries', which had been created out of the break-up of the Soviet Union (known as the 'Eastern European and New Independent States'). These states received official assistance but not ODA. The two lists have since been (rightly) combined.

2 Weforum.org/press/2019

3 By 1960, public and private capital flows from the rich countries amounted to 0.83% of their GNI. Around three-quarters of this was official bilateral aid.

4 Marcel Mauss' famous words were that "on est obligé de donner parce que donner oblige" (one is obligated to give because giving obligates).

5 oecd-ilibrary.org/sites/e3c30a9a-en/1/3/3/index.html?itemId=/content/publication/e3c30a9a-en&_csp_=8cdd8991f371dde0be547aab4112527a&itemIGO=oecd&itemContentType=book#figure-d1e6971

6 By far the largest Chinese project was the Tamzam railway, which covers more than 1,750 km and connects the Tanzanian port of Dar-es-Salaam with the Zambian city of Kapiri Mposhi.

7 The only official condition is that the recipient country may not give Taiwan diplomatic recognition.

8 From the 1899 poem of that name by the British novelist and poet Rudyard Kipling.

9 The British talked in terms of 'responsible trade unionism' and 'constructive co-operativism' to make it clear that these social organisations were definitely not supposed to act against vested interests.

10 The essay of the Governor-General of the Belgian Congo (1934–1946) published in 1948 and titled *Dominer pour Server* ('dominate to serve') tells a lot about the spirit in which Belgian colonials accepted the need for a more welfare-oriented policy.

11 Originally, the Société Générale kept itself aloof from Leopold II's colonial project and only in the early years of the 20th century did it develop into an active, pro-colonial enterprise.

12 This refers to the colonies and territories that were run by the colonial countries which had lost the First World War.

13 Even so, real changes were taking place in the South at that time. Indonesia declared its independence in 1945, the League of Arab States was created in the same year, India gained its independence in 1947, the state of Israel was established in 1948 and Mao Zedong rose to power in China in 1949.

14 The proposal to set up another international trade organisation was rejected. However, the General Agreement on Tariffs and Trade was created.

15 Named after the then US Secretary of State, George Marshall, who devised the plan.

16 Only USD 13.5 billion was actually used during the five-year Marshall Plan.

17 The European Recovery Plan functioned as a 'countervalue fund'. The money at the USA's disposal could be converted into loans, but 70% was used to purchase goods from the USA: USD 3.5 billion was used to purchase raw materials; USD 3.2 billion for food, cattle fodder and fertiliser; USD 1.9 billion for machines and vehicles and USD 1.6 billion for fuel. Every country indicated its requirements and the Organisation for European Economic Co-operation (OEEC) decided who got what. The American suppliers were paid in USD, while the European recipients had to make payments in local currency into a countervalue fund for the goods. That money could be used by the recipient countries for investment projects.

18 Quoted in *The Guardian*, 16 February 1996.

19 See e.g., the Structural Adjustment Participatory Review International Network (www.saprin.org).

20 Debt was regarded as intolerable when its net discounted value was more than 150% of the country's export income.

21 The realist school in the study of international relations in fact consists of realists and neorealists. The assumptions that they share are as follows: (1) states are the primary actors in the international system; (2) the state acts as a unit; (3) the international system is anarchical and there is no entity with a monopoly on the legitimate use of violence (although the neorealists accept that a certain structure can be identified in the international system); (4) all states try to maintain or extend their power and interests via the international system. The idealist or liberal school works on the following assumptions: (1) individuals are the primary international actors; (2) states are pluralistic actors which have internal divisions and have to take account of elections and negotiations between groups; (3) states have multiple interests, which they seek to defend/extend via the international system, but they also take account of the interests of others.

22 Omoruyi took the view that the French aid regime was still inspired to a large extent by the *besoin de rayonnement*. France was the most generous donor in sub-Saharan Africa, but its aid was concentrated in its former colonies. There was also a positive correlation between French aid and the value of French goods and services imported by the recipient country.

23 public.tableau.com/views/CPA-Donor/CPA-Donor?amp%3B%3Aembed=y&%3Adisplay_count=no&%3AshowVizHome=no

24 www.developmentaid.org

25 In Belgium, for example.

26 The Maastricht Treaty of 1992 introduced three new principles, the so-called three Cs: coordination, complementarity and coherence. The Treaty of Amsterdam, signed five

years later, added the principle of consistency, with a view to ensuring that all the different aspects of its external relations, such as foreign relations, security, trade and development cooperation policies, would be oriented in the same direction.

27 The UK had not yet left the Union.

28 Belgium, France, Germany, Italy, Luxembourg and the Netherlands were then the member states of the European Economic Community.

29 The ACP Group was created due to a number of common interests that were shared by the African, Caribbean and Pacific states (especially with regard to the export of sugar to the European market), but also because the countries from the Caribbean and the Pacific Region wanted to take advantage of the African countries' negotiating strength.

30 Between the nine European member states and 56 ACP countries.

31 See e.g., ECDPM, 2001.

32 There was talk about Eurafrica first when German supporters of European integration called for an amalgamation of African colonies in the early 20th century. It was suggested as a first step towards a federal Europa. Later, the term 'Eurafrica' was associated with a desired privileged access to minerals and other African natural resources.

33 In 2018, China and the USA had a share of 17% and 6%, respectively, of Africa's trade in goods.

34 At the ACP Summit in December 2019, the ACP Group of States adopted the revised Georgetown Agreement, which resulted in a change of name. In April 2020, the ACP Group of States became the Organisation of African, Caribbean and Pacific States (OACPS).

35 Eritrea is the only country that did not sign the African Continental Free Trade Area agreement.

36 In the future, these institutions, such as the joint Council of Ministers, the joint Committee of Ambassadors or Senior Officials and the joint Parliamentary Assembly, will operate at two different levels: a plenary format when the dialogue involves the EU and the entire ACP group, and a regional format where specific ACP issues will be dealt with.

37 https://www.un.org/en/pdfs/un_system_chart.pdf

38 However, collectively, sovereign states outside the DAC only account for 5% of total funding to the UN Development System, for a total of USD 1.5 billion in 2016 (OECD, 2018).

39 oecd-ilibrary.org/docserver/9789264308831-en.pdf?expires=1595930586&id=id&acname=guest&checksum=F565A8F6D650F8EC71FE9444DE0016B8

40 For instance, it has over 200 projects in Mauritania alone, another 200 in neighbouring Senegal, 130 in Gambia, 150 in Niger…

41 education-progress.org/en/articles/access/ (retrieved July 2020).

42 un.org/press/en/1998/19980714.sgsm6638.html

43 oecd-ilibrary.org/docserver/51eb6df1-en.pdf?expires=1610089724&id=id&acname=guest&checksum=9F12DB6C2193223AC3F12E2F964AD429

44   These percentages should be considered as estimates rather than exact amounts as there are some differences in how OECD-DAC donors report CSO spending.

45   This is an interactive data collection process conducted at the local level or with a specific target group (e.g., women). Participatory rural/rapid appraisal, as the term indicates, does not normally take much time and energy from the donor nor the potential beneficiaries of the project. But if taken seriously, it is applied at the design and final evaluation phases of a project cycle. It can also be used to make a collective mid-term evaluation.

46   Objective-oriented project planning is a participatory but pretty rigid planning technique, in which all parties involved identify and analyse the problems to be addressed in the project, and prepare a concrete and realistic project plan together. Once some form of consensus has been reached, the problems are organised into a logical sequence. Subsequently, they are reformulated into objectives to be attained. A part of the objectives is selected to be the focus of the project. These objectives are then translated into a project planning matrix or logical framework. This planning matrix describes the objectives at different levels, referred to as the general objective, immediate objective, project outputs and project activities.

47   buildingstatecapability.com/the-ddd-manifesto/ (retrieved November 2015).

48   oxfamblogs.org/fp2p/thinking-and-working-politically-update-where-have-aid-agencies-consultants-etc-got-to/ (retrieved November 2015).

49   For its development work, FC Barcelona, aspiring to be 'más que un club' (more than a club) has created a specialised foundation, the Barça Foundation. The different programmes developed by the foundation are deployed in 59 countries, mainly in Africa, America and Asia. According to the data provided by the foundation, the total number of beneficiaries had reached more than one million internationally in 2018. The different programmes are financed by FC Barcelona, which donates 0.7% of its annual budget, but also by professional players and trainers who contribute 0.5% of their income. Members (*socios*), supporters (*culés*) and other individuals can directly donate via the foundation's official website. Numerous private companies and other foundations, such as Shell and la Caixa, also provide programme funding.

50   In this, they follow Schuyt et al. (2009) who define philanthropy as "contributing money, goods and/or time, voluntarily supplied by individuals and organisations (funds, companies, churches) mainly to support the aims of public advancement".

51   vierdepijler.be

52   Programme of the ITUC, adopted by the Funding Congress of the ITUC. Vienna, 1–3 November 2006.

53   worldmapofmicroinsurance.org/

54   It is important to note that the IMF data used by the World Bank also includes the "Compensation of employees": this refers to income earned by temporary migrant workers in the host country and the income of workers who are employed by embassies,

international organisations and foreign companies. The entire income of temporary migrant workers is included in this definition, although that income may never actually be transferred (at least not entirely) to the origin country as migrants still have to cover their own living costs.

55 It has to be noted that the growth in remittances globally in recent years may have actually, at least partly, derived from changes in how remittances are measured, rather than actual increases in such financial flows.

56 This happened in the context of 'La mission Barrio Adentro' ('into the neighbourhood mission'), a plan launched in the early 2000s to provide healthcare to poor, urban neighbourhoods and poor, remote rural areas.

57 In the literature, a movement or support base with these characteristics is termed a 'public interest group', as opposed to a 'private interest group' such as a professional federation. This public interest group is interested in development cooperation as a public good.

58 developmentcompass.org/

59 https://www.radiaid.com/about

60 worldhungerindex.org

61 It will come as no surprise that this kind of provocative thesis did stir up some academic commotion (see, for example, Bergrenn, 2018).

62 Smallpox, or variola, was eradicated by the end of the 1970s; rinderpest, or cattle plague, by 2010.

63 https://www.oecd.org/dac/financing-sustainable-development/datavisualisations/

64 www.outcomemapping.ca

65 This is apparent, for example, from the analysis of structural adjustment programmes. Dollar and Svensson (1998, quoted in Martens et al., 2002) found that around a third of all World Bank structural adjustment loans failed to achieve their policy goals but were issued anyway. This shows that the Bank does not rely purely on altruistic motives with regard to economic development but also takes account of its own interests. A country also needs to be supported to be able to repay the foregoing loans to the Bank. Other donors and creditors put pressure on the Bank to give financial resources to developing countries so that they can repay their loans to them.

Bibliography

Acharya, A. et al., Proliferation and fragmentation: Transaction costs and the value of aid. *Journal of Development Studies* 2006, 42(1): 1–21.

Addison, T., Structural adjustment. In C. Kirkpatrick, R. Clarke, & C. Polidano (eds.), *Handbook on development policy and management*. Cheltenham: Edward Elgar, 2002, pp.42–50.

Adelman, C., Schwatz, B., & Riskin, F., *Index of global philanthropy and remittances 2016*. Washington: Hudson Institute, 2016.

Aidt, T., & Tzannatos, Z., *Unions and collective bargaining: Economic effects in a global environment*. Washington D.C.: World Bank, 2002.

Albrecht, L., The Giving Pledge turns 10: These billionaires pledged to give away half of their wealth but they soon ran into a problem. *Market Watch*, 10 August 2020.

Al-Dahash, H., Thayaparan, M., & Kulatunga, V., Understanding the terminologies: Disaster, crisis and emergency. *32nd Annual Association of Researchers in Construction Management (ARCOM) Conference*, 5–7 September 2016, Manchester, 2016.

Alford, R., The Nobel effect: Nobel Peace Prize laureates as international norm entrepreneurs. *Virginia Journal of International Law* 2008, 49: 62–151.

Al-Yahya K. & Fustier, N. *Saudi Arabia as a humanitarian donor: High potential, low institutionalisation*. GPPI Research Paper 14, 2011.

Angus, L., Teaching within and against the circle of privilege: Reforming teachers, reforming schools. *Journal of Education Policy* 2012, 27(2): 231–251.

Appe, S., & Telch, F., Grassroots international NGOs: Using comparative interpretive policy analysis to understand meanings in private development aid. *Journal of Comparative Policy Analysis: Research and Practice* 2020, 22(1): 30–46.

ARC, Faith in Finance. *Faith-consistent investing and the Sustainable Development Goals*. Bath: Alliance of Religions and Conservation, 2016.

Atim, K., *Towards better health in Africa: A comparative study of community financing and mutual aid insurance*. Brussels: Worldsolidarity, 1995.

Awiah, E., & De Tavernier, J., Dealing with proselytism in development cooperation: A rights-based and pluralistic approach. *Journal of Church and State* 2020, 62(3): 525–543.

Ayittey, G.B.N., *Africa unchained: The blueprint for Africa's Future*. New York: Palgrave/MacMillan, 2005.

Balasz, S.I., *Aid allocation of the emerging Central and Eastern European donors*. Munich: MPRA Paper 30234, 2011.

Bamutese, M.-C., *Rwanda en Burundi: 'donor darling' versus 'donor orphan'; volgt het Belgisch ontwikkelingsbeleid de international trend?*. Leuven: KU Leuven, unpublished master's thesis, 2020.

Banerjee, A.V. & Duflo, E., *Poor economics: Rethinking poverty and the ways to end it*. London: Random House, 2014.

Barder, O., & Birdsall, N., *Payments for progress: A hands-off approach to foreign aid*. Washington: Center for Global Development, 2006.

Bauer, P., *Equality, the Third World and economic delusion*. Harvard: Harvard University Press, 1981.

Benček, D., & Schneiderheinze, C., *More development, less emigration to OECD countries: Identifying inconsistencies between cross-sectional and time-series estimates of the migration hump*. Kiel: Kiel Institute for the World Economy, Working Paper 2145, 2019.

Bergrenn, C., *Good things on the rise: The one-side worldview of Hans Rosling*. Linköping: Linköping University, 2018.

Birn, A., Backstage: the relationship between the Rockefeller Foundation and the World Health Organisation, Part I 1940–1960s. *Public Health* 2014, *128*(2): 129–140.

Block, T., *Pitfalls of the SDGs*. Gent: Centre for Sustainable Development, Ghent University, 2018.

Bloom, D., Canning D., & Chan K., *Higher education and economic development in Africa*. Harvard: Harvard University, 2005.

Boas, M., & McNeill, D., *Multilateral institutions: A critical introduction*. London: Pluto Press, 2003.

Boidin, J.-C., *ACP-EU relations: the end of preferences? A personal assessment of the post-Cotonou Agreement*. Discussion Paper 289, Brussels: European Centre for Development Policy Management, 2020.

Bond, *Financial trends for UK-based INGOs. An analysis of Bond members' income between 2006 and 2016*. 2018. Retrieved online from: bond.org.uk/sites/default/files/resource-documents/financial_trends_for_uk-based_ingos.pdf

Booth, D., *Fighting poverty in Africa. Are PRSPs making a difference?* London: Overseas Development Institute, 2003.

Borrel, J., *Identifying socio-political and economic priorities to fight inequalities*. Brussels: Socialist and Democrat Africa Week, S&D Group, 2020.

Bourn, D., *The theory and practice of development education: A pedagogy for global social justice*. New York: Routledge, 2015.

Bourn, D. (ed.), *The Bloomsbury handbook of global education and learning*. Bloomsbury Publishing, 2020.

Bouzoubaa, H., & Brok, M., *Particuliere initiatieven op het gebied van ontwikkelingssamenwerking*. Nijmegen: Radbout Universiteit Nijmegen, 2005.

Brauman, R., *Le Tiersmondisme en question*. Paris: Olivier Orban, 1986.

Brautigam, D., *China, Africa and the international aid architecture*. Working Papers Series 107, African Development Bank, 2010.

Bretos, I., & Marciello, C., Revisiting globalisation challenges and opportunities in the development of cooperatives. *Annals of Public and Cooperative Economics* 2017, 88(1): 47–73.

Bristol, N., Military incursions into aid work anger humanitarian groups. *The Lancet* 2006, 367(9508): 384–386.

Broadman, H., China and India go to Africa. *Foreign Affairs* 2008, 87: 95–109.

Brockington, D., & Banks, N., *Changes in expenditure, income, and income sources for development NGOs based in the UK*. Report from University of Sheffield, 2017. Retrieved online from: sheffield.ac.uk/news/nr/development-ngos-charitable-expenditure-research-1.747024

Brown, S., The instrumentalisation of foreign aid under the Harper Government. *Studies in Political Economy* 2016, 97(1): 18–36.

Brown, T., Negotiating the NGO/social movement dichotomy: Evidence from Punjab, India. *VOLUNTAS* 2014, 25: 46–66.

Browne, S., *Aid and influence: Do donors help or hinder?* London: Earthscan, 2006.

Bruce, J., Service learning as a pedagogy of interruption'. *International Journal of Development Education and Global Learning* 2013, 5(1): 33–47.

Bryan, A., Using development-themed film to promote a pedagogy of discomfort. In M. Liddy, & M. Parker-Jenkins (eds.), *Education that matters: Teachers, critical pedagogy and development education at local and global levels*. Oxford: Peter Lang, 2013, pp.75–104.

Bryant, J., *Mapping local capacities and support for more effective humanitarian responses*. Policy Brief 75, Humanitarian Policy Group, ODI, November 2019.

Burrell, J. C., Riot Games Social Impact Fund. *Riot Games*, 16 October 2019. Retrieved online from https://www.riotgames.com/en/news/riot-games-social-impact-fund

Burrell, J. C., 2019 Social Impact – Year in Review. *Riot Games*, 2020. Retrieved online from https://assets.contentstack.io/v3/assets/blt731acb42bb3d1659/bltdabe471a2eb-ca287/5eb9bb02ee88132a6f6cffba/Riot-Social-Impact-YIR-2019.pdf

Burnside, C., & Dollar, D., Aid, politics, and growth. *American Economic Review* 2000, 90(4): 847–868.

Byatnal, A., Is COVID-19 magnifying colonial attitudes in global health. *DEVEX*, July 2020. Retrieved online from: https://www.devex.com/news/is-covid-19-magnifying-colonial-attitudes-in-global-health-97499

Campbell, J., *Trump's Africa policy is better than it looks*. Council on Foreign Relations, 6 April 2020. Retrieved online from: https://www.cfr.org/in-brief/trumps-africa-policy-better-it-looks

Care USA, *The changing times: A plan for change*. CARE USA Annual Report, 2007.

Castells, M., *The rise of the network society: The information age: Economy, society and culture Vol. I*. Oxford: Blackwell, 1996.

Castells, M., *End of millennium: The information age: Economy, society and culture Vol. III*. Oxford: Blackwell, 1998.

Castro, M., Melluish, S., & Lorenzo, A., Cuban internationalism: An alternative form of globalisation. *International Review of Psychiatry* 2014, 26(5): 595–601.

CCIC, *The Paris Declaration on Aid Effectiveness: Donor commitments and civil society critiques*. Canadian Council for International Cooperation, 2006.

Center for Global Development, *Commitment to development index 2007*. Washington D.C.: Center for Global Development, 2008.

Center for Global Prosperity, *The index of global philanthropy and remittances 2010*. Washington D.C.: Hudson Institute, 2010.

Chenery, H., *Redistribution with growth: Policies to improve income distribution in developing countries in the context of economic growth*. London: Oxford University Press, 1974.

Churchill, C., *Protecting the poor: A microinsurance compendium*. Geneva: International Labour Organisation, 2006.

Claymone, Y., *A study on one village one product project (OVOP) in Japan and Thailand as an alternative of community development in Indonesia: A perspective on Japan and Thailand*. Zhejiang University, 2011.

Clifford, D., International charitable connections: The growth in number, and the countries of operation, of English and Welsh charities working overseas. *Journal of Social Policy* 2016, 45(3): 453–486.

Cole, T., The white-savior industrial complex. *The Atlantic*, 21 March 2012.

Collier, P., *The bottom billion*. Oxford: Oxford University Press, 2007.

Conrad, J., *An outpost of progress and other stories*. New York: Dover Thrift Editions, 2019.

Cox, A., Healey, J., & Koning, A., *How European aid works. A comparison of management systems and effectiveness*. London: Overseas Development Institute, 1997.

Crane, B., & Maguire, E., First: Aid – The future of US foreign aid in the Trump administration. *Conscience Magazine* 2017, 38(1): 19–31.

CRED & UNDRR, *Human cost of disasters: An Overview of the last 20 years, 2000–2019*. Brussels/Geneva: Centre for Research on the Epidemiology of Disasters and the UN Office for Disaster Risk Reduction, 2020.

Currion, P., *Network humanitarianism*. Humanitarian Policy Group Working Paper, ODI, London: Overseas Development Institute, 2018.

Curtis, D., *Politics and humanitarian aid: Debates, dilemmas and dissension*. London: Overseas Development Institute, 2001.

Curtis, D., Development assistance and the lasting legacies of rebellion in Burundi and Rwanda. *Third World Quarterly* 2015, 36: 1365–1381.

DAC, Aid extended by Local and State Governments. *DAC Journal* 2005, 6: 1–53.

DAC, *2007 progress report on untying ODA to Least Developed Countries*. Development Assistance Committee, 2007.

DAC, *2008 Survey on monitoring the Paris Declaration: Effective aid by 2010? What it will take*. Organisation for Economic Co-operation and Development, 2008.

Darko, E., *Private sector and NGO engagement*. London: Overseas Development Institute, 2014.

Deacon, B., & Stubbs, P., Global social policy studies: Conceptual and analytical reflections. *Global Social Policy* 2013, 13(1): 5–23.

De Bruyn, T., New development philanthropists? The effects and characteristics of the (Flemish) fourth pillar of development cooperation. *Mondes en Développement* 2013, 41(1): 33–48.

De Bruyn, T., *Remittances from Belgium as a lever for development*. Leuven: HIVA, KU Leuven, 2017.

De Bruyn, T., & Develtere, P., *Het potentieel van de diasporafilantropie – Onderzoek naar het geefgedrag van Belgische migrantengemeenschappen*. Brussels: Koning Boudewijnstichting, 2008.

De Haas, H., *Engaging diasporas: How governments and development agencies can support diaspora involvement in the development of origin countries*. Oxford: International Migration Institute, University of Oxford, 2006.

Della Porta, D., Building bridges: Social movements and civil society in times of crisis. *VOLUNTAS* 2020, 31: 938–948.

Devarajan, S., (ed.), *Aid and reform in Africa: Lessons from ten case studies*. Washington D.C.: World Bank, 2000.

Develtere, P. (ed.), *Het draagvlak voor duurzame ontwikkeling; wat het is en wat het zou kunnen zijn*. Antwerp: De Boeck, 2003.

Develtere, P., *De Belgische Ontwikkelingssamenwerking*. Leuven: Davidsfonds, 2005.

Develtere, P., The unbearable lightness of public support for traditional development cooperation. *Europe's World Debating Forum*, Autumn 2008.

Develtere, P., Towards a whole-of-society approach. Presentation at DG DEVCO, European Political Strategy Centre Workshop, Brussels: European Commission, 2019.

Develtere, P., How can we move from payers to players in our relation with Africa? *Friends of Europe*, 5 May 2020.

Develtere, P., & De Bruyn, T., The emergence of a fourth pillar in development aid. *Development in Practice* 2009, 19(7): 912–922.

Develtere, P., & Huybrechts, A., The impact of microcredit on the poor in Bangladesh. *Alternatives* 2005, 30(2): 165–189.

Develtere, P., & Huybrechts, A., The movement for the abolition of child labour as an example of a transnational network movement. *Work, Organisation, Labour and Globalisation* 2008, 2(1): 165–179.

Develtere, P., Huyse, H., & Van Ongevalle, J., *How do we help? The free market in development aid*. Leuven: Leuven University Press, 2012.

Develtere, P., & Michel, A., *Bilan d'un demi-siècle de coopération belge*. Brussels: DGOS, 2009.

Develtere, P., Pollet, I., & Wanyama, F., *Cooperating out of poverty: The renaissance of the African cooperative movement*. Geneva/Washington: International Labour Organization/World Bank Institute, 2008.

Develtere, P., & Stessens, J., *De vierde pijler van de ontwikkelingssamenwerking in Vlaanderen: de opmars van de levensverbeteraar*. Leuven: HIVA, KU Leuven, 2007.

Dijkstra, G.A., *The impact of international debt relief*. Routledge, 2008.

Doherty, D., Bryan, A.C., Hanania, D., & Pajor, M., The public's foreign aid priorities: Evidence from a conjoint experiment. *American Politics Research* 2020, 48(5): 635–648.

Dollar, D., & Pritchett, L., *Assessing aid: What works, what doesn't and why?* Washington: World Bank Policy Research Report, 1998.

Doucouliagos, H., Hinz, T., & Zigova, K., *Bias and careers: Evidence from the aid effectiveness literature*. Bonn: IZA Institute of Labor Economics, 2020.

Doucouliagos, H., & Paldam, M., The ineffectiveness of development aid on growth: An update. *European Journal of Political Economy* 2011, 27(2): 399–404.

Dowla, A., & Barua, D., *The poor always pay back: The Grameen II Story*. Bloomfield: Kumarian Press, 2006.

Dragusanu, R., Giovannucci, D., & Nunn, N., The economics of fair trade. *Journal of Economic Perspectives* 2014, 28(3): 217–236.

Dreher, A. et al., Apples and dragon fruits: The determinants of aid and other forms of state financing from China to Africa. *International Studies Quarterly* 2018a, 62(1): 182–194.

Dreher, A. et al., *Buying votes and international organisations: The dirty work-hypothesis*. London: CEPR Discussion Paper 13290, 2018b.

Eade, D., Editorial overview. *Development in Practice* 2004, 14(1–2): 5–12.

Earl, S., & Carden, F., Learning from complexity: The International Development Research Centre's experience with outcome mapping. *Development in Practice* 2003, 12(3-4): 518–524.

Easterly, W., *The elusive quest for growth: Economists' adventures and misadventures in the tropics*. Cambridge: MIT Press, 2002.

Easterly, W., & Williamson, C.R., Rhetoric versus reality: The best and worst of aid agency practices. *World Development* 2011, 39(11): 1930–1949.

ECDPM, *Cotonou infokit: History and evolution of ACP-EU cooperation*. Maastricht: European Centre for Development Policy Management, 2001.

ECDPM & ActionAid, *Whither EC aid? The code of conduct on complementarity and division of labour*. Maastricht: European Centre for Development Policy Management, 2007.

Edgren, G., *Capacity development, incentives and brain drain*. New York: Bureau for Development Policy, United Nations Development Programme, 2002.

Editorial, global health: Time for radical change? *The Lancet* 2020, 396(10258): 1129.

Edwards, M., *Civil Society*. Hoboken, NJ: John Wiley & Sons, 2014.

Elsen, B., Pollet, I., & Develtere, P., *Compass for intercultural partnerships*. Leuven: Leuven University Press, 2007.

EuropeAid, *Thematic evaluation of the water and sanitation sector: Synthesis report*. Brussels: EuropeAid, 2006.

European Commission, *Special Eurobarometer 318: Development aid in times of economic turmoil.* 2009. Retrieved online from: ec.europa.eu/public_opinion/archives/ebs/ebs_318_en.pdf

European Commission, *Innovative financing at a global level.* Commission staff working document, Brussels: European Commission, 2010a.

European Commission, *Special Eurobarometer 352: Europeans, development aid and the Millennium Development Goals.* 2010b. Retrieved online from: ec.europa.eu/public_opinion/archives/ebs/ebs_352_en.pdf

European Commission, *Special Eurobarometer 494: EU citizens and development cooperation.* Brussels: European Commission, 2019a.

European Commission, *Budget support: Trends and results 2019.* Brussels: European Commission, 2019b.

European Commission & OECD, *Reshaping decentralised development cooperation. The key role of cities and regions for the 2030 Agenda.* Brussels/Paris: European Commission/OECD, 2019.

FTF, *Report on trends in the North American fair trade market.* Lancaster: Fair Trade Federation, 2009.

Fang, J., China's tobacco industry is building schools and no one is watching. *The Conversation*, 11 August 2019. Retrieved online from: theconversation.com/chinas-tobacco-industry-isbuilding-schools-and-no-one-is-watching-120961

Fang, J., Wan, X., & Yang, G., "Pro-tobacco propaganda": A case study of tobacco industry-sponsored elementary schools in China. *Tobacco Induced Diseases* 2018, 16(S1): 73.

FAO, *The state of food security and nutrition in the world.* Food and Agricultural Organization, 2020.

Fejerskov, A.M., From unconventional to ordinary? The Bill and Melinda Gates Foundation and the homogenising effects of international development cooperation. *Journal of International Development* 2015, 27(7): 1098–1112.

Fieldhouse, D.K., *The West and the Third World.* Oxford: Blackwell, 1999.

Fonteneau, B., & Koval, S., *Evaluation de la loi du 25 mai 1999 relative à la coopération internationale belge.* Louvain-la-Neuve: Leuven, UCL and HIVA-KU Leuven, 2008.

Fore, H.H., & Biegel, S., *How impact investing can help girls shatter the glass ceiling.* 2020. Retrieved online from: devex.com/news/opinion-how-impact-investing-can-help-girls-shatter-the-glass-ceiling-97838

Foresti, M., Less gratitude, please. How COVID-19 reveals the need for migration reform. *Future Development Blog, Brookings*, 22 May 2020. Retrieved online from: brookings.edu/blog/future-development/2020/05/22/less-gratitude-please-how-covid-19-reveals-the-need-for-migration-reform/

Fowler, A., Distant obligations: Speculations on NGO funding and the global market. *Review of African Political Economy* 1992, 20(55): 9–29.

Friedman, T., *The world is flat: A brief history of the twenty-first century.* New York: Picador, 2005.

Furness, M., Ghica, L., Lightfoot, S., & Szent-Iványi, B., EU development policy: Evolving as an instrument of foreign policy and as an expression of solidarity. *Journal of Contemporary European Research* 2020, 16(2): 89–100.

Gallin, D., *Trade unions and NGOs: A necessary partnership for social development.* Geneva: United Nations Research Institute for Social Development, 2000.

Gaspar, V. et al., *Fiscal policy and development: Human, social and physical investments for the SDGs.* Staff Discussion Notes 19/03, Washington: International Monetary Fund, 2019.

Gereffi, G., & Lee, J., Economic and social upgrading in global value chains and industrial clusters: Why governance matters. *Journal of Business Ethics* 2016, 133(1): 25–38.

Ghandour, A.R., *Jihad humanitaire: Enquête sur les ONG islamiques.* Paris: Flammarion, 2002.

Gibson, C., Andersson, K., Ostrom, E., & Shivakumar, S., *The Samaritan's dilemma: The political economy of development aid.* Oxford: Oxford University Press, 2005.

Global Humanitarian Assistance, *Global Humanitarian Assistance report 2020.* Delaware: Global Humanitarian Assistance, 2020.

Gomanee, K., Girma, S., & Morrissey, O., *Aid and growth in Sub-Saharan Africa: Accounting for transmission mechanisms.* Credit Research Paper, University of Nottingham, 2002.

Griffin, K., & McKinley, T., *New approaches to development co-operation.* New York: United Nations Development Programme, Office of Development Studies, 1996.

Gulrajani, N., & Calleja, R., *Understanding donor motivations: Developing the Principled Aid Index.* London: Overseas Development Institute working paper 548, 2019a.

Gulrajani, N., & Calleja, R., *The Principled Aid Index.* Overseas Development Institute policy briefing, 2019b.

Hadwiger, F., The phenomenon of global framework agreements. In F. Hadwiger (ed.), *Contracting international employee participation: Global framework agreements, international law and economics.* Cham: Springer International Publishing, 2018, pp. 21–60. https://doi.org/10.1007/978-3-319-71099-0_3.

Hajer, M. et al., Beyond cockpit-ism: Four insights to enhance the transformative potential of the sustainable development goals. *Sustainability* 2015, 7(2): 1651–1660.

Harrigan, J., El-said, H., & Wang, C., The economic and political determinants of IMF and World Bank lending in the Middle East and North Africa. *World Development* 2006, 34(2): 247–270.

Harvey, P., *Cash-based responses in emergencies.* London: Humanitarian Policy Group, Overseas Development Institute, 2007.

Hayes, L., & Pereira, J., *Turning the tables: Aid and accountability under the Paris framework: a Civil Society Report.* Belgium: Eurodad, 2008.

Heap, S., *NGOs engaging with business: A world of difference and a difference to the world.* Oxford: International NGO Training and Research Centre, 2000.

Heinzel, M., *More than the sum of its parts. The role of staff experiences in World Bank project performance*. Potsdam: Chair of International Organisations, University of Potsdam, 2020.

Heinzel, M. et al., Birds of a feather? The determinants of impartiality perceptions of the IMF and the World Bank. *Review of International Political Economy*, 2020.

Henrickx, J., *Alsof de weg ons zocht. Jeanne Devos en haar strijd voor de dienstmeisjes in India*. Tielt: Lannoo, 2019.

Hoang, T.L., Ta, N.L., Nguyen, D.L., & Ho, T.M.H., One village one product (OVOP): A rural development strategy and the early adaption in Vietnam. *Sustainability* 2018, 10(12): 4485.

Holden, P., Irreconcilable tensions? The EU's development policy in an era of global illiberalism. *Journal of Contemporary European Research* 2020, 16(2): 101–119.

Holvoet, N., & Renard, R., *Breaking with the past: Belgian development at the turn of the century*. Antwerp: Institute for Development Policy and Management, 2002.

Hudson, J., Hudson, D., Morini, P., & Anders, M., *Debunking the engagement 'journey': What drives public engagement with global poverty?* Brief 6. Engagement Lab 2018–2023. London: University College London and University of Birmingham, 2020. Retrieved online from: developmentcompass.org/storage/stickiness-inbrieflayoutfinal-1606209819.pdf

Howell, J., *Working beyond government: Evaluation of AUSAID's engagement with civil society in developing countries*. AusAID, 2012.

Huffington Post UK, *Muslims 'give most to charity', ahead of Christians, Jews and atheists, poll finds*. Huffington Post, 21 July 2013.

Hurt, S.R., African agency and EU-ACP relations beyond the Cotonou Agreement. *Journal of Contemporary European Research* 2020, 16(2): 139–162.

Huyse, H., & De Bruyn, T., *New trends in governmental funding of Civil Society Organisations: A Comparative Study of 9 OECD-DAC Donors*. Leuven: HIVA, KU Leuven, 2015.Huyse, H., & Van Ongevalle, J., *Fulfilling the expectations? The experiences with the M&E-part of outcome mapping in an education for sustainability project in Zimbabwe*. Leuven: HIVA, KU Leuven, 2008.

IDA, *Aid architecture: An overview of the main trends in official development assistance flows*. Washington D.C.: International Development Association, 2007.

IDA & IMF, *Heavily Indebted Poor Countries (HIPC) Initiative and Multilateral Debt Relief Initiative (MDRI): Status of implementation*. Washington D.C.: International Development Association/International Monetary Fund, 2010.

IFRC, *World disasters report: Focus on urban risk*. Geneva: International Federation of Red Cross and Red Crescent Societies, 2008.

IFRC, *World disasters report: Leaving no one behind*. Geneva: International Federation of Red Cross and Red Crescent Societies, 2018.

Igoe, M., Exclusive: Philip Morris International continues its development charm offensive. *DEVEX*, 31 October 2019.

Igoe, M., Disrupt and compete: How Trump changed US foreign aid. *DEVEX*, 21 August 2020.

Information Office of the State Council, *China's foreign aid*. Beijing: White Paper, 2011.

IOM, *Mobility for health professionals to, from and within the European Union*. IOM Migration Research Series 48, Geneva: International Organization for Migration, 2014.

Ion, J., *La fin du militantisme?* Paris: Editions de l'Atelier, 1997.

Jad, I., NGOs: Between buzzwords and social movements. *Development in Practice* 2007, 17(4–5): 622–629.

Jamali, D., & Keshishian, T., Uneasy alliances: Lessons learned from partnerships between businesses and NGOs in the context of CSR. *Journal of Business Ethics* 2009, 84(2): 277–295.

Janssen, R., *Ontwikkelingssamenwerking door subnationale autoriteiten. Een context van multi-level governance*. Leuven: KU Leuven, 2008.

Jiang, C.L., Les relations de la Chine et l'Afrique: Fondements, réalités et perspectives. *Monde Chinois* 2006, 8: 7–26.

Joint Research Centre, *Many more to come? Migration from and within Africa*. Luxembourg: Publication Office of the European Union, 2018.

Jolly, R., The history of development policy. In C. Kirkpatrick, R. Clarke, & C. Polidano (eds.), *Handbook on development policy and management*. Cheltenham: Edward Elgar, 2002, pp.15–21.

Jones, A., Keijzer, N., Friesen, I., & Veron, P., *E.U. development cooperation with Sub-Saharan Africa 2013–2018: Policies, funding, results*. Brussels/Berlin: European Centre for Development Policy Management and Deutches Institut für entwicklungspolitik, 2020.

Juchtmans, G., & Vandenbroucke, A., *10 jaar gelijke onderwijskansen op school: tussen trouw aan het beleid en aanpassingsvermogen*. Steunpunt Studie- en Schoolloopbanen, 2013.

Kamstra, J., *Dialogue and dissent: Theory of change 2.0*. Ministry of Foreign Affairs, The Netherlands, 2017.

Kapur, D., The Janus face of diasporas. In B.J. Merz (ed.), *Diasporas and development*. Harvard: Harvard University Press, 2007, pp.89–118.

Karkare, P., Calabrese, L., Grimm, S., & Medinilla, A., *European fear of 'missing out' and narratives on China in Africa*. Brussels: European Think Tanks Group, 2020.

Khagram, S., Riker, J., & Sikkink, K., *Restructuring world politics: Transnational social movements, networks and norms*. Minneapolis: University of Minnesota Press, 2002.

Kharas, H., *The new reality of aid*. Wolfensohn Center for Development, 2007a.

Kharas, H., *Trends and issues in development aid*. Wolfensohn Center for Development, 2007b.

Kharas, H., *Development assistance in the 21st century*. Wolfensohn Center for Development, 2009.

Kharas, H., & Hamel, K., A global tipping point: Half the world is now middle class or wealthier. *Brookings: Future Development*, 27 September 2018.

King K., 'New actors: Old paradigms?', *NORRAG News* 2010, 44: 8–12.

Kinsbergen, S., *Particuliere initiatieven op het gebied van ontwikkelingssamenwerking: De Risi-co's van het vak*. Nijmegen: Center for International Development Issues Nijmegen, 2007.

Kinsbergen, S., 'The legitimacy of Dutch do-it-yourself initiatives in Kwale county, Kenya.' *Third World Quarterly* 2019, 40(10): 1850–1868.

Kinsbergen, S., & Schulpen, L., 'From tourist to development worker: Private development initiatives in the Netherlands.' *Mondes en Développement* 2013, 161(1): 49–62.

Kinsbergen, S., Schulpen, L., & Ruben, R., 'Understanding the sustainability of private development initiatives: What kind of difference do they make?' *Forum for Development Studies* 2017, 44(2): 223–248.

Kivimäki, T. (ed.), *Development co-operation as an instrument in the prevention of terrorism.* Copenhagen: Nordic Institute of Asian Studies, 2003.

Knack, S., & Rahman, A., Donor fragmentation and bureaucratic quality in aid recipients. *Journal of Development economics* 2007, 83(1): 176–197.

Kollar, P., The past, present and future of League of Legends studio Riot Games. *Polygon*, 2016. Retrieved online from: https://www.polygon.com/2016/9/13/12891656/the-past-present-and-future-of-league-of-legends-studio-riot-games

Kragelund, P., Back to basics? The rejuvenation of non-traditional donors' development cooperation with Africa. *Development and Change* 2011, 42(2): 585–607.

Kruesmann, M., Now showing: Using film as an educational medium in British schools. *Policy & Practice: A Development Education Review*, 2014, 18: 1–14.

Kruyt, D., & Vellinga, M. (eds.), *Ontwikkelingshulp getest: resultaten onder de loep*. Muiderberg: Coutinho, 1983.

Kull, S., American public support for foreign aid in the age of Trump. *Brookings Blum Roundtable Brief*, 31 July 2017.

Kumaran, M., & Pappas, J., Managing voluntourism. In T.D. Connors (ed.) *The volunteer management handbook: Leadership strategies for success*. Hoboken, 2012.

Lampert, M., & Papadongonas, P., *Towards 2030 without poverty. Glocalities: think global, act local*. Amsterdam: Motivaction International, 2016. Retrieved online from: oxfamsol.be/sites/default/files/documents/towards_2030_without_poverty-glocalities2016-2-new.pdf

Lamy, P., *L'Europe en première ligne*. Paris: Éditions du Seuil, 2002.

Lancaster, C., *The Chinese aid system*. Washington D.C.: Center for Global Development, 2007.

Lancaster, C., *George Bush's foreign aid: Transformation or chaos?* Washington D.C.: Center for Global Development, 2008.

LeagueFeed. How many people play League of Legends? *LeagueFeed*, 12 January 2021. Retrieved online from: https://leaguefeed.net/did-you-know-total-league-of-legends-player-count-updated/#

Levich, J., The Gates Foundation, Ebola, and global health imperialism. *The American Journal of Economics and Sociology* 2015, 74(4): 704–42.

Levine, M., Big bets and the Gates Foundation: How's that working for us? *Non Profit Quarterly*, 12 February 2020.

Li, J., #The struggle is real: The West and the white savior complex. *The Harvard-Westlake Chronicle*, 27 February 2018.

Lindenberg, M., & Bryant, C., *Going global: Transforming relief and development NGOs*. Bloomfield: Kumarian Press, 2001.

Lloyd, T., *Why rich people give*. London: Association of Charitable Foundations, 2004.

Madounga, N., & Fonteneau, G. *Le mouvement syndical en Afrique noire. Contributions pour une histoire*. Brussels: Solidarité Mondiale, 1998.

Makundi, H., Huyse, H., Develtere, P., Mongula, B., & Rutashobya, L., Training abroad and technological capacity building: Analysing the role of Chinese training and scholarship programmes for Tanzanians. *International Journal of Educational Development* 2017, 57: 11–20.

Mana, K., 'Chine-Afrique: Les enjeux d'une coopération', *Congo-Afrique*, XLVIII, n° 425, 2008, 391–401.

Marchetti, R., Civil society, global governance, and the quest for legitimacy. In M. Telò (ed.), *Globalisation, Multilateralism, Europe: Towards a better global governance?* Routledge, 2016, pp. 341–56.

Marijsse, S., L'évolution récente des relations économiques belgo-zaïroises. L'achèvement de la décolonisation. In G. de Villers (ed.), *Belgique/Zaïre: Une histoire enquête d'avenir*. Paris: L'Harmattan, 1994.

Marijsse, S., & Geenen, S., *Win-win or unequal exchange? The case of the Sino-Congolese 'cooperation' agreements*. Antwerp: Institute of Development Policy and Management, 2009.

Martens, B., Mummert, U., Murrell, P., & Seabright, P., *The institutional economics of foreign aid*. Cambridge: Cambridge University Press, 2002.

Martinez-Zarzoso, I., Nowak-Lehmann, F., Parra, M.D., & Klasen, S., Does aid promote donor exports? Commercial interests versus instrumental philanthropy. *Kylos International Review for Social Sciences* 2014, 67(4): 559–587.

Medinilla, A., & Teewan, C., *Beyond good intentions: The new EU-Africa partnership*. Brussels: European Centre for Development Policy Management Discussion Paper N° 267, 2020.

Meredith, M., *The fortunes of Africa*. London: Simon & Schuster, 2014.

Merry A., *Landscape of microinsurance in Africa 2018: Focus on selected countries*. Microinsurance Network, 2019.

Mesa Peinado, M., Evolution and future challenges of development education. *Revista Internacional de Investigación en Educación Global y para el Desarrollo* 2011: 41–160, 2011. Retrieved online from: educacionglobalresearch.net/en/manuelamesa1issuezero/

Milford, A., Market failure, coffee cooperatives and sustainable labeling: The case of Chiapas, Mexico. In J. Defourny, P. Develtere, B. Fonteneau, & M. Nyssens (eds.) *The worldwide making of the social economy*. Leuven: ACCO, 2009: 55–86.

Miller, D., Sachs, Easterly and the banality of the aid effectiveness debate: Time to move on. *Mapping Politics* 2011, 3: 72–86.

Ministerie van Buitenlandse Zaken, *Resultaten in ontwikkeling: rapportage 2005-2006.* The Hague: Ministerie van Buitenlandse Zaken, 2007.

Mitchell, I., Ritchie, E., & Rogerson, A., *Finance for international development (FID): A new measure to compare traditional and emerging provider countries' official development finance efforts, and some provisional results.* Washington D.C.: Center for Global Development, Working Paper 529, 2020.

Molenaers, N., & Renard, R., *Ontwikkelingshulp faalt: Is participatie het redmiddel?* Leuven: ACCO, 2007.

Morrissey, O., British aid policy in the 'Short-Blair' years. In P. Hoebink, & O. Stokke, (eds.), *Perspectives on European development co-operation: Policy and performance of individual donor countries and the EU,* Routledge, 2005, pp.161–183.

Motivaction, *Barometer internationale samenwerking 2010.* Amsterdam: Motivaction, 2010.

Moyo, D., *Dead aid: Why aid is not working and how there is a better way for Africa.* Vancouver: D & M Publications, 2010.

Museru, M., Toerien, F., & Gossel, S., The impact of aid and public investment volatility on economic growth in Sub-Saharan Africa. *World Development* 2014, 57: 138–147.

Nancy, G., & Yontcheva, B., *Does NGO aid go to the poor? Empirical evidence from Europe,* Washington D.C.: International Monetary Fund, 2006.

Nyonkuru, D., *Pour la dignité paysanne. Expériences et témoignages d'Afrique.* Réflexions, Pistes Méthodologiques, Brussels : GRIP, 2018.

OECD, *Survey on monitoring the Paris Declaration: Making aid more effective by 2010.* Paris: OECD, 2008a.

OECD, Mozambique. *African Economic Outlook*, OECD/African Development Bank, 2008b. Retrieved online from: oecd.org/dataoecd/13/6/40578303.pdf

OECD, *Progress report on implementing the Paris Declaration.* Paris: OECD, 2009.

OECD, *Multilateral development finance: Towards a new pact on multilateralism to achieve the 2030 Agenda together.* Paris: OECD, 2018.

OECD, *Development cooperation report 2019: A fairer, greener, safer tomorrow.* Paris: OECD, 2019a.

OECD, *Decentralised development cooperation: Unlocking the potential of cities and regions.* OECD Development Policy Paper 22, Paris: OECD, 2019b.

OECD, *Private philanthropy for the SDGs: Insights from the latest OECD DAC statistics.* Paris: OECD, 2020a.

OECD, *Six decades of ODA: Insights and outlook in the COVID-19 crisis.* Development Co-operation Profiles, Paris: OECD Publishing, 2020b.

OECD-DAC, Aid extended by local and state governments. *DAC Journal* 2005, 6(4): 7–56.

OECD-DAC, *Scaling Up: Aid Fragmentation, Aid Allocation and Aid predictability.* Paris: OECD, 2008a.

OECD-DAC, *DAC list of ODA recipients*. Paris: OECD, 2008b.

OECD-DAC, *Aid statistics*. OECD, 2010a. Retrieved online from: oecd.org/dac/stats

OECD-DAC, *Development aid at a glance*. Paris: OECD, 2010b.

OECD-DAC, *Development co-operation report 2010*. Paris: OECD, 2010c.

OECD-DAC, *Beyond the DAC. The welcome role of other providers of development co-operation*. OECD-DCD Issues Brief 2010d. Retrieved online from: oecd.org/dac/beyondthe-dacthewelcomeroleofotherprovidersofco-operation.htm

OECD-ODI, *Untying aid: is it working?* Aarhus: Danish Institute for International Studies, 2009.

OECD & UNDP, *Making development cooperation more effective: 2019 progress report*. Paris: OECD, 2019.

Oggier, L., The effectiveness of debt relief: Assessing the influence of the HIPC initiative and MDRI on Tanzania's health sector. *American Journal of Undergraduate Research* 2019, 16(2): 31–44.

Olela, D., Le secteur informel et le syndicalisme des résistants. Esquisse d'une autre facette du phénomène au travers la quotidienneté congolaise. *Mouvements et enjeux sociaux* 2007, 38: 63–81.

Omoruyi, L.O., *Contending theories on development aid. Post-Cold War evidence from Africa*. Aldershot: Ashgate, 2001.

OPHI & UNDP, *Charting pathways out of multidimensional poverty: Achieving the SDGs*. New York & Oxford: UN Development Programme & University of Oxford, 2020.

Orozco, M., Transnationalism and development: Trends and opportunities in Latin America. In S. Munzele Maimbo, & D. Ratha (eds.), *Remittances. Development impact and future prospects*. Washington D.C.: World Bank, 2005, pp.307–330.

Oxfam. *Thinking and Working Politically update: where have aid agencies, consultants etc got to?* Oxfam Blogs, 23 September 2014. Retrieved online from: oxfamblogs.org/fp2p/thinking-and-working-politically-update-where-have-aid-agencies-consultants-etc-got-to/

Özkan, M., *Turkey discovers Africa: Implications and prospects*. SETA Foundation for Political, Economic and Social Research, 2008.

Paquot, E., *International solidarity organisations and public authorities in Europe: Comparative study on national and European aid and consultation schemes*. Paris: Ministère des Affaires Étrangères, 2001.

Pearson, L.B., *Partners in development. Report of the Commission on International Development*. London: Pall Mall, 1969.

Pérez, A., *The international aid of subnational governments: The case of Spain*. Working Paper 10, Madrid: Elcano Royal Institute, 2018.

Pevehouse, J., et al., Tracking organisatioins in the world: The Correlates of War IGO Version 3.0 datasets. *Journal of Peace Research* 2019, 57(3): 492–503.

Pieniazek, M.A., Ubuntu: Constructing spaces of dialogue in the theory and practice of global education. In D. Bourn (ed.), *The Bloomsbury Handbook of Global Education and Learning*. 2020, pp.76–89.

Piot, J., & Heylen, M., *Eat, love, volunteer: Hoe vrijwilligers ondersteunen*. Kalmthout: Pelckmans Pro, 2017.

Pollet, I., *General barometer of the support for development cooperation. Survey on the support for development cooperation among the Belgian public: Synthesis report*. Leuven: PULSE Research Platform & HIVA, 2010.

Pollet, I., *Barometer draagvlak ontwikkelingssamenwerking. Rapport van de enquête en focusgroepsgesprekken in 2013 over het draagvlak voor ontwikkelingssamenwerking bij de Belgische bevolking*. Leuven: HIVA, 2014.

Pollet, I., & Develtere, P., *Het draagvlak voor ontwikkelingssamenwerking in Vlaanderen. Resultaten van een enquête in 2003*. Leuven: HIVA, 2003.

Pollet, I., & Develtere, P., *Het draagvlak voor ontwikkelingssamenwerking in Vlaanderen. Resultaten van een enquête in 2004*. Leuven: HIVA, 2004.

Pollet, I., Habraken R., Schulpen L & Huyse H. *The accidental aid worker: A mapping of citizen initiatives for global solidarity in Europe*. Leuven/Nijmegen: HIVA KU Leuven – CIDIN, 2014.

Pollet, I., & Huybrechts, A., *Het draagvlak voor ontwikkelingssamenwerking in Vlaanderen. Resultaten van een enquête in 2007*. Leuven: HIVA, 2007.

Pollet, I., Steegen, B., & Goddeeris, I., Giving religion a place in development cooperation: The perspective of Belgian NGOs. *Forum for Development Studies* 2020, 47(3): 555–576.

Porter, M., LoL players raised $2 million for charity during Worlds. *Mail Online*, 18 November 2017. Retrieved online from: https://www.dailymail.co.uk/sport/esports/article-5095785/LoL-players-raised-2-million-charity-Worlds.html

Prahalad, C.K., *The fortune at the bottom of the pyramid: Eradicating poverty through profits*. Pennsylvania: Wharton School Publishing, 2006.

Ratha, D., Mohapatra, S., Vijayalakshmi, K.M., & Xu, Z., *Revision to remittance trends 2007*. Development Prospects Group, 2008.

Reed, P., Mukherjee, A. *Business regulation and non-state actors: Whose standards? Whose development?* Routledge, 2013.

Reisen, H., Ownership in the multilateral development-finance non-system. In OECD, *Financing development 2008: Whose ownership?*, Paris: OECD Development Centre, 2008, pp.42–61.

Renwick, N., *China and humanitarian aid cooperation*. Institute of Development Studies Policy Brief 170, 2020.

Riddell, R.C., *Does foreign aid really work?* Oxford: Oxford University Press, 2008.

Riot Games, 2017 worlds charity fundraiser. *Riot Games*, 2017. Retrieved online from: https://www.riotgames.com/en/who-we-are/social-impact/2017-worlds-charity-fundraiser

Rist, G., *Le Développement. Histoire d'une croyance occidentale.* Paris: Presses de la Fondation Nationale des Sciences Politiques, 1996.

Roodman, D., *An Index of Donor Performance: Working Paper 6.* Washington D.C.: Center for Global Development, 2010.

Rosling, H., Rosling, O., & Rosling Rönnlund, A.R., *Factfulness: Ten Reasons we're wrong about the world – and why things are better than you think.* London: Sceptre, 2018.

Sachs, J., *The end of poverty; How we can make it happen in our lifetime.* London: Penguin Books, 2005.

Sachs, J., Achieving the Sustainable Development Goals. *Journal of International Business Ethics* 2015, 8(2): 53–62.

Sachs, J., Schmidt-Traub, G., Kroll, C., Lafortune, G., Fuller, G., & Woelm, F., *The Sustainable Development Goals and COVID-19*, Sustainable Development Report 2020, Cambridge: Cambridge University Press, 2020.

Sardan, O. de, Devarajan, S., Dollar, D., & Holmgren, T. (eds.), *Aid and reform in Africa: Lessons from 10 case studies.* Washington: World Bank, 1997, 2002.

Sautman, B., & Hairong, Y., Friends and Interests: China's Distinctive Links with Africa. *African Studies Review* 2007, 50(3): 75–114.

Smelts, D. Daalder, I.H., Friedhoff, K., Kafura, C., & Helm B., *Divided we stand: Democrats and Republicans diverge on US foreign policy.* Chicago Council on Global Affairs, 2020.

Frame, Voice, Report!, *How to engage citizens with the Sustainable Development Goals.* Retrieved online from: https://www.framevoicereport.org/media/8705/how-to-engage-citizens-with-the-sustainable-development-goals.pdf

Schnable, A., New American relief and development organisations: Voluntarising global aid. *Social Problems* 2015, 62: 309-329.

Schneider, S.H., & Gleser, S.H., *Opinion monitor for development policy 2018: Attitudes towards development cooperation and sustainable development.* 2018. Retrieved online from: oecd.org/derec/germany/Monitor-development-policy.pdf

Schraeder, P., Hook, S., & Taylor, B., Clarifying the foreign aid puzzle: A comparison of American, Japanese, French and Swedish aid flows. *World Politics* 1998, 50(2): 294–323.

Schulpen, L., & Gibbon, P., Private sector development: Policies, practices and problems. *World Development* 2002, 30(1): 1–150.

Scott, S., Philanthropic foundations and development co-operation. *DAC Journal* 2003, 4(3).

Sharman, T., *The trade escape: WTO rules and alternatives to free trade economic partnership agreements.* Action Aid International, 2005.

Shaw, T., Global/local: States, companies and civil societies at the end of the twentieth century. In K. Stiles (ed.), *Global institutions and local empowerment. Competing Theoretical perspectives.* New York: St. Martin's Press, 2000.

Shomba, S., The problematic contribution of the revival churches towards sustainable development in the DR Congo. In J. Defourny & P. Develtere (eds.), *The worldwide making of the social economy.* Leuven: ACCO, 2009.

Shomba, S., *Comprendre Kinshasa à travers ses locutions populaires*. Leuven: ACCO, 2009.

Shomba, S. et al., *Rapport de l'enquête menée dans le cadre du projet d'appui à la structuration et au développement des capacités de production agricole des populations rurale défavorisées au nord de la province de l'Equateur en République Démocratique du Congo*. Kinshasa: CDS, 2008.

Shomba, S., & Develtere, P., COVID-19 en Afrique: Un couteau dans du beurre, *Journal Du Développement* 2020, 372: 11–14.

Soors, W., Devadasan, N., Durairaj V., & Criel, B., *Community health insurance and universal coverage: Multiple paths, many rivers to cross*. World Health Report 2010, Background Paper, 48. Geneva: World Health Organisation, 2010.

Sotero, P., *Brazil as an emerging donor: Huge potential and growing pains*. Washington D.C: World Bank Institute, 2009.

Stanford, V., *Aid dependency: The damage of donation*. University of Edinburgh, 2015.

Stein, S., Pluralising possibilities for global learning in Western higher education. In D. Bourn (ed.), *The Bloomsbury handbook of global education and learning*, 2020, pp.63–75

Stein, S., Hunt, D., Suša, R., & de Oliveira Andreotti, V., The educational challenge of unravelling the fantasies of ontological security. *Diaspora, Indigenous, and Minority Education* 2017, 11(2): 69–79.

Stephen, M., & Martini, A., *Turning the tables: Insights from locally-led humanitarian partnerships in conflict-affected situations*. London: Saferworld and Save the Children, 2020.

Stessens, J., Gouet, C., & Eeckloo, P., *Efficient contract farming through strong farmers' organisations in a partnership with agri-business*. Leuven: HIVA, 2004.

Storeng, K., The GAVI Alliance and the 'Gates approach' to health system strengthening. *Global Public Health* 2014, 9(8): 865–79.

Swiss, L., A sociology of foreign aid and the world society. *Sociology Compass* 2016, 10(1): 65–73.

Takyi-Amoako, E.J., Towards an alternative approach to education partnerships in Africa: Ubuntu, the confluence and the post-2015 agenda. In E.J. Takyi-Amoako & N.T. Assié-Lumumba (eds.), *Re-visioning education in Africa*. Cham: Palgrave Macmillan, 2018, pp. 205–227.

Tartar, A., & Sam, C., How the rise of developing countries has disrupted global trade. *Bloomberg New Economy*, 7 May 2019.

Tatham, P.H., & Pettit, S.J., Transforming humanitarian logistics: The journey to supply network management. *International Journal of Physical Distribution & Logistics Management* 2010, 40(8/9): 609–622.

Taupiac, C., Humanitarian and development procurement: A vast and growing market. *International Trade Forum*, October 2001, 7–12.

Telford, J., & Cosgrave, J., The international humanitarian system and the 2004 Indian Ocean earthquake and tsunamis. *Disasters* 2006, 31(1): 1–28.

Thorbecke, The evolution of the development doctrine and the role of foreign aid 1950-2000. In F. Tarp (ed.), *Foreign aid and development*. London/New York: Routledge, 2000, pp.17–47.

Thys, A., *L'expansion colonial belge*. Conference on November 3 in Liège, Brussels, 1905.

Tostensen, A., Søreide, T., & Skage, I.A., *The challenge of per diem misuse: Training and travel as extra pay*. Bergen: Chr. Michelsen Institute U4 Brief 8, 2016.

Trimmel, J., Concord's reaction to Juncker's speech "State of the Union" 2018. *Concord Newsroom*, 12 September 2018.

TUDCN, *Trade union principles and guidelines on development effectiveness: TUDCN development papers*. Brussels: Trade Union Development Cooperation Network 2011. Retrieved online from: ituc-csi.org/IMG/pdf/TU_develop_EN.pdf

UN, *Funding compact: Report of the Secretary-General*. New York: Economic and Social Council, 2019.

UNCTAD, *The least developed countries report*. Geneva: UNCTAD, 2010.

UNDP, *Annual statistical report 2006*. United Nations Development Programme, 2007.

UNDP, *Creating value for all: Strategies for doing business with the poor*. New York: United Nations Development Programme, 2008.

UNDP, *Worldwide trends in the Human Development Index 1970-2010*. United Nations Development Programme, 2010. Retrieved online from: hdr.undp.org/en/data/trends/

University of Birmingham, *Development aid: how do you convince the public that progress is possible?* 2020. Retrieved online from: https://www.birmingham.ac.uk/research/quest/towards-a-better-society/Attitudes-towards-aid.aspx

Urpilainen, U., *Statement during the informal meeting of Development Ministers*, 29 September 2020.

Vaes, S., & Huyse, H., *Private sector in development cooperation. Mapping international debates, donor policies, and Flemish development cooperation*. Leuven: HIVA, KU Leuven, 2015. Retrieved online from: https://lirias.kuleuven.be/retrieve/333199

Van Bilsen, J., *Kongo 1945–1965: het einde van een kolonie*. Leuven: Davidsfonds, 1993.

Vandemoortele, J., From simple-minded MDGs to muddle-headed SDGs. *Development Studies Research* 2018, 5(1): 83–89.

Vansina, J., *Being colonised: The Kuba experience in rural Congo, 1880-1960*. Madison: University of Wisconsin Press, 2010.

Vaux, T., Humanitarian trends and dilemmas. *Development in Practice* 2006, 16(3–4): 240–254.

Vencato, M.F., *The development policy of the CEECs: the EU political rationale between the fight against poverty and the near abroad*. Doctoral thesis, Leuven: KU Leuven, 2007.

Vlaminck, Z., & Huyse, H., Development aid and transnational solidarity with African trade unions: Walking the thin line, *Globalizations* 2021, 0(0): 1–16.

Von Grebmer, K., et al., *2020 Global Hunger Index: One decade to zero hunger*. Bonn/Dublin: World Hunger Hilfe & Concern Worldwide, 2020.

Voorst, A. van, *Draagvlak voor ontwikkelingssamenwerking binnen Nederland en de rol van de NCDO*, Voorstrategie, 2005.

Vossen, M., & Van Gorp, B., The battle of ideas about global poverty in the United Kingdom, The Netherlands, and Flanders. *The European Journal of Development Research* 2016, 29(4): 707–724.

Waghid, Y., African philosophy of education as a response to human rights violations: Cultivating Ubuntu as a virtue in religious education. *Journal for the Study of Religion* 2014, 27(1): 267-282.

Walker, C., & Kirk, E.J., Alternatives – Pitfalls of polarised internationalism: Protest against Cuban medical solidarity. *Studies in Political Economy* 2017, 98(1): 82–92.

Walker, P. et al., The impact of COVID-19 and strategies for mitigation and suppression in low- and middle-income countries. *Science* 2020, 369(6502): 413–422.

Wang, J.-Y., *What drives China's growing role in Africa?* IMF, 2007.

Wenham, C., & Kittelsen, S.K., Cuba y Seguridad Sanitaria Mundial: Cuba's role in global health security. *BMJ Journals* 2020, 5(5): e002227.

Wertheim, W.F., Ontwikkelingshulp als neo-kolonialisme. *De Nieuwe Stem* 1967, 22: 461–83.

Westerwinter, O., Transnational public-private governance initiatives in world politics: Introducing a new dataset. *The Review of International Organisations* 2019, 16(4): 137–174.

Wheatly, J., & Kynge, J., China curtails overseas lending in face of geopolitical backlash. *Financial Times*, 7 December 2020.

Williams, S., *Unfinished business: Ten years of dropping the debt*. London: Jubilee Debt Campaign, 2008.

Williamson, J., *The Washington Consensus and beyond*. Washington: Institute for International Economics, 2003.

Wojtowicz, L., & Hanania, D., Americans support foreign aid, but oppose paying for it. *Chicago Council on Global Affairs*, 2017. Retrieved online from: thechicagocouncil.org/about/press-release/poll-americans-support-foreign-aid-oppose-paying-it

Woodward, B., *State of denial*. London: Simon & Schuster, 2006.

World Bank, *Worldwide Governance Indicators*. Retrieved online from: http://info.worldbank.org/governance/wgi/

World Bank, *2010 World Development Indicators*. Washington D.C.: World Bank, 2007.

World Bank, *Boards of Directors: Voting Powers*. 2010. Retrieved online from: https://www.worldbank.org/en/about/leadership/votingpowers

World Cooperative Monitor, *Exploring the cooperative economy: 2019 report*. Brussels: EURICSE/ICA, 2020.

WHO, *Drinking-water*. World Health Organisation Fact Sheet, June 2019. Retrieved online from: https://www.who.int/news-room/fact-sheets/detail/drinking-water

Yang, M., Moralities and contradictories in the educational aid for Tibet: Contesting the multi-layered saviour complex. *Journal of Multilingual and Multicultural Development* 2019, 41(7): 620–632.